Cambridge Studies in Medieval Life and Thought

ENGLAND'S JEWISH SOLUTION

This is a detailed study of Jewish settlement and of seven different Jewish communities in England between 1262 and 1290, offering in addition a new consideration of the prelude to the Expulsion of the Jews in 1290.

The book estimates the extent of Jewish residence and settlement; it evaluates the tallage payments made by those communities; and finally by a close discussion of prevailing attitudes towards usury and moneylending it considers the Edwardian Experiment of 1275. The impact of Edward I's legislation and Jewish policy on his Jewish subjects is then examined. Changes are measured on a local level by a detailed study of seven Jewish communities. It is possible to follow the business transactions of Jewish financiers in these different provincial communities over a period of almost thirty years; and a thorough and detailed study is made of the type of people who borrowed from the Jews. Finally a survey is made of the possible motives and continental parallels which influenced the Expulsion in 1290 and the subsequent dissolution of the Jewries.

Cambridge Studies in Medieval Life and Thought
Fourth Series

General Editor:

D. E. LUSCOMBE

Leverhulme Personal Research Professor of Medieval History, University of Sheffield

Advisory Editors:

R. B. DOBSON

Professor of Medieval History, University of Cambridge, and Fellow of Christ's College

ROSAMOND MCKITTERICK

Professor of Early Medieval European History, University of Cambridge,

and Fellow of Newnham College

The series Cambridge Studies in Medieval Life and Thought was inaugurated by G. G. Coulton in 1921; Professor D. E. Luscombe now acts as General Editor of the Fourth Series, with Professor R. B. Dobson and Professor Rosamond McKitterick as Advisory Editors. The series brings together outstanding work by medieval scholars over a wide range of human endeavour extending from political economy to the history of ideas.

For a list of titles in the series, see end of book.

ENGLAND'S JEWISH SOLUTION

Experiment and Expulsion, 1262–1290

ROBIN R. MUNDILL

CAMBRIDGE
UNIVERSITY PRESS

PUBLISHED BY THE PRESS SYNDICATE OF THE UNIVERSITY OF CAMBRIDGE
The Pitt Building, Trumpington Street, Cambridge CB2 1RP, United Kingdom

CAMBRIDGE UNIVERSITY PRESS
The Edinburgh Building, Cambridge, CB2 2RU, United Kingdom
40 West 20th Street, New York, NY 10011–4211, USA
10 Stamford Road, Oakleigh, Melbourne 3166, Australia

First published 1998

Printed in the United Kingdom at the University Press, Cambridge

Typeset in Bembo 11/12 pt   [CE]

A catalogue record for this book is available from the British Library

ISBN 0 521 58158 8 hardback

For my parents
Derrick Arthur
and Anne

CONTENTS

FIGURES

xi

TABLES

PREFACE

When I embarked on the study of medieval Anglo-Jewry in late 1980 it seemed that I had come across a comparatively quiet backwater. Much research had been done on the topic by members of the Jewish Historical Society of England (JHSE). This work was dominated by the studies of Michael Adler, Cecil Roth, Vivian Lipman, Canon Stokes, James Parkes and Sir Hilary Jenkinson. This had been augmented by the works of H. G. Richardson in 1961 and 1972 and more recently of Professor Barrie Dobson who published two papers on the York Jewry in the 1970s. The latter finally brought the Anglo-Jew more clearly into mainline medieval history. I hope that this book will strengthen the bridge across the divide between what has been traditionally considered Jewish history on one side and medieval British history on the other.

As my own work progressed I found that the study of medieval Anglo-Jewry had a much wider appeal and interest than I had believed. I encountered much research and scholarship. Sometime in late 1981 I met Dr Zefira Rokeah in the small dark coffee bar at the Public Record Office, Chancery Lane, London. It is fair to say that as we sat there we thought ourselves not only to be kindred souls in search of a small community of some seven hundred years standing, but also somewhat alone! We have been in touch ever since and I not only am indebted to Dr Rokeah's work but have also benefited from her enthusiasm and advice. As my thesis came to a conclusion in 1987, I made the aquaintance of Vivian Lipman. He was a gentle and careful scholar. His death in March 1990 was a great loss to students of Anglo-Jewish history. I was privileged to be invited by the JHSE to give a lecture in his honour in June 1990.

Ten years after I commenced my studies it had become clear to me that there had been many different local studies of Edwardian Anglo-Jewry but little had been done to pull the work together and to view the medieval Anglo-Jews as a single community. The records of the actual Expulsion had not been closely examined; the Receipt Rolls and records of tallages had been neglected for too long. The debtors of the Jews had not received enough attention and the actual procedures of the Expulsion itself had not always prompted the right sorts of questions.

From 1990 the study of medieval Anglo-Jewry seems to have opened up and is now maturing at such a pace that even as this book goes to press there are many other studies about to be published. The JHSE has continued to try to finish the editing of the Plea Rolls of the Exchequer of the Jews under the distinguished editorship of Dr Paul Brand. In America Dr Paul Hyams, Professor Gavin Langmuir and more recently Professor Robert Stacey have all contributed immensely to our knowledge of the subject. In Israel Zefira Rokeah has continued her important researches and in particular her magisterial efforts to produce an edition of the Jewish entries in the Memoranda Rolls. Other contributions have been made by Professors Kenneth Stow and Sophia Menache of the University of Haifa. In England Professor Barrie Dobson was honoured by the JHSE and became its president for 1990–1. The subject has also attracted the attention of Professors Jack Watt and Colin Richmond and more recently of Dr Nicholas Vincent. Archive work and research has been forthcoming from Joe Hillaby, and Volume v of the Plea Rolls of the Exchequer of the Jews is a testimony to the patience and efficiency of Dr Paul Brand. In Germany, under the guidance of Professor Alfred Haverkamp of the University of Trier, important contributions have been made by Drs Gerd Mentgen and Christoph Cluse; interest in the Jews and their history has accordingly started to blossom there. On all these influences I have drawn.

It is hoped that what follows will stimulate both debate and interest within this fascinating field. However before passing to the study there are several points which are worthy of mention. The very fact that I take 1262 as a starting point has a significance. First, I believe that this is the start of Edward I's real contact with his Jewish subjects and the roll of Jewish debts dating from 1262 gives a view of the Jewish community just before the Baronial rising, a decade before Edward I's accession. Second, although chapter 6 considers nine separate Jewish communities the fact that Norwich has been ommitted is due partly to the vagaries of the records but mainly to the fact that Vivian Lipman's study of the Norwich Jewry was so thorough. I hope that he would have approved of this present work.

ACKNOWLEDGEMENTS

This book naturally has its origins in my thesis 'The Jews in England 1272–1290' which was completed in 1987 at the University of St Andrews. The decision to carry out further research and to write a book which examined Edward I's reign was fostered by the encouragement of both Vivian Lipman and Professor Barrie Dobson.

Over the years I have come to owe many debts of gratitude to many different people and the full list is a very long one. For both their undergraduate teaching and supervision during research on my thesis I would like to thank Anne Kettle and David Corner. Special thanks must go to Barrie Dobson for his patience, advice and incisiveness. Since 1987 he has read many versions of articles and chapters with both dedication and constructive criticism. As noted in the Preface, encouragement has also come from Zefira Rokeah, who has visited me whenever she has been in this country and who has inspired me as a fellow researcher to continue to work on this topic.

I would like to thank the Twenty-Seven Foundation of the Institute of Historical Research for financial assistance for further research. In 1988–9 they gave me the support to widen my knowledge of the Nottingham, Devizes and Exeter communities. In 1992–3 they helped me to tackle the scribal jottings of the 1262 tallage. I am thankful for the patience and help of the staff of many record offices both in London and throughout the country. In particular I would like to thank the staff of the University Library of my *alma mater*. I would also like to convey my gratitude to Selwyn College, Cambridge for electing me to a Bye Fellowship during 1996.

I am particularly grateful to Professor Robert Stacey, Dr Paul Brand, Dr Gerd Mentgen and Dr Zefira Rokeah for allowing me to see unpublished papers and work. I am also grateful for discussion and criticism from audiences at many lectures and from readers of my work.

xvii

Acknowledgements

I owe much not only to my own teachers but also to my pupils for keeping my interest in history alive.

Perhaps more immediate is the debt that I owe to my family and, in particular, to my wife, Elaine, who not only married a thesis but has also had to put up with a book ever since. I hope that the outcome is worthy of all her trust and encouragement. I hope too that my daughters, Emma and Catriona, will grow up to read of the medieval Anglo-Jew and above all to avoid hatred of any kind throughout their lives. The greatest debts that I have cannot be repaid. My mother, who died while I was engaged on my thesis, not only shared my interest in the subject but believed in my ability to bring my work to a successful conclusion. Similarly my father, who died while I was writing this book, would have been delighted that I saw it through to fruition.

Any mistakes or erroneous statements are entirely of my own making.

ABBREVIATIONS

BIHR	*Bulletin of the Institute of Historical Research*
BL	British Library
CCA	Canterbury Cathedral Archives
CCR	*Calendar of Close Rolls*
CFR	*Calendar of Fine Rolls*
Concilia	D. Wilkins, 1737, *Concilia Magnae Britanniae et Hiberniae, a Synodo Verolamiensi, A.D. 446 ad Londiniensem A.D. 1717. Accedunt Constitutiones et Alia ad Historiam Ecclesiae Anglicanae Spectantia*, 11 vols., London, 1810–28
CPR	*Calendar of Patent Rolls*
EcHR	*Economic History Review*
HCA	Hereford Cathedral Archives
JHS	*Jewish Historical Studies*
JHSE	Jewish Historical Society of England
JJS	*Journal of Jewish Studies*
JQR	*Jewish Quarterly Review*
Misc JHSE	*Miscellanies of the Jewish Historical Society of England*
PRO	Public Record Office
PREJ1	*Calendar of the Plea Rolls of the Exchequer of the Jews Preserved in the Public Record Office*, vol. I, *Henry III 1218–1272*, ed. J. M. Rigg, 1905 (Jewish Historical Society of England)
PREJ2	*Calendar of the Plea Rolls of the Exchequer of the Jews Preserved in the Public Record Office*, vol. II, *Edward I 1273–1275*, ed. J. M. Rigg, 1910 (Jewish Historical Society of England)
PREJ3	*Calendar of the Plea Rolls of the Exchequer of the Jews Preserved in the Public Record Office*, vol. III, *Edward 1 1275–1277*, ed. H. Jenkinson, 1929 (Jewish Historical Society of England)
PREJ4	*Calendar of the Plea Rolls of the Exchequer of the Jews Preserved in the Public Record Office and the British Museum*, vol. IV,

	Henry III 1272 and Edward I 1275–1277, ed. H. G. Richardson, 1972 (Jewish Historical Society of England)
PREJ5	*Plea Rolls of the Exchequer of the Jews Preserved in the Public Record Office*, vol. V, *Edward I 1277–1279*, ed. S. Cohen, revised P. Brand 1992 (Jewish Historical Society of England)
RO	Record Office
Rigg	*Select Pleas, Starrs and other Records from the Rolls of the Exchequer of the Jews 1220–1284*, ed. J. M. Rigg, 1902 (Selden Society 15, London)
SCBM	*Starrs and Jewish Charters in the British Museum*, vols. I–III, ed. H. Loewe, H. P. Stokes and I. Abrahams, 1930, Cambridge
Statutes	*Statutes of the Realm, Printed by Command of His Majesty King George the Third in Pursuance of an Address of the House of Commons of Great Britain from Original Records and Authoritative Manuscripts*, 4 vols., London, 1737
TJHSE	*Transactions of the Jewish Historical Society of England*
WAM	Westminster Abbey Muniments

WEIGHTS AND MEASURES

1 peck = $\frac{1}{4}$ bushel
1 truges = $\frac{2}{3}$ of a bushel
8 bushels = 1 quarter
1 soam = 1 quarter

The term *trugum* was in common usage in the Welsh Marches from 1257.

Ladum or *summum* normally represented a quarter. They were both a recognised and legal measure for dry goods from Richard I's assize in 1197. A soam came to mean a pack saddle full or horse load.

AVOIRDUPOIS

16 ounces = 1 pound
7 pounds = 1 nail or clove
14 pounds = 1 stone
2 stones = 1 quarter
4 quarters = 1 hundredweight
20 hundredweights = 1 ton

Weights and measures varied not only from district to district but from merchant to merchant and from transaction to transaction. The author of *Seneschausie* claimed that the right stone of wool was 12 lbs but in Flanders it was 13 lbs. Peglotti claimed that the nail or clove was in common usage for wool, cheese and butter. The clove or nail was the weight carried over a horse's back. When the merchant wished to make up a larger denomination than the 7 lbs he carried either side of his horse he simply took two nails or cloves and sought and shaped a convenient-looking natural stone and balanced it on an arm; this would weigh approximately 'one stone'.

However, it will never be possible to trust medieval weights and measures entirely and it is unlikely that any standards really prevailed for very long. The *Eastern Daily Press* recorded on 19 April 1921 that there were still twenty-five local corn weights and measures, twelve different bushels, thirteen different pounds, ten different stones and nine different tons.

CEREAL

1 qtr of wheat weighs approximately 36 stone.
1 bushel of wheat weighs approximately $4\frac{1}{2}$ stone.
1 bushel of wheat would weigh 60 lbs.
1 bushel of barley would weigh 56 lbs.
1 bushel of oats would weigh 42 lbs.

1 qtr of wheat would require approximately 1.5 acres. In 1987 1.5 acres would yield approximately 480 qtrs of wheat. $4\frac{1}{2}$ qtrs would be enough to feed one person for one year. 1 qtr of cereal would make approximately 400 lbs of bread which could feed four people for approximately three weeks.

WOOL

One sack of wool would normally comprise 300 fells. Medieval sheep yielded fleeces weighing approximately $2\frac{1}{3}$ lbs. To obtain enough wool for one sack it was necessary to have a flock of 158–76 sheep.

In 1271 Isabella de Forz's estates sold 38 sacks of wool for £215 6s 8d.

In 1277 Isabella de Forz's estates sold $37\frac{1}{2}$ sacks of wool for £275 0s 0d.

Between 1284 and 1306 the abbot of Gloucester increased the abbey's sheep until they numbered 10,000; he was able to sell 46 sacks of wool in a single year.

The bishop of Winchester's estates yielded:

$93\frac{1}{2}$ sacks of wool in 1273
79 sacks of wool in 1278
33 sacks of wool in 1283
28 sacks of wool in 1289
47 sacks of wool in 1291.

1275 and 1276 saw an outbreak of scab. By 1279 prices began to level off but wool was a commodity with a value which was on the increase from an investor's point of view. A rough guide would be that a sack cost £4 13s 8d in 1272, rose to £6 2s 2d by 1280 and stayed at around £6 9s 8d by 1290.

JEWISH NOMENCLATURE

It was common amongst Ashkenazi to name a child after a deceased relative. Most Jewish children would probably have been given a Hebrew name at birth. Certainly males would be named at circumcision and females at any time during the first month of their life. As they grew up an adjustment would be made from the biblical name to the orthography of the language of the country of their residence. They would be careful to preserve their Hebrew names for 'sacred purposes': marriage, blessings, bar mitzvah. Ashkenazi Jews did not tend to use cognomens or surnames until the nineteenth century. As demonstrated by the names which will be encountered throughout this book, a wife used her husband's name. However, some surnames do appear: le Eveske, l'Evesk, *Episcopus* le Blund, le Petit, Mouton, Menahem, Levi (patronymic). Other names which reflect the offices of the community can also be found: *Parnass, Hazzan, Gabbay, Capellanus*. Interestingly Adler comments that most Jewesses appear to have been given French names whilst men were usually satisfied with biblical names.

The orthography of Jewish names in either Latin, Anglo-Norman or, indeed, English is another extremely difficult problem. Because of this no attempt has been made to standardise Jewish names completely. Different versions of spellings exist for the following names and, at times, just the difference of one letter may be enough to identify a separate individual.

Aaron	Aron	
Avigaye	Avegaye	
Belasset	Bellasset	Belassez
Bonami	Bonamy	
Bonefey	Bonfy	Bonefie
Bonne	Bona	
Cresse	Deulecresse	Dieulecresse

Diay	Diey	
Hak	Hakelm	Hake
Isaac	Isac	Izaak
Lumbard	Lombard	
Manasser	Manser	
Meir	Mayre	Meyre
Peytevin	Pet	
de Provyns	de Provincia	
Solomon	Soloman	Salaman

Jewish nomenclature is further complicated because of the use of sacred names or *Shem Hakkodesh* and the use of business names *Kinnui*.

Some of the names which are common throughout the text naturally have their Hebrew equivalent:

Avigaye = Abigail
Anita = Hannah
Belita = Belle
Bellasset = Rachel
Bonamy = Benjamin
Copin = Jacob
Dielecresse (May God increase) = Josce = Jesse
Hagin = Vives = Haim
Mollin or Molkin = Samuel

CHRONOLOGY

1262	February	Earl of Derby storms Worcester and carries off *archa* to Tutbury.
	4 June	Henry III grants Prince Edward the receipts from the Jewry for the next three years.
1264	January	The Award of Amiens.
	Easter week	London Jewry sacked by de Montfort supporters. Gilbert de Clare captures Canterbury and takes the *archa* away.
	14 May	Victory at Lewes.
1265		John Dayville, leader of the 'Disinherited', storms Lincoln and sacks the Jewry.
1266		Jews expelled from Romsey.
1268	April	Council in London. Ottobuono's peace mission. *Turbato corde* Inquisition given power to deal with the Jews.
1269		Provisions of the Jewry.
1271	25 July	Mandate to the Jews.
1272	2 April	Richard of Cornwall dies.
	April	Tallage assessed on the Jews.
	16 November	Henry III dies. Regency: Walter Giffard, Robert Burnell, Roger Mortimer.
1273	February	General *archae* scrutiny.
	April	Tallage assessed on the Jews.
	18 June	Prohibition of Jewish settlement in Winchelsea.

	October	Prior Joseph de Chauncy appointed Treasurer.
	December	Great Tallage ordered.
1274	2 August	Edward I returns to England.
	21 September	Burnell appointed Chancellor.
	October	Prohibition of Jewish settlement in Bridgnorth.
1275	January	Anti-usury campaign against merchants.
	18 January	Jews expelled from queen mother's dower towns. Jews of Marlborough move to Devizes; Gloucester to Bristol; Worcester to Hereford; Cambridge to Norwich.
	25 April	Parliament promulgates the Statute of the Jewry. *Domus Conversorum* enlarged and poll tax instituted on Jews. Settlement restricted to *archa* towns.
1276–7		War in Wales.
1276	January	*Archa* scrutiny ordered. Followed by tallage.
	September	Jewish Exchequer moves to Shrewsbury. Tallage. Hugh of Digneuton's enquiry on Jewish settlement.
1277	November	The Treaty of Conway. Edward turns a Jew over to Parliament for blasphemy.
1278		Tallage. Bishop of Lincoln excommunicates Lincoln Christians who have Jews working for them. *Vinei soreth velut* Franciscans and Dominicans to give conversion sermons to the Jews. Compulsory for Jews to attend.
	November	Campaign against coin-clipping. Renewal of coinage and allegations against the Jews.
1279	25 January	John Pecham becomes archbishop of Canterbury.
	May	Edward grants general amnesty for Jews accused of coin-clipping.
	11 May to 19 June	Edward in France.
1280		Edward issues instructions that Jews must attend Dominican sermons.

1281		*Ad fructus uberes* grants mendicants the right to make public sermons.
1283		The Statute of Acton Burnell.
	October	Jews expelled from Windsor.
1287		Council of Exeter.
	May	Edward ill at Blanquefort. Publicly takes the cross at Bordeaux.
	May	The Jews of England arrested.
	June	Edward meets King of Aragon at Oleron. Both stay with Dominicans.
	August to November	The expulsion and dissolution of the Gascon Jewry.
	Late September to February 1288	Last Edwardian tallage on English Jewry.
1288	October	Charles II of Anjou released from captivity after Edward I intervenes.
1289	12 August	Edward's return.
	11 October	Edward arrives in London. State trials begin: Weylaund, Stratton, Bray, Hengham, Ludham and Rochester arrested.
1289	8 December	Expulsion of the Jews from Anjou and Maine.
1290	January to 17 February	Parliament meets.
	28 April	Edward visits mother at Amesbury.
	29 April	Easter Parliament.
	30 April	Marriage of Joan of Acre to Gilbert de Clare.
	20 May	Philip the Fair expels Jews from Saintonge and Dives.
	21 May	*Quo Warranto* issued.
	14 June	Summonses issued to all shires to send knights for Parliament by 15 July.
	18 June	Secret orders issued to sheriffs to seal all *archae* by 28 June.
	8 July	Margaret married to John of Brabant. *Quia Emptores* issued.
	18 July	Expulsion of the Jews from England declared.

Late July	Cinque Ports alerted about safe passage of the Jews.
24 August	Safe passage granted for Bonamy of York.
September	William de Marchia appointed to prepare *Valor Judaismus*.
1 November	All Jews to leave England.
5 November	Official statement published at King's Clipstone.
26 November	All *archae* brought in to Westminster.
27 December	Hugh of Kendal sells former Jewish property.

'The number of new writers doing important work
are evidence of the maturation of the field
of Jewish history.'

Norman Cantor, *The Sacred Chain*, London, 1995

Chapter 1

THE ENGLISH EXODUS RE-EXAMINED

'You have achieved in one day what the Pharaohs of Ancient Egypt failed to do', commented one contemporary chronicler on the occasion of Edward I's Expulsion of the Jews from England.[1] In 1272 Edward I became king; in 1290 he expelled the Jews from England. On his accession, Edward styled himself 'Edwardus, dei gratia, Rex Angliae, dominus Hiberniae, et dux Aquitaniae'. He subsequently received such titles and historical epithets as the Hammer of the Scots, the English Justinian, the Conqueror of the Welsh, but rarely has he been considered as the instigator of one of the earliest European expulsions of the Jews.[2] During his reign the Anglo-Jews were indeed, as contemporaries noted, 'condemned to wander the earth and to be cut off'.[3] The English Exodus has subsequently received comparatively little attention. It is mentioned by contemporary chroniclers in just a few curt lines.[4] Perhaps typical of the type of comment was the observation made by John of Oxnead, who noted that:

The Lord the King condemned all Jews of whatever sex or age living throughout England into perpetual exile without any hope of return. In truth, out of all that large number of Jews, whose total number from young to old was reckoned to be 17,511, no one who would not be converted to the Christian faith either by promise or allurement remained beyond the fixed and decided day of departure.[5]

Another anonymous chronicler indicated that the Jews were a widespread feature of English society at the time:

---

[1] *Chronicles of the Reigns of Edward I and Edward II, Commendatio Lamentabilis*, vol. II, p. 14.

[2] Jenks 1902; Salzman 1968; Prestwich 1988.

[3] Ross, *Annales Lincolniae*, vol. III, pp. 248–9, Manuscript in Ross Collection, Lincoln Public Library; *Concilia*, vol. II, p. 180.

[4] *Monumenta Franciscana*, vol. II, p. 143; *Eulogium (Historiarum)*, vol. III, p. 305; Walsingham, *Historia Anglicana*, vol. I, p. 31.

[5] *Chronica Johannis de Oxenedes*, p. 277.

I

About that time an irritatingly large number of Jews who lived in many different towns and strongholds, in view of what had happened in the past, were ordered, albeit in a faltering fashion, to leave England with their wives and children and with their goods and moveables at about the Feast of All Saints; this date had been imposed on them as a limit and they did not dare break this under threat of punishment.[6]

The deadline for expulsion passed and was soon forgotten. However, it was at least noted along with the other major events of 1290, the deaths of Margaret of Scotland and Queen Eleanor.

For almost three hundred years thereafter few Jews were to be seen in England, and references to their presence in British medieval society almost disappear. A renewed interest in the Jews seems to have been stimulated only in the late sixteenth and early seventeenth centuries, when Spanish Marrano Jews began to return.[7] But even then, antiquarians made nothing more than passing references to the Expulsion of 1290, even if they showed slightly more curiosity and interest than some modern historians. John Speed noted that

to purge England from such corruptions and oppressions as it groaned under and not neglecting therein his own particular gaine the King banished the Jews out of the realme confiscating all their goods leaving them (as they by their cruel usuries had eaten his people to the bones) nothing but money to bear their charges.[8]

John Stow remarked that 'the number of Jews now expulsed was 15,060 persons whose houses being sold the King made a mighty masse of money'.[9] Earlier in the sixteenth century John Leland commented that the Jews' loss was the king's gain: 'Afterwards in the reign of this King Edward (Longshanks surnamed) all their riches were confiscated to the King's treasury and their persons banished.'[10] An anonymous seventeenth-century anti-Jewish pamphleteer also suggested that the Crown gained from the Expulsion:

Some say they had only money given them to bear their charges over into France. Others say that all goods not moveable with their Tallies and Obligations being confiscate; all other moveables as gold and silver they were licensed to carry over. The number of them when they departed was about 16,511. Many more than at their first coming, an increasing misery to the land where ere they came.[11]

---

[6] BL Cotton Nero D II, fo. 183 which also notes that the Jews had previously been exiled from parts of Aquitaine.
[7] Roth 1960; Wolf 1928, pp. 1–91.
[8] Speed, *History of Great Britain*, p. 545; Tovey 1738, p. 25.
[9] Stow, *Annales of England*, p. 204.   [10] Leland, *Commentarii*, p. 321.
[11] H. W., *Anglo-Judaeus*, p. 25.

Although in the early sixteenth century there was a growing interest in the study of Hebrew, a consequence of the growth of humanism and the spread of the Reformation, most historians were aware only of the bare facts of the Expulsion.[12] Fresh debate on the position of the Jew in society accompanied the rise of the Puritans and was fostered by movements towards religious toleration in the early seventeenth century.[13] Many realised that although religious differences would always remain, there was no reason why Jews could not be loyal citizens within a Christian commonwealth. Under the Commonwealth, application was accordingly made for the re-admission of the Jews to England. Indeed, Edward Nicholas blamed the tribulations which the country had recently suffered on the fact that the people of God had themselves been maltreated.[14] It was Menasseh ben Israel's *Spes Israelis* and subsequent petition to the Lord Protector that eventually swayed opinion in England.[15] Yet it also started a Jewish debate which was taken up by William Prynne. Prynne's *Short demurrer to the Jewes...* is still a fundamental source for historians of Anglo-Jewry.[16] To the lawyers of the seventeenth century the Expulsion had been an act of royal prerogative and as far as they were concerned there was no law in existence which forbade the return of the Jews. After delay due to the death of Cromwell the Jews finally returned to England with the monarchy in 1660.[17]

However it was not until the eighteenth century that a proper history of the Jews in England appeared. De Bloissiers Tovey, a vicar and later the Principal of New Inn Hall, Oxford, lamented the lack of attention to this aspect of history in his introduction to his *Anglia Judaica*:

> you would think that even the tiniest detail of their history was worth recording. Yet it seems either the majority of English historians knew almost nothing about their history, or they simply could not be bothered to write it down. The result is that all we have is a mass of disparate and sketchy details from various chronicles and histories written through the ages, plus a huge collection of public records. Therefore to make life easier, I have put all of these together and have compiled a complete history in one volume, just for you, my dear Reader.[18]

Thus, in 1738, the man who is well entitled to be called the 'Father of Anglo-Jewish Studies' published a work covering the history of the Jews from 1066 to the early eighteenth century.

[12] Tuchman 1982, p. 93; Roth 1978, pp. 146–7. The chair of Hebrew was founded at Cambridge in 1549.
[13] Katz 1982; 1992.   [14] Roth 1978, p. 153.
[15] Israel, *Spes Israelis*; Wolf 1901, pp. xviii–lxxvii.   [16] Prynne, *A short demurrer.*
[17] Roth 1978, pp. 173–4.   [18] Tovey 1738, introduction; Pearl 1990, p 1.

However, much of Tovey's work was ignored. On this topic modern Christian historians have tended to be just as laconic as the medieval chroniclers. If anything, they only emphasised the financial side of the medieval Anglo-Jews' life. This, as we shall see, is perhaps understandable given the nature of the records the medieval Anglo-Jews have left behind; but many later historians also ignored the lives of the Jews who left these shores over seven centuries ago. The task of piecing together the evidence, of considering the fact that England was the first state to exile the Jews in the Middle Ages, and of examining this sad epoch in their history has until recently been left primarily in the hands of Jewish historians.[19]

It is not of course surprising that Christian historians have tended to neglect the Expulsion of 1290. It has been regarded by some as a slightly taboo subject. It could also be, as Professor Colin Richmond has observed, that 'Englishness' has clouded the issues.[20] The English solution is a topic which deserves closer attention, as it opens up many questions about thirteenth-century England as a whole. The sudden expulsion of a Jewish minority has not prompted many general questions, sociological or otherwise, about thirteenth-century English society. Nor has the apparent financial gain of the Crown stimulated further questions, economic or otherwise, about royal finances. The meticulously prepared financial and legal records, which have survived in abundance, have not inspired many Christian historians to look further into Edward I's 'Final Solution'. The evidence is plentiful and must be examined as a whole. The revival of the study of medieval Anglo-Jewry has only slowly evolved; and this too should be considered before any attempt is made to put the English Exodus into context.

Despite the fact that the Expulsion was so thorough, the first Anglo-Jewish community has left a legacy behind it. Place-names, charters, rolls, the first archives, and the method of trading by bonds used widely by merchants in the thirteenth and fourteenth centuries, were all part of the Anglo-Jewish heritage.[21] Small Jewish colonies that had in some cases existed for almost 200 years were totally suppressed, sometimes leaving only a street name as evidence of their existence, for instance in Canterbury, Winchester and of course London. A few sites remain. Tradition had it that St Stephen's and St Mary Colechurch in London, the Church of the Holy Sepulchre in Cambridge, Moyses Hall at Bury St Edmunds and St Giles at Bristol were once synagogues.[22] A *mikvah*, or ritual bath, which may well date back to the eleventh century has been discovered in

---

[19] Stacey 1987a, pp. 61–2; Mundill 1991a.   [20] Richmond 1992.   [21] Mundill 1990b.
[22] Jacobs 1896, pp. 162–91; Essex 1782; Samuel 1974; Adler 1928, pp. 122–3.

Bristol.[23] A few place-names perhaps connected with the Jews still lie cryptically on the map: Jew's Hollowcombe, Jews' Meadows, Jewry Wall all point to a Jewish presence.[24] Lincoln preserves not only its Jew's House at No. 8 Steep Hill and Jew's Court, allegedly the oldest synagogue in England, but also much tradition and folklore, regrettably often centred on the alleged ritual murder of Little St Hugh in 1255.[25] Apart from Jewbury at York, other Jewish burial grounds have been located and excavated.[26] The Anglo-Jews also left behind the *Domus Conversorum* or House of Converted Jews, situated in London, which continued in existence until the seventeenth century.[27] The only other tangible remains of Anglo-Jewry are quintessentially religious objects: the Bodleian ewer, a *shofar* and a small number of prayer books.[28]

Most of the heritage that the medieval Anglo-Jew has left behind is documentary. This evidence is so voluminous that it provides a very clear picture of Jewish life for just over two centuries. Many of the documents themselves form several special series which were kept apart from the main governmental records. The majority of these are housed in the Public Record Office, which itself (until recently) was situated on the former site of the *Domus Conversorum*.[29] The documents tend to be mainly financial and judicial records kept by Christian scribes for administrative purposes. The financial records comprise mostly details of taxation through tallages, of income through fines, and of Jewish financial activities which were for a century closely monitored by the Crown. The judicial records reveal details of legal cases brought by and against the King's Jews. The medieval Anglo-Jew posed many different problems for the successive governments of twelfth- and thirteenth-century England. An early response to the need to record Jewish financial dealings was the creation of the *Scaccarium Judaeorum* or Exchequer of the Jews, a department for Jewish affairs. It is due to the existence of this department and its staff that so many records remain.[30]

---

[23] *The Independent*, 6 July 1987, p. 4; *The Jewish Chronicle*, 19 January 1996 gives details of what is thought to be a medieval synagogue in Guildford.

[24] Jew's Hollowcombe in Devon, Devon RO, Crediton tithe map 1891; Jews' Meadows in Horsham, West Sussex; Levy 1902a.

[25] Jacobs 1893b; Langmuir 1972; Lincoln Public Library, The Banks Collection; Lethieullier 1700; Tuck 1934, pp. vii–ix; Roth 1934, pp. 20–5.

[26] Pearson 1983; Addyman 1984; Lilley *et al.*, 1994; Honeybourne 1964; Roberts 1992.

[27] Adler 1903; Richmond 1992, pp. 56–7.

[28] Beit-Arie 1985. Both the Bodleian ewer and the *shofar* were exhibited at the Anglo-Jewish Historical Exhibition of 1887; *Catalogue of Anglo-Jewish Historical Exhibition, 1887*, p. 7; Lipman 1967, pp. 33, 313–14; Davis 1887.

[29] An original arch from the *Domus Conversorum* can be seen in the wall behind the bicycle sheds at the former PRO, Chancery Lane; Atkinson 1912, plate iv, p. 15.

[30] PRO E/101/249 and E/101/250 series, PRO E/9 series and PRO E/401 series. Mundill 1993, pp. 25–7.

The Jewish Exchequer regulated all Jewish affairs. It generated many records in scribal shorthand which contain minutiae about Jewish life. At first it kept all of its records on the Pipe Roll of the king's main exchequer. However, it soon developed its own specific, specialised records to do with the day-to-day running of the provincial Jewish communities of England. After the widespread riots and the general massacre of *Shabbat ha Gadol* in 1190, and because of financial loss of revenue, it became necessary for the Crown to protect the financial dealings of its Jewish citizens by formally enrolling them.[31] In 1194 the Crown gained more control over the Jews as it tried to tighten up on running the affairs of its Jewish subjects. The Crown had customarily profited from the Jews and made them render unto Caesar that which was Caesar's. The Ordinances of the Jewry of 1194 comprised six vital pieces of legislation. The first was that all financial bonds between Jews and Christians should be legally registered. It then set up a series of centres where the bonds could be deposited in a large chest, or *archa* as the repository was known. It appointed two Jewish and two Christian officials in the major towns to witness all contracts being made. It made the format and legal jargon of the bond universal. All bonds had to be enrolled by a government official. The initiative behind these ordinances for setting up archives throughout the country was that of the justiciar, Hubert Walter, and it is probably to him that we owe our wealth of medieval Jewish records. The Ordinances of 1194 legalised, systematised, regulated as well as condoned Jewish moneylending and created the vast amount of specifically Jewish records that are available to the historian. If there had not been this preoccupation with recording and depositing records of individual transactions which concerned Jews in the thirteenth-century *archae*, there might have been precious little to reconstruct their sojourn in this country and even fewer repositories containing other deeds.[32]

The Jewish Exchequer was a working department housed at Westminster. It is known that in 1225 workmen were paid for putting a window in 'the Jews' chamber at Westminster'.[33] The Jewish Exchequer had its own royal seal and also kept its own separate records in both Latin and Hebrew.[34] It had its very own Justices, clerks and sergeants. The records of this special office, which has been described as 'both a judicial tribunal and a financial bureau', have preserved a fairly complete picture of Jewish affairs both in terms of cases brought by Jews or against Jews and in terms of the financial aspects of taxation and

---

[31] Cramer 1940; 1941; Miller 1957; Clanchy 1979, pp. 50–1.
[32] Scott 1950; Jenkinson 1918.   [33] Meekings 1955, p. 179.
[34] Sayles 1936, pp. clv–clix; PRO E/101/249/15.

tallage.[35] When referring to these particular financial records, Sir Hilary Jenkinson noted that 'it is remarkable that the records, dull, no doubt, and repetitious at times but plentiful and detailed, have not been comprehensively worked'.[36] Thus the records of the Jewish Exchequer reveal two main types of record: legal records on the Plea Rolls of the Jews and financial records on the Receipt Rolls of the Jews. The survival of the Jewish Plea Rolls from 1219 to 1287 has allowed historians to observe the workings of the Justices of the Jews and the lives of the Jews who colonised thirteenth-century England.[37] Historians have studied these records intermittently for over a century. Perhaps it is because the records are so specific that researchers have often been confused by them and have sometimes become slightly constricted in their approach to the history of the medieval Anglo-Jew. However, the work of publishing such records has been undertaken by the Jewish Historical Society of England. The resulting editions of the Plea Rolls contain almost as much of interest for the thirteenth-century historian as they do for the 'Jewish' historian.[38]

The Jewish Receipt Rolls were mainly used to account for the monies raised from Jewish tallages. Their survival has allowed historians to examine the Crown's income from its Jewish subjects.[39] This particular series of documents is primarily concerned with the negative side of the Jews' financial activities: their unpaid loans, deficits and payment of taxes. These financial records received attention many years ago from Charles Gross. Gross divided the fiscal operations of the Jewish Exchequer, or the 'Engine of Extortion' as he preferred to call it, into four main categories: tallages, fines, reliefs and escheats.[40] Subsequent historians have concerned themselves especially with the tallages, the easiest category with which to deal. The thirteenth-century tallages on the Jews have been closely considered by Peter Elman, Cecil Roth, Sir Hilary Jenkinson and, more recently, H. G. Richardson.[41] The tallages are especially important because the information provided in them gives clear indicators about Jewish society at the time the payments were collected. In articles published in 1985 and 1988, Professor Robert Stacey has used the actual records of the 1244 tallage receipts and has shown that the Jewish community then suffered a major blow to the capital it had and could provide: so much so that he agrees with Professor Barrie Dobson and calls the period 1240–60 a

---

[35] Miller 1957.   [36] Jenkinson 1918, p. 20.
[37] PRO E/9 series. *PREJ1*; *PREJ2*; *PREJ3*; *PREJ4*; *PREJ5*; Cohen 1951.
[38] Dobson 1992.   [39] PRO E/401 series. Jenkinson 1918.   [40] Gross 1887, pp. 192–4, 205.
[41] Elman 1938a; Roth 1978, chapter 3; Jenkinson 1918; 1922, pp. 185–7; 1955; Richardson 1960, pp. 213–337.

watershed in Anglo-Jewish relations.[42] Professor Stacey has also lamented the fact that 'very little serious work has been done on the 1275–1290 period'.[43] It is naturally crucial to an understanding of the motives behind the Expulsion that the Jewish tallages of Edward's reign are considered in detail. These Edwardian tallages will be discussed below.

The Jewish inhabitants of medieval England have also left behind them another form of documentary evidence. 'Bills', observed Mr Micawber in the nineteenth century, 'a convenience to the mercantile world, for which, I believe, we are originally indebted to the Jews.'[44] Micawber was in his own way correct. Historians are indebted to the Anglo-Jew for the 'bills' they left behind them. Many details of Jewish financial transactions have survived under various names, guises and forms such as obligations, chirographs and tallies. Some have survived as separate records in isolation. Many separate bonds, predominantly from Henry III's reign, have also survived in the Public Record Office.[45] The collection of Jewish documents in the muniments of Westminster Abbey also contains many pre-Edwardian and early Edwardian bonds.[46] However, few Edwardian bonds dating from after 1275 have survived.[47] It is known that many bonds were destroyed and cut up and used as seal tags for other official documents. Many must also have been burnt along with the tallies in the nineteenth century.[48] Although the bonds may have been destroyed, the Public Record Office holds a further class of financial records that apply specifically to the Jews.[49] Many of these documents are simply lists or scrutinies of the financial transactions made by the Jews which were deposited in the *archa* in each town. These lists of bonds made by the Jews contain details of over 3,000 individual transactions carried out in the thirteenth century.

Many other details of transactions, particularly sales of lands, mortgages and quitclaims, have survived elsewhere. Contemporaries called them *starra* (sing. *starrum*), which was the Latin equivalent of the Hebrew *shetar*. *Starra* are held at the Public Record Office, the Westminster Abbey Muniments and the British Library.[50] However,

---

[42] Stacey 1988; 1985; Dobson 1979.

[43] Stacey 1987b, pp. 61–2; Mundill 1987, pp. 58–100; see chapter 4 below.

[44] Dickens, *David Copperfield* 1983 edn, p. 630.

[45] PRO E/101/249 and E/101/250 categories as well as some *archae* which have survived amongst the PRO C/47/9. PRO E/101/249/5 and E/101/249/7. There are also many other Henrician bonds amongst the Ancient Deeds series PRO C/146 category; *Catalogue of Ancient Deeds*, vol. III–V. See Table 6 below.

[46] Tanner 1936, pp. 62–3; Davis 1888; Lipman 1967, pp. 187–312.

[47] Hereford and Worcester RO MS AH81/34; PRO C/146/1360; Mundill 1990a, pp. 6–7.

[48] Rokeah 1971; Giuseppi 1963, p. 98.   [49] PRO E/101/249, E/101/250.

[50] Davis 1888; *SCBM*, vols. I–III; PRO E/250/13; PRO E/9 series reveals many records of *starra*.

many other *starra* exist in cathedral archives and in the muniments of some Oxford and Cambridge colleges as well as in the archives of St Bartholomew's Hospital.[51] In addition the Anglo-Jew has left behind a variety of other records. The accounts of the *Domus Conversorum* provide a range of records that enables us to chart the history of the House for over six centuries.[52] Using these, the Reverend Michael Adler wrote a full history of the *Domus Conversorum* in 1903.[53] The bulk of what is known about medieval Anglo-Jewry is indeed naturally drawn from these specifically Jewish records. Without such records historians would have been condemned to working from far more fragmentary evidence in order to build a history of the first Anglo-Jewish community. However, the pre-Expulsion Anglo-Jew was a well-established feature of medieval society and so references to Jews and Jewish affairs pervaded other governmental records. Because of the medieval Jews' importance to government and officialdom in general, reference to Jewish affairs can be found in major governmental records such as the Pipe Rolls, the Chancellor's Rolls, the Close Rolls, the Patent Rolls, the Fine Rolls, the Justices' Rolls, the Forest Rolls, the Hundred Rolls and the Miscellanea of the Chancery, and amongst the collections of Ancient Deeds and Ancient Petitions. It is far too easy to forget that on a local level incidental references to Jewish affairs can be found, admittedly with great difficulty, among records as diverse as Manorial Court Rolls, Bailiffs Accounts, Cartularies and the odd survivals of deeds and bonds.[54] The charter which Simon de Montfort obtained, banning the Jews from Leicester, was sold at Sotheby's in 1904.[55] Other documents, like the Pollard Starrs, connected exclusively with one piece of land, were discovered in the hands of a firm of Norwich solicitors, Messrs Bignold and Pollard, only in 1932.[56] It is likely that many other incidental references to Jews and their affairs are still to come to light.[57]

The actual Expulsion of the Jews in 1290 was carried out so efficiently that it has left behind it much written evidence. The ensuing Dissolution of the Jewries has also left a comprehensive set of documents. So much so that these particular groups of records richly deserve the title of *Valor Judaismus*.[58] Such detailed records, made by the King's Remembrancer, an official of the king's own Great Exchequer, have

---

[51] Adler 1937; Hilton 1989, pp. 22–3; Roth 1957; Stokes 1913, pp. 159–61; Loewe 1932.

[52] PRO E/101/250/15–30, E/101/251/1–32, E/101/252/1–30, E/101/253/1–29, E/101/254/1–30.

[53] Adler 1903; Stacey 1992a.   [54] Mundill 1993, pp. 25–7.   [55] Levy 1902a, pp. 40–1.

[56] *SCBM*, vol. II, pp. 305–18.

[57] Mundill 1990a, pp. 7–8. Hereford and Worcester RO MS AH81/34; PRO C/146/1360.

[58] Mundill 1993, pp. 25, 43 note 6; PRO E/101/249/7 and E/101/250/1–12; BL Additional MS 24,511 and Lansdowne MS 826 fos. 28–64.

enabled historians to examine in detail the final Dissolution of the Jewries and the redistribution of their lands. The documents include the original orders for the sheriffs of each county to close the *archae* and to bring them into Westminster, and for them to value all Jewish properties in the major towns and to make final scrutinies of the various *archae*.[59] This clearly reveals the state of the separate Jewries in 1290. These records show that Edward received at least £1,000 from the sale of Jewish-held properties.[60] They also contain details of over 1,000 bonds deposited in the *archae* in 1290 of which Edward now became the creditor. The Crown subsequently held on to these debts until 1326 when they were finally written off.[61]

Detailed interest in Jewish records and the English Exodus was awakened by the Anglo-Jewish Historical Exhibition in 1887, in itself a catalyst for the subsequent foundation of the Jewish Historical Society in 1894.[62] It was these two events, above all, which led nineteenth-century historians to re-examine and to print the sources. Thus in 1893 Joseph Jacobs published a widely read compendium of records, selected from many Latin, Hebrew and French sources.[63] Jacobs stopped at 1206, but his work is still of much use to the historian of the twelfth century. It encouraged others to return to the sources which had never been properly exploited before. The *Valor Judaismus* was studied for the first time in detail, and published, in part, by B. Lionel Abrahams in 1896.[64] This led him to write his award-winning essay, 'The Expulsion of the Jews from England in 1290'.[65] Many have followed and accepted his work, yet few have revised it. Meanwhile, an increasing number of sources continued to be printed. Mayer Domnitz Davis edited many of the *shetar* which were extant in English archives. In 1898 he published them as the second in a series of papers connected with the Anglo-Jewish Historical Exhibition.[66] However, despite these initiatives and other attempts at establishing a history of the medieval English Jewry, historians still seemed to ask few questions about what they regarded as a by-way of British social and economic history.

Renewed interest in the central governmental records made the subject of medieval Anglo-Jewry more accessible. Although many local historians and antiquarians, using occasional local references or deeds in their town or county histories, had noted the fact that there had formerly been Jewish communities present in a particular area, few had carried out thorough local investigations. As a direct result of the publication of Jewish records many histories of individual Jewish

---

[59] PRO E/101/250/1 and BL Additional MS 24,511.   [60] *Ibid.*
[61] *Statutes*, vol. I, p. 255.   [62] Stacey 1987b, p. 61.   [63] Jacobs 1893a.
[64] Abrahams 1896.   [65] Abrahams 1894b.   [66] Davis 1888.

communities were constructed. Local histories exist in some form or other for Bristol, Cambridge, Canterbury, Exeter, Hereford, Leicester, Lincoln, London, Northampton, Norwich, Oxford, Southampton, Winchester, Worcester and York.[67] The idea of publishing the records did not stop with local and governmental records. In 1930 the Starrs and Charters in the British Library were catalogued and printed. They still contain much of general interest to the medievalist and the local historian alike.[68]

The task of producing a full history of medieval Anglo-Jewry was left to a distinguished historian who completed his authoritative history of Anglo-Jewry from medieval to modern times in 1941. The late Dr Cecil Roth remains, as he was once described, 'the colossus of Anglo-Jewish history'. In particular, Roth carried out an enormous amount of work on all of the different species of records.[69] More recently the late Dr Vivian Lipman, in his study of the Norwich Jewry, worked extensively on the Westminster Abbey Muniments and also published some of them in print.[70] H. G. Richardson considered the English Jewry as a whole and, in his last chapter on the Expulsion, began to point the way towards a more complete study of Edwardian Anglo-Jewry.[71] Such a study has been made possible by the publication of the Plea Rolls by the Jewish Historical Society of England. More recently Dr Zefira Rokeah has carried out much research on the unedited and unprinted Chancellor's Rolls as well as the Justices' Rolls and has also added to the history of the medieval Anglo-Jew during Edward's reign from more general records. She has examined in detail the records which concern the coin-clipping allegations of 1279 and those which involve the Jews as either victims of or perpetrators of crime.[72] Nevertheless, the wider implications of the Jews' financial transactions and how Jews fared during Edward I's reign have still received comparatively little attention.

There is yet a further aspect of the Jews' financial activities that has perhaps not been examined closely enough. Historians of the thirteenth century have tended to ignore the impact of Jewish finance on the rural economy. When writing in connection with more general issues, however, they have raised questions about the many Christian clients of

---

[67] Adler 1928; Dobson 1993; Stokes 1913; Adler 1914; 1931; Hillaby 1984; 1985; 1990b; 1990c; Levy 1902a; Davis 1881; Jacobs 1893b; Roth 1934; Jacobs 1896, pp. 162–91; Hillaby 1993a; Collins 1946; Jolles 1996; Lipman 1967; Cohen 1932; Roth 1951; Allin 1972; Turner 1954; Hillaby 1990a, pp. 73–122; Brunskill 1964; Dobson 1974; 1979. Mundill 1987, chapters IV, V, VI considers the communities of Canterbury, Hereford and Lincoln.

[68] *SCBM* vols. I–III.   [69] Mundill 1991a, p. 205.

[70] Lipman 1967, pp. 187–312.   [71] Richardson 1961.

[72] Rokeah 1971; 1972; 1973; 1974; 1975; 1982a; 1982b; 1984; 1990; 1993.

the Jews. Dr Paul Hyams, in a discussion of moneylending at village level, hinted that much might be revealed by examining the local business dealings of the provincial Jewish communities.[73] This possibility had been raised by the late Professor Michael Postan, who suggested that Jewish moneylenders did not seem to operate in villages but might well have been lending money to peasant freeholders.[74] Any full-scale study of the Jewry under Edward I must accordingly encompass a consideration of exactly who the clients of the Jews were and where they lived. There are several studies which have tried to ascertain who the local clients of specific Jewish communities were. In 1894, B. L. Abrahams published a list of the surviving Jewish bonds in the two Hereford *archae* of 1290. For the first time, he not only transcribed the name of the Jewish creditor but also that of the Christian debtor.[75] This initial study was later followed in 1932 by Dr Sarah Cohen, who utilised the law suits recorded in the Plea Rolls of the Jewish Exchequer to analyse what types of person were indebted to the Jews and to ascertain whom the Jews were prosecuting for default of debt in Oxfordshire.[76] A few years later Peter Elman used several lists of bonds deposited at various times in the Cambridge *archae* and the list of debts to Abraham of Berkhamstead in 1255 to investigate more thoroughly the Jews' Christian clients. Elman proved that, whilst the Jew was generally urban based during the thirteenth century, his clientele was primarily rural.[77] In 1967, Vivian Lipman also tried to define the types of person who borrowed from Norwich Jews. His analysis of debtors was confined to the information supplied by the Norwich Day Book of 1225–7 which revealed some 300 debtors. His conclusions were that only a very small percentage of the debtors were 'great noblemen' or 'religious houses' and that most of them appeared to be 'members of the rural gentry'.[78] More recently Joe Hillaby has investigated the debtors of Hamo and Aaron le Blund of Hereford as well as other Hereford Jews and, as will be seen, has provided some more concrete solutions to the questions which have been raised about the Jews' debtors.[79]

Naturally the new interest in the medieval Jewish community during the nineteenth century led to attempts to explain the Expulsion. B. L. Abrahams thought that Edward I was moved by religious and other motives and in particular was responding to a papal Bull of 1286 which

[73] Hyams 1970, p. 30. [74] Postan 1972, pp. 152–3. [75] Abrahams 1894a.
[76] Cohen 1932.
[77] Elman 1936, pp. 113, 140–7; 1938a; Stokes 1913, appendices 4, 5, 6; *CCR 1254–1256*, pp. 170–2.
[78] Lipman 1967, pp. 93–4; Levy 1902b.
[79] Hillaby 1984; 1985; 1990c; Mundill 1987, chapters v and vii.

was sent by Honorius IV.[80] In 1891, George Leonard suggested that the Expulsion was agreed to by the people in return for a voted tax of a fifteenth by the people and of a tenth by the clergy. He saw it as a result of religious bigotry and baronial hatred as well as jealousy of Jewish financial success and wealth.[81] In 1903, James Rigg, who transcribed many of the Plea Rolls of the Exchequer of the Jews, saw Edward I's *Statutum de Judeismo* of 1275 as a crucial prelude to the Expulsion. He believed that it was because the Jews failed to comply with the full letter of the law set out in the Statute that they were expelled. He drew particular attention to the fact that the Jews did not become agriculturists within the fifteen-year period that the Statute of the Jewry allowed them and that they continued to practise usury by concealing it with apparently commercial transactions. This failure, he claimed, led directly to their Expulsion.[82] Certainly the Statute of 1275 is central to any discussion of the English Exodus and will receive attention below. Subsequently several different interpretations and explanations have been made which will need further consideration below.

The most commonly accepted argument is that of Peter Elman, who was the first to try and see the Expulsion in purely financial terms. His explanation was adopted and accepted by Cecil Roth.[83] Vivian Lipman expanded the financial theory. He believed that the reasons why the Jews were expelled were given in a document, dated after the Expulsion, which accused the Jews of continuing to practise usury in the form of *curialitas*.[84] Looking further afield, H. G. Richardson backed the view of ecclesiastical culpability and royal innocence.[85] More recently Barnett D. Ovrut claimed that the Expulsion was 'a conscious act of an aggressive government which was made in response to a number of political and constitutional factors'. He saw the decision to banish the Jews as a blow not against the Jews but against the greater lords. According to Ovrut the Expulsion helped the lesser landowners who were playing an increasing role in the development of the English state.[86] By contrast Dr Paul Brand pointed to the importance of rising anti-semitism.[87] He can be supported by the work of Professor Gavin Langmuir, who examined Jew-hatred, and who put forward a far more sociological explanation. Such an argument can naturally be strengthened by Joshua Trachtenberg and Norman Cohn's work.[88] In 1985,

[80] Abrahams 1894b.   [81] Leonard 1891.   [82] Rigg 1903.
[83] Elman 1936; 1938b; 1938a; 1952; Roth 1978, pp. 38–90, 273.
[84] Lipman 1967, p. 163; Mundill 1991b, pp. 150–4.
[85] Richardson 1961, pp. 213–33.   [86] Ovrut 1977.
[87] I refer to a lecture given by Paul Brand to the Jewish Historical Society of England on 16 July 1980.
[88] Langmuir 1963; 1971; Trachtenberg 1943; Cohn 1975.

Professor Sophia Menache examined the expulsions from France and England and pointed out that there was a link between an expulsion decreed by a king and the stereotype of the diabolic perfidious Jew in contemporary society. She saw expulsion of the Jews as a step forward in the growth of a national identity and as a political action designed to weaken internal opposition.[89] Recently, historians like Professors Robert Stacey and Sophie Menache have started to become more interested in the motives behind the Expulsion.[90] Many of these views and interpretations must be borne in mind as possible explanations for the English Exodus but they can only be rediscussed after a more thorough examination of Edwardian Anglo-Jewry itself.

There are many other questions that remain. Why was the Expulsion decided upon in 1290 and not 1272? Why did Edward bother to make important anti-Jewish legislation in the early part of his reign? If Expulsion was as inevitable as the differing theories of ecclesiastical pressure, Jewish financial inadequacy and rising anti-semitism would seem to indicate, why did some Jews manage to survive Edward's legislation in 1275? The immediate circumstances that led to the final decision may never be known, as the decision for the English Final Solution was taken in secret. However, a new analysis of Edward's rule over his Jewish subjects between 1262 and 1290, based upon a synthesis of previous work and a re-examination of the available documentation, will lead to some probable answers.

Such a study must combine the general historical themes and issues alongside the town histories and naturally must utilise the surviving financial and administrative records in detail. Many factors need to be considered; but it is above all imperative to examine Edward's policy towards the Jews themselves and to establish finally what he was trying to do when he started what has been dubbed the 'Edwardian Experiment'.[91] The Statute of the Jewry is indeed central to an understanding of the Expulsion itself and this particular Statute has often been misinterpreted. It is rightly accepted that it was directed against the Jews as usurers and moneylenders, but it is perhaps ironic that some of the latter seem to have survived to become commodity brokers with a keen interest in what we might call 'futures'. This shift of Jewish financial interest tends to militate against the economic explanation of the Expulsion as championed by Peter Elman, accepted by Cecil Roth and used by Vivian Lipman. In any re-examination of the Expulsion of the Jews a start must be made with a consideration of the position of the

---

[89] Menache 1985.   [90] *Ibid.*; Stacey 1997.
[91] Lipman 1967, pp. 162–85. Vivian Lipman was the first to use the term 'Edwardian Experiment'; Mundill 1991b, p. 147.

Jewish community within Edwardian society. The Jewish community's financial commitments in the form of tallages and fines also need to be closely examined. Finally, the Jews' relations with their clients must also be discussed before any proper attempt to reach a conclusion about England's Jewish solution can be made.

Chapter 2

JEWISH SETTLEMENT, SOCIETY AND ECONOMIC ACTIVITY BEFORE THE STATUTE OF THE JEWRY OF 1275

Any attempt to analyse the nature of medieval Anglo-Jewry during the last years of its existence must naturally involve a consideration of the Jewish community before the start of Edward I's reign. Jews had always been a small minority within the Christian population of the realm. Yet it is important to consider how widespread the Jewish community had been throughout the country, how influential, and how closely related to various strata of English society. Such factors will throw light on the Jewish community's internal structure and contacts. They will also reveal how the Jewish community made its living and what kind of business the Jews conducted prior to Edward's reign, and will expose some of the social and commercial consequences of that business.

As is well known, the medieval Anglo-Jewish community was a Norman importation. There can be little doubt that it was the Conqueror himself who first encouraged Jewish immigration from Rouen to England in the late eleventh century.[1] By the twelfth century the Jewish pioneers had begun to inhabit the major trading towns of the country. At the end of that century it appears that the separate Jewish communities in each provincial town had started to conduct business in more rural districts. It is even possible that their moneylending activities and their search for clients made them at least partly itinerant. After the dislocation of Stephen's reign, the chronicler William Fitz Stephen observed that 'Peace was everywhere and there emerged in safety from the towns and castles both merchants seeking fairs and Jews seeking creditors.'[2] Towards the end of the twelfth century, a contemporary noted the special position of the English Jew:

Under our first three sovereigns they had been to a certain extent left alone; they had been loyal and industrious subjects, and had ministered much to the

---

[1] *Gesta Regum Anglorum*, vol. II, p. 371 note.
[2] *Materials for the History of Thomas Becket*, Rolls Series 67, 1875–85, vol. III, p. 19; Streit 1993.

prosperity of the country of their adoption; they worshipped in their synagogues in peace, bought land and amassed riches; their lives had fallen in pleasant places and they concluded that the future would be as the past had been.[3]

One of the best-known, most fortunate and industrious of medieval Anglo-Jews, Aaron of Lincoln, had a business which was carried out on a local as well as a national level. His financial activities included buying the debts of other Jews, lending both large and small sums, securing rent charges, pawnbroking and even speculating in corn. It was a business which involved a wide range of clients from all over the land. In 1186, when Aaron died, his debts were worth well over £15,000 and his debtors included the kings of England and Scotland, various earls, abbots, priors, towns, sheriffs and even the archbishop of Canterbury.[4] The list of Aaron of Lincoln's debtors clearly proves that the lending of Jewish capital meant that to be a successful Jewish business man the creditor had to be well travelled. It was primarily for business reasons too that other Jews dispersed throughout England and became more familiar with roads, rivers, towns and villages. However, it was not to be a pleasant and peaceful existence. At the end of the twelfth century the Augustinian canon, William of Newburgh, who left a full account of the massacre of 1190, complained about the position that the Jews had allegedly made for themselves: 'By an absurd arrangement they were happy and renowned far more than Christians, and swelling very impudently against Christ through their good fortune, did much injury to Christians.'[5]

The general massacres of 1190 were widespread, and many Jewish communities were subjected to the pogroms which began at Richard I's coronation in London in September 1189. Massacres of Jews at this time took place in small towns such as Ospringe in Kent, Thetford in Suffolk and Stamford in Lincolnshire, as well as in major trading centres like Norwich, Bury St Edmunds and York.[6] From other sources it seems clear that, by the late twelfth century, a Jewish presence in England was widespread and centred not just on a small handful of towns but also within smaller communities such as Bungay, Dunstable and Lynn.[7] Nor

[3] Atkinson 1912, p. 8.
[4] Richardson 1960, p. 9. The Lincoln Jewish community contributed £40 to a *donum* levied by Henry II in 1159. Hill 1979, pp. 25, 33; 1965, pp. 218–21; Jacobs 1899; Hunter 1828, p. 269; *Cartularium Rievallense*, pp. 200, 203, 204; *Memorials of Fountains Abbey*, vol. II, p. 18; Jacobs 1893a, p. 264; Srawley, *The Book of John de Schalby*, 1966, p. 8; Davis 1881, p. 187.
[5] *Historia Rerum Anglorum*, vol. I, p. 280.
[6] Dobson 1974, pp. 25–31 gives the most recent account of the massacres of *Shabbat ha Gadol*.
[7] Roth 1978, pp. 21–2; Lipman 1967, pp. 20–2, 57, 58; *Historia Rerum Anglorum*, vol. I, p. 280; Streit 1993.

is it surprising, as Vivian Lipman observed, that Jewish communities were rarely far away from royal castles.[8] The fact that the Jews were a Norman importation, French-speaking and alien to the indigenous population, meant that for most of the twelfth century they would have found it hard to be assimilated into local society, even if they had personally wished to be so. Quite apart from the religious barriers which separated them from Christian society, they must have been resented as much as any other aliens. It was for reasons of security, self-preservation and social welfare as well as the preservation of their religion that they tended to live in centres which had a royal representative or a powerful protector close at hand. The Jews needed protection from Christian society from their arrival in England until they were expelled. Joe Hillaby has suggested that the links between the Jews and their protectors were at times so strong that the former sometimes moved with the latter. When the Bigods' castle at Bungay was demolished in 1174 it is possible that the small Jewish community moved with the earls of Norfolk or their followers to Norwich, Lincoln, Northamptonshire and Hereford. Certainly, in the early thirteenth century, it seems that Marcher Lords like Walter de Lacy took Jews like Hamo of Hereford under their protection. For in 1218 Hamo and other Jews received encouragement and the promise of future protection to settle in Hereford and other places.[9]

By the early thirteenth century the Jews were accordingly widely established throughout the realm. Their business of lending money naturally linked them directly or indirectly to the land in the surrounding countryside as their security for their loans. As creditors using land for security these Jewish business men must have had an intimate knowledge of its value. They must have inspected or at least known the lands which had been offered as security for their loans by their debtors. The evidence of their activities in the local land markets and in mortgaging at this period is plentiful and widely spread over many shires. It also seems that in the twelfth and early thirteenth centuries their clients were generally of a high landholding status.[10] It was their business which occasionally took them further afield. In Kent there was a community of Jews at Canterbury by 1187. By 1190 some of them had evidently settled at Ospringe, where they were to be massacred by the local populace. By 1194, it is likely that Jews were living or conducting business in Rochester because some meadows

---

[8] Lipman 1984.   [9] Hillaby 1984, pp. 363, 367–8; 1985, p. 212; *CPR 1216–1225*, p. 157.
[10] Jacobs 1893a, p. xiv; Hillaby 1985, p. 262; Richardson 1960, pp. 83–102.

had been mortgaged to them by the priory of Rochester.[11] In the early thirteenth century it may be that some Jews began to migrate further afield, encouraged, like the Hereford Jewry, by promises of protection.

Throughout the period of Jewish presence in medieval England, forced migrations and local expulsions also dictated where Jews settled. They were, for example, expelled from Bury St Edmunds as early as 1190.[12] However, Jewish families or communities still migrated in search either of new clients or merely of a more peaceful existence. During the thirteenth century, Jews lived or conducted business in the mid-west of the country, in towns like Bridgnorth, Caerleon, Gloucester, Ludlow, Tewkesbury, Warwick, Worcester, Hereford and Bristol.[13] They lived, or certainly travelled, as far north as Shrewsbury, for between 1284 and 1289 they were forced to pay a special toll for using Montford Bridge.[14] Nearer to Hereford, where a community appears to have been established as early as 1179, it is evident that in the 1280s Jews lived in Weobley and later possibly on the small manor of Much Markle.[15]

Local migration can also be seen within large counties like Lincolnshire, where there were two distinct Jewish colonies from quite an early date. Throughout the thirteenth century tallage payments and receipts were made by the sheriff of Lincolnshire for the Jewish *communae* of both Stamford and Lincoln. There was an *archa* at Stamford and Jews lived there, in the parishes of St Michael and of St John's and All Saints, until the Expulsion. There was also a synagogue in Stamford, which was

[11] Roth 1978, p. 21; *Pipe Roll 1191–1192*, pp. 147, 203, 213; *Registrum Hamonis Hethe*, p. 2; Jacobs 1893a, pp. 73, 90.

[12] Jacobs 1893a, pp. 141–2; Stacey 1987b, p. 65 calls for a re-examination of these early local expulsions; Scarfe 1986, pp. 99–109; Mundill 1997.

[13] PRO E/101/249/10, E/101/249/29, E/101/250/4, E/101/250/5; *PREJ1*, pp. 9, 150; *PREJ3*, p. 319; *CCR 1272–1279*, pp. 49–50; *Abbreviatio Rotulorum Originalium*, vol. 1, p. 243; *Historia Sancti Petri de Gloucester*, pp. xxxix–lii, 20–1; Tovey 1738, p. 151. *Episcopal Registers of Worcester – Register of Godfrey Giffard 1268–1301*, pp. xvi and introduction, preserves a story of a Jew who fell into a cess pit at Tewkesbury. Richard de Clare refused permission for the unfortunate Jew to be helped out of the cess pit as it was the Sabbath. The Jew, for religious reasons, refused help. In any case Richard de Clare then refused him help on the Sunday, and by the Monday morning the Jew was dead.

> Tende manus Salomon, ut te de stercore tollam
> Sabbata nostra colo, de stercore surgere nolo
> En ruit altra dies, nunc me stercore tollis
> Sabbata nostra cola de stercore tollere nolo.

[14] *CPR 1281–1292*, p. 116. The pontage charge granted for five years was to be ½d for any Jew or Jewess to cross the bridge, or 1d if they were on horseback. Montford is one mile north of Shrewsbury on the River Severn. For a similar grant of pontage cf. *CCR 1272–1281*, p. 331.

[15] PRO E/101/250/5; PRO Justices Itinerant 1/303/ m. 63 dorse, kindly communicated to me by Dr Z. E. Rokeah.

forfeited in 1290.[16] Stamford was clearly a Jewish colony of some importance in the south of the county. In the north, Lincoln had been the headquarters of Aaron of Lincoln's financial empire by at least the 1190s, and also possessed an *archa* and at least one synagogue. Within this eastern area of the country it was not only Stamford and Lincoln that were hosts to Jewish communities. Toponymic evidence and taxation records suggest that there were some Jews present in other outlying towns in Lincolnshire and Yorkshire, including Tickhill, Doncaster, Hedon, Retford, Grantham and Holme, and Brodsworth.[17] Places such as these were frequented by Jews who had strong links with the communities of Lincoln, Nottingham and York. Indeed, for some years, the Lincoln Jewry shared a burial ground called 'Le Jewbury' at York with these other communities.[18] The Lincoln Jews also seem to have had connections with the Jews of Colchester and naturally with the largest and most important community of the realm, London.[19] Thus, at one time or another in the thirteenth century, communities of Jews existed from Newcastle upon Tyne to Exeter and from Hereford to Colchester.[20]

A very rough impression of the distribution of the most substantial Jewish settlements by the mid-thirteenth century can be gained from records of tallage assessments and collections. The tallage assessments of July and October 1255 reveal that there were Jewish communities in the following areas: Bedford, Bristol, Cambridge, Canterbury, Colchester, Exeter, Gloucester, Hereford, London, Lincoln and Stamford, Marlborough and Wilton, Northampton, Nottingham, Oxford, Warwick, Winchester, Worcester and York.[21] The records of tallage receipts made in 1253 and 1260 refer to many of these same towns, and also reveal other areas of settlement. Payments were made by Jews in the following towns and counties: Bedford, Berkshire, Bristol, Cambridge, Canterbury, Colchester, Dorset, Exeter, Gloucester, Hereford, Lincoln and Stamford, London, Northampton, Norwich, Nottingham,

---

[16] PRO SC/11/46; Royal Commission on Historical Monuments – Stamford, p. xli.

[17] Tickhill: Rigg, p. 53 and Hunter 1828, vol. I, pp. 225, 237; Doncaster: PRO E/101/249/16 and E/401/1582; Hedon: WAM nos. 6831 and 9145; Retford: *CCR 1272–1281*, p. 389; Grantham: PRO E/101/249/4; Holme: Rigg, p. 68; Brodsworth: Hunter 1828, vol. I, p. 314 and PRO E/101/250/12.

[18] Honeybourne 1964, p. 157; Adler 1933, p. 149; Davies 1875, p. 186. Nottingham RO M/24/182–8, The Lassman Papers.

[19] Davis 1887, 12 August, p. 10; PRO E/101/249/10, a roll connected with Lincoln Jews, reveals the names of three Jews 'of Colchester'.

[20] Guttentag 1977, pp. 1–24 examines the brief history of the Newcastle community; Stephenson 1984, pp. 48–52 briefly outlines the history of the Colchester Jewry.

[21] The assessment made in July 1255 can be found in *CPR 1247–1258*, pp. 439–40. Details of the arrears and further assessments in October 1255 can be found in *CPR 1247–1258*, pp. 441–4.

Oxford, Sussex, Warwick, Wiltshire, Winchester, Worcester and York.[22] By the mid-thirteenth century it seems that the great majority of Jews lived in towns which could offer protection of some sort and an *archa* in which to deposit their transactions. Yet some were still apparently able to live further afield and away from an *archa*.[23]

The evidence accordingly suggests that the vast majority of medieval Anglo-Jews lived in communities in towns.[24] Thus the Jewish properties mentioned in Hugh of Kendal's post-Expulsion accounts are all situated in *archa* towns. The distribution of known Jewish synagogues and burial grounds also confirms that Jews usually lived in towns which had *archae*.[25] Moreover a survey of the towns in which *archae* were still situated in 1290 makes it clear that the urban centres in which the Jews were concentrated were often county towns, cathedral cities, towns with castles and mercantile centres.[26] It is thus tempting to think of medieval Jews as town-dwellers and indeed some historians have gone as far as to describe them as an 'urban phenomenon'.[27]

However, despite the close Jewish association with towns in the thirteenth century, a few historians have acknowledged the possibility that Jews lived in smaller towns and even villages.[28] Dr Paul Hyams, for instance, while accepting that the pattern of Jewish settlement was urban based, at the same time gave credence to the possibility that more rural settlements could have flourished.[29] Despite the twelfth-century evidence to this effect, his views have not been universally accepted. Professor R. B. Dobson found it difficult to believe that small numbers of Jews could live harmoniously with Christians as isolated residents. Yet he accepted that the traditional view, expressed by the Reverend James Parkes, that village Jewries were practically non-existent in

---

[22] Evidence for the tallage receipts for 1253 are derived from PRO E/401/20 and for 1260 from PRO E/401/43.

[23] Roth 1978, pp. 276–7 published a 'tolerably comprehensive list of Jewish settlement in the medieval period'. *CPR 1258–1266*, p. 442 reveals an order to fifteen burgesses of Bridport to protect Abraham fil Miles and Moses his son-in-law Jews of Bridport, while Mundill 1991b, p. 139 shows that despite the Statute of 1275 a Jew or Jewish family lived at Cricklade and Highworth between 1276 and 1281 where they paid annually for this privilege; *CPR 1258–1266*, p. 613 shows an expulsion from Romsey; *CCR 1259–1261*, p. 381 reveals an expulsion from Derby. See also Appendix 1, 'Places of Jewish Settlement 1262–1290'.

[24] Mundill 1987, pp. 12–13 (map), 'Towns with *archae* in late thirteenth century England'; Hillaby 1984, p. 360; 1990b, pp. 23–4. Three basic attempts have been made to list the places where Jews lived during the period of the first Anglo-Jewish colony. Jacobs 1893a, pp. 373–81; Roth 1978, p. 277; Gilbert 1976, p. 40.

[25] PRO E/101/250/1; BL Additional MS 24,511 fos. 48–9; Honeybourne 1964, p. 158.

[26] IPRO E/101/250/1; BL Additional MS 24,511 fos. 48–9; Honeybourne 1964, p. 158; Lipman 1984.

[27] Hyams 1974, p. 271; Richardson 1960, p. 83.

[28] Richardson 1960, pp. 20–2; Lipman 1968, pp. 67–8. [29] Hyams 1974, p. 271.

England and France, might still be proved.[30] In France this view has been revised and the works of Henri Gross, Professor Robert Chazan and Professor Norman Golb have reopened the issue.[31] Naturally, some modern orthodox Jews have found it hard, on religious grounds, to accept that their forebears could have lived, without a synagogue, in the countryside. They would claim that a Jew must, of necessity, live close to a synagogue and that, to have a synagogue, a large distinctive urban community is implied. However, medieval Judaism must have been flexible and no doubt it was acceptable and possible for Jews to live in rural areas and to use the burial grounds and synagogues of the larger communities for burials or high festivals. If in thirteenth-century France there were places where only 'two Israelites' lived, why should this not be the case in England?[32] Professor Dobson, despite his doubts, seems swayed by the work of Professor Chazan on northern French Jewry, with its emphasis on this sort of scattered rural settlement.[33]

In the light of such considerations the problem of Jewish residence in more rural and remote areas must be reviewed. Many historians have been attracted to H. G. Richardson's interpretation of Jewish toponyms, in which he claims that the obviously rural surnames that the Jews often took originated not from their places of residence but from the places where they pursued their business.[34] Although toponyms are not always to be trusted they are perhaps an indication and at times even a proof of habitation. Moreover, H. G. Richardson's interpretation of Jewish toponymic surnames and Jewish settlement can be challenged by evidence all over the country.[35] Records show beyond a doubt that some Jews actually lived in places as remote as Abergavenny in Wales, Bridport in Dorset, Cricklade in Wiltshire, Dunwich in Suffolk, Maldon and Rayleigh in Essex, Retford, Royston, Sandwich and Tewkesbury.[36] To strengthen his argument concerning Jewish toponymic surnames, H. G. Richardson claimed that permanent residence outside the *archa* towns was illegal without the king's licence.[37] This seems not to have been always the case. In 1249, Deulecresse the Jew of Wilton (where there was an *archa*) held a property in Salisbury, where there is no record of any *archa* at any time.[38] Deulecresse actually lived in the property, as he was involved in a plea for a right of way to the

---

[30] Dobson 1979, pp. 37–8; Parkes 1962, p. 63.   [31] Gross 1897; Chazan 1969; Golb 1985.
[32] Rabinowitz 1972, p. 31.   [33] Dobson 1979, p. 37; Chazan 1969, p. 59.
[34] Lipman 1967, pp. 19–22; Richardson 1960, pp. 13–14.
[35] Richardson 1960, p. 13 and following.
[36] *CPR 1258–1265*, p. 442; Parker 1979, p. 151; *PREJ3*, p. 43; Mundill 1991b, p. 139.
[37] Richardson 1960, p. 13 and following.
[38] In 1249 William Bonard of Salisbury was summoned to answer Deulecresse the Jew of Wilton. Deulecresse was trying to enforce his rights of way over Bonard's land in Salisbury to get to

water. Any challenge to Richardson's views on Jews being domiciled, legally or illegally, outside an *archa* town will have to be based on a detailed analysis of the evidence for smaller settlements and of the repeated attempts of the government to control Jewish settlement.

Government legislation to limit the residence of Jews to *archa* towns in itself naturally suggests that some Jews were accustomed to live in communities which did not have *archae*.[39] The Crown had always monitored Jewish settlement and constant attempts had been made before Edward I's reign to restrict the Jews to the *archa* towns. In 1253 the Jews were confined to living only in the towns where they had been 'accustomed to live'. Certainly it is clear that in the early 1270s, when Prior Joseph de Chauncy issued orders to seventeen sheriffs to the effect that all Jews should come into the main towns from the 'vills outside', some Jews lived in remoter places outside the main towns of each shire.[40] In Edward's reign the pattern of Jewish settlement was to change fairly drastically in 1275, when the Jews were expelled from the towns which were under the jurisdiction of the queen mother: provision was made for the Jews to be deported from Marlborough to Devizes, from Gloucester to Bristol, from Worcester to Hereford, and from Cambridge to Norwich.[41] The *Statutum de Judeismo*, issued in the same year, again stipulated that the Jews must live only in the *archa* towns.[42] Dr Cecil Roth pointed out that periodic orders to arrest Jews not residing in *archa* towns exist.[43] Hugh of Digneuton was commissioned in 1277 to investigate how far the new legislation was being observed but unfortunately his report has not survived.[44] Again, in 1284 new legislation confining Jewish residence to the *archa* towns was issued.[45] However, any settlement was subject to the influence of local protectors and also to special royal licence. After the *Statutum de Judeismo* in 1275, which restricted the Jews to the *archa* towns, Edward granted licences to individual Jews, 'to trade and ply merchandise and to live' in

water. These rights, for a term of ten years, had been written down in a chirograph. Deulecresse lost the claim: Meekings 1961, p. 138.

[39] Roth 1978, p. 72. Jews did live in non-*archa* towns. For this privilege they had, of course, to pay for special licences. In 1272, Jews from Bottisham and Holme paid such fines: Rigg, pp. 68–9. In 1272, there were at least two Jews living in Basingstoke: *PREJ1*, p. 277. Another paid to live there in 1273: *PREJ2*, p. 104. Hagin fil Isaac, *qui vocat* Benedict Bateman was also living in Basingstoke: *PREJ2*, p. 297. Another Jew paid to reside at Berkhamstead: *PREJ2*, p. 144. In 1275, Josce Bundy of Rayleigh in Essex was arrested for having dwelt there without a licence: Rigg, p. 82. In 1275, at least one Jew lived in Abergavenny: *PREJ2*, p. 144. Gross 1887, pp. 188–90. See Appendix 1, 'Places of Jewish settlement 1262–1290'.

[40] Rigg, p. xlix; Rokeah 1997, p. 189.

[41] *CPR 1272–1281*, p. 76; Rigg, p. 85; *Seventh Report of the Deputy Keeper of the Public Records*, 1846, p. 240; Mundill, forthcoming.

[42] *Statutes*, vol. 1, pp. 220–1.   [43] Roth 1978, p. 72.

[44] *Ibid.*; *CPR 1272–1281*, p. 240.   [45] *CCR 1279–1288*, p. 256.

places like Baldwin Wak's town of Thrapston in Northamptonshire and Gilbert de Clare's town of Caversham near Reading, as well as Rochester, Southampton, Ipswich, Dorchester, Royston and Retford.[46] Exceptions such as these, the repeated attempts in 1253, 1275, 1277 and 1284 to control the settlement of Jews, and the periodic orders to arrest Jews not obeying the relevant legislation all suggest that Jewish settlement was not as polarised within a small number of *archa* towns as historians have customarily believed.[47]

There are other incidental references which demonstrate that some Jews did live in towns and villages which did not have *archae*. The accounts and surveys of the Wiltshire lands of Adam de Stratton reveal that Jews contributed to the farm and lived on the manors of Cricklade from 1269 until at least 1281 and at Highworth from 1277 until 1281.[48] Various payments from Jews in remote places, and special payments for residence in small towns, also appear in the Jewish Plea Rolls. On the receipt roll of the main Exchequer for the Easter term 1275, Belia and Ursell of Gloucester paid 12s 0d so that they could remain at 'Brocstred' (Bread Street); Vyves fil Moses of Clare paid 6s 8d to remain at Maldon; and Samuel fil Jacob and Samuel fil Manser paid 4s 0d to remain at Wickham.[49] The Salisbury gaol deliveries for 1275 record that William Page of Warminster, who had stolen a green mantle, a woman's coat, a tapet and a linen sheet, had sold them to Michael, a Jew of Fisherton Anger, for 5s 0d.[50] Other evidence shows that in 1278 Sampson of Norwich was killed by thieves and his goods were carried off from his house in Farningham in Kent. Amongst the shopholders and tenants revealed by Sir John Clapham's study of Linton in Cambridgeshire in the 1270s was a single Jew called Adam Caiphas.[51] In the early 1270s, there is evidence that Norwich Jews were dealing in the east coast port of Dunwich.[52] In 1275 Josce fil Aaron of Colchester and his wife were living at Dunwich; they were fined £22 16s 2d for having taken the chattels of Isaac Gabbay, a deceased Jew there. Similarly there is evidence that a Jewess called Reyna paid £2 to remain in Dover between 1272 and 1274.[53] Thus, there is good evidence that some Jewish families did live, in small numbers, both in coastal ports and in

---

[46] *CCR 1272–1279*, pp. 259–60; *CCR 1272–1279*, pp. 362, 370, 376, 382, 385, 389.
[47] Hyams 1974, p. 271; Lipman 1968, pp. 66–7; Hillaby 1990a, p. 73.
[48] Farr 1959, pp. xviii–xix, 14, 31, 39, 50, 62, 73, 83, 93, 102, 121, 202, 212, 221.
[49] PRO E/401/75. Bread Street is 1½ miles north-west of Stroud.
[50] Pugh 1978, p. 35.
[51] Rokeah 1982a, p. 14; Clapham 1933, pp. 198–9; Harding 1993, p. 116.
[52] Parker 1979, p. 151.
[53] *PREJ3*, p. 43; I am particularly grateful to Dr Rokeah for bringing to my attention this reference to Dover: PRO E/352/67 membrane 3.

the countryside. Clearly, families who dwelt in such isolated communities did so at great risk and it is likely that they had the protection of patrons in the form of their major clients. They would easily be distinguished from their Christian contemporaries even without the badge which was enforced at various times throughout the thirteenth century.[54]

The majority of the English Jews, however, would presumably have preferred the safety which an important town offered them and the social intercourse and succour which living amongst their brethren provided. Yet at the start of Edward's reign, toponymic evidence suggests that there were Jews living in places like Beverley, Buckingham, Brodsworth, Burford, Caerleon, Calne, Chippenham, Clare, Colton, Doncaster, Dorking, Evesham, Hedon, Hendon, Ilchester, Kingston, Knaresborough, Lambourne, Newbury, Newmarket, Newport, Rising, Romney and Shoreham. Other references prove that there were Jews living in smaller places such as Alcester in Warwickshire, Arundel, Basingstoke, Bottisham, Chesterton near Cambridge, Chichester, Chipping Campden, Cricklade, Dorchester, Guildford, Hatcham, Highworth, Holme, Lewes, Odiham, Seaford, Sudbury and Wallingford.[55] It is also known that the Jews were expelled from Derby in 1261, Romsey in 1266, Winchelsea in 1274, Eleanor of Provence's dower towns and Andover in 1275 and Windsor in 1283; none of these was an *archa* town or appeared to have had significantly large Jewish communities living there.[56] Thus before and during Edward's reign there were Jews living in *archa* and other major towns as well as in smaller and perhaps more remote places. Jewish settlement in the early years of Edward I's reign was clearly not just centred on the *archa* towns.[57] Yet if, before Edward's reign, Jews had colonised remoter places, then by the 1280s Jewish settlement was clearly in geographical retreat.

Even within the larger English towns the small Jewish communities would have been an easily distinguished homogenous group. Demographic details of these more urban-based Jews are difficult to interpret. However, it has been suggested that they made up about 1 or even 2 per cent of the urban population. It has also been suggested that the Jewish community in England, even at its height during the early

---

[54] Synan 1965, p. 104; Roth 1978, pp. 40, 78; *Concilia*, vol. I, p. 591 and vol. III, p. 155; Rigg, p. xlix; *Statutes*, vol. I, pp. 220–1.

[55] See Appendix I.

[56] *CCR 1258–1266*, pp. 153, 613; *CCR 1272–1279*, p. 50; *CCR 1279–1288*, p. 241; Cooper 1850, p. 20 makes a passing reference to there having been a building called Jew's hall there. Mundill forthcoming.

[57] Hyams 1974, p. 271; Hillaby 1990b, p. 23; Richardson 1960, p. 83; Langmuir 1963, pp. 210–21.

thirteenth century, never exceeded some 5,000 souls.[58] It is certainly clear that the contemporary estimates of the numbers of Jews who were expelled in 1290 were exaggerations. According to the chronicles of the day, the number of Jews who left England varied between 15,000 and 17,000.[59] More recently, it has been suggested that 2,000 is a more acceptable figure for the number of Jews who were forcibly exiled.[60] Several pieces of evidence give clues as to the size of Jewish population during Edward's reign. Such evidence, naturally, only offers very rough figures, but it does seem to confirm that the lower estimate of the number of Jews who were expelled is correct, and it also demonstrates that a decline in the Jewish population occurred not only between the start of the thirteenth century and the Expulsion but also throughout Edward I's reign.

One such indication of Jewish population decline in Edward's reign comes from 1279 when all the Jews of England were arrested.[61] Although Cecil Roth was suspicious of contemporary chroniclers' reports that during the coin-clipping allegations of 1278 and 1279 all Jewish householders (some 680) were imprisoned, this claim now seems to be authenticated by the recent work of Zefira Rokeah.[62] If only 680 Jewish householders existed in the late 1270s, then a total Jewish population of only about 2,720 (or more, if non-householders are considered) could be expected. If an allowance is made for Jews who were hanged or who may have fled the country, then a figure of just under 4,000 for the total Jewish population might be proposed for the late 1270s. It is also quite clear that, as a result of the coin-clipping allegations, the Jewish population again decreased. It can be confirmed, for example, that 293 Jews were executed in London alone in 1279 for alleged coin-clipping. Dr Lipman provided evidence of a serious population decline in Norwich; and repeated references to *suspensi* and *damnati* in the contemporary records only serve to substantiate what might be termed a pogrom during those years.[63] Thus it can be assumed that by 1279 the total Jewish population did not exceed 4,000 but was probably above 2,000.

---

[58] Lipman 1968, pp. 68–9 suggests between 5,000 and 6,000. Hyams 1974, p. 270 qualifies this by pointing to a shrinking community and surmises that by 1290 the population was probably 2,500–3,000. Mundill 1987, p. 16 estimates a figure of about 4,000 for the late 1270s. Rokeah 1990, p. 97 has recently suggested a figure of between 2,000 and 3,000 at the Expulsion.

[59] *Chronica Johannis de Oxenedes*, p. 277 intimates a total Jewish population of 16,511; Stow, *Annales*, vol. I, p. 204 gives the figure of 15,060; H.W., *Anglo-Judaeus*, p. 25 accepts the figure of 16,511.

[60] Lipman 1968, p. 65 suggests around 2,500–3,000; Mundill 1987, p. 16; Rokeah 1990, p. 97.

[61] Roth 1978, p. 78; Richardson 1960, pp. 217, 219–20.   [62] Rokeah 1990, p. 96.

[63] Lipman 1968, pp. 65 note 12 and 76–7.

The only national evidence for the total population of Anglo-Jewry in the 1280s derives from the poll tax accounts for the early part of the decade. This tax was to be paid by all male and female Jews over the age of twelve. The returns that survive for the period 1280–3 indicate that between 1,135 and 1,179 Jews paid the tax each year. However, the returns occasionally exclude some communities, as in 1280 when the London and Canterbury communities do not appear to have paid.[64] It is also likely that many Jews in rural areas escaped this particular tax or could not be found to pay it. The possibilities for tax evasion were great and certainly collection was neither welcomed nor helped by the local communities. At least one official who was appointed to collect the tax was assaulted by members of the Oxford Jewry.[65] Despite these problems, however, the figures from the poll tax accounts again confirm a figure of a Jewish population of about 2,000 in the early 1280s.

The governmental records at the time of the Dissolution of the English Jewries give many indications as to the assets held by the Jews, but it is not possible to use this evidence to reach any figure of total population. The suppression of the Jewries brought about the redistribution of the lands of approximately only 120 Jewish property holders. This might have indicated a population of 600 were it not for the fact that the surviving bonds suggest a higher figure.[66] The financial bonds in the *archae* at Bristol, Canterbury, Cambridge, Devizes, Exeter, Hereford, Lincoln, Norwich, Nottingham, Oxford and Winchester reveal approximately 262 Jews who had registered their transactions in 1290.[67] Taking into account the fact that some of these Jews were possibly already deceased as well as the lack of evidence for Jewish creditors in other major *archa* towns, an estimate of Jews who had bonds registered in the *archae* in 1290 would indicate 500 and certainly no more than 600. Allowing for Jews who had perhaps fled or gone into hiding, and for Jews who did not make bonds, the figure of Jewish population prior to the Expulsion might again be about 2,000. Thus, although it is virtually impossible to determine the exact number of Jews who were exiled or to come to any firm conclusions about the size of the total Jewish community, it is certainly possible to conclude that in population terms Edwardian Jewry was an insignificant minority. However, it was a minority that was under constant surveillance, regulation, intimidation and harassment from the host society at large.

[64] See chapter 4 below. *CPR 1272–1281*, p. 371; Adler 1939, p. 300; PRO E/101/249/24.
[65] Stacey 1992a, p. 280; Roth 1951, p. 162.
[66] PRO E/101/249/27; PRO E/101/249/30; BL Lansdowne MS 826, 4, fos. 28–64.
[67] PRO E/101/250/2–12.

Such small Jewish communities within contemporary English society must necessarily have had close contacts with their fellow Jews within their own immediate region, but they must also have had similar contacts with satellite communities and other Jews in more distant major towns. Jews naturally married Jews; and mobility between the different communities for marriage purposes if nothing else could not have been uncommon. In Canterbury, during the period 1251–3, Bona, a Jewess, paid 2 shillings for permission to go to her husband at Cheriton (a few miles north of Folkestone); and Salle paid 6s 8d to attend a wedding in London. Clearly, personal relations as well as business matters entailed a fairly high degree of mobility between the Jewish communities in England.[68] However, it was their shared religion and their shared perceptions of Gentile society that bound the Jews together as small interconnected homogenous communities. As Norman Cohn observed, 'they persisted through so many centuries of dispersion as a clearly recognizable community, bound together by an intense feeling of solidarity, somewhat aloof in its attitude to outsiders and jealously clinging to the tabus which had been designed for the very purpose of emphasizing and perpetuating its exclusiveness'.[69] This aloofness and enthusiasm for Judaistic culture distinguished the Jew from his contemporaries and gave him a common bond with his fellow Jews.

In the first place English Jews were linguistically different. The majority of males were probably trilingual in Latin, Norman–French and Hebrew. The Jews' legal language and the language of contracts was Latin; and the fact that the majority of the documentary evidence regarding the Jews was in Latin is, in itself, evidence that they were fluent in it. However, it seems that they also spoke and wrote in French and it is possible that the majority preferred to use it as their everyday language.[70] Cecil Roth claimed that it was necessary to translate the domestic service which was used on the Eve of the Passover into the vernacular for the benefit of women and children.[71] But it was not the Jews' ability to converse and write in both Latin and Norman–French which set them apart from society. As Professor Michael Clanchy has

---

[68] *PREJ4*, pp. 139–43.   [69] Cohn 1975, p. 77.

[70] Loewe 1953, p. 235; Dobson 1974, p. 5; Roth 1978, p. 93; Jacobs 1889. Surviving examples of letters from Jews which are written in French are: PRO SC/8/54/2655 (From Bonamy of York); SC/1/13/106; SC/8/180/8966; SC/311/15531 (From Deudone Crespyn of York); SC/8/219/10906 (From Bonamy of York); SC/8/220/10970 (From Bonefy of Cricklade); E/101/250/13 (A *Starrum* issued by Gamaliel of Oxford). Other examples can be found in WAM nos. 9115, 6806 and 6812 (in this particlar *starrum* the early English forms of east, west, north and south are repeated in Hebrew characters after the words themselves). CCA MSS A68, A93, A90, Letter Book II 4. See also the 'Great Paxton' *starrum* which is claimed to be the work of an amateur; *Registrum Antiquissimum*, vol. III, pp. 197–201 (Lincoln Record Society, 29).

[71] Roth 1978, p. 125.

observed: 'At all social levels except that of the King's court native French speakers seem to have rapidly and repeatedly assimilated into the local population. The only exception to this rule are the Jews who remained separate because of their different religion and scriptural language and not because of their French origins.'[72]

The major linguistic difference between Jew and Gentile was the Jews' use of Hebrew. This was widely used and is found in epitaphs and graffiti as well as in transactions made between Jews, and their own signatures.[73] Legal transactions and loans between Jews were clearly drawn up by Jewish scribes, several of whom must have been employed in every community. Jewish scribes were also employed in London at the *Scaccarium Judaeorum* where a Hebrew copy of the Plea Roll was compiled. Such Jews would also have been responsible for the Hebrew written on the stocks of tallies used in the Exchequer.[74]

The Jews of England also had their own cultural achievements which set them apart from their Christian neighbours. Moses of London, who died in 1268, wrote the *Darkhe ha-Nikkud veha-Neginah*, the most competent work on Hebrew punctuation and accentuation for many centuries. He had three sons who all produced scholarly works during Edward I's reign: Elijah Menahem of London, Benedict of Lincoln and Jacob of Oxford.[75] In 1287, Jacob fil Jehudah of London produced his *Etz Chayim*, a collection of the whole body of Jewish law which made available the rabbinical responses of scholars such as Rabbi Elijah of Warwick, and of two of Moses of London's scholarly sons, Rabbi Joseph of Bristol and Rabbi Moses of Dover.[76] The poems of Meir of Norwich have also survived and bear witness to the events leading to the Expulsion: the massacres, imprisonments and sequestration of property.[77] The Edwardian Jew, therefore, actively perpetuated an intellectual and literary culture that set him apart from Christian society. The Jews' linguistic ability, literature, nomenclature, diet and laws all separated them from Gentile society and gave them points of contact with their fellow Jews.

The main focal point for any Jewish community was naturally the synagogue.[78] This multi-purpose building was the centre of the cultural, social and religious differences between Jew and Christian and was also a tangible representation of these differences. The importance of the

---

[72] Clanchy 1979, p. 168.
[73] Fuss 1975, pp. 229–45; Adler, 1935, pp. 8–23; 1937, pp. 15–33; Roth 1953, pp. 283–6; Davis 1888; CCA MSs A 68, A 93, A 90, Letter Book II 4 (all Hebrew quitclaims); WAM no. 9015 (Hebrew signature on the back).
[74] Roth 1946, pp. 31–3; 1948. [75] Marmorstein 1928; 1931; Kaufman 1893; Stokes 1914.
[76] Haberman 1967, pp. 157–9. [77] Shohet 1931, p. 43 and following.
[78] *PREJ2*, pp. 34, 42, 53, 56, 126, 146, 153, 165, 250; Hillaby 1993a, p. 186.

synagogue in Edwardian England is, as Joe Hillaby has recently observed, underlined by the fact that the government used the synagogue as the medium through which it made proclamations to its Jewish subjects.[79] The English synagogue was used as a place of prayer, study and assembly. It also housed the ritual bath or *mikvah*.[80] In contrast to the grandness and size of the continental synagogues at Cracow, Regensburg, Toledo and Worms, the English synagogues were generally quite simple.[81] All that was required for a service to take place was an ark for the Torah and a partition, which might be represented by a curtain, to keep men and women apart. The surviving synagogue at Lincoln reflects this simplicity of Judaism's basic needs.[82] In some cases the synagogues or *bethels* were possibly even small establishments maintained by wealthy patrons in private houses.[83] But it is abundantly clear that in most towns the synagogue was a building recognisable to both Jew and Christian alike. In most of the major towns during the Barons' Wars the rebels singled out the synagogue and sacked it. Within some towns the Church was aware of the possible religious competition offered by the synagogues and at various times tried to shut them down or confiscate them.[84] After 1290 it is possible that several were sequestered for the benefit of the Christian Church.

Documentary evidence of several communal and a few private synagogues has survived.[85] The details concerning the actual buildings show that they were often quite central and were nearly always easily distinguished from neighbouring buildings. The Canterbury antiquarian, William Somner, showed that the synagogue there was still recognisable in the seventeenth century when he observed 'that the Stone Parlour of the Saracen's Head which was mounted upon a vault and ascended by many stone-steps is the remains of a good part of that which was our Canterbury Jews' school or synagogue'.[86] The synagogues at Colchester and Hereford were recognisable because they had adjoining shops. It is possible that these were rented by Jewish shopkeepers to provide victuals for the Jewish community at large.[87] At

[79] Roth and Wigoder, 1975, pp. 1814–18; Hillaby 1993b, p. 184.
[80] Shohet 1931, p. 24.
[81] Metzger 1982, pp. 59–86; Kedourie 1979, p. 139.
[82] Jews Court, Steep Hill, Lincoln; Roth 1934; Rosenau 1936; Hillaby 1993b, p. 183.
[83] Roth 1978, p. 77. There is a possibility that a type of *bethel* might well have been found at Guildford; *The Independent* 16 January 1996, p. 7; *The Jewish Chronicle*, 19 January 1996, p. 6 where Edgar Samuel expresses his doubts and Joe Hillaby expresses arguments for it being a *bethel*.
[84] Roth 1978, p. 77; Richardson 1960, pp. 194–5.
[85] Mundill 1987, pp. 31–2; Hillaby 1993b, pp. 185–6.
[86] Somner 1640, p. 145; Haes 1903, pp. 230–2.
[87] BL Lansdowne MS 826, 4, fos. 28–64; PRO E/101/249/27, 30; Abrahams 1896, pp. 76–105.

Lincoln the surviving synagogue is still a very substantial stone building. Although there were two other synagogues in Lincoln, little detail of them survives.[88] The Norwich synagogue seems to have been an unusual building which was situated in the very centre of the town. Vivian Lipman showed that it had at least three entrances and was possibly constructed with stone columns and glazed roof tiles.[89] The synagogue at Nottingham was near the marsh on the edge of town on the south-west corner of Castle Gate and Lister Gate. It was reached by crossing the property of Jacob fil Menahem the Florid in the parish of St Peter's. In 1261 it was described as 'a house and a courtyard with a cellar and a synagogue on it'. It is just possible that one stone which was found during the last war was either from its construction or from a nearby Jewish cemetery.[90]

Only the locations and annual values of the other medieval English synagogues are known. Interestingly the Jewish communities of Northampton and Winchester also probably had burial grounds. The Winchester Jewish cemetery was outside the Westgate and must have included a small building which had a laving stone for corpses.[91] At York it appears that there were at least two synagogues in existence during Edward's reign. The first was granted to John Sampson and Roger Basy on 15 November 1279 by Queen Eleanor and was described as 'the whole land with buildings and appurtenances and with a school built therein and with steps leading to the entrance of the said land'. It was clearly raised up, possibly because it backed onto the River Ouse. The second York synagogue was probably in a private house adjoining Le Jewbury.[92] Joe Hillaby has done much to add to the list of medieval English synagogues. He concluded that many of them were close to Jewish houses which probably belonged to Jewish patrons.[93] The picture which now emerges in most towns is almost that of a synagogue complex which would have been easily identified by all Jews and townspeople alike.

These synagogues were not just important for their outward appearance. Inside, the *scolae* were both centres of worship and seats of Jewish learning. Each community was exposed to Jewish education from a young age until death. Jewish children were taught the elements of religious knowledge by the *hazzan* or 'reader' in the *Beth ha Sepher* or the 'House of the Book'. For the male adult's more advanced education there were the *yeshivahs* or *Beth Talmud*, of which the *scola* of Peytevin

---

[88] Roth 1934, pp. 20–5; Johnson 1978, pp. 35–7.   [89] Lipman 1967, pp. 123–5.
[90] WAM nos. 6799, 6800; Nottingham RO M/24/182/188, The Lassman Papers.
[91] Honeybourne 1964, p. 157; Turner 1954, p. 18; Collins 1946, pp. 151–64.
[92] *CPR 1272–1281*, p. 334; Adler 1933, pp. 120, 149–50.   [93] Hillaby 1993b, p. 195, 197.

Magnus at Lincoln in the 1250s was presumably one.[94] As a result of the influence of the synagogues, the three basic religious codes of Judaism, the Torah, Talmud and Responsa, all circulated widely throughout the Anglo-Jewish colonies and were used every day of the year. The use of the Torah or Scrolls of the Law apparently aroused little opposition from Gentiles. In fact, as Canon Stokes observed, 'We meet with it in the synagogue, the home, in public seats of learning, in private libraries as well as in courts of law and in various tribunals as well as in the pledge shop.'[95] The Jew was allowed to swear on the Torah as the Christian was on the Vulgate. The Talmud, however, had a different reception from Gentile society. The Papacy strongly disapproved of it and as late as 1286 Archbishop Pecham received a papal command to pass on to his bishops, 'that the books commonly called *Thalamud* which the Jews of England were putting forth as of greater authority than the Law of Moses were to be confiscated'.[96] Suppression of some Jewish literature did take place and as the Reverend James Parkes observed, 'It is evidence of the ruthless efficiency of the medieval Church that among the tens of thousands of medieval manuscripts which fill the libraries of Europe, America and Israel today there is only one complete medieval copy of the Talmud.'[97] The third precept, the rabbinical Responsa, was not outlawed. Along with their cabbalistic writings, the Jewish communities presumably managed to conceal it or else Gentiles remained ignorant of it for many centuries. However, all the texts and tenets of Judaism as well as a religious education were widely available for the medieval Anglo-Jews.

Two Ketubboth that have survived from the thirteenth century bear witness to the importance English Jews placed on religious education. The contract made between Yomtob fil Moses and Solomon fil Eliab regarding the marriage of the former's daughter, Ziona, to the latter contains a promise that Yomtob will engage a teacher to instruct Solomon during the first year after his marriage as well as to provide clothes for the weekday and the Sabbath and to support the couple for a year in his house.[98] Another contract made in 1271 in Lincoln shows that the bride's mother gave the couple a monetary dowry and 'a volume on calf skin containing the whole 24 books of the Hebrew Bible properly provided with vowel points and the *Masorah*, each leaf containing six columns and also having a separate portion with the *Targum* of the *Pentateuch* and the *Haftaroth*'.[99] Thus, Jewish education and religion were clearly paramount in Jewish social life, and the

[94] Keith 1959, p. 49; Rabinowitz 1972, pp. 213–24; Roth 1978, p. 279; Hillaby 1993b, p. 193.
[95] Stokes 1914, p. 79.   [96] Synan 1965, pp. 111–12.   [97] Parkes 1962, p. 73.
[98] WAM no. 6847.   [99] WAM no. 6797.

synagogue as purveyor of them was the basis of a significant difference between Jewish and Gentile culture.

Relatively little is known of relations between Jews and Christians in the towns or how the Jewish communities were regulated. It is clear that, despite repeated attempts by the Church to prevent it, the Jews lived in 'open' rather than 'closed' Jewries.[100] There were no ghettos in England. In general the Crown was not concerned about where Jews actually lived inside the *archa* towns, but only became concerned with enforcing its rights to Jewish properties when a Jew died.[101] There are, regrettably, many instances of friction between Christian and Jew and of riots or burnings of various Jewries.[102] A little more is known of the relationships between those who were appointed to look after the Jewish communities and their charges. A unique piece of local evidence survives from Canterbury which shows how the Jews lived their lives as a minority beside a relatively hostile majority. In the years 1251–4 the sheriff of Kent, Reginald of Cobham, recorded the receipts which he took from the Jews of Canterbury.[103] Cobham's receipts reveal in minute detail how the Canterbury Jewry was governed and how the Jewish community reacted to its Christian guardians.

Under Cobham's three-year custodianship the Canterbury community and twenty-one individual Jews made payments to him which amounted to just over £329. The responsibility of protecting a Jewry was not without substantial benefits. Out of the collections of money and valuable objects, Cobham was able to pay himself and his officials. In 1254, he was even able to use £80 collected from the Jews as a loan to John Geldewin and Richard Derde of Rochester.[104] Cobham was assisted in his work by an under-constable who obviously had a significant role to play in the running of Jewish affairs, for when John of Northwood's term of office as under-constable was complete the Jewish community paid £2 because they did not wish him to be re-elected as under-constable.[105] The sheriff and the under-constable must have had very close, almost daily, contact with the Jewish community. This close contact may be reflected by the fact that the receipts are written in Norman-French rather than in the language of Latin officialdom.

The Canterbury Jews made payments to the officials for a variety of reasons: for not attending inquests, for getting inquests held, for not attending the Justices of the Jews in London, for help with the payment

---

[100] Hyams 1974, p. 273.   [101] Mundill 1987, pp. 178–81.
[102] Hillaby 1990a, pp. 105–6; Adler 1928, pp. 158–61; Cohn-Sherbok 1979, p. 32; Cohen 1932, pp. 301–5.
[103] PRO E/101/249/8; printed in *PREJ4*, pp. 139–43; Lipman 1984, pp. 12–13.
[104] *PREJ4*, p. 143.   [105] *PREJ4*, p. 142.

of dues, for assistance in claiming their debts from Christians, for obtaining exeats from Canterbury to go to Higham, Cheriton and London, for marrying their daughters to Jews of other communities, for gaining official appointments, for obtaining justice, for special permission to eat the sheriff's lamb at Easter, and even for the right to employ what were presumably Christian wet-nurses.[106] Perhaps, however, the most significant feature of this record is the way in which the Jews of Canterbury can be seen to be acting as a community. It was in this communal capacity that the Jews of the town paid to have their bonds received and valued when the *archa* was sealed, paid to delay the payment of Queen's Gold, paid to obtain several concessions related to the collection of tallage, possibly paid to have their corn ground at the king's mill at Ospringe and paid for several other kinds of service rendered by the sheriff.[107] It accordingly seems that, by implication at least, the Canterbury Jewry had a *bursa communis* in order to be able to pay its fines and bribes, make loans and look after its poorer brethren.[108] It is similarly evident from these entries that the Jewish community in Canterbury was well organised, that it had a degree of autonomy, and that it could be effective when it came to influencing the election of Christian officials.

The Canterbury Jewry also provides some evidence of the power of the leaders of the local community. It shows that they too had an interest in deciding which Jews should be admitted to their community. Soon after the barons' wars, in 1266, the Canterbury Jewish community seems to have begun to protect the interests of its existing members. This is evidenced by a unique surviving English example of the *Herem ha yishub* or prohibition of settlement.[109] This prohibition on Jewish settlement in Canterbury is unparalleled even amongst the bounteous records of the continental Jewries. In 1937, Dr Louis Rabinowitz claimed that it was 'probably the only document extant giving the formula of an institution which persisted in southern France, Germany, Italy and eastern Europe for some seven centuries'.[110] The document itself, which was signed by seventeen Canterbury Jews, sets forth in solemn terms that:

the Jews of Canterbury had come to the resolution and thereto bound themselves by oath, that no Jew of any other town than Canterbury shall dwell in the said town, that is to say, any liar, improper person or slanderer, and that should anyone come to dwell there by writ of their lord the king, the whole

---

[106] *PREJ4*, pp. 139–43.
[107] *PREJ4*, pp. 139–43; *PREJ3*, p. 295 shows Moses de Doggestrete paying 10 bezants, in 1277, for the community so that they may have the sheriff's writ not to pay for the gates of Canterbury.
[108] Lipman 1968, pp. 73–4.   [109] Rigg, pp. 35–6.   [110] Rabinowitz 1937.

community shall pay to the king such sums as Salle fil Josce, Abraham fil Leo and Vives of Winchester, whose seals are attached to this *shetar*, shall lay upon the community in order that the person may be disqualified by the king from residing there; and if any of the community should oppose the disqualification of such a Jew who has shown himself a liar, an improper person and a slanderer, or has obtained such a writ from the king, let them be disqualified together.[111]

Michael Adler interpreted this document as an attempt to deal with the problem of an influx of refugees from other Jewries which may have been devastated during the troubles of the early 1260s.[112]

There is, however, no evidence of this prohibition having actually been used in Canterbury; and there are indeed problems in assessing how it was likely to have been implemented, for medieval Jews on the continent, where the custom persisted, clearly had difficulties themselves in interpreting the exclusion custom.[113] Rabbi Tam, for example, in the twelfth century, had claimed that 'the Talmudic law forbidding strangers to settle in a town against the will of the inhabitants applied only to such persons who refused to pay their share of the taxes', and had gone on to rule in his *responsa* that no Jew could be refused admission into a Jewish community if he was willing to abide by the community's rules.[114] The problem as to whether the Canterbury *Herem* was ever implemented does not, however, detract from the document's significance as an expression of the wishes and fears of the community of Canterbury at the time of its issue. Rabbi Dan Cohn-Sherbok sees the *Herem* as basically an attempt to deal with certain unscrupulous members of the Jewish community in order to improve the image of Jewish financial dealings.[115] Such an interpretation supports Louis Rabinowitz's view that it was not solely a reaction to a political emergency.[116] There can, however, be little doubt that the *Herem* was intended, in Rabinowitz's words, 'to bring about the economic protection of the community and the establishment of a virtual trading monopoly', in a time of difficulty.[117] It does prove that the Jewish communities were in some ways autonomous when it came to their internal affairs and that they were at times prepared to exclude other Jews who might bring disaster upon them by bad financial dealings or otherwise cause tension within the ecclesiastical capital of England.

Despite the caution of the Canterbury Jewish community, the very fact that the Jews provided credit facilities inevitably led to the indebtedness of many Christian institutions and individuals. By 1220, the abbey of St Augustine in Canterbury was 'so burdened with debts,

---

[111] Rigg, pp. 35–6.   [112] Adler 1914, p. 43.   [113] Finkelstein 1924, pp. 13–15.
[114] *Ibid.*   [115] Cohn-Sherbok 1979, pp. 23–37.   [116] Rabinowitz 1937, p. 79.
[117] Rabinowitz 1938.

that to the great scandal of the Church and the reproach of religion the daily allowances (*corridia*) of the monks were being sold to the enemies of the Cross of Christ – the Jews'.[118] St Augustine's was not free from Jewish debts until 1267 when Brother Adam of Kingsworth paid off the large sum of £133 6s 8d owed to Jewish creditors.[119] By 1223, Christ Church also owed several Jews £12 9s 4d.[120] Indebtedness to Jewish financiers and the problems which it caused were widespread over the whole country.

The deep involvement of the Jews in local economies all over England has long been acknowledged. H. G. Richardson has shown that Jewish economic activity in the twelfth and early thirteenth centuries included moneylending on the security of land, the sale of corrodies, prebends and rentcharges, occasional credit dealings in corn and other commodities and also pawnbroking.[121] Whilst evidence is plentiful for all but the last, it is clear that it was the loan on security of land or mortgage which caused particular resentment on the debtor's part. Naturally financial obligation to a Jewish creditor turned into odium when the debtor lost his lands completely. Examples of the subsequent problems of indebtedness, particularly in the early decades of the thirteenth century, are multifarious. Amongst other individual cases, H. G. Richardson examined the dealings of William of Husborne. Sometime in the first decade of the thirteenth century, William borrowed money from Jewish moneylenders on the security of a prebend, then on his land and then on a corrody. He was unable to keep up repayments and was helped out of his impossible financial situation by Prior Richard de Morins of Dunstable, who paid off the Jewish creditors. Naturally the priory gained Husborne's security from the transaction as well as taking over his debt.[122] Similarly in the early thirteenth century men like Robert and Henry Braybrooke were able to acquire land by paying off Jewish creditors in return for the conveyancing of the original security.[123] Using Richardson's work, Professor John Hatcher illustrated how what he termed 'ecclesiastical business acumen' extended the lands of abbeys, priories and individuals in the late twelfth and early thirteenth centuries.[124]

---

[118] *Chronicles of St Augustine's Canterbury*, p. 1,872. [119] *Ibid.*, p. 1,916.
[120] Mate 1973, p. 194. Mate also reveals borrowings from Jacob the Jew in 1240 and Bonamy in 1242 and 1244.
[121] Richardson 1960, pp. 74–108. [122] *Ibid.*, pp. 259–63.
[123] *Ibid.*, pp. 270–80, 73. Richardson also reveals the involvement in land acquisition of Sir Adam de Stratton; Walter of Merton; a royal counsellor, Robert Walerand; a steward of the royal household and lieutenant in Gascony, Roger Leyburn; barons William of Valence and Gilbert of Clare; ministers and future bishops, Robert Burnell and Godfrey Giffard.
[124] Hatcher and Miller 1978, p. 171.

Trafficking in Jewish debts must have caused distress in many of the rural communities around the urban centres where Jews had settled. Such business shows the so-called Jewish moneylenders in a different light and led Professor Gavin Langmuir to call them 'real estate agents'.[125] No doubt they entered into this type of business primarily because they required security for their loans. To the Jewish money-lender there was probably not much difference between a moveable pledge and the use of land as a security, but it was in this pledging of land that Christian entrepreneurs, be they clerics, nobles or petty labourers, saw the opportunity for augmenting their estates, often at the Jews' expense. Long ago, Professor Maitland commented that Jewish business caused a reaction: 'land is being brought to the market and feudal rights are being capitalized'.[126] H. G. Richardson also saw this development as having very serious consequences: 'This complex system provided the solvent which broke down the apparent rigidity of the structure of feudal land tenure and facilitated the transfer of estates to a new capitalist class, the religious communities or *novus homo*.'[127]

There is little doubt that Jewish activities did have an impact on the structure of land tenure and did cause financial difficulties for those individuals who unsuccessfully dabbled in debts, as well as providing growing resentment against the Jewish moneylenders.[128] As Professor Alan Harding recently observed, 'Jewish money-lenders introduced abbeys, lay magnates and the growing race of stewards and royal clerks to the opportunities of investment in the property of indebted knights.'[129] Such introductions were widespread over the whole country.

Perhaps one of the best-documented examples of ecclesiastical business acumen and mounting indebtedness is that of Peter de Bending, who lived in Kent in the 1230s. A nineteenth-century antiquarian described de Bending's plight in detail: 'he became entangled step by step with those merciless money-lenders, who exacted an enormous interest, and were ever binding his estates more and more; till he was driven to alienate them all to the Priory of Christ Church Canterbury to pay off his debts and release him from his thraldom'.[130] The Pollard Starrs show that, in 1230, de Bending was forced, presumably through his indebtedness, to mortgage his manor of Westwell (near Ashford) to the priory of Christ Church, Canterbury in return for £171 17s 0d and the manor of Little Chart which he was to hold at rent. By January 1234, de Bending was £33 6s 8d in arrears with the rent for Little

[125] Langmuir 1963, pp. 214–21. [126] *Ibid.*, p. 218; Maitland and Pollock 1952, p. 475.
[127] Richardson 1960, p. 94. [128] Coss 1975. [129] Harding 1993, p. 198.
[130] Larking 1866, p. 306.

Chart; the priory, in return for all rights to the manor of Westwell, dissolved the debt.[131]

It was because of his debts that de Bending turned to Jewish financiers. Not all of de Bending's borrowings from Jews are known. In 1234 he borrowed £2 4s 0d from Moses Crispin at the rate of interest of 2 pence in the pound per week. In November 1234, he borrowed a further £5 a year for the next ten years at the same rate of interest from Benedict Crispin. In March 1235, by two bonds, he borrowed another £19 from Jacob Crispin. All the loans were made on the security of de Bending's land and chattels. Still insolvent in 1236, de Bending mortgaged the manor of Little Chart to Bonami, a Jew of Canterbury, reserving the right of a quitrent of one pound of pepper a year. Bonami paid de Bending £200. Finally in 1237, having mortgaged his property and run out of Jewish creditors, de Bending approached the priory of Christ Church and asked in return for his seisin of the manor of Little Chart and £133 6s 8d to release him from his debts.[132]

The priory paid off de Bending's debts and received quitclaims from Benedict and Jacob Crispin, Isaac fil Benedict and Jacob fil Isaac, Aaron Blundin, Joseph fil Moses and Moses fil Jacob and Bonamicus, and Cresselin who was described as 'of Little Chart'. Perhaps Cresselin had actually gone to live on the mortgaged lands, which were some miles from Canterbury. De Bending's dealings show a typical case whereby a large Christian institution aggrandised itself by paying off Jewish debts. In a period of about seven years the priory of Christ Church had gained Westwell and recovered Little Chart at a cheap price and the Jews had gained their interest.[133] There are many other illustrations of the uneasy alliance of Jewish finance and local Christian financial aid. Christ Church Priory continued to profit by paying off at least three Jewish debts in the 1230s. The convent gained the land of Adam de Garewinton which was near Adisham by paying off de Garewinton's debts to Isaac fil Mayer.[134] It also gained the land of Nicholas de Borne in Hildinge by paying off his debt of £25 6s 8d to Benjamin fil Mayer and gained a further 10 acres of land in Gare for paying £6 13s 4d to deliver Henry de Hok of his debts to Solomon fil Jesse.[135]

Such mortgaging of land in rural areas and trafficking in Jewish bonds were also common in the Marcher counties of Hereford and Worcester. There the religious houses, while on the one hand condemning the Jews, were also content to transact business with them. Such business also led to friction between uneasy partners. For example, Leo, a Jew of

[131] *SCBM*, vol. II, pp. 305–18; Larking 1866, pp. 305–18; Adler 1914, pp. 31–2.
[132] *Ibid.*   [133] *Ibid.*   [134] CCA MS A 68.   [135] CCA MS A 90, A 93.

Worcester, was arrested for forcible entry into the Hospital of Worcester when he tried to get his 'partner', the abbot of Pershore, to pay up monies that were owed to him.[136] Earl Richard de Clare of Gloucester not only allowed Jews to live on his estates but also bought the exclusive right to collect the debts of another Jew in Gloucestershire. Nevertheless, in 1248 Richard de Clare, who needed to borrow money to go on crusade, went to the monks at Tewkesbury and got them to negotiate on his behalf with the Jews.[137] Yet it was not only religious houses and great nobles who benefited from others' indebtedness. By the 1230s Hugh Freman of Shelwick (near Hereford) was in debt to the Jews. He was forced to grant his land in Shelwick to Thomas de Geyton for the low sum of £3 6s 8d in return for being acquitted of a Jewish debt. A little later he was forced to grant another 5 acres of land to Thomas de Geyton for £2 to pay off another Jewish debt.[138] In Hereford itself land was also pledged to the Jews: Emma, the widow of Hugh le Taillur, was obliged to release her land in the city to Isaac the Jew of Worcester.[139] In 1248, Philip de Kynemaresbur, who was indebted to the Jews, was forced to lease his land called Yondercumb to the abbey of St Peter's, Gloucester for a consideration of £6 13s 4d to pay off his Jewish creditors.[140] In the 1260s, James Beauchamp rounded off his estate at Acton Beauchamp by purchasing the land of John son of Robert of Abetot. In return Beauchamp paid John's debts to Isaac of Worcester, provided a pension for John's mother of a tunic and promised her as much grain as she required.[141] In 1267, Leo fil Preciosa, a London Jew, possibly operating from Hereford, sold all rents and debts that he had contracted with James de Helyun in the county of Hereford to a Christian, William de Chysulle. Leo also sold William the right to levy the debts on James de Helyun's land and even offered to help William collect them.[142] By such collaboration, Christian laymen and clerics were able to make a profitable living from Jewish business at the expense of their fellow Christians.

A similar picture can be detected in Lincolnshire. In the 1220s, the church of St Mary and the monks of Kirkstead received 4 bovates with three tofts in Great Sturton by paying off the debts of William of Barkwith, who had been indebted to a Jew, Ursell fil Pucella. Ursell gave a Hebrew quitclaim for the land.[143] Similarly, in 1230, the abbey

---

[136] Jacobs 1893a, pp. 154–5.
[137] *Annales Theukesberia*, p. 137. Abrahams 1894a, p. 139.
[138] HCA MS no. 335. Shelwick is approximately 2½ miles north-north-east of Hereford; HCA MS no. 334.
[139] HCA MS no. 110. The only Jewish *starrum* remaining in Hereford.
[140] HCA MS no. 1635.   [141] Harding 1993, p. 197.   [142] *PREJi*, p. 157.
[143] *SCBM*, vol. I, p. 34. Great Sturton is 5½ miles north-north-west of Horncastle.

of Newhouse paid William de Silvedune £8 for 6½ bovates of land and his fields in Kelby. The abbey again paid off the debts on the land, 'if there had been any', and received a quitclaim from Josce fil Elias of Lincoln.[144] Newhouse also gained more land in 1240 when Geoffrey Berner of Harborough granted three selions of land in Harborough as well as other land to the abbey. The documentation was accompanied by quitclaims from Jacob fil Leon, in Hebrew, who signed the document on behalf of his father Leon who was in London at the time, and from Leon himself who wrote a formal quitclaim in Latin.[145] In the 1250s the convent of Greenfield gained two nearby woods from Jacob fil Sampson Levy of Lincoln who subsequently issued a quitclaim.[146] In 1275, Bullington Priory, by having paid off the debts of Peter le Kendow of Helmswell, gained the right and claim on the land, tenements and rent that Isaac Gabbay had had in the village of Hackthorn.[147] Interestingly, many of Isaac Gabbay's debtors came from nearby places such as Holme, Langton, Donnington and Stenigot. Isaac was an example of the Jewish business men who were lending in a small rural area outside Lincoln.[148] Local individuals like John de la Launde also gained from indebtedness. In April 1268, John paid off the debts of one of the baronial rebels, Hugh de Nevill of Lesseby, and gained in return the right to the demesnes, homages, services, villeinages, the advowsons of the church, the woods, the meadows, the pastures, the mills, the gardens and the fisheries as well as all other things belonging to the manor. All this cost John £10 16s 0d which de Nevill had owed the king and a further £28 which de Nevill owed Manasser of Brodsworth.[149] It is perhaps ironical that, by 1290, a John de la Launde, another member of the same family with the same name, was himself indebted to another Lincoln Jew.[150]

It was through such land transactions that the Jews no doubt acquired a knowledge of the rural economy, of the farms, manors and meadows, and of potential customers. As they became more familiar with such detailed information the Jewish business men were able to extend their financial dealings and lay the foundations which might later be used for dealing in commodities. Certainly these contacts in the rural areas outside the *archae* towns show that the Jews were familiar with their locale and had a good knowledge of their likely clientele. In particular,

---

[144] *SCBM*, vol. I, pp. 47–53.
[145] *SCBM*, vol. I, pp. 56–60. Harborough is 8 miles north-north-west of Grimsby.
[146] *SCBM*, vol. I, pp. 79–80.   [147] *SCBM*, vol. I, pp. 30–4.
[148] Mundill 1987, pp. 348–52.
[149] Foster 1920, p. 225, no. 6; *PREJ1*, p. 210; Moor 1930, pp. 249–50.
[150] Foster 1920, p. 225, no. 6; *PREJ1*, p. 210; Moor 1930, pp. 249–50; Mundill 1987, p. 261.

the prevalence of unofficial 'partnerships' between the Jews and the local monasteries proved successful for both parties. The monasteries acquired land cheaply. The Jews were able to lend knowing that other capital was present to pay off the debts of a defaulting debtor. Such a situation prompted the barons to complain that Jews transferred the debts and lands which had been pledged to them to magnates and powerful men in the kingdom who kept them even when the debtor was ready to pay.[151] The distress which land alienation caused to the debtor led to more and more special clauses being written into land transactions. The clause forbidding land alienation to Jews seems to have evolved between 1240 and 1260 and to have anticipated in spirit the later Statute of Mortmain.[152] Such a clause simply forbade the recipient of the land to alienate the land to either Jew or religious institution. Examples can be found in land transactions in both town and countryside all over the country. It was not until the enactment of the Provisions of the Jewry by Walter of Merton in 1269 that it was forbidden for the Jews to take land on a mortgage. The Provisions finally put a stop to land being alienated at the expense of the debtor.[153] Ironically, they had not stopped Walter of Merton acquiring Cuxham and three other manors by paying off the debts of Stephen de Chenduit.[154] Neither had they stopped Sir Geoffrey de Langley from acquiring lands which had been mortgaged to Jews in Warwickshire.[155]

Despite the inclusion of warranties against alienation to the Jews or religious institutions, the problems of indebtedness were not eased. It is not surprising that bitter hatred for the moneylender and the sin of usury grew. As debts mounted so it seems did hatred for the creditors. The baronial hatred for Jews between 1258 and 1265 is well known and was probably fired by the fact that the magnates saw the Jews as royal pawns and as partly if not wholly responsible for their personal financial crises.[156] In Easter week 1264 five hundred London Jews were massacred by the followers of de Montfort.[157] John fitz John, 'one of the most ruthless and vigorous of Earl Simon's henchmen', led the attack on the London Jews and is said to have killed Isaac fil Aaron, one of the leading Jews of the time.[158] Many London Jews had their houses burnt and looted. The Jewish survivors of the pogrom and the official records of the financial transactions of the London Jewry were saved by the justiciar and the mayor and were subsequently sent to the Tower for protection.[159] During these troubles baronial troops occupied Bristol,

---

[151] Harding 1993, p. 198. [152] Plucknett 1949, p. 98. [153] Rigg, pp. xlix–li.
[154] Harding 1993, p. 198. [155] Coss 1975. [156] Lieberman 1983, pp. 66–8.
[157] Jenks 1902, pp. 129–30; Hillaby 1993a, pp. 134–7. [158] Roth 1978, p. 61.
[159] Powicke 1947, p. 461.

Bury St Edmunds, Cambridge, Canterbury, Hereford, Northampton, Leicester, Lincoln, Norwich and Oxford.[160] At Oxford it is clear that congregations of Jews were flocking into the city from the surrounding countryside for protection. After the wars, the English Jewry was undoubtedly in a deplorable state.[161]

Because of the upheavals many Jewish creditors had lost touch with their debtors. The dislocation to financial records and the collection of loans and tallages was enormous. In the west much damage was done when the earl of Derby stormed Worcester in February 1262 and seized the *archa*. Most of the Worcester Jews who were still there were massacred. The *archa* was subsequently taken to the earl's castle at Tutbury.[162] When Prince Edward, after the fall of Northampton, finally took Tutbury he broke the *archa* open and sent the documents for safe-keeping to Bristol.[163] In the south-east in 1261, the Canterbury Jewry was attacked and many of its inhabitants were violently assaulted.[164] Worse followed when, in 1264, Gilbert de Clare, the earl of Gloucester, captured the town. De Clare sacked the Jewry and, according to Gervase, 'at this same time nearly all the Jews were destroyed and exiled'.[165] Certainly the *archa* was stolen, for the earl's followers entered the house of Simon Pabley, one of the Christian chirographers, and took it away.[166]

The hatred and fury that had shown itself in other towns also manifested itself in Cambridge and Lincolnshire. In 1265, John Dayville, the leader of a party of the 'Disinherited', the renegade rebel barons who had been sheltering in the Isle of Axholme to the north of Lincoln, raided the city. The rebels entered the city and besieged the castle. The king sent his son, the Lord Edward, to deal with them. Unfortunately, for the Jews of Lincoln it was too late. The band of rebels had taken the opportunity to march down from the Bail and to sack the Jewry.[167] According to Walter of Hemingburgh, they entered the synagogue, tore up the scrolls of the Law, killed many Jews and, as a final gesture, seized all the bonds and charters belonging to the Jews and set fire to them.[168] After the event, the king ordered twenty-four citizens of Lincoln to protect the Jews and their goods.[169] However, the business

---

[160] *Ibid.*, p. 450; Dobson 1993, pp. 15–16.   [161] Roth 1978, p. 61.
[162] *Annales Monastici*, vol. IV, p. 448; Hillaby 1990a, pp. 105–6.   [163] Powicke 1947, p. 487.
[164] *CCR 1258–1266*, p. 229; Cohn-Sherbok 1979, p. 32.
[165] *Gervase of Canterbury*, vol. II, p. 235; Adler 1914, p. 40; Rigg, p. 51.
[166] PRO E/101/249/22, printed in *PREJ4*, pp. 148–71. It seems that some Jews were also imprisoned in the castle at Canterbury during this period: Adler 1914, pp. 53, 78; Hasted 1800, vol. XI, p. 61.
[167] Victoria County History, *Lincolnshire*, vol. II, p. 262; Hill 1965, p. 209.
[168] Hemingburgh, *Chronican*, p. 327.   [169] *CPR 1258–1266*, pp. 421–2.

records had been thoroughly destroyed. Almost as a last act, in 1266 the 'Disinherited', who had been using Cambridge as a supply base, massacred some Cambridge Jews and took the *archa* to Ely.[170]

Such actions caused major problems for Jewish finance and for the Jewish creditors. The dislocation is best evidenced by several cases which followed the destruction of the Lincoln *archa*. When Moses of Clare sued Henry of Whaddon for a fee rent of £4 which should have been paid annually from 1264, Henry claimed that it was unlawful because the bond had been outside the *archa* at the time it was burnt. An inquest by the chirographers claimed that the bond had been in the chest when it was burnt.[171] In July 1266, Henry III granted Benedict fil Magister Moses and his brother Hagin a special dispensation which allowed for the bonds in their hands or their debtors' hands to be valid. These Jews, together with other Lincoln Jews such as Manser of Brodsworth, Isaac fil Benedict and Elias of Doncaster, were thus allowed to claim their pledges as normal and to secure the payment of them in the usual fashion.[172] It seems that recovery from the sacking of the Jewry and the reclamation of debts which had in effect been annulled by fire was slow. At Wilton the Jewish losses had been so severe that the king, 'out of compassion', appointed a number of burgesses to be their guardians and defenders.[173] The Crown was forced to act to help its Jewish subjects. In January 1266 Henry confirmed the rights of the Jew.[174]

The Jewish communities who suffered during the turbulent 1260s were the victims of general odium for two major reasons. First, their religious beliefs and customs increasingly left them separated and cut off from the mainstream beliefs of contemporary society. Second, a large majority of Jews were engaged in the provision of finance. The provision of financial credit over a period of time naturally leads to the unpopularity of the creditor with the debtor. The provision of credit on the security of land had also involved an unpopular third party. The involvement of entrepreneurs who gained land in return for providing the payments for Jewish creditors made the Jewish moneylender even more unpopular than the Cahorsins, the Italians, the rent collectors and the bailiffs put together.

The Jews, already a minority amongst a hostile host population, had added unpopularity to their insularity by their moneylending and use of the mortgage. The Jewish financier had indirectly benefited many ecclesiastics, monasteries and individuals who, in the first half of the

---

[170] Dobson 1993, pp. 15–16.   [171] Rigg, p. 41.
[172] *CPR 1258–1266*, p. 617; *CPR 1266–1272*, p. 95; Hill 1965, p. 209; Roth 1948, p. 69.
[173] Powicke 1947, p. 516.   [174] *CCR 1264–1268*, p. 163; Powicke 1947, p. 517.

thirteenth century, had profited from the Jews' dealings in rural mortgages. As indebtedness grew and as debtors lost their lands to other parties the Jews were singled out as the cause. The anger against and hatred of the Jew which manifested themselves during the baronial revolt were soon to be accompanied by a change in attitude by the Church. Although religious institutions had often been content to gain from Jewish usury in a material way, they were now forced to reform and curtail their involvement in the land market. The prevention of land alienation by the Provisions of 1269 also put a stop to the Church making gains from Jewish usury. Now the Church no longer gained materially from Jewish business activities, it was ready to make a more enthusiastic attack on the Jews and to demand conversion. This change in attitude was also followed in Edward I's reign by a change in attitude towards usury. The Edwardian Anglo-Jew was in desperate need of protection and of economic redirection if the increasing hostility of the baronial and knightly classes, as well as the Church, was not to succeed.

Chapter 3

'THE KING'S MOST EXQUISITE VILLEINS': THE VIEWS OF ROYALTY, CHURCH AND SOCIETY

Having seen how the Jewish communities became established in England during the twelfth and thirteenth centuries it is now important to see how they were perceived by their royal protectors and the Church, as well as by the population at large. It was the Jews' business dealings such as the mortgaging of land and the lending of money that brought them into contact with officials, nobles, clergy and townspeople as well as those living in the country-side.[1] From time to time, their business resulted in a 'partnership' with abbeys and Church institutions as well as with individuals who benefited from the traffic in Jewish debts.[2] Early in the thirteenth century, lay and clerical entrepreneurs who gained land by paying off Jewish debts clearly did not have troubled consciences about dealing with Jews. On the other hand the debtors who lost their land were certainly troubled. Their indebtedness and loss caused resentment and fuelled hatred for the Jew and possibly even for their new landlord. However there must also have been a group of debtors of whom little is known, who managed to repay their debts and who might well have actually gained from transacting business with Jewish financiers. Thus, there were many Christians who were directly or indirectly involved with Jewish finance and who naturally had varying attitudes towards the Jews. Yet, as debtors started to fail on their repayments and as the lawlessness which accompanied the mid-century rebellion spread, so the protection of those who had tolerated

---

[1] Richardson 1960, pp. 13–22; Nottingham RO M24/182–8, the Lassman Papers.

[2] Lieberman 1983, p. 56 shows that amongst other religious houses Meaux, Fountains and Peterborough launched active campaigns to acquire property. She also gives examples for Holy Trinity, London; Newhouse Priory; Worcester Cathedral Priory; Waltham Abbey; St Mary's Osney; Bildewas Abbey; Christ Church Canterbury; Durham Priory; Abbey Dore; Malton Priory; St Albans; Llanthony Priory; Abbey of Old Warden; Darley Abbey; Cirencester Abbey; Westminster Abbey; Ramsey Abbey; and St Peter's Gloucester. For individuals see Meekings, 1981, pp. lxiv–lxvi; Mundill 1993, p. 28. See also Harding 1993, chapter 4, note 140.

the Jews proved inadequate.[3] This chapter will consider the attitude of both Church and state towards the Jewish communities and the canonical and constitutional position of the Jew within contemporary society. It will also examine the close relationship between the royal family and the Jews and the relationship which Edward had with his Jewish subjects in England before he became king as well as his contacts with Jews in Gascony where he was their duke.

After the unrest of 1265–9, Henry III and the Lord Edward were eager to restore peace and the royal protection of the Jews rather than to turn the Jewish community over to the wrath of their debtors. Although the Crown tried to restore the status quo as far as the Jewish communities were concerned, both Henry III and Edward I were gradually forced to bow to changing attitudes. After the baronial revolt and the destruction of many of the Jewries Henry III guaranteed the Jews' rights and even allowed them to profit from business transactions which had been destroyed during the rebellion.[4] Edward I found that he was confronted by changing attitudes towards the Jews. He was first subjected to a change in attitude by the Church. The Church had altered its stance; whereas it had profited from the partnership in land mortgages, the Provisions of 1269 put a stop to this. The complaints of the magnates were matched by canonical and state legislation concerning usury and moneylending.

Naturally these changing attitudes needed to be taken into consideration by the Crown.[5] As faithful and pious leaders of the country, both Henry III and Edward I had to listen to their leading bishops and indeed to the papal legates. This also meant that both kings, although personally ready to lend and borrow, became acutely aware of the current feeling on usury. Secondly, they also had to consider the financial rewards that they themselves could gain from the Jewry. Thirdly, it was important to both kings to re-establish the exact constitutional position of the Jew within society after the unrest. After all, Jews were royal property, a position which led William Prynne, writing in the seventeenth century, to dub them 'the King's most exquisite villeins'.[6] Many of these different issues and attitudes in the mid-thirteenth century were unclear and thus any 'policy' towards the Jewish community was necessarily ambivalent.[7] Such was also the case with the clerical view of the Jew.

To the whole of Catholic Christendom the Jews were an embarrassment and a threat to its creed. Nevertheless, the Church's view of the Jew remained ambiguous. Joshua Trachtenberg observed that 'Christian

---

[3] Lieberman 1983, p. 66; Coss 1975, p. 31–4.   [4] See above, chapter 2.
[5] Watt 1987; Stow 1981; 1992b, pp. 237–40.   [6] Prynne 1656, p. 128.
[7] Stacey, 1992b, pp. 13–14.

policy towards the Jews is a paradox. Bitterly condemned and excoriated they were yet to be tolerated on humanitarian grounds and indeed preserved on theological grounds as a living testimony to the truth of Christian teaching.'[8] Nowhere is this paradox more noticeable than in the views and actions of two thirteenth-century English prelates, Bishop Grosseteste of Lincoln and Archbishop John Pecham. Grosseteste seems to have held a scholarly view of the Jews.[9] In 1233, when writing to Margaret de Quinci, countess of Winchester, on whose lands some Jews had settled, he described them thus: 'They are a wandering people because of the *diaspora* and exiled from their proper home, namely Jerusalem; they wander because of the uncertainty of how long they can stay in one place and are fugitives through their fear of death.' He claimed that they were the Lord's reminder of the Passion, and 'to this end they are witnesses of the Christian faith against the unfaithful Pagans'. He stated that they should be protected and should not be killed but should be made to work the fields and earn an honest living, oppressing no one with their usuries, for 'Truly, at the end of time, when the large number of races will have entered in, just as it is written in the scriptures, then all Israel, that is the Jewish people, will be saved because of their faith, because of the same faith of Christ, and will return from captivity to true freedom.'[10]

By contrast Archbishop Pecham was not at all interested in preserving Jews as a reminder of the efficacy of Christianity but carried out a very active campaign for their wholesale conversion, a campaign which may have had a major influence on their final expulsion from England.[11] The dogmatic conflict between Christianity and Judaism centred around the ancient Jewish refusal to acknowledge Christ as the Messiah and to accept the Immaculate Conception.[12] The deepening of this particular conflict led R. W. Hunt to observe: 'Controversial literature directed against the Jews reappeared at the end of the eleventh century and was vigorously maintained throughout the twelfth, as the Jewish problem became more acute.'[13]

The disputation between Christian and Jew became a common theme which has left a series of tracts behind it. One of the earliest was Gilbert Crispin's *Disputatio Judaei cum Christiano* of about 1093; and there were to be many other twelfth-century variations on a

---

[8] Trachtenberg 1943, p. 164.
[9] Friedman 1934, p. 22; Southern 1986, pp. 244–9; Stacey 1992a, p. 268.
[10] Bishop Robert Grosseteste, *Epistolae*, Rolls Series, 1861, pp. 33–7; Maddicott 1994, pp. 15–16.
[11] Logan 1972; Pecham, *Epistolae*, vol.I, pp. 212–13, 239; vol II, pp. 407–10; vol III, p. 937; Abrahams 1894b, p. 437.
[12] Abulafia 1989; Loewe 1953.   [13] Hunt 1948, p. 146.

theme.[14] One such tract was the anonymous *Dialogus inter Christianum et Judaeum de fide catholica* which was dedicated to Alexander, bishop of Lincoln (1123–48).[15] Later in the century the *Dialogus contra Judeos ad corrigendum et perficiendum destinatus* by Bartholomew, bishop of Exeter (1180–1184) and the rather bullying *Invectiva contra perfidiam Judaeorum* by Peter of Blois appeared.[16] There were also the *Dialogi cum Judaeo* of Petrus Alphonsi, a converted Spanish Jew, who came to England during the reign of Henry I and whose works were widely known in England during the second half of the century.[17] Similar literature was also available during the thirteenth century. For example a brief anonymous tract from the library of Rochester priory called *Arma contra Iudeos* was written in about 1202.[18] In the thirteenth century Peter of Cornwall, the prior of Holy Trinity, Aldgate, London, wrote his *Liber disputationis Petri contra Symonem Iudeum de confutatione Iudeorum* by which he managed to convert Symon the Jew, who then became a canon of Holy Trinity.[19] This desire to combat Judaism with argument even affected the Oxford Franciscan, Roger Bacon, who urged the study of Hebrew because he claimed that large numbers of Jews were being held back from Christianity because no one knew how to preach to them in their own language.[20]

The writers of these disputations were of course concerned with converting Jews, but they were also equally concerned with providing a collection of arguments which would arm Christians when their faith was attacked. Whilst Christianity had in fact nothing to fear from Judaism as an alternative religion, conversion to Judaism was not unknown. Intermarriage between Jew and Christian was not entirely impossible, or so it would seem from two celebrated cases. As is well known, in 1222, for the love of a certain Jewess, a deacon converted to Judaism and even circumcised himself. He was subsequently burnt at Oxford.[21] Similarly, in 1275 a Dominican, Robert of Reading, married a Jewess and was circumcised. He later died in prison.[22] If there was no distinction and division between Jews and Christians such as the *tabula*, or badge of shame, then how could relations be stopped other than by

---

[14] Abulafia and Evans, *The Works of Gilbert Crispin*, pp. xxvii, 1–61; Williams 1935; Abulafia 1989, p. 107.

[15] Abulafia 1989.   [16] Loewe 1953; Hunt 1948.

[17] Loewe 1953; Hunt 1948; Hermes, *Disciplina Clericalis*, pp. 3–90; Jones and Keller 1969, p. 16.

[18] Hunt 1948, p. 146, particularly note 3.   [19] Hunt 1948.

[20] Loewe 1953, p. 226; Roth 1978, p. 129; Stacey 1992a, p. 267; Nottingham RO MS M 24/182–8: the Lassman Papers.

[21] Hyams 1974, p. 277; Maitland 1912.

[22] Although it is possible that both converts were called Robert it appears that folklore has confused them. A plaque was laid in the ruins of Osney Abbey in 1931 to commemorate the martyrdom of the previous unfortunate: Cohen 1932, p. 298; Hyams 1974, p. 275.

argument? But it was not just for worldly love that Christians were attracted to Judaism. Prior to 1200, Giraldus Cambrensis mentions the conversion of two Cistercians to Judaism.[23] Clearly the Church could not tolerate the risk of such conversions to Judaism and was anxious to bring the Jews into the body of the Church. The disputations were works which represented the Church's views; they were also alas responsible for the growth of hatred against the Jews.[24]

In many ways medieval English society was well prepared to try to convert the Jews. Robert fitz Harding, mayor of Bristol, opened a school for converted Jews there as early as 1154.[25] The prior of Bermondsey opened a similar institution in 1213.[26] Henry III, who delighted in witnessing the baptism of Jews in his personal presence, founded the *Domus Conversorum* or House of Converted Jews in London in 1232.[27] Apparently, a converted Jew was acceptable to court society and could make his own way in later life. Thus Sir Henry of Winchester, bearing his sponsor's Christian name, was a converted Jew who did well for himself after his conversion in the early 1250s.[28] Elias l'Eveske, formerly the royally appointed leading member of the Jewish community or Archpresbyter, also converted to Christianity sometime in the mid-1250s.[29] Roger le Convers, the king's serjeant at arms in the 1270s, was a converted Jew.[30] Recently Dr Joan Greatrex has shown that in 1255 there were 150 *conversi* assigned to 125 religious houses up and down the land.[31]

If they could not convert all the Jews by disputations or by the offer of a place in the *Domus Conversorum* or in an abbey, then the English clergy were directed to control them. The rulings against the Jews made at the Fourth Lateran Council in 1215 were introduced into England in 1222 at the Council of Oxford by Archbishop Stephen Langton at the same time as he was responsible for the burning of the converted deacon.[32] Henceforth no cohabitation between Christian and Jew was to be allowed, no Christian was to be employed by a Jew in any capacity, and the *tabula* was to be worn. There is evidence that these early anti-Jewish measures were strictly enforced, especially in the dioceses of Lincoln and Norwich.[33] The English bishops were well aware of the Jewish presence in their sees and the problems which they thought this presence brought with it. In 1240, Bishop William de

---

[23] Giraldus Cambrensis, vol. IV, p. 139.   [24] Stacey 1992a, p. 263–4.
[25] Adler 1928, pp. 124–5.   [26] Tovey 1738, p. 94.
[27] Powicke 1947, vol. I, p. 125; Adler 1939, p. 279; Stacey 1992a, p. 269.
[28] Stacey 1992a, pp. 276–7.   [29] Stokes 1913, pp. 30–3; *CCR 1257–1300*, p. 16.
[30] Stacey 1992a, p. 279.   [31] Greatrex 1992, p. 137.
[32] Maitland 1912, pp. 260–4; *Concilia*, vol. I, p. 591.   [33] *Concilia*, vol. I, p. 693.

Cantilupe of Worcester decreed that no Christian woman should be employed as a wet-nurse by the Jews, that no Christian should give money to the Jews to use for purposes of usury and that no Jews' goods should be kept or received in any church.[34] In the late 1240s, the bishop of Chichester, Richard de la Wich, issued orders that the Jews of his diocese should not build any new synagogues, and that they should wear the *tabula*. He also prohibited his Christian flock from living with Jews.[35] In 1256, the bishop of Salisbury complained bitterly that the prohibition that stopped Christian women from acting as wet-nurses to Jewish children was not being observed and threatened future transgressions with excommunication.[36] In 1261, the Council of Lambeth tried to further the Church's power over the Jews and ruled that a delinquent Jew should reply in things ecclesiastical to Church law.[37] Finally, three years before the Expulsion, in 1287, the Council of Exeter once again banned Christians from working in Jewish households, forbade eating meals with Jews, prohibited sick Christians from accepting medicine from any Jew, restricted the Jews to their houses on Good Friday, even making them keep their windows shut, curtailed the erection of new synagogues and again enforced the *tabula*.[38] Such restrictions show clearly the change in attitude towards the Jews. Many of the restrictions were inspired by Rome and were then promulgated in England by ecclesiastics like Langton and Pecham. However, the constant repetition of these and other restrictions by the English Church upon the Jews reflects both the Church's concern and the fact that its policy of segregation was not wholly successful.

Thus, the English Church saw the Jews both as a people to be converted and as a religion to be frowned upon and discouraged. It naturally railed against usury (whilst at the same time being happy to profit by it where it could) but it also did what it could to foster and promulgate an image of the Jew in the eyes of the faithful. True to their faith, contemporary chroniclers reflected this hatred for the Jew. Many openly fanned a deep odium for the Jew by making constant references to Jews as 'perfidious'. Matthew Paris thought of them 'as sign of Cain the accursed'.[39] Richard of Devizes referred to them as 'bloodsuckers' and 'worms'.[40] The Jew was also commonly referred to as the 'Devil's disciple' and this association had not died out by Shakespeare's day.[41]

---

[34] *Ibid.*, p. 675.   [35] *Ibid.*, p. 693; Watt 1987.   [36] *Concilia*, vol. I, p. 719.
[37] *Ibid.*, p. 751.   [38] *Concilia*, vol. II, pp. 430–3.
[39] Matthew Paris, *Historia Anglorum*, vol. III, p. 103. Useful throughout this next section are Rokeah 1988; Menache 1996, pp. 319–20.
[40] Devizes, Richard of, *Chronicles of the Reign of Stephen, Henry II and Richard I*, vol. III, p. 383.
[41] Shakespeare, *The Merchant of Venice*, II; ii; 27 and III; i; 22.

The ritual murder allegations that first manifested themselves in medieval England are symptomatic of the vast, abysmal and intense hatred
that the host majority had for the Jewish minority.[42] Although
connected with the Church, these accusations were of the type that
passed into the popular psyche. 'Jew hatred' had many aspects and was
not solely an ecclesiastical product but the Church was only too happy
to market it to the faithful. As well as unpopular moneylender, a
stereotypical view prevailed of the Jew as a sorcerer, murderer,
necromancer, cannibal, poisoner, blasphemer, international conspirator
and Devil's disciple.[43]

Jew hatred was also manifest in what Joshua Trachtenberg termed
'popular subjective and non-natural beliefs'.[44] The belief of the power
of Jewish magic, stirred by fear of the *kabbalah*, the Jewish mystical
movement, and particularly by the suspicion of the *mezuzah*, was
common.[45] Such irrational ideas led to tales which spread orally. Such a
story was that of Abraham of Berkhamstead, who in 1250 was alleged to
have bought an image of the Madonna and Child and to have placed
the icon in the bottom of his privy. He then defecated on it and
commanded his wife to do likewise. The Jewess took the icon out from
the jakes and cleaned it. Her husband found out and killed her.[46] The
common belief that before selling meat to Christians the Jews had their
children urinate on it to induce sickness and death led to prohibitions
against Christians buying food from Jews.[47] Circumcision was itself
open to misinterpretation and provided more fuel for absurd accusations.[48] The belief that the Jew had a distinguishable smell was also
common, possibly owing to the eating of garlic or the use of chemicals
to remove hair because the Jew was forbidden by his religious law to
use a blade on his beard.[49] Inevitably any unusual or inexplicable disaster
could be blamed on the Jews.

Recent work by Professors Bob Moore and Gavin Langmuir as well
as others has examined the growth of anti-semitism with increasing
sophistication. They have also tried to distinguish between anti-Judaism
and anti-semitism.[50] It is unlikely, however, that the medieval mind
could have constantly made such a distinction. Any anti-Jewish feeling,
be it lay or clerical, was ultimately manifested as pure 'raw' hatred of

[42] Trachtenberg 1943, p. 12.   [43] Langmuir 1971, p. 387; Menache 1985, pp. 351–8.
[44] Trachtenberg 1943, pp. 6, 12.
[45] Scholem 1969; 1976; see under '*Mezuzah*', *Encyclopaedia Judaica*, vol. 11, pp. 1,474–7.
[46] Langmuir 1972, p. 463.   [47] Trachtenberg 1943, p. 100.
[48] Lipman 1967, pp. 59–62; Jacobs 1893a, p. 216.
[49] Trachtenberg 1943; Pearl 1990, p. 55. The *foetor Judaicus* is a belief which lasted in Europe until
the late 1950s.
[50] Moore 1987, pp. 27–9, 80–5; 1992; Langmuir 1990a, pp. 275–95; 1990b, pp. 301–9, 311–13.

the Jews. Nor can there be any doubt that both the general hatred for the Jews and the clerical attempts to convert them were fired by the awareness of the allegations of ritual murders that had evolved in England. It has long been acknowledged that medieval England began or rekindled the ritual murder allegations.[51] The kingdom boasted several shrines to boy saints who had allegedly been 'done to death' by the Jews.[52] The first case occurred in Norwich in 1144 and was recorded by a Benedictine monk, Thomas of Monmouth, who came to Norwich Priory soon after the event. He labelled the murderers of St William of Norwich as 'Christian-killing Jews'. He also records the fervour with which the prior of St Pancras, Lewes, tried to receive the body of the child martyr rather than leave it at Norwich. From 1144 to about 1155 various miracles occurred at the shrine.[53] In 1168, St Harold of Gloucester was allegedly tortured to death by the Jews and a shrine was erected at the abbey there.[54] In 1181 a similar accusation was made at Bury St Edmunds; in this case the boy was also named St Robert.[55] In 1183 another boy, Adam of Bristol, was allegedly sacrificed by a renowned killer, Samuel of Bristol, who also killed his wife, and then repented of the deed and converted the next day.[56] In 1192 in Winchester, described by Richard of Devizes as the 'Jerusalem of the Jews', the martyrdom of a French boy, employed by a Jewish cobbler, took place.[57] These allegations made excellent tales for a receptive public.

The accusations continued into the thirteenth century. Suspicion was raised against the Jews of Lincoln in 1202 when the body of a dead child was found outside the city walls.[58] In 1220 it was claimed that the Jews of Stamford had played a game that mocked Christianity.[59] In 1225 a jury in Winchester found two Jews guilty of murdering a child; in the same year a Jew was also accused of murdering a girl, but when she turned up alive and well he was freed on bail.[60] Again, in 1232 the suspicion of ritual murder was raised against the Winchester Jews and the community was imprisoned; they were later released and the boy's mother was charged with the murder.[61] In 1244 a shrine to a dead baby, found in St Benet's cemetery, was established at St Paul's. It was alleged

---

[51] Rokeah 1988, pp. 104–9; Menache 1985, p. 357.

[52] Amongst others: St William 1144; St Harold 1168; shrine at St Paul's in 1244; St Hugh 1255. Langmuir 1972.

[53] Richmond 1992, pp. 53–4; Langmuir 1984a; 1984b.

[54] *Historia et Cartularium Monasterii Sancti Petri Gloucesteriae*, vol. I, pp. xxxix–xl, 20–1.

[55] Rokeah 1988, p. 107 note 40.

[56] BL Harleian MS 957; Jacobs 1893a, p. 152; Cluse 1995a.

[57] Rokeah 1988, pp. 107–8; Allin 1980.   [58] Stenton 1926, no. 996; Hill 1965, p. 223.

[59] Langmuir 1972, pp. 462–3.   [60] Rokeah 1988, p. 108.   [61] *Ibid.*

and confirmed by the testimony of two converted Jews that the marks on the body were Hebrew words.[62] However the most well-known and scandalous example of the Jews committing ritual murder on a Christian child occurred in Lincoln in 1255. In the late summer of that year the dead body of a nine-year-old boy turned up in a well in Lincoln. It was taken to the cathedral with speed and a shrine was soon established there. Miracles started to happen. Henry III investigated the allegations in person and a Jew in fact claimed that the murder had been carried out by other Jews. Some ninety-three Jews were imprisoned, of whom about nineteen were executed and the rest later freed. As is well known, the repercussions of and belief in the alleged ritual murder of Little St Hugh have continued through many centuries.[63]

For all these reasons the image of the ever-unpopular Jew was present for all Christians to experience. Stories of his perfidiousness must have been widely circulated.[64] Some of these stories, like the case of Little St Hugh, became highly popularised. Many were widely known amongst a broad spectrum of thirteenth-century society. Common tales of the Christ killers and the killers of Christian children circulated. In a society with an insatiable thirst for such tales and for the triumph of Christianity over evil, the population became increasingly ingrained with hatred for the Jew. In the *Legenda Aurea* the story of the Jewish glass blower of Bourges who attempted to kill his son for having attended a Christian mass was brought to the attention of the literate public, who passed it orally to the masses. Naturally such a tale had a popular hagiographical Christian heroine. Having seen her son confined to flames, the boy's mother screamed and a crowd gathered. The boy was miraculously shielded and saved by none other than the Virgin Mary. The crowd who had gathered threw the father into the flames; but he was not to be saved.[65] Despite the fact that the story can be traced to Byzantium in about 550 it is clear that it was well known across Europe. It was included by Gregory of Tours in his *De gloria martyrum* in 593.[66] It was transmitted to and recorded in a manuscript in the Old Sarum scriptorium during the early twelfth century.[67] Depictions of the miracle are extant in the Lady Chapel at Winchester.[68] Such tales and widely circulating rumours and beliefs about the Jews naturally helped to increase resentment of the Jewish presence.

[62] Pearl 1990, pp. 65–6; Rokeah 1988, p. 109.   [63] Langmuir 1972; Jacobs 1893b.
[64] Cohen 1983, pp. 1–27; Rubin 1992.
[65] Rubin 1992, p. 173; Ryan, *Jacobus de Voragine*, vol. II, pp. 87–8; for other stories concerning the Jews see Streit 1993, pp. 184–5 and Jacobs 1893a, p. 153.
[66] *Ibid.*; Southern 1958.   [67] Salisbury Cathedral MS 165 fos. 177a/b.
[68] Winchester Cathedral, Lady Chapel.

As a result of the odium on the part of the Church, the superstitious beliefs of the people, the Jewish involvement in providing credit and their own individual culture and religion, the Jews accordingly became entirely set apart from the Gentile populace, and co-existence became virtually impossible. The Jew was distinguished from society not only by his religious beliefs and physical appearance but by what became the very marks of his Judaism: the *tabula* and the spiked hat or *cornutum pileum*.[69] The caricatures of thirteenth-century Anglo-Jews drawn by the Exchequer scribes as they laboured over Jewish matters bear these distinctions of hatred.[70] Even artists who portrayed biblical Jews began to depict them anachronistically.[71] Religious sculpture, whilst showing an awareness of the Jews' relationship to the Old Covenant, always depicted the Church Triumphant and the Synagogue Broken. A late example of this genre is still extant at Rochester. There was also a similar depiction at Lincoln. The chapter house at York Minster carries another example.[72] Jew hatred manifested itself throughout the medieval period, but the thirteenth century was a time when the distinctions between Jew and Christian were particularly emphasised in art and popular culture.

Jew hatred was also coloured by jealousy of the Jews' privileged position in society, a position which was more than apparent to the masses. In the towns Jews came under the protection of the sheriff or the bailiffs. In legal cases they were administered by a special Justice. Within medieval English society, the Jew held a peculiar protected position of his own. It was in this context that, probably from their arrival, the Jews had their own individual royal charter of rights. H. G. Richardson observed that a charter may have existed in Henry I's reign.[73] Although there were subsequent changes in the legal status of the Jew, in essence his position in relation to the Crown remained the same. The Jew was Crown property. Bracton gave the contemporary

---

[69] Mellinkoff 1973, pp. 155–67; Strauss 1942; Kisch 1957. The *cornutum pileum* was supposedly never worn in England but it is clearly depicted on PRO E/401/87. The *tabula* (in England the Ten Commandments) is clearly visible on PRO Essex Forest Roll 1277 and BL Cotton MS Nero D II.

[70] Rokeah 1972; Roth 1950; Lipman 1966.   [71] Kiewe 1946.

[72] Various examples of this genre are still extant. There are two statues on either side of the 'Judgement Porch' on the south side of Lincoln Cathedral which may have represented 'Church' and 'Synagogue'. The porch was begun in the late 1250s soon after the Little St Hugh Affair (1255) and was completed in 1280. There are also two statues dating from the fourteenth century on the chapter house doorway at Rochester Cathedral. European examples are extant at Strasburg (Cathedral), Trier (Liebfrauenkirche) and Paris (Notre Dame). A painting on a panel from the roof of the chapter house at York has also survived showing 'Synagogue' – exhibited at 'The Age of Chivalry', Royal Academy, London, 1987. Edwards 1958.

[73] Richardson 1961, pp. 109–11; Parkes 1937.

view: 'Truly the Jew can have nothing which belongs to himself, because whatever he acquires he acquires not for himself but for the king because they do not live for themselves but each acquires for others and not for themselves.'[74]

This was the special position that William Prynne recognised and railed against in the seventeenth century. Despite his obvious hostility to the Jews, Prynne's appraisal of their status as 'the King's most exquisite villeins and bondslaves' is still helpful in understanding their position in medieval society.[75] This relationship was also later clarified by Cecil Roth who saw the Jew as *servus camerae regis* or 'serf of the royal chamber'.[76] Long ago Professor Maitland illustrated the technical ambiguity of the Jew's position when he claimed that the Jew was a quasi-slave but that 'the servility was a relative servility – in relation to all other men the Jew is free'.[77] Both Maitland and William Prynne recognised the ambiguity of the Jews' relationship to the Crown but to contemporaries the special treatment and protection afforded to the Jews by the Crown was even simpler to understand. The Jew was the king's Jew and it is clear that this special status was often the cause of resentment. As early as 1164 the clergy complained that the Jew had special privileges: 'So that for the Jews by the proposed law their oath is the end of all lawsuits whether civil or criminal. Would it not seem to thee unworthy of my lord, the King, unless the clergy were granted a privilege which is indulged to lay citizens or Jews?'[78]

Over a century later, in 1282, the vanquished Welshmen, the sons of Maredud of Penliti, wrote and complained to Archbishop Pecham: 'It is truly significant that all Christians have laws and customs in their own lands; truly the Jews keep their laws whilst living amongst the English...'[79] In 1287, when a knight whose manor had been mortgaged to a Jew went to Gascony to seek a judgement from the king himself, Edward I, according to several chroniclers, replied, 'but I grant to you and to all others in my kingdom an equal law so that I do not appear to favour a Jew rather than a Christian'.[80] There was clearly much jealousy and animosity concerning the legal position of the Jew within contemporary society.

The special constitutional status of the Anglo-Jews was no doubt resented by many of the king's subjects, but it was maintained because

---

[74] Schechter 1914, p. 128; Maitland and Pollock 1952, vol. I, pp. 472–3.

[75] Prynne, *A short demurrer*, p. 128.

[76] Roth 1978, p. 96; Langmuir 1963, pp. 196–204; Picciotto 1922, p. 69; Watt 1991, pp. 153–8, 172.

[77] Maitland and Pollock 1952, vol. II, p. 468.   [78] Jacobs 1893a, pp. 42–3.

[79] Pecham, *Epistolae*, vol. II, p. 454.   [80] Triveti, *Annales*, pp. 312–13.

of their economic relationship with the Crown. The status of the Jews and whether they were serfs, of servile position or had rights at all has fuelled much discussion.[81] Professor Jack Watt has recently reopened the debate.[82] Whatever the true relationship between the Crown and the Jews was, it is clear that they were of special status. This is evidenced by various pieces of legislation which were primarily concerned with the protection of the Jew as financier and trader. The earliest surviving general charter to the Jews, granted by Richard I at Rouen on 22 March 1190, clearly illustrates their place within society.[83] The Jews were to be allowed to 'reside in our land freely and honourably and to hold lands, fiefs, pledges, gifts and purchases'. It provided them with legal rights, to have justice from royal courts, as well as rights of burial and inheritance. It also granted them the right 'to receive and buy at any time whatever is brought them except things of the church and blood stained garments'. They were allowed to swear oaths, 'upon their book and on their roll', and to sell their pledges after a year and a day. There was no restriction of movement and they enjoyed exemption from customs. The charter finally clarified the Jews' status: 'And we order that the Jews throughout all England and Normandy be free of all customs and of tolls and of taxes on wine just like our own chattels and we command you to ward and defend them and protect them.'[84]

Four years later, in the Ordinances of the Jews, all financial dealings involving Jews were regulated and the *archa* system was established. With a series of chests, which were for keeping records of money-lending activities, Hubert Walter had effectively established an early national archive. The first official archivists were the two Jewish and two Christian chirographers who were to witness the making of all loans and maintain lists of the transactions in each of six or seven centres. Hubert Walter's Ordinances also laid down the standard format of the bipartite bond which was to be a record of how much was lent and to whom it was lent. Standard charges of 3d for drawing up each bond were established; the two scribes were to receive 2d and the keeper of the roll 1d.[85]

In 1201, John reconfirmed the charter of the Jews and virtually granted judicial independence to the Jewish communities. It was established that any 'breaches of right' that should occur amongst the Jewish community were to be 'examined and amended amongst themselves according to their law so that they may administer their own justice amongst themselves'.[86] Jealousy of the Jewish position increased.

[81] Langmuir 1963, pp. 196–204; Picciotto 1922, p. 69.   [82] Watt, 1987; 1991; 1992.
[83] Jacobs 1893a, pp. 134–6; Parkes 1937.   [84] Jacobs 1893a, pp. 134–6.
[85] *Ibid.*, pp. 156–7.   [86] *Ibid.*, pp. 212–15.

Many, including the Londoners, could not understand what made the Jew so special. The Crown even went out of its way to protect Jewish rights: 'If we have given our peace even to a dog', wrote King John, in 1203, when rebuking the Londoners for having molested Jews, 'it shall be inviolably preserved.'[87]

The early Henrician legislation on the Jews, contained in the Statute of 1233, did not alter the Jews' position but was again concerned with their business. It confined itself to modifications of lending practice. The final clause of the Statute concerned pawnbroking and forbade any Jew to make a loan on security of church plate or blood-stained clothes or any clothes which had clearly been obtained by force. The Statute also reversed previous policy about Jewish immigration: in 1218 the Crown had actually encouraged the Jew to settle in England, but it now stipulated that he should only remain if 'he is such a man that he is able to serve the king and find pledges in good faith'. Those Jews who were to be exiled were to leave by 29 September 1233 or be detained in prison at the royal pleasure.[88]

In 1239, further government legislation seems to have been specifically aimed at regulating the day-to-day running of the London *archa*. A copy of the legislation has survived because it was to remain 'in the custody of the aforesaid chirographers as an example of their duties'. It established that *archa* officials and clerks were to be appointed regularly. It also stipulated that the *pes* of the tripartite chirograph must now be placed in an *archa* within ten days of its date of execution to be valid. It forbade both Christian and Jew to withhold the chirograph from the *archa* after the tenth day: the Christian was to be 'in our severest mercy' and the Jew to have his chattels forfeited if they did not comply. It stipulated: 'Likewise, let the seal of the Christian, who had mutually accepted that debt, contain the proper name of he who is borrowing it and let that part which ought to be replaced in the chest be sealed for that reason.' Profit was again regulated at 2d in the pound per week and the Crown now declared a moratorium on Jewish debts. Usury was not allowed to run upon debts payable between 24 June 1239 and Christmas Day 1240. The 1239 legislation also declared a restriction on residence: all Jews were to remain wherever they lived with their whole family from 29 September 1239 for the period of one year and they were not to be allowed to move without special licence from the king.[89] It seems that the Crown may have been trying to round up the Jewish community for a census. The Lincoln roll of Jewish debts taken in 1240

[87] Clanchy 1979, p. 69.
[88] Richardson 1938, pp. 392–4; 1960, pp. 293–4; Vincent 1992, pp. 125–6.
[89] *Cronica Maiorum*, pp. 237–8.

shows that a scrutiny was taken in that year and the summoning of leading Jews to Worcester in 1240 in order to exact a tallage also points to an attempt to enumerate and evaluate all Jewish assets within the whole country.[90]

By the mid-century, it was not only the Crown that had an interest in running Jewish affairs and trying to establish the official status of the Jewish communities. In 1244, the barons demanded that their council should be allowed to nominate one of the Justices of the Jews. By 1250, they demanded the reform of the *Scaccarium Judaeorum*.[91] It seems that as the Crown became unpopular, so the unpopularity of the Jew became greater and, as a result, anti-Jewish legislation became harsher. Finally, at the end of January 1253 the Crown issued an official mandate to the Justices of the Jews which laid down edicts which 'were to be strictly adhered to'. It banished all Jews, 'unless they did service', it stopped the erection of any new synagogues and it ordered that 'they could only celebrate their rituals in quiet voices so that Christians could not hear them'. It made the Jews subject to paying parochial dues, forbade them to employ Christian wet-nurses or servants and banned Christians from eating or meeting with them. The sale of meat to Jews during Lent was forbidden. The Jew was banned from disparaging the Christian faith or entering any church or chapel except for the purpose of transit. Sexual intercourse between Christian and Jew was utterly forbidden. The *tabula* was now to be enforced by the state. Jewish colonisation was officially limited, except by special licence, to the towns where they 'had been accustomed' to live. Attempts to dissuade any potential converts to Christianity now carried a penalty. The year 1253 was a major turning point in the constitutional status of the Jew.[92]

Shortly afterwards, the Lord Edward became involved in Jewish affairs. From 1262 he played an ever-increasing role with the Jews. Once peace was restored after the barons' wars, the Crown tried to reconstruct the *archa* system and build a new confidence in its royal Jews. It was, however, also aware of the problems caused by land alienation and indebtedness. In 1269, the new Provisions of the Jewry, drawn up by the Lord Edward and Sir Walter of Merton and endorsed by Henry III, attempted to solve some of the complaints of the baronial party. The Provisions decreed that all debts to the Jews which took the form of fees which had not been assigned or sold to Christians were to be quit only to the debtors who had used them as security. The Jew was then banned from taking any other fee debts and from selling off any

---

[90] PRO E/101/249/4; Roth 1978, p. 45; Stacey 1985, p. 176.   [91] Roth 1978, p. 59.
[92] Rigg, pp. xlviii–xlix.

existing ones he owned except with royal licence.[93] Two years later, on 25 July 1271, a further mandate was issued to the Justices of the Jews which forbade Jews to enjoy a freehold in manors, lands, tenements, fees or tenures of any kind. This effectively only left the Jews cash and commodities in which they could legally deal and quite possibly resulted in higher interest charges on loans. According to the mandate, the Jews were allowed to continue dwelling in their own houses but any other houses in their possession were only to be let to Jewish tenants. The mandate also stipulated that all fee debts, lands and tenures which the Jews had been enfeoffed of before 1271 were to be discharged as quickly as possible and that the Christians involved were to pay off the principal only. A final clause forbade Christians to serve Jews as nurses, bakers, brewers and cooks, 'because the Jews and Christians are different in the cult of faith'.[94] It was against the background of all these legislative measures that Edward I was to deal with Jewish problems during his reign. Edward's attempts to bring about change to this legal situation undoubtedly deserve the description of 'experiment'. The *Statutum de Judeismo* of 1275 and the *Chapitles Tuchaunz le Gewerie*, if they were ever issued, were both attempts to revise the position and status of the Jew in society as it had been established before Edward's reign. This Edwardian 'experiment' will be considered in greater detail in chapter 5.

Before making an examination of Edward's attempts to alter the social position and business practice of the Jews, it is necessary to consider Edward's own personal attitudes to the Jews. Professor Tout stated categorically that Edward disliked the Jews on both religious and economic grounds. Edward, he claimed, strongly held the medieval belief in the harmfulness and sinfulness of usury; his own embarrassed finances and constant burden of debt did not make him the more friendly to the moneylender.[95] Accordingly his personal views on usury and his dislike of creditors are both good reasons for his wish to change the Jews' role in society, but they do not explain why he tried to bring about change before he finally expelled them or why he did not banish the Jews on his return to England in 1274. Edward's own personal views, and the influences of those close to him, must obviously be considered if a true impression of his motives for expelling the Jews from England is ever to be reached. In the first place, Edward's background and upbringing must naturally have coloured his view of the Jews. His mother Eleanor has long been acknowledged as 'the

---

[93] Rigg, pp. xlviii–li; Denholm-Young 1947, p. 143; Prestwich 1988, p. 62.
[94] Rigg, pp. l–lv.
[95] Prestwich 1972, p. 10; Tout 1920, p. 161. By November 1263 Edward was in debt to Jacob of Oxford for £66 13s 4d, *CCR 1261–1264*, p. 315.

steady enemy of the Jews'; and her uncle Boniface had also been their enemy.[96] It was Eleanor of Provence who, in 1275, had all Jews banished from the towns which she held in dower.[97] Edward's own uncle and former tutor, Simon de Montfort, made his hatred of the Jews clear by expelling them from Leicester, 'for the good of his soul and the souls of his ancestors and successors'.[98] Edward's own feelings towards the Jews were also influenced by his father's attitude towards them. Henry III's own interest in the Jews has been described as 'almost morbid'. The late Sir Maurice Powicke went on to claim that Henry:

could not do without them, and at times tried to be just to them. He was keenly interested in attempts to convert them. But in times of stress, when he was apt to take refuge from his anxieties or his conscience in religious exercises, the ruthless exploitation of the Jews would seem to him a duty as well as a means of profit.[99]

Certainly Henry realised their value and used them to finance his extravagant way of life. It is now well known that in 1240, at Worcester, Henry squeezed the largest tallage of the thirteenth century from his Jewish subjects.[100] Edward must, at the very least, have been aware of the Jews as an obvious source of income.

Another influence of which the Lord Edward must have been aware was the attitude of his uncle, Richard of Cornwall, towards the Jews. Richard appeared to favour the Jews as financiers rather than the Italians or the Cahorsins.[101] The relationship between Richard and the Jews seems to have been one in which Richard utilised their financial expertise, for as N. Denholm-Young observed, 'whatever the nature of his transactions with the Jews, Richard did not come to them as a borrower'.[102] Richard first appeared as a patron of the Jews in 1231, when he began to protect certain Jews at Berkhamstead. It was probably at Richard's instigation that in 1235 Henry III granted the Jews who had settled at Berkhamstead, without royal permission, the right to remain there with their chirographer's chest. In 1242 Richard was given permission to move the Jewish community and to set up an *archa* at his new castle of Wallingford. In return for royal protection Richard of Cornwall used Jewish financiers to provide financial backing for his own crusade. In June 1236 Richard took the cross and in January 1237 the Jews were asked to grant him £2,000 in aid of his expedition.[103]

[96] Stokes 1918, pp. 163–4; Biles 1983, pp. 129–30; Howell 1987, pp. 375–6.
[97] Mundill 1993, p. 48, Dobson 1993, p. 18.
[98] Levy 1902a, pp. 40–2; Maddicott 1994, pp. 14–17.   [99] Powicke 1947, p. 313.
[100] Stacey 1985; 1988.   [101] Denholm-Young 1947, pp. 68–9.   [102] *Ibid.*, p. 31.
[103] *Ibid.*, pp. 21–2, 31–2; *CCR 1242–1247*, p. 393.

Richard of Cornwall was an individual who had a reasonably good relationship with certain Jews. When, in 1249, Abraham of Berkhamstead fell foul of the authorities and his chattels were confiscated, it was Richard who intervened and saved him.[104] At Richard's instance, Abraham was allowed to keep the residue of his chattels. In 1254, when Abraham was accused of murdering his wife, he was imprisoned in the Tower. This time in serious trouble, Abraham apparently offered to betray all the other Jews in England. The Jewish community offered Richard £666 13s 4d to keep Abraham in prison. Richard supported Abraham and he was allowed to make his peace with the king for a fine of £466 13s 4d in 1255. Abraham of Berkhamstead was now described as Richard's Jew and was granted to him bodily. A list of the debts owed to Abraham amounting to £1,800 was compiled and these were to be collected for Richard's personal use.[105] Thus, like other members of the royal family, Richard of Cornwall now had his own 'royal' Jew.

Richard was also prepared to help other Jews. In 1255, it was Richard who intervened to stop the execution of the Lincoln Jews who had been accused of the alleged murder of Little St Hugh. As a result of the allegations, eighteen Lincoln Jews were put to death at Christmas 1255. Twenty-one Jews were finally released at Richard's instance in May 1256.[106] Richard was probably well acquainted with many members of the Oxford, Lincoln and London Jewish communities. In 1256, before he left for Germany, he lent the government £3,333 6s 8d on the security of the whole Jewry.[107] Richard also called in all the debts from the Jews that he could, as well as those from his own Jew, Abraham of Berkhamstead. After the wars and because of his absence Richard was unable to protect the Jews any longer. His own son, Henry of Almain, and Prince Edward both clearly had different attitudes towards the Jews. It was these two younger men who were probably responsible for the Statute of the Jewry in 1269. N. Denholm-Young saw this particular piece of legislation as a turning point in the fortunes of the Jews: 'The attitude of Edward to the Jews is in strong contrast to the favourable treatment that they had learned to expect from Richard.'[108]

By the late 1260s Richard of Cornwall was powerless to protect the Jews. Prince Edward and Henry of Almain were insistent upon changing the Jews' constitutional position. However it is important that, at this time, not all the magnates of the realm seem to be as much against the Jews as the young prince and his legislators. It does seem that

---

[104] Denholm-Young 1947, pp. 69–70.
[105] *Ibid.*, p. 70; PRO E/101/249/14; Langmuir 1972, p. 463.
[106] Langmuir 1972, p. 479.
[107] Denholm-Young 1947, p. 70.
[108] *Ibid.*, p. 143.

there was what might be called a pro-Jewish party, which had included Richard of Cornwall and which was now over-ruled. The attack on the Jews' position begun in Richard of Cornwall's absence by Prince Edward and Henry of Almain was renewed and the *Provisio Judaismi* of 1271 (when Richard was present) was finally passed. This finally changed the status of the Jews; they were now forbidden to hold free tenements.[109] 'At a stroke', as Cecil Roth commented, 'their status was virtually reduced to that of pawnbrokers.'[110]

Despite this attack on their legal rights the Jews were still seen by the Crown to be a source of royal income and as a guarantee against which money might be raised. In 1271, in order to provide funds for the Lord Edward's crusade, Henry III mortgaged the Jewry to his brother for a second time.[111] In return Richard of Cornwall lent the Lord Edward £1,333 6s 8d which was secured upon a pledge of the Jewries for one year.[112] When Richard died, on 2 April 1272, Henry III resumed the ownership of the Jewry.[113] Thus it was not only Richard of Cornwall who had found Jewish finance and contact with the Jewish communities to be a useful source of income but both Henry III and the Lord Edward who used their relationship with their Jewish subjects to raise finance. Similarly their queens, Eleanor of Provence and Eleanor of Castile, also provided patronage for particular Jews and profited by them. In 1275, after he had been effectively excommunicated from the Jewish community, Cok Hagin or Hagin fil Deulecresse became the 'Jew of the King's Consort', Eleanor of Castile.[114] In 1281 she even recommended him for the position of Archpresbyter of the Jews.[115] Queen Eleanor seems to have dealt in particular with Jacob of Oxford and Hagin fil Magister Moses, who had been Archpresbyter in 1280.[116] She certainly profited from the Jewish communities; it seems that her Queen's Gold (a due on every tenth mark paid to the king, as a 'voluntary' fine for the royal goodwill in the renewal of leases on Crown lands) was often paid to her in Jewish debts.[117]

It is little wonder that Eleanor was later accused by Archbishop Pecham of acquiring land by 'utilising the whirlpools of Jewish usury'. In 1281 she gained lands worth a total of over £380 per annum from nine knights who were deeply involved in debt with London Jews.[118] The unfortunate debtors had over the years amassed debts worth over

[109] Rigg, pp. xlviii–li.   [110] Roth 1978, p. 66.
[111] Stokes 1918, p. 169; Prestwich 1988, p. 80.   [112] Stokes 1918, p. 169; Roth 1978, p. 67.
[113] Roth 1978, p. 67.   [114] Stokes 1918, p. 166; Parsons 1995, p. 140.
[115] Stokes 1913, pp. 35–7.   [116] Stokes 1918, pp. 164–7; Mundill 1993, pp. 72, 86.
[117] Stokes 1918, pp. 157–8; Stacey 1985, p. 180 note 24; Byerly 1986, pp. xiii–xiv; Parsons 1995, pp. 121–3.
[118] Stokes 1918, pp. 167–8; Mundill 1993, p. 34; Parsons 1995, pp. 128–35.

£3,996 13s 4d to Jews like Jacob of Oxford and Hagin fil Magister Moses as well as other London-based Jews.[119] The queen had, during a decade of dealing with the London Jews, acquired these debts and now tried to liquidate them by taking over the debtors' lands in return for either, in some cases, making extra cash payments or, in others, granting partial remission of the debts. She gained the manor of Burgh in Suffolk worth £30 annually, the manor of Quendon in Essex worth £40, the castle of Leeds worth £30 and the manor of Westcliffe in Kent worth £60, and the manor of Nocton in Lincolnshire for a term of fourteen years worth £60, as well as the manors of Torpeyl and Upton in Northamptonshire worth £80 per annum. From payments of Queen's Gold she also obtained the manor of Scottow in Norfolk worth £40, the manors of Westham, Fobbing and Shenfield in Essex, and the manor of Longele worth £40 per annum.[120] The queen was not alone in her dealings with the Jews. Edmund, earl of Lancaster, the king's brother, also seems to have had connections with and offered protection to one of the richer London Jews, Aaron fil Vives. Aaron remained Edmund's personal Jew until the Expulsion in 1290.[121]

Edward's immediate family had clearly seen the value of the Jews and how to exploit them. Not only had they protected individual Jews and gained by taking over Jewish transactions but they had also profited from the tallages and fines which were imposed on the whole Jewish community. Edward I's predecessors had made legislation to protect the Jewish credit facilities in the kingdom. It is clear that there were also many at the royal court who either had dealings with Jews or profited from them. These included Edward's Chancellor, Robert Burnell, the Jewish officials of the Exchequer, leading knights and even members of the royal household.[122] On a personal level Edward had had much contact with the Jews. He had even borrowed private loans from certain of them.[123] He was not only aware of his own family's attitude towards the Jews but must also have been aware of the feeling of the barons and the knightly class who accompanied him on crusade and who fought for

---

[119] *CCR 1279–1288*, pp. 80–1.

[120] Although there were many small sums also owed in the Exchequer the main debts show that Sir John de Burg was in debt to Manasser le fiz Aaron for £266 13s 4d; Sir Bartholomew de Redham owed Agin £200; Sir William de Montchesney owed Hagin £250 and the king £100; Sir Robert Canvil owed a debt to various Jews and had seemingly had his debt taken over by the prior of Romely; Sir William de Leyburn owed £680 to Hagin who had given the debt to the queen; Sir Gilbert Peche owed the queen £333 6s 8d for a debt to Aaron le fiz Vives and £30 to the king; Sir Stephen de Cheyndut owed various Jews £666 13s 4d; Sir Norman de Arcy owed Master Elias and Mansel le fiz Aaron £950; Sir John de Cameys owed Hagin £333 6s 8d. Parsons 1995, pp. 157–97.

[121] Mundill 1993, pp. 64–5, 75–6, 85. [122] Mundill 1987, p. 135; see chapter 5 below.

[123] *CCR 1261–1264*, p. 315.

him in Wales. In fact during his reign he was able to pardon or cancel their debts as a reward for faithful service.[124] Edward was also aware of the popular hatred of the Jews and the Church's view of them. His personal hostility towards the Jews must have increased in 1255 when the affair of Little St Hugh inflamed popular conceptions of them.[125] Edward had actually witnessed an act of blasphemy committed by a Jew. On Ascension Day 1268 Edward was in Oxford when a Jew stopped a procession going towards St Frideswide's where the annual sermon was to be preached. The Jew tore the rood from the bearer and trampled it under foot in the presence of the Chancellor, Masters and Scholars of the University and the parochial clergy. It was Edward who sent the news of the event to his father at Woodstock. It is quite possible that, as Dr Christoph Cluse has recently commented, this had a profound effect on the young prince, who had just taken the cross.[126] Edward was personally only too well aware of the prevalent religious and lay feelings towards the Jews.

Edward's first real encounter with Jewish financial affairs came when he was still a prince in 1262. On 4 June, Henry III made what Professor Michael Prestwich has recently called a radical step by granting Edward the receipts from the Jewry in England for a three-year period.[127] Edward immediately entrusted the Jewry to some merchants from Cahors, presumably farming it out in return for a fixed annual sum possibly because he was afraid of being tainted by usury.[128] Edward had probably first encountered some of the problems which Jewish communities posed in his role as ruler of Gascony. Much of Edward's time was spent on Gascony and his policy towards the Jewish communities there is crucial to an understanding of his attitude to the Jewish communities of England. In 1249 the revenues from Gascony had first been given to him. In 1252 he received the title of duke. In 1254 at the age of fifteen, he made his first visit to his duchy and was also married there. In 1261, he made his second visit and set about restoring order and justice. He first entered the duchy as king of England in August 1273, when an early attempt at a *Quo Warranto* enquiry was made. This was later carried out in an improved way on his English subjects in 1278. Margaret Wade Labarge has intimated that Edward had always used Gascony as a place for experimental policies, 'which were later applied in England in a more fully developed form'.[129] It is, as H. G.

---

[124] Lieberman 1983, p. 221; Mundill 1993, pp. 38–9.
[125] Langmuir 1972; Roth 1978, pp. 56–7.
[126] Stokes, 1918, p. 163; Cluse 1995b, pp. 396–405, 419–23, 436–42.
[127] Prestwich 1988, p. 38.   [128] *CPR 1258–1266*, pp. 233, 283; PRO E/101/249/10.
[129] Wade Labarge 1980, pp. 41–4.

Richardson observed, even possible that the expulsion of the Jews from Gascony in 1287 was a model for what followed in England on 1 November 1290.[130] The likelihood of this will be discussed at greater length below but it is important to establish here that Edward had had early contacts with his Jewish subjects elsewhere in Europe in the capacity of duke rather than king.

In Gascony there was no organisation resembling the English Exchequer of the Jews and it was necessary for Edward's agents to rely for their information on the Jews' own records. The Gascon Jews, like their brethren in France, lived under the protection of the duke or king. In Gascony this protection was carried out by a special organisation composed of a judicial system and particular judges, nominated jointly by the constable and the seneschal or sheriff.[131] It is clear that, even during his busy reign as king of England, Edward still found time to monitor the fortunes of his Jewish subjects in Gascony. In June 1275, when there were complaints of abuses in the justice given to the Gascon Jews, Edward entrusted two officers to hear the complaint and to see that justice was given to the Jews, 'as it was to the Christians and according to the custom of the land'.[132] After further Jewish complaints of being harassed by their Christian neighbours, Edward ordered the seneschal of Gascony and the constable of Bordeaux to have Jewish causes tried by good and lawful Christians.[133] In the early 1280s he also showed favour to the Jews of Lectoure (near Toulouse) when he granted them a remission of a claim of £100.[134] In Gascony, the Jews were even protected by the intervention of local custom. On 29 December 1281 Gerard de Monlezun, bishop of Lectoure, the town council and the citizens wrote to Edward I and claimed that Josce, Leon and Samuel of Toartre, their wives and their children had been living as citizens there for over twenty-five years and that they lived under the protection of the liberties and franchises of their town. They claimed that a new financial imposition should not be made on them and that they should be treated as subjects of the king and that the king should intervene and respect the liberties and the franchises of Lectoure.[135]

Despite the fact that they received some respect for their liberties from Edward, Gascon Jews were naturally subject to ducal taxation. Tallages were imposed in 1275, in 1281 (when a particularly large levy was assessed) and in 1282.[136] The policy of tallage collection in Gascony was always subject to negotiation and it seems that over these particular tallage payments Edward even had some compassion for the Jews.

---

[130] Richardson 1960, pp. 225–9, 233. See chapter 8 below. [131] Trabut-Cussac 1972, p. 264.
[132] Trice Martin 1895, pp. 170–1. [133] *Ibid.*, p. 173. [134] *Ibid.*, p. 174.
[135] Trabut-Cussac 1972, p. 313, note 228. [136] *Ibid.*, pp. 312–13.

Clearly tallage assessment in Gascony was made even more difficult by the fact that there were no official *archae* or scrutinies on which to base such assessments. The fact that Edward often acquitted such tallage payments led Charles Trice Martin to comment that Edward showed a desire to treat the Jews of Gascony with favour.[137] The reason for this, as the king himself wrote, was that he did not wish the Jews to be oppressed with too heavy taxes lest their number should diminish.[138] So it seems that at this date Edward had no desire to reduce his Gascon Jews to poverty. In 1275 the constable of Bordeaux recommended moderation of the amount of tallage demanded from the Jews. Edward accordingly ordered the constable of Bordeaux and the seneschal of Gascony not to burden the Jews of Gascony, because 'of the dearness of grain and wine this year'.[139] It is evident that in the mid-1270s Edward showed some concern for his Jewish subjects in Gascony.

In 1277 a special immunity from tallage for life was granted to Bonamy and Isaac of Bordeaux and their families for an annual payment of £13 6s 8d and they were allowed to dwell where they pleased.[140] Similarly, Elias fil Benedict of London and his wife were granted the same privileges for an annual payment of 13s 4d.[141] During the severe tallage of 1281, Edward also granted a special licence to Aaron of London and his wife Rose of aquittance of tallage for a payment of £1 6s 8d annually for the next six years.[142] He even instructed the constable of Gascony and Bordeaux to relax the tallage payments on other Jews in 1282.[143] Another royal exemption from tallage was made on 1 May 1283 to some Jews in return for an annual payment of £1 6s 8d.[144] In 1283 the Jews of Agenais also obtained a fixed tax for five years.[145] Without any means of controlling or keeping a pulse on the financial dealings of the Gascon Jews it is perhaps not surprising that both they and Edward preferred a fixed rate of payment for tallage. However, while in the early years of his reign Edward might even perhaps be seen as compassionate in the way in which he treated the Gascon Jewry, this was not to last. Four years later, in 1287, a general expulsion of the Jews from the duchy and the seizure of their goods was ordered.[146] Because of the similarities between his action in Gascony in 1287 and that in

[137] Trice Martin 1895, p. 170.   [138] *Ibid.*, p. 174.   [139] Mundill 1993, pp. 49–50.
[140] *Ibid.*, p. 57.   [141] *Ibid.*, p. 58.
[142] Trice Martin 1895, p. 174; Trabut-Cussac 1972, p. 313.
[143] Trice Martin 1895, p. 175.
[144] Trabut-Cussac 1972, p. 289. Two instalments were to be paid to the Exchequer of Bordeaux, half at Michaelmas and half at Easter.
[145] *Ibid.*, p. 313.
[146] *Ibid.*, pp. 85–6; Richardson 1960, pp. 225–6; Salzman 1968, pp. 94–5.

England in 1290 the reasons and motives for this change of policy and ideas will be considered further below.

In England, when it came to the administration of Jewish affairs Edward I also took a very personal role. He certainly must have led the deliberations of the royal council over the state of English Jewry in the late 1260s. The preamble to an ordinance made at Hilary term 1269, which prevented Jews from selling debts that they were owed to any Christian, stated that it was made by the king, and by the royal counsel of Edward and other wise men.[147] The late H. G. Richardson held that in England Edward cannot have failed to take a lively interest in the Jews because of the financial pressures from which he suffered in the 1270s.[148] However, whatever his personal feelings and his general awareness of the Anglo-Jewish communities, in the early part of his reign Edward I probably did not have the time to come properly to grips with the Jewish problem. When he eventually did try to do so it seems that he required either conversion or the assimilation of the Jews into Christian society. He wanted English Jews to forsake usury and to become legal traders. It does not seem that he wished them to be killed. In 1279, when the executions of Jews for coin-clipping had got out of hand, he let those Jews who were still accused pay fines rather than be imprisoned or killed.[149] This may of course have been because of his strong sense of justice. Yet in England he clearly wished to find some sort of solution to the Jewish problem without creating widespread pogroms or genocide. It is also clear that the Jewish problem was probably never high on his agenda. Any firm policy which Edward I may have had towards the Jews was delayed by his deep involvement in strengthening the laws which affected all of his subjects, by wars with Wales, problems in Gascony, international affairs and corruption amongst his officials.

When Henry III died, Edward was absent on crusade; he did not return to England until 1274.[150] In 1275, he set about a major overhaul of the common law and the problems which he perceived to be afflicting his country: 1275 saw the instigation of the Hundred Rolls as well as the Statute of Westminster to tighten judicial procedure. The Statute of the Jewry of 1275 may be seen as part of the overall measures that Edward saw as necessary for the smooth running of the country, not necessarily as a separate piece of legislation for his Jewish subjects.[151] Further legislation and the implementation of the Statute itself at this

---

[147] Rigg, pp. xlviii–li; Denholm-Young 1947, p. 143; Prestwich 1988, p. 62.
[148] Richardson 1961, pp. 214–15.   [149] *CCR 1272–1279*, p. 529.
[150] Prestwich 1988, pp. 82–90.
[151] Salzman 1968, pp. 52–3; Prestwich 1988, pp. 267–79; Stacey, 1997, pp. 77–9.

period was made impossible by the problems with the Welsh: in 1276 and 1277 punitive expeditions had to be dispatched to Wales.[152] By 1278 and 1279 Edward was trying to renew his coinage.[153] It was as a result of inquiries into the poor state of the coinage that much blame fell upon the Jews. Whilst the crisis of the coin-clipping allegations came to its height Edward was busy trying to produce the Statute of Gloucester in 1278 and the Statute of Mortmain in 1279.[154] In 1280 he seems to have found time to turn briefly to the Jewish problem and revitalised the *Domus Conversorum* by providing it with some finance.[155] By 1282 and 1283, the years which might well have seen more vital legislation for the Jews, he was again deeply involved with the Welsh wars.[156] However, in 1283 he managed to remedy the problems which confronted 'legal merchants' and in the Statute of Merchants copied the Jewish *archa* system to ensure the quick repayment of debt. In 1285, the Statute of Winchester attempted to provide better public safety. In May 1286, he set out for Gascony and did not return until August 1289, only ten months before issuing the orders for the Expulsion of the Jews from England.[157]

On a more personal level Christian piety, as Professor Michael Prestwich has observed, informed many of Edward's actions and provided much of his personal faith.[158] He must have discussed the Jews and their situation with fellow crusaders and as he travelled in Europe, and as he met with other rulers with Jewish subjects in their lands. Edward took his part in the last crusade with St Louis of France, who also had many Jewish subjects.[159] On Edward's return from the Holy Land, he must have been well aware of the Council of Lyons and its resolutions against usury.[160] In 1280, he waived his claim to the Jewish poll tax and every forfeiture which came to him from a Jewish source for a period of seven years in order to endow the *Domus Conversorum*. His officers noted that the reason behind this gesture was that 'the king believes that the conversion of Jewish depravity to the Catholic faith would specially be to the increase of faith and worship of the name of Christ... in order that they be turned from their blindness to the light of the Church and may be strengthened in the firmness of their

---

[152] Prestwich 1988, pp. 174–82.   [153] *Ibid.*, pp. 244–8.
[154] *Ibid.*, Gloucester – pp. 97, 271, 291; Mortmain – pp. 251–325, 274, 522.
[155] Mundill 1993, pp. 68–9; Stacey 1992a, p. 276.
[156] Prestwich 1988, pp. 188–201, 255; Abrahams 1894a, p. 158.
[157] Prestwich 1988, pp. 278, 280–1, 287, 305–7, 523; Plucknett 1949, pp. 138–47.
[158] Prestwich 1988, pp. 111–14; 1985.
[159] Prestwich 1988, pp. 67, 72, 80; Jordan 1989, pp. 144–8 and note 25 on p. 148; Cluse 1995b, p. 419.
[160] Parkes 1938, p. 286; Stow 1989, pp. 131–2.

faith'.[161] Even despite what might be considered to be rhetoric it is still likely that Edward I's own faith might have had a significant influence on his final solution.

Edward I's own instructions in the early 1280s make it clear that he was 'led on by the love of God, and wishing to follow more devoutly in the path of the Holy Church'. Certainly Edward took firm action against blasphemy by introducing strict laws. The Jews were warned under peril of life and limb to avoid any blasphemous utterance against Christ and the Blessed Virgin Mary or the Holy Sacraments.[162] Edward also approved the attempts to make Jews attend sermons. In 1280, in accordance with the papal Bull *Vineam Sorec* of 1278, he issued instructions compelling Jews to attend sermons aimed at their conversion by the Dominicans.[163] In 1277, at the request of Archbishop Kilwardby, himself a Dominican, Edward ordered that a ribald Jew who had masqueraded as a Franciscan should undergo a severe punishment for his blasphemy.[164] In 1287, whilst in Gascony, Edward I once again took the cross. Soon afterwards his frustration and crusading ardour were turned against the Jews of both Gascony and England. At about the same time, the queen mother took the veil.[165] Perhaps it was because he had realised that he could not afford to make another warlike pilgrimage to the Holy Land that he turned against the Jews, who ironically had partially financed his first crusade.[166]

Surprisingly perhaps, many of Edward's actions towards the English Jewry were clearly conducted in person. H. G. Richardson showed that many of the Chancery Rolls give clues as to Edward's own interests in the Jews. The phrase, 'it has come to our ears' is common in the commissions of oyer and terminer.[167] Richardson also states that when the tallages of 1277 and 1278 were imposed on the Jewish community Edward gave verbal instructions to the assessors and collectors in person.[168] In 1279 Edward, in a special audience, instructed William de Brayboef just before the latter was appointed to take over the handling of the goods and chattels from the Jews who had been hanged for coin-clipping allegations.[169] In February 1286, before his departure for Gascony in the following May, Edward gave verbal instructions for a scrutiny of the *archae* in London and in the Exchequer at Westminster.[170] A ruler who took so much interest in the administration of the

---

[161] Mundill 1993, pp. 68–9; Stacey 1992, pp. 279–83.   [162] Mundill 1993, pp. 68–9.
[163] Roth 1978, p. 79; Adler 1939, p. 300; Abrahams 1894b, p. 435.   [164] PREJ3, pp. 311–12.
[165] Prestwich 1988, p. 123. Eleanor had resided at Amesbury from 1276 and took the veil in 1286.
[166] Salzman 1968, pp. 85, 95.   [167] Richardson 1960, p. 223.
[168] Ibid., pp. 223–4, particularly note 2.   [169] Ibid., p. 224.
[170] Ibid., p. 224; Mundill 1993, pp. 82–3.

Jewry and who did not ignore the Jewish problem must therefore have reached the decision for a final solution with difficulty. Edward I tried to experiment with the Jews' position in society before reaching his final solution. On a personal level, he can be seen as both pious and sometimes compassionate towards the Jews rather than as a bitter anti-semite in the modern sense.[171] He can also be seen as annoyed and angry that those Jews who did not take heed of his experimental ideas had disobeyed his laws. He clearly wished for nothing more than to make them abandon usury and to entice them into the Christian fold by conversion. It is therefore very possible that the final Expulsion was the result of Edward's own anger because his personal experiment failed and his orders had been disobeyed. However, such conclusions must wait until a fuller discussion of motives can be made in a later chapter.

Edward I was probably rarely out of touch with the situation his Jewish subjects were in. He regularly travelled through the towns in which Jewish communities lived: in 1274 Northampton, in 1275 Windsor, in 1276 Winchester, Lincoln, Chichester and Canterbury, in 1277 Woodstock, in 1280 Winchester and Marlborough (where Jews had been living), Lincoln, Abingdon, in 1281 Devizes and Gloucester, in 1283 Worcester, at Christmas 1285 and in January 1286 Exeter.[172] As king of his Christian subjects he naturally listened to their particular problems and local complaints when he visited their towns. As king of the Jews, Edward also knew the unusual position of his Jewish subjects within the realm and of their 'liberties' and standing in society as a whole. He certainly must have met with Jewish leaders in London and possibly at court.[173] As king, Edward was well aware of his responsi-bilities to both Jew and Gentile alike. However, he was naturally forced to leave local problems to others such as sheriffs to deal with and often needed to delegate to men like Hugh de Digneuton and the commis-sioners appointed to hear the allegations of 1278–9. For administering the Jews he had to use his officials appointed to the *Scaccarium Judaeorum* but from time to time he still took a deep personal interest in what could be termed the Jewish situation.

Before Edward I's reign, medieval English Jews were a recognisable and widespread community who were hated primarily because of their religion, their involvement in moneylending and the irrational accusa-tions of ritual murder. Despite various attempts and initiatives they

---

[171] Richmond 1992; Aronsfeld 1990; Stacey 1992b, Jerusalem, p. 15.

[172] Mundill 1993, pp. 46–87 provides an approximate itinerary of the towns visited by Edward.

[173] Although there is no actual proof of a specific meeting it is hard to believe that Edward and one of the leaders of the Jewish community, Rabbi Elias Menahem, never met. See Mundill 1997.

usually would not convert or assimilate. They remained as a clearly visible different minority group in society. They had special immunities, special courts and the Crown's protection. They enjoyed a degree of religious toleration and self-government. They were widely unpopular within a xenophobic mono-religious society. Added to this they were resented and had incurred the wrath of those, like Peter de Bending and many others, who had lost their lands through debt. In many ways it is surprising that they had lived and remained in England amidst such conditions through almost two centuries.[174] The reason for their continued presence can only be explained by the Crown's protection and in their special economic relationship with the Crown. After all, they were the King's Jews, his 'most exquisite villeins', and it was this special relationship which had protected them for so long and had given them their own constitutional rights. Reasons for their expulsion must partly lie in the deterioration of this relationship, Edward's own motives and the failure of his 'experiment'. Having examined the attitudes of the general populace, of the royal family and Edward's own special relationship with both English and Gascon Jews we must now consider the English Jews' special financial and fiscal relationship with the Crown in further detail and see if any deterioration or reason for their final expulsion can be traced

[174] Roth 1978, p. 47; Stokes 1913, p. 32.

Chapter 4

THE ROYAL TRIBUTE

'Did the forefathers of this miserable people think you meet with more rigorous Taskmasters in Egypt? They were only called upon to make brick: but nothing less than making gold seems to have been expected from the Jews in England.'[1] Thus de Bloissiers Tovey, writing in the eighteenth century, described the financial pressures on the medieval Anglo-Jew. His type of interpretation has left behind it a historiographical stereotyping which remains current even in the twentieth century, namely the association of Judaism and capital. Such a concept, linking Judaism inseparably to wealth, has coloured historians' and many contemporary views for several centuries. One of the most forceful proponents of this attitude was William Shakespeare who put the following couplet into the mouth of Shylock's servant in *The Merchant of Venice*: 'There will come a Christian by/Will be worth a Jewesses' eye.'[2]

Almost four hundred years after the Bristol tallage of 1210, the event to which this particular verse alludes, Shakespeare and the general populace still considered the Jews to be uniformly wealthy.[3] Such sentiments continued through the course of English literature and are expressed by Sir Walter Scott, who, in his *Ivanhoe*, portrayed Isaac the Jew as the great northern moneylender.[4] The stereotyping also continued into the novels of Dickens whose Fagin became almost as infamous as Shylock.[5] Rudyard Kipling took up a similar image in his *Puck of Pook's Hill*.[6] This notorious misrepresentation, linking Judaism so inseparably to great wealth, has had much influence on our own society's view of the Jew. It is represented not only in jokes, playground abuse and racial comments but also in the way in which the financial

---

[1] Tovey 1738, p. 199.   [2] Shakespeare, *The Merchant of Venice*, II, v; Abrahams 1916.
[3] Usher 1992; Adler 1928, pp. 141–2.   [4] Scott 1830, *Ivanhoe*.
[5] Dickens 1849–50, *Oliver Twist*.
[6] Kipling 1906, *Puck of Pook's Hill*, 1951 edn, pp. 283–304.

value of the English Jewish community has always been emphasised. More than one twentieth-century writer has referred to medieval Anglo-Jewry as being 'The golden goose that laid the golden egg.'[7] In the context of such obvious bias it is not surprising that general preconceptions of the Jews' wealth have also influenced many historians. It is accordingly understandable that the Expulsion of 1290 has itself usually been explained away in predominantly economic terms. In order to try to understand the real motives for the Expulsion it is necessary to examine exactly how valuable the medieval Jewry was and more importantly the financial significance the Jewish community had for royal revenues, particularly in the reign of Edward I; for if economic issues dictated the Expulsion then the amount of revenue Edward took from his Jewry is clearly of vital import.

As has been indicated, many historians of Anglo-Jewry have alluded to the financial importance of the Jews to the Crown's revenues. Indeed there is a historiographical tradition on this very subject. Joseph Jacobs, in the last century, paraphrased a seventeenth-century pamphleteer and referred to the Jews as a 'financial sponge' which the Crown could squeeze when money was short.[8] Similarly, Charles Gross claimed that the king 'fleeced them to the quick', but was also eager to point out that the people would have 'flayed them to the bone'.[9] In this century, Cecil Roth referred to the medieval Anglo-Jewish community as the 'King's milch cow'.[10] However, until recently relatively few historians have ventured further than cursory investigations of the financial importance of the Jews which gave rise to both the literary sentiments and the historical observations, and few have actually tested the Stubbsian/Sombartian linkage of Jews and capital.[11] The records of the Jewish Exchequer have preserved a reasonable picture of royal revenues arising from Jewish affairs. These sources for Edward I's reign will now be investigated in greater detail.

'Dull, repetitive and complicated', as Sir Hilary Jenkinson once described them, these records nevertheless form the corpus of the evidence of the financial relationship between the Jews and the Crown during the thirteenth century.[12] Through close examination it is possible to use them to establish an idea of how much capital the Jews still had before the Expulsion, how much wealth had been eroded and finally whether in 1290 the Jews were still of financial importance to the

---

[7] Arkin 1955, pp. 16–20.   [8] Jacobs 1893a, p. xix; H.W., *Anglo-Judaeus*, p. 6.

[9] Gross 1887, p. 206.   [10] Roth 1978, chapter 3.

[11] Abrahams 1916, pp. 176–7; Stubbs 1929, vol. II, pp. 459, 580; Elman 1939, pp. 91–2; Rosten 1968, pp. 530–1; Sombart 1913.

[12] Jenkinson 1918, p. 20.

Crown or not. In order to achieve this it is necessary to make a wide-ranging examination of all the surviving records. As was observed earlier, Charles Gross conveniently divided the fiscal operations of the 'Engine of Extortion' (as he called the Jewish Exchequer) into four main categories: tallages, fines, reliefs and escheats.[13] All these categories must be considered. Any investigation of these different sources of income has to be based on two types of record: first, the Receipt and Plea Rolls of the Jewish Exchequer and secondly, the Receipt, Plea, Patent and Close Rolls of the other numerous governmental departments which sometimes recorded Jewish business. The specifically 'Jewish' records, the Plea Rolls and the Receipt Rolls of the Exchequer of the Jews, naturally abound with mentions of fines, tallages, amercements, confiscations, licences and other penalties imposed on the Jewish community. Yet it is an impossible task to enumerate the number of cases in the Plea Rolls of the Jews or indeed the other mainstream governmental records which ended in fines or financial gain for the Crown. The latter sources only contain occasional mentions of Jewish revenues; and only in a few cases is it possible to isolate information from the more general records and to link it with what is available from the more 'Jewish' records. Such a task would be a gargantuan one and indeed as impossible as seeking the proverbial needle in a haystack.[14] However, an attempt will be made here to use some of these sources to show approximately how much Edward I gained from his Jewry before the Expulsion.

A good starting point for any general investigation into Jewish finances was provided by Peter Elman in 1938. He broke down the thirteenth-century Jewish tallages into four chronological phases and then drew conclusions concerning the average amount of tallage assessed per annum. He also detected a pattern in the tallages: 'The imposition of tallage became severer and more frequent towards the forties of the century; it fell off during the baronial wars to rise to its apex around the year 1275. There appears to have been a more or less close synchronization between the rise and fall of the Jewish tallages and the general history of the thirteenth century.'[15] At first sight, such synchronisation seems to be correct and can easily be verified. Certainly in Edward's reign, his crusade, his works on the royal castles and his Welsh wars can be used to explain increases in tallage assessment. However, those who accept this interpretation at face value rely too much on the evidence of the tallage assessed rather than the tallage

---

[13] Gross 1887, pp. 192–4, 205.   [14] Mundill 1993, pp. 25–7.
[15] Roth 1978, pp. 272–3; Elman, 1938b, p. 112.

collected. By contrast, H. G. Richardson was more cautious and concentrated upon the actual amounts received by the Exchequer.[16] To gain a better idea of the Jews' financial value to the Crown, records of actual receipt rather than assessment must clearly be consulted. To do this accurately is extremely complicated because between the opposite poles of tallage assessed and tallage collected there existed a vast range of intricate negotiation, mystery and unanswered questions. The whole task is made more difficult because payments for tallage do not necessarily appear on one special roll; not all tallage payments were in cash. Tallage payments could unwittingly be hidden in payments made by officials and labelled by the Exchequer scribes as simply 'from many Jewish debts'.[17] Despite these pitfalls, it is still worth trying to pick out the relevant tallages and to attempt to examine the Crown's actual income from them.

Isolating different tallages is a difficult exercise mainly because the payments and the records tend to overlap each other. The sorts of evidence that testify to a tallage on the Jewry can be of several kinds. First, the actual document recording part or all of the financial gain for the Crown has in some cases survived.[18] Second, the Patent, Close and Memoranda Rolls have preserved the orders to and appointments of special commissioners for the tallage.[19] Third, in general each tallage was nearly always preceded by a general scrutiny of the *archae* which represented the Crown's great interest in the state of Jewish finances.[20] Fourth, in some cases chronicle sources and other evidence record that a tallage took place.[21]

Although each tallage generated much bureaucracy, relatively little is known of the actual mechanism of collection. A tallage was an arbitrary tax, by definition, which the Crown declared that it was going to levy, ordered officials to collect, and then simply took from its Jewish subjects and transferred to royal coffers.[22] The original instructions to levy a tallage were, as Professor Robert Stacey has recently observed, made

---

[16] Richardson 1960, pp. 214–15, particularly note 5.   [17] Jenkinson 1918, pp. 31–7.

[18] *Ibid.*; Jenkinson's list is still used as a guide to the special Jewish rolls within the PRO E/401 category in the Public Record Office today; Elman 1938a, pp. 153–4.

[19] *CPR 1272–1281*, pp. 61, 154, 273; Rokeah, 1997.

[20] Apart from the *archa* scrutinies taken after the Expulsion several other Edwardian scrutinies have survived in part: Hereford: *PREJ3*, pp. 230–8; Colchester: PRO C/47/9/48; York: (in part) PRO C/47/9/49; Exeter: (in part) PRO E/101/249/31; Oxford: PRO E/101/249/32; Northampton: PRO E/101/249/33. The Memoranda Roll for Hilary 1275 (PRO E/101/249/19) records information from the 1276 scrutinies about bonds in eleven different *archae*. Printed in *PREJ4*, pp. 13–70.

[21] References to early tallages can be found in *Annales Monastici*, vol. II, p. 300; Matthew Paris, *Chronica Majora*, vol. III, p. 543; vol. IV, pp. 260, 373; vol. V, pp. 274, 458.

[22] Gross 1887, pp. 194–202.

with great secrecy. They were probably issued orally in the first instance, the privy seal later being used to prevent creditors from removing, or not depositing, bonds in the local *archae*.[23] It has also become clear that the process of collection directly involved Jews, who were appointed to aid the Exchequer officials.[24] In each town a Jewish *talliator* was appointed to apportion the burden of the tallage as fairly as he could upon his brethren.[25] The cash collected was paid either to a local official or to a man of standing, like an abbot, a prior or the sheriff of the county; in some cases, it was paid directly to the Jewish Exchequer at Westminster.[26]

What has clearly emerged from previous studies of Jewish finance is that the capital which the Jewish community possessed at the end of the twelfth century had declined by Edward I's reign. It also becomes patently clear that tallage assessments are not necessarily a good yardstick for Jewish ability actually to pay tallage. The Northampton *Donum* of 1194, assessed at £3,333 6s 8d, produced payments of £1,742 9s 2d.[27] The famous Bristol tallage of 1210, estimated at £40,000 (the second largest ever assessed upon Anglo-Jewry), has left no record other than the story of the treatment of one Jew by King John.[28] The *auxilium* of 1221, assessed at £1,000, only apparently yielded £643 1s 10d.[29] The largest tallage of Henry III's reign, in 1241, was assessed at £13,333 6s 8d. As Professor Stacey has conclusively shown, almost 70 per cent of this tallage was collected in full. The Crown actually collected over £9,052 10s 3½d.[30] This particular tallage collection must have had great impact on Jewish wealth. If such a massive collection is coupled with the other Henrician tallages, then Robert Stacey's observations on Jewish capital during Henry III's reign must be accepted as a good

---

[23] Stacey 1985, pp. 185, 194, particularly note 45.

[24] In a paper given by Dr P. Brand to the JHSE on 23 March 1983 University College London it was intimated that the Archpresbyter of the Jews had an advisory capacity to the *Scaccarium Judaeorum* on all matters of finance. For further discussion of the role of Archpresbyter see Gross 1887, pp. 178–9; Richardson 1960, pp. 121–4; Stacey 1985, pp. 190–3 and appendix v, pp. 248–9.

[25] PRO E/101/249/12. This documents the appointment of six Jewish assessors and six wealthy Jews who were responsible for assessing the tallage. It also names local Jews who were responsible for tallage collections in Bedford, Bristol, Cambridge, Canterbury, Colchester, Exeter, Gloucester, Hereford, Lincoln, London, Northampton, Norwich, Nottingham, Oxford, Somerset, Stamford, Warwick, Worcester and York. This document is printed in part in Stokes 1913, p. 250 who erroneously dated it to 1219; Richardson 1960, p. 214 note 5 corrected the dating although, as Stacey 1985, pp. 248–9 points out others persisted in dating it to 1219.

[26] *PREJ4*, pp. 33 and 47–9; PRO E/101/249/25 and E/101/249/26; Rokeah, 1997, appendix II.

[27] Abrahams 1925.

[28] Brewer 1970, p. 587; *Chronica Johannis de Oxenedes*, pp. 125–6; Bartholomew de Cotton, *Historia Anglicana*, p. 99; Matthew Paris, *Historia Anglorum*, vol. II, p. 121; Matthew Paris, *Chronica Majora*, vol. II, p. 528; Adler 1928, pp. 141–2.

[29] Chew 1928.   [30] Stacey 1985, pp. 169, and 199, table 2.

impression of the damage done to the financial reserves of Jewish business men before Edward I's reign. Professor Stacey pointed out that: 'The double blows of the 20,000 mark tallage of 1241–1242 and the 60,000 mark tallage of 1244–1250 ruined the financial magnates of England, and effectively decapitated the class structure of medieval Anglo-Jewry. In so doing Henry broke the financial backbone of the English Jewish community, and permanently reduced its financial value to the crown.'[31]

Not all Henrician tallages had such high yields. In November 1252 a tallage of £2,666 13s 4d was assessed but apparently only £321 10s 3½d was collected. This inability to pay the 1252 tallage serves to underline Professor Barrie Dobson's suggestion of a watershed at that time in the Jews' financial ability to make their tallage payments. In his study of the York Jewry, Professor Dobson observed: 'The corrosive effects of excessive tallage on the one side and of increased anti-Jewish propaganda and blood-libel accusations on the other seem to have made the mid-1250s a real watershed in the history of Anglo-Jewish relations.'[32] Certainly, the 1250s can be seen as a watershed not only for Gentile–Jewish relations but also for Jewish wealth. It is the 1250s which probably mark the start of a catastrophic decline in Jewish wealth. Recovery was greatly hampered by the civil war and further demands made by Henry III on his Jews. Certainly, many Jews and their businesses were damaged during this period. It could well have been that, as Professor Robert Stacey's work demonstrates, cash returns for tallage were no longer easy to find. Stacey noted that one of the features of the 1241 tallage, as must have been the case with other tallages, was that payments were collected in cash rather than bonds, or by forcing Christian debtors to pay their dues. He also shows that this did the greatest damage to any potential business recovery:

In this respect the 'cash-only' policy in 1241–1242 may even have proved economically counter-productive in the long run. By concentrating the tax burdens on the Jews alone instead of on the realm through the Jews, the king not only ruined the great Jewish financiers; he also choked off one of his most effective conduits for the indirect taxation of the kingdom as a whole.[33]

Before examining the tallages of Edward's reign it is worth bearing in mind the fact that after the 1240 tallage the Jewish community had found difficulty in paying cash for tallage payments, that tallage payments were not necessarily made on time and that perhaps all they had to offer were unredeemed bonds as payment. It is even more

---

[31] *Ibid.*, p. 205.   [32] Dobson 1979, p. 36.   [33] Stacey 1985, p. 207.

important to see who actually paid the tallage after the watershed had been passed. If the Jews could not pay, did the onus fall to their debtors? Certainly the Edwardian Jew still had to render unto Caesar that which was Caesar's, and throughout Edward's reign was never free from financial demands. In order to answer this question a far more detailed study of payments from the Jews during Edward's reign is necessary than has yet been produced.[34]

In the early months of 1272, Henry III had ordered a new tallage of the Jews to be made. This was probably designed to contribute towards the expense of the Lord Edward's crusade. It was assessed at £3,333 6s 8d.[35] By this time many Jews were either unable or unwilling to pay and many were subsequently imprisoned in the Tower of London. On 20 November 1272, when Henry died, the royal council carried over a substantial balance of arrears of tallage upon the Jews. By January 1273 only £1,289 10s 0d had been collected.[36] Some of the cash was used to pay royal officials by an authorisation of the late king.[37] The actual payments show that in 1272 there was considerable financial hardship amongst the Jewish community. There was, for instance, only one contributor from the Hereford community, Aaron le Blund, who was imprisoned in the Tower because he had failed to pay in full. He managed to contribute a total of £60 in five payments. The fact that four of the payments were made on his behalf by his clients, William de Sholle, John of Norwich and Adam Beraud, only serves to prove Aaron's inability to pay cash.[38] The contribution from the Canterbury community was £71 which was paid by only four Jews.[39] Only three Jews paid for the Lincoln community: Sampson fil Magri who gave £15 at Lincoln; Elias fil Manasser who gave £10 at Lincoln; and Diey of Stamford who gave £10 at Stamford.[40] The payments of the London community which rendered a total of £404 1s 3d also revealed problems with cash payments.[41] Financial pressures on the wealthier Jews made it necessary for the burden to fall on their Jewish debtors. Leo fil Preciosa made three payments: two on his own behalf (totalling £12 13s 4d) and one large payment of £20 paid by the hand of Robert Waler.[42] A massive contribution of £304 was paid on behalf of Hagin fil Magister

---

[34] Stacey 1985, p. 170 particularly note 3; 1987b, pp. 67–8.   [35] Elman 1938a, p. 154.
[36] Richardson 1960, p. 214; Elman 1936, p. 30; PRO E/401/1567.   [37] PRO E/401/1567.
[38] PRO E/401/1567. William de Sholle's indebtedness to Aaron le Blund of Hereford is also recorded on PRO E/101/250/5. See also *CCR 1268–1272*, p. 517; Rigg, p. 70; Mundill 1987, pp. 330, 332.
[39] PRO E/401/1567.
[40] Sampson fil Magri and Elias fil Manasser were also forced to make further contributions of £15 and £10 respectively at Stamford for the Jewish community of Stamford: PRO E/401/1567.
[41] PRO E/401/1567; Hillaby 1993a.   [42] PRO E/401/1567.

Moses in four instalments by his Christian debtor Walter de Furneus.[43] Financial hardship was evident elsewhere in the country. In Devonshire one Jew, Jacob Copin, made the only tallage contribution for the Exeter community. He made two payments totalling £19.[44] Similarly, Moses de Pavely made the only contributions for the Nottingham community and gave £13 6s 8d in two payments. Three Jews made payments from Southampton totalling £16 13s 4d. It is no surprise that the roll also reveals smaller contributions. The Northampton community offered £1 paid by 'two poor Jews of Northampton'.[45] By 1272 the Jewish community was clearly finding difficulty in meeting the financial demands made on it. It is clear that not all Jews contributed to tallage payments and in some cases their debtors were starting to foot the Jewish tax bill.

Yet a single record does not reveal the whole effect of a tallage. To get a fuller picture of the effect of any tallage it is necessary to use other records. The tallage contribution of Benedict of Winchester remained unpaid until June 1275 when Edward himself allowed £60 of Benedict's personal assessment of £100 to be paid by a bond made between the Jew and William de Appletrefeld and which the king then acquitted. The bond was accepted as part payment, 'for the £100 that remain to be rendered of his tallage of the 5,000 marks assessed upon the community of the Jews of London in the late king's time'. Once the king had accepted £60 by bond he then ordered the Justices of the Jews 'to cause the remaining £40 to be levied of the more clear debts of Benedict for the king's use'.[46]

Apparent financial difficulties did not mean that the Crown's ministers let the Jewish community have any respite. After Henry III's death, in December 1272, a scrutiny of the king's chest of the Jewry at Westminster was ordered.[47] This scrutiny, made at the very hub of the organisation of the king's Jewry, illustrated some of the administrative methods used by the officials concerned with the Jews on Edward's behalf. It revealed two large rolls of fines to be paid, two large rolls of various sheriff's accounts, six rolls of various debts to Jews in a bag and one large roll of the same debts which formerly had been sent to Henry III. It also referred to a canvas bag with all the charters from the Treasury, both sealed and unsealed, and one official seal pertaining to the Jewish Exchequer. Finally, it mentioned a pyx which contained the king's writ for levying the tallage (presumably the writ of Henry III for the previous tallage).[48] Yet this scrutiny was not just a stocktaking

---

[43] *Ibid.*   [44] *Ibid.*   [45] *Ibid.*   [46] *CCR 1272–1279*, pp. 199–200.
[47] Cohen 1951, pp. civ–cix.   [48] PRO E/101/249/15.

exercise. In February 1273, special commissioners were appointed to make a scrutiny of the *archae* in nineteen towns. As Dr Rokeah has recently pointed out, in early October 1273 Prior Joseph de Chauncy was appointed as Edward's Treasurer and by December of that year he had issued orders which must have heralded the first tallage of Edward I's reign. The arrangements for the first Edwardian tallage were methodical: de Chauncy had sent out orders which required the Jews to come into the main towns and to remain there until April 1274.[49]

The official receiver of the first Edwardian tallage was the bishop of Waterford, Stephen de Fulburn.[50] The bishop was helped in the collection of the tallage by two of the king's clerks, Adam de Stratton and William de Middleton, the officials who had made the scrutiny of the king's chest of the Jewry in the preceding December of 1273.[51] Once again the tallage meant pecuniary difficulties for some Jews. In February 1274, Aaron de la Rye of London was granted a licence to sell some of his houses after he had already made a payment of over £18 6s 2d as a contribution by the London community.[52] By June 1274 Edward was in urgent need of money and he ordered Stephen de Fulburn to pay £2,000 to Luke de Lucca so that the king's merchant might send it to Paris to await Edward's arrival there. A few days later, at the instance of de Chauncy, Warin the treasurer of the New Temple was also ordered to supply Luke de Lucca with £2,000, 'of the tallage assessed upon divers Jews'.[53] It is clear that the collection of the tallage was not as easy as de Chauncy or Edward had estimated. De Fulburn, Stratton and Middleton were again ordered in October 1274 to levy the arrears of the tallage.[54] They were granted the power to levy the money on the Jews' debts and goods and to threaten them with exile. In November 1274 Edward reappointed Stephen de Fulburn, this time to be assisted by Brother Luke de Hemmington and William de Middleton, to levy the arrears of the tallage. On this occasion non-payment was to be dealt with in the following manner:

And if any Jew fail to pay on the day appointed him, they shall cause him to leave the realm with his wife and children except those children which are in tallage and have paid; and they shall assign such Jews the Port of Dover within three days after the day of payment to depart never to return, their lands, houses, rents and all the goods of them and theirs to be saved to the king.[55]

No record of expulsion of any Jew for inability to pay exists at this

---

[49] Rokeah 1997.   [50] *CPR 1272–1281*, p. 51.
[51] *CPR 1272–1281*, pp. 51, 52, 61, 62, 63; Elman 1936, p. 31.
[52] *CPR 1272–1281*, p. 62.   [53] *CPR 1272–1281*, p. 51; Rokeah 1997.
[54] *CPR 1272–1281*, pp. 61–2.   [55] *Ibid.*, p. 62.

time. Payment of this tallage was made at the New Temple sometime in January 1275. It was clearly put to immediate use as on 18 and 27 March 1275 the treasurer of the New Temple was ordered to deliver the residue of the tallage to Master Thomas Bek.[56]

The New Temple tallage raised in excess of £1,400. The actual roll recording these tallage payments had a unique format. It contained a list of approximately 362 entries of payments. The entries were not under county headings, as was more normal with tallage records, but were listed only by each contributor's name. The tallage was highly organised and on the dorse of the second membrane there is a breakdown of the contributions of nineteen towns. It is also clear that certain local agents were to collect the tallage in cash and then they were to make payment to the king. Thus the Lincoln contribution was made by the prior of St Catherine's, the Wilton contribution was to be delivered by the abbot of Walton and the Hereford contribution was delivered by the Master of the Hospital of Dinmore.[57] Some of the payments were made on behalf of the Jewish communities through Jewish *talliatores*: Isaac the son of Abraham of Berkhamstead paid £1 for the Marlborough tallage and Aaron fil Josce paid the same amount for the Stamford community. Such payments might represent the total collections from poorer communities. Again the pressure of this tallage was not only on the Jews. Even Stephen de Fulburn, the receiver of the tallage, paid £6 13s 4d for the tallage contribution of Master Elias, a Jew of London. There were also forty other payments made by Christians for debts to Jews. Even if the tallage had not made the target of the assessment it was still money that Edward urgently needed. This urgency might account for the unusual form of the Receipt Roll and the fact that it was to be paid at the New Temple.[58]

It is clear that even whilst making the collection at the New Temple, Edward and his Treasurer, de Chauncy, had further plans to tallage the Jews. Edward's return to England in August 1274 meant even greater financial pressure for the Jewish communities. It seems that the collection of the New Temple tallage also shades over into the collection of what has been called 'the Great Tallage'. The earliest indication of the Great Tallage comes from a roll of tallage returns which commenced in September 1274. It is headed 'Receipts of a tallage assessed at a third

---

[56] *Ibid.*, pp. 83–4;   [57] PRO E/101/249/16; *PREJ4*, p. 33.
[58] Receipts of a tallage on the Jews paid at the New Temple, London in 1274. Canterbury £327 2s 0½d; Winchester £218 8s 1d; Oxford £180 10s 0d; Exeter £100; Lincoln £67 13s 6d; Northampton £64 16s 6d; Nottingham £60 13s 11d; York £60; Norwich £48 10s 11d; Bristol £46 10s 11d; Cambridge £43 0s 0d; Hereford £40 5s 4d; Warwick £39; Colchester £37 17s 7d; Marlborough £35 7s 1½d; Worcester £27 14s 3d; Bedford £17 10s 0d; Wilton £10 0s 1d; Gloucester £9 6s 7d. Rokeah 1997.

part of all their goods'.[59] This tallage is aptly named 'the Great Tallage' not only because it was assessed at a third of all Jewish goods but also because it has left behind it the largest amount of documentary evidence for any Jewish tallage. Four lists (excluding duplicates) of the tallage receipts, two Memoranda Rolls (primarily concerned with payment and collection), many fragments of lists, and evidence that many Jews were imprisoned for failure to pay the tallage serve as reminders of the pressure put upon the Jews to fill the royal coffers.[60] One of the lists of the actual tallage collections in each county has survived from this period. The return from Bedfordshire and Buckinghamshire is extant but is in bad condition.[61]

The four lists of tallage receipts reveal several different methods of payment. Cash payments were clearly preferred and they were made either directly by the Jew concerned, on his own behalf or on behalf of the community, or by one of his clients who was later obliged to pay up his debt in full because the Crown had in effect enforced repayment. Another type of payment was a lump sum paid either by a Jewish *talliator*, by the community of Jews or by a local Christian official presumably acting as a collector.[62] The roll records a total payment of £1,225 4s 7d. It records payments made between September 1274 and early 1275. The Kent contribution was £87 15s 6d and was paid by twenty-three Jews and seventeen Christians. Once again a 'Jewish' tallage forced Christians to pay up part of their debts to Jews. Englesche filia Leonis made a personal contribution of £1 5s 3d, while her client, Henry Joce, paid 16s 0d for a debt which he owed her. Other Christians, like Master Jacob de Helles and Thomas his brother, paid £6 of their debts to Hagin fil Magister Moses. Benjamin Brunning was forced to pay 13s 4d for his debt to Dyey fil Benedict and 10s 0d towards his debt to Jacob of Oxford. Geoffrey Harloc paid two instalments totalling £1 12s 6d for his debts to Gamaliel of Oxford. Robert de la Forde paid £1, William Reynegod paid £1 16s 0d and Richard Godibure, a carpenter, paid 4s 6d for their respective debts to Aaron de la Rye of London. The Jews themselves paid sums varying from Isaac fil Benedict's £40 to Josce fil Samuel's 2d. In total the Jews paid £64 7s 9d whilst Christian debtors contributed £23 7s 9d. For Herefordshire the tallage contribution was paid entirely by the Jews

---

[59] Cohen 1951, pp. cix; PRO E/401/1568; Richardson 1960, pp. 214–15.

[60] PRO E/401/1568, E/401/1569, E/401/1570, E/401/1571 (a partial duplicate of E/401/1568 exists as E/101/249/18 and of E/401/1570 as E/101/249/21). The Memoranda Rolls are PRO E/101/249/19 and E/101/249/20 and are printed in *PREJ4*, pp. 13–88. Some evidence of imprisonment can be found in PRO E/101/249/22 which is also printed in *PREJ4*, pp. 148–95 cf. pp. 157, 180.

[61] PRO E/101/249/17.   [62] PRO E/401/1568–71.

themselves. Thirteen Jews of Hereford raised a total of £16 7s 10d. Some clearly had difficulties. Benedict fil Elye was only able to raise 1s 8d in cash and so the sheriff, John la Ware, sold his chattels and raised a further 10s 0d. Other Hereford Jews also had their chattels sold in this manner. Moses fil Isaac's chattels fetched 5s 0d, Belia the widow's brought 10s 0d, Blanche the widow's brought 3s 0d, Elias le Ardre's only 5s 0d and Bona the widow's 4s 0d. The Lincolnshire Jewish communities seem to have been more affluent at this time and were able to contribute a total of £213 3s 2d. Two instalments were paid in lump sums by local officials: the prior of St Catherine's Lincoln paid 10s 1d for the Lincoln community and the prior of St Leonard's outside Stamford paid £60 7s 1½d for the Stamford community. Amongst the Lincolnshire tallage payments there were only two payments made by Christian clients: Robert fil Everard de Pylton who paid 10s 0d and Robert fil Simon of Boston who paid £5 4s 0d. The largest individual contribution was made by Isaac fil Benedict, a Lincoln Jew, who rendered £46 15s 4d. Again in Lincolnshire some Jews were forced to sell their chattels. The chattels of Elias of Doncaster realised £3 6s 1d whilst the goods of Bonefey fil Breton fetched £5. Overall, some twenty-two Lincolnshire Jews contributed.[63]

A second roll bore evidence of a further sum of £284 3s 6½d collected for the Great Tallage.[64] This time contributions for the Kentish Jewry were made entirely by Christian debtors. The Herefordshire Jews' contributions included payments from five Jews who had not paid on the preceding roll and a Christian, Walter de la Walle, who paid 15s towards Abraham fil Aaron's tallage. The Lincolnshire contribution included payment by six Jews who had not contributed previously. A particularly large contribution was made by Bonefey fil Breton whose chattels, according to the previous roll, had been sold. At Stamford he paid a further £6 10s 6d. A Christian client, Robert fil Radulph, also paid a debt of £2 16s 8d to Bonefey's daughter Juetta and this was taken as payment for tallage. A third roll recorded some relatively small payments. The Kent contribution was made once more by Master Jacob de Helles and Thomas his brother for their debts to Hagin fil Magister Moses. The Herefordshire contribution of 4s 0d was made by Robert fil John Fabri for a debt to Aaron fil Bonamy, and in an entry for Warwickshire Vyves fil Vyves de Hereford paid 6s 8d. The Lincolnshire contribution of 10s 0d was paid by Jacob fil Jacob. The

---

[63] Bonefey fil Breton was still able to supply a further £1 9s 3½d in cash: PRO E/401/1568.
[64] PRO E/401/1569.

payments recorded on the whole roll amounted to only £32 1s 4d.[65] It is clear that the tallage collectors were persistent.

A fourth roll contained details of £49 2s 2d worth of tallage receipts for this period.[66] The Kentish Jews made four contributions: Aaron fil Elias paid £1 13s 4d, Aaron of Winchester paid 6s 8d, Hagin *genus* Leon 6s 8d and Benedict fil Elias 4s 5d. Again Master Jacob de Helles and his brother paid £6 for their debt to Hagin fil Magister Moses. Thus in two years Master Jacob de Helles and his brother had been forced by the tallage to repay up to £24 for their Jewish debts. The Herefordshire Jews made only a single contribution by Benedict fil Elye who rendered 8s 11d. However, another entry for Warwickshire again records that Vyves fil Vyves of Hereford rendered a further 2d towards the tallage. The Lincolnshire Jewry yielded three payments. One of them for £2 11s 0d was rendered by the abbot of Thornton who was the tenant of Simon de Veer. It appears that de Veer was indebted to Solomon fil Benedict and Manser of Brodsworth and presumably he could not pay, so that his tenant, the unfortunate abbot, paid for tallage. Bonefy fil Breton of Stamford was able to contribute a further £2 and Sampson fil Solomon yielded £2 3s 4d.[67]

From these rolls, it is clear that not all the Jews of any one community were expected to pay the tallage at any one time. It seems that a tallage involved payments by other Jews who perhaps were not the wealthiest of moneylenders. It also seems likely that many Christian debtors must have viewed the tallage commissioners with the same odium as did the Jews because they were forced to pay up their debts to finance tallage payments for their Jewish creditors.[68] There were also many difficulties in collecting the tallage. In June, August and December of 1275 officials were appointed to make a scrutiny of the London *archa*.[69] If it was ever made, it has not survived, and there are very few indications that the London Jews actually paid a contribution. As with any medieval fiscal record it is difficult to assess if these four rolls represent the total of the tallage which was collected. Quite clearly the Great Tallage of 1274 was still being levied in June 1278 when officials were ordered to levy the arrears connected with it.[70] Thus, historians are only left with an approximate indication of the total amount paid.

That the Great Tallage caused further hardship and economic dislocation for Jewish business is clear. As with all tallages, if the Jews could not pay their tallage and if Christian debtors could not be found to pay their debts for them, there were only two options: prison, or

---

[65] PRO E/401/1570.   [66] PRO E/401/1571.   [67] PRO E/401/1571.
[68] Stacey 1988, pp. 140–1, 145–6.   [69] CPR 1272–1281, pp. 148, 158, 184.
[70] *Ibid.*, p. 51; Rokeah 1997.

bartering with the Crown to pay their tallage in negotiable bonds. Prison faced many before an agreement with the Crown could be made. One such Jew secured his freedom from imprisonment in the Tower of London on 13 May 1275, when the tallage commissioners were ordered to cause Bateman of Stamford to be acquitted of his payments because he had offered the king his lands, goods and chattels throughout the realm for the king's personal use.[71] Similarly, on 10 July 1275 the Treasurers and Barons of the Exchequer were ordered to deliver Sampson fil Master Miles of Stamford, Samuel fil Manasser of Lincoln, Vives fil Garseyas, Abraham fil Diey of Holme, Elias fil Ursel of Lincoln and Abraham fil Samuel from their imprisonment at the Tower. Their tallage was to be levied from their more collectable debts and if it was still unpaid in September they were to be re-imprisoned.[72]

The two surviving Memoranda Rolls reveal some of the confusion involved in collection and the intricate administration which was required.[73] The first roll records many of the problems from January 1275 onwards.[74] It records orders to the chirographers to produce certain bonds and documents involved with the tallage. It also records the delivery of bonds from the provincial *archae* to the king's Treasury and even the names of the Jews who had no bonds registered in the *archae*. It registers the bonds which the Christians had paid up and records that the paid bonds were cancelled and returned to the debtor.[75] In the case of a Jew who had paid tallage, the roll provides lists of the bonds which were returned to the payee. Eight of Jacob of Brancegate's bonds were sent from Lincoln to London and six of them were returned to Lincoln after he had satisfied the officials by the payment of his tallage.[76] The confusion over who had paid and who had not done so is reflected in the legal suits that ensued when the sheriffs distrained Christian debtors or a bond was hotly disputed.[77] There were clearly many problems in getting the final payments into the Receipt.

The second Memoranda Roll bears similar entries, but is dominated by details of reports of inquests as to whether debts have been paid to the Jews.[78] It includes a writ dated 18 May 1275 which tries to sort out the debts owed to certain Jews in Worcester, Gloucester and Hereford.[79] According to the Justices' records, a third part of a debt of £30 in the names of Richard Pauncefoot and Aaron le Blund was owed to Ursel fil Isaac and a third of a debt of £12 in the same names was owed

---

[71] *CCR 1272–1279*, p. 166.   [72] *Ibid.*, p. 201.
[73] PRO E/101/249/19 and E/101/249/20. Both are printed in *PREJ4*, pp. 13–88.
[74] PRO E/101/249/19.   [75] *PREJ4*, pp. 13–15, 17, 25–7.
[76] *Ibid.*, p. 26 (for other similar examples see pp. 29 and 62–3).   [77] *Ibid.*, pp. 28, 31, 34.
[78] PRO E/101/249/20; *PREJ4*, pp. 70, 74–7, 83, 88.   [79] *Ibid.*, p. 71.

to Belia of Gloucester. The Justices were ordered to levy the debts for the arrears of tallage and to acquit both Jews. Belia's arrears of tallage as well as Ursel's amounted to £18 13s 3d. The bonds which were in the king's hands amounted to £22, therefore Belia and Ursel were quit of their tallage and the sheriff was ordered to distrain Richard Paunce-foot.[80] This roll also shows how some tallage payments were made by the transfer of bonds. It records that Robert of Billesdon paid three bonds for the tallage of Sampson fil Rabbi and the cancelled bonds were delivered to him.[81] The evidence once again suggests that the financial pressure of a tallage affected both Jews and their clients alike.

The climax of Edwardian tallage collections was not in 1275, as Peter Elman once indicated, but came later in the reign.[82] H. G. Richardson claimed that fresh tallages were levied in 1276, 1277 and 1278.[83] Certainly a general scrutiny of the *archae* was ordered in January 1276. This is indeed one of the few instances where historians have some details of an organised *archae* scrutiny before a tallage was imposed. Not only have the orders to officials to inspect the *archae* survived but some of the actual scrutinies have also survived.[84] The tallage of 1276 was nominally £1,000 which was, as Richardson observed, paid in cash by the Jews, and with 'remarkable promptitude'.[85] Payment was due by September 1276 and at the end of September 1276 only £27 of the amount was still outstanding. The Receipt Roll for this particular single tallage has survived.[86] It reveals that the London Jews paid their tallage of over £115 to Giles de Oudenarde, the constable of the Tower of

---

[80] *CCR 1272–1279*, p. 169.   [81] *Ibid.*, p. 83.

[82] Elman 1938b, p. 112; Mundill, 1987, pp. 60–78, 99; Stacey 1987b, p. 71 note 65 where Professor Stacey calls for a new study and draws attention to the Elman hypothesis as being erroneous.

[83] Richardson 1960, pp. 215–16.

[84] *CCR 1272–1279*, pp. 126, 263; *PREJ3*, pp. 230–8; PRO C/47/9/48; WAM nos. 6698, 9056, 9052, 9017, 9059, 9031; PRO C/47/9/49. PRO E/101/249/33 lists some of the debts of Moses of Northampton, Solomon fil Sampson, Josce Babstar of Northampton and Avigaye filia Vives; PRO E/101/249/31. The roll consists of three membranes, two of which were added in 1974. It records the debts of Aunta the wife of Samuel fil Moses (35), Isaac fil Moses (1), Jacob Crespyn (13), Aaron de Caerlion (13), Solomon fil Solomon (4), Tertia the wife of Lumbard (3), Copynus fil Lumbard (2), Ursellus fil Manser (2), Jacob Copyn (36), Deulecresse *capellanus* (17). This new evidence contradicts Richardson's statement that in 1276 there were only two Jews involved in moneylending in Exeter: Richardson 1960, p. 18. See chapter 6 below for fuller discusssion. PRO E/101/249/32 reveals those bonding in Oxford in 1275: Isaac fil Leon de Polet, Jew of Oxford (47) worth £225 8s 4d and ½ quarter and 2 bushels of cereal; Lumbard of Cricklade (23) worth £103 3s 4d; Vives fil Bonefey (6) worth £14 13s 4d; Diay, Jew of Burford (5) £13 16s 8d; Vives fil Bonenfaunt of Gloucester (4) worth £10 0s 0d and 1 qtr of cereal; Jacob of Oxford (1) worth £10 0s 0d; Mokke the wife of Benedict of the Synagogue (4) worth £9 1s 8d; Vives fil Vives of Clare (1) worth £5 0s 0d; Jew of Lambourne (1) worth £2 13s 4d; Moses fil Abraham, Parnass (1) worth £2 10s 0d; Benedict fil Abraham (1) worth 13s 4d. The total value of the ninety-four bonds was £397 0s 0d plus 1½ qtrs and 2 bushels of cereal.

[85] Richardson 1960, pp. 215–16.   [86] PRO E/401/1572.

London. For the Jews of Kent only two entries from the community of the Jews of Canterbury survive, totalling £120. The Jews of Hereford made a payment which totalled £60. It appears that this was not enough, as on 13 December 1276 the Hereford community paid £3 6s 8d so that they should not be imprisoned in the Tower of London. The Jews of Lincolnshire paid several payments towards this new tallage. The community of the Jews of Stamford yielded £24, Master Benedict of London £5, Abraham of Kent, Senior £20, and Isaac de Provyns £5, Isaac fil Isaac de Provyns £10 and the Lincoln community £20. Interestingly no Christians appear to have paid sums of money on this roll. It is most surprising that after the exactions of the Great Tallage, which was still in fact being levied, the Jews were able to find further financial resources to pay to their royal master. By 13 December 1276, £954 8s 3d had been collected and a further £22 6s 8d, as well as the Hereford fine, was collected by 14 February 1277. For once a target assessed by the Crown had almost been realised.[87]

The Jews were again tallaged in 1277. However, as H. G. Richardson correctly noted, the amount of this tallage does not appear to be recorded either in specific records of the tallage or upon the Chancery Rolls.[88] For the first time during Edward's reign there thus appears to be a *lacuna* in the tallage evidence. A roll headed 'Receipts of a tallage of the Jews 25,000 marks' has however survived.[89] It is similar to the previous roll, but has only three payments on it. The sum total of the roll between September 1276 and February 1277 was £10 5s 7d.[90] Thus for the 1277 tallage little evidence remains, although the Jewish Exchequer was certainly kept busy that year. In April 1277, now preoccupied by the Welsh wars, Edward ordered the governmental departments of state to move to Shrewsbury.[91] It is known that sometime during the year the Jewish Exchequer moved to take up residence in the abbey at Shrewsbury where it was situated by September 1277. Although there is no evidence of a general scrutiny it was also in May 1277 that the king empowered Hugh de Digneuton to make an inquiry throughout the land as to where the Jews were living and also to enforce the wearing of the *tabula*.[92] Perhaps this inquiry was so that Edward could enforce and maintain the regulations which he had set down in the Statute, but perhaps he was preparing another tallage in order to supply his financial needs at a time of war. Whatever the reason behind Digneuton's inquiry, later in the same month Edward

---

[87] *Ibid.* [88] Richardson 1960, p. 216. [89] PRO E/401/1573.
[90] PRO E/401/1575; *Select Cases in the Court of King's Bench under Edward I*, vol. II, Selden Society 57, 1938, p. lxiii.
[91] *Ibid.* [92] *CPR 1272–1281*, p. 240.

ordered John de Cobham, Philip de Willoughby and William de Middleton to assess another tallage on the Jews.[93] In June, Roger de Northwood was sent to Canterbury to reopen the *archae* which had presumably been sealed since the last scrutiny. Roger was empowered to transcribe all the charters in it and to deliver those which were quit to the Christian debtors.[94] However, even though the Exchequer of the Jews was clearly very active during this period, no other evidence of tallage returns has survived for 1277.

If there is little evidence of the collection of the tallage in 1277 there is even less for the tallage of 1278 which both Peter Elman and H. G. Richardson claim was assessed at £2,000.[95] It is possible, despite the upheavals of the Welsh wars, that it was still collected: as Richardson has pointed out, the London community whilst in the Tower paid a contribution towards a tallage of £2,000.[96] Further, there is an order dated 12 November 1278 to Antony Bek to pay £2,000 that was lately assessed and received from a tallage on the Jews of England to Reynier de Lucca and Orlandinus de Podio.[97] Thus, although no actual records of the 1278 tallage survive, there can be little doubt that in that year Edward did not let the opportunity to provide the royal coffers with welcome funds slip away.

Excluding the lack of evidence for the receipt of the 1277 and 1278 tallage, and bearing in mind that the Receipt Rolls are clearly not comprehensive, it emerges that by 1278 the Jews of England had paid at least a total of £5,301 8s 8½d into Edward's coffers in a period of just six years.[98] Although other sources indicate that during the same period a total of £18,000 had been assessed on them, it is still possible to claim from the figures of tallage *known* to have been received by 1278 that the Jews' ability to pay tallage was not past its climax at this point in time.[99] H. G. Richardson's comments upon Edward I's early Jewish tallages demonstrate that the Jews were now left alone for a while:

In estimating the severity of the exactions of the 1270s it must have borne in mind that the total population of all the Jewish communities in the country at the time can scarcely have reached 3,000 souls, and that the great majority of them were poor and moreover that the burden of taxation fell upon a small number of wealthy families who were deprived of a large part of their working capital by the 'great' tallage and whose business was further restricted by the

---

[93] *Ibid.*, p. 211.   [94] *Ibid.*, p. 215.
[95] Richardson 1960, p. 216; Elman 1938a, p. 154; *CPR 1272–1281*, p. 274.
[96] Richardson 1960, p. 216 note 3.   [97] *CPR 1272–1281*, p. 282; Kaeuper 1973, p. 182 note 29.
[98] PRO E/401/1567, E/101/249/16, E/401/1568–73.
[99] Elman 1938a, p. 154; 1938b, p. 139.

prohibition of overt usury by the Statute of the Jewry of 1275. It is significant that the tallage of 1278 was the last for nearly a decade.[100]

There is evidence for at least one other Jewish tallage in Edward's reign. It is perhaps significant that again this tallage coincides with a rising in Wales. Peter Elman referred to the tallage assessment of 1287 for £13,333 6s 8d as the final turn of the screw but claimed that there is little evidence that it was collected.[101] However, on 20 August 1287 Lumbard fil Cressaunt of Winchester was to be aided by the sheriff of Southampton in recovering debts due to him because he was indebted to the king for a large sum by 'reason of the king's Tallage lately made throughout the whole Jewry within the realm'. Cecil Roth also pointed out that on 2 May 1287 there was a sudden reversal to the harsher methods of past reigns in that all the leading Jews were arrested and imprisoned as a preliminary to exacting a fresh tallage.[102] H. G. Richardson correctly claimed that there was evidence for the tallage, but remained sceptical about the imprisonment.[103] However, most tallages involved imprisonment for non-payment and there is evidence for widespread general imprisonment during these years.

Some evidence of the actual payment of the tallage is recorded on two different Receipt Rolls dating from 1287–8.[104] The first records general payments made in late 1287 whilst the second covers the early months of 1288. The rolls are predominantly records of amercements paid by Christians and Jews and at first sight are not concerned with tallage payments. However there are several entries recording the levying of tallage. Instead of being preceded by the county for which the payments were made, the entries are simply introduced by 'England' in the margin. As Dr Rokeah has correctly pointed out, four different entries note that Randulph de Sandwich, William de Carleton and Gregory de Rokesle paid £3,100 for tallage of the Jews. The second roll records four further payments made for the tallage on the Jews of England by the three commissioners. The payments are £645 17s 2d, £183 4s 11d, £30 and £13 6s 8d, a total of £872 8s 9d. Thus the tallage of 1287–8 seems to have raised £3,972 8s 9d. Even though it was only almost a quarter of the tallage assessed, it was still a large payment and is in fact the peak of recorded tallage payment in Edward's reign.[105]

Thus it is possible to reconstruct not only the tallages assessed on the Edwardian Jews, but also the surviving details of the payments they

[100] Richardson 1960, p. 216.   [101] Elman 1938a, p. 146.
[102] *CCR 1279–1288*, p. 456; Roth 1978, p. 79.
[103] Richardson 1960, p. 227; Roth 1978, p. 275; Capgrave, *Liber de Illustribus Henricis*, p. 167; *Annales Londinienses* in *Chronicles of the Reigns of Edward I and Edward II*, p. 96.
[104] PRO E/401/1584, E/401/1585.   [105] Rokeah, forthcoming.

Table 1. *Known tallage payments received during Edward I's reign*

1272	£1,289	10s	0d
1274	£1,434	6s	7d
1274–5	£1,225	4s	7d
1275	£ 284	3s	6½d
1275 to February 1276	£ 32	1s	4d
1276	£ 49	2s	2d
September 1276 to 1277	£ 976	14s	11d
September 1276 to 1277	£ 10	5s	7d
September 1287 to December 1287	£3,100	0s	0d
January 1288 to February 1288	£ 872	8s	9d
	£9,271	17s	5½d

Sources: PRO E/401/1567, E/101/249/16, E/401/1568–73, E/401/1584, E/401/1585.

made to the Crown. The sums received are given in Table 1. It is obviously necessary to compare these figures with the amount of tallage assessed. Peter Elman's figures for the tallage assessments for Edward's reign have been widely accepted and make comparison easy. He claimed that a tallage of £3,333 6s 8d was assessed in April 1272. There is evidence that £1,289 10s 0d, well under half the sum assessed, was recorded. Another tallage was assessed in April 1273 at £666 13s 4d; there seems to be little evidence for the collection of this tallage. In 1274 the amount assessed was £2,666 13s 4d; only £1,434 6s 7d, again well under half the amount, was apparently received. The tallage between 1274 and 1276 was assessed at £8,333 6s 8d; evidence remains which shows that a total of £1,590 11s 7½d, under a fifth of the amount, was probably collected. Following the general *archae* scrutinies, a tallage of £1,000 was again assessed in September 1276. Between 1276 and 1277 £987 0s 6d was collected. This seems to be the only Edwardian tallage which was collected almost in full. During the period 1277–8 a further tallage for £2,000 was required: no evidence for collection remains. Finally, in May 1287, came what Elman had called 'the last turn of the screw', when a tallage of £13,333 6s 8d was demanded. There is evidence that £3,972 8s 9d was collected, or just under a quarter of the amount.[106]

Having considered the available evidence, what can be established from such a close study of the Edwardian tallages? It can be seen that the tallage payments were relatively high for the first three years of Edward's

[106] Prestwich 1988, p. 344. Using different sources Michael Prestwich places the total for 1287 at £4,023 rather than £3,972; PRO E/159/48, m.4.

reign, that they increased in late 1276 and 1277 and that then they did not feature for another ten years, until the impositions of 1287–8. Without any doubt the payments of 1287–8 were the highest of the reign and indeed the highest for almost fifty years: this would hardly indicate Jewish financial decline. From this evidence, and particularly that of the last tallage, it seems that, although under financial pressure, the Jews' ability to pay did not necessarily disintegrate; the Statute of the Jewry of 1275 had not yet reduced them to total poverty, because in 1287 they were able to pay a huge sum, just under half of the total tallage that Edward had apparently managed to collect from the Jewish community during his reign. Certainly, there is evidence early in Edward's reign that some pressure was indirectly being put on Christian debtors, rather than Jews. The fact that tallage assessments were not always realised is not of course an index to Jewish impoverishment. In general, medieval tax assessments were often not fulfilled. After all, only half of the Northampton *Donum* (1194) and the *Auxilium* (1221) were ever collected.[107] Through tallage during his reign Edward actually collected £9,271 17s 5½d from his Jews. He collected a further £11,000 from the confiscated property of Jews who had been accused of coin-clipping in the period 1278–9. This in itself shows that their wealth had not been totally depleted by tallage payments.

How poor the Edwardian Jews were and how much effect the tallages had had on the community is however difficult to establish. It is made even more difficult by the pogroms and coin-clipping accusations of 1278–9. Before this date, there were certainly Jews who were forced to pay in bonds, who had to sell property to meet tallage payments and who were genuinely poor; and there were certainly Jews who tried to avoid paying the tallage. Overall the early tallages of Edward's reign might not have had a crippling effect on Jewish resources, but coupled with the confiscations in 1278–9 and finally a large demand for tallage in 1287, when Edward himself was out of the country, these exactions must have had great impact on the Jewish community's wealth. In order to confirm whether wealth was indeed in total decline it is, however, important to consider what can be known about the lending capacity of Jewish financiers and the frequency and value of Jewish financial transactions, as well as the other ways in which the Jewish community was subjected to financial levies during the reign. The former will be considered in chapter 6; the latter can usefully be considered by referring to the Jewish Receipt Rolls themselves as well as to other sources.

Charles Gross' second category of 'cogs in the Engine of Extortion'

---

[107] Abrahams 1925; Chew 1928.

was described by him as 'small amercements for transgressions and payments for liveries and concessions'.[108] Clearly this definition covers a wide range of payments by the Jewish community as well as a fairly unquantifiable income for the Crown's revenues. An examination of all these payments and fines is again made very difficult because many such payments can be found recorded in many different sources. Examples of such payments can be found not only in the Jewish Plea Rolls and the Jewish and ordinary Receipt Rolls but also occasionally in other manuscripts such as bailiffs' accounts. The majority of such payments are found in the surviving Jewish Receipt Rolls which contain and reflect the most consistent record of what might be termed 'overheads' or everyday payments.[109] An examination of these rolls will give some indication of the additional financial burdens imposed on the Jewish community and how much the Crown benefited from this particular source of income.

The Jewish Receipt Rolls form a body of documents that are worthy of especial consideration.[110] The rolls contain details of payments that can best be described as the outcome of various transgressions, of which some of the most frequent are *persona non habet, quia non habet* (not having the culprit to hand), *pro plegio suo* (for not having a pledge), *pro non est presens* (for not being present when the Court was sitting), *per falsam clamam* (for making a false claim or wasting the court's time) and *pro iniusta detentione* (for being unjustly detained).[111] The most common payment, however, is simply described as *de debitis* (from debts). This term is generally used in the case of a Christian who owes money to a Jewish creditor, paying the Jew's debt to the Crown, presumably in return for acquittance of part or all his debt to the Jew in question. From the entries on the rolls it also seems that the Christian or the Jew who was forced by the Justices to make the payment sometimes had to make these payments by instalments. Debtors and clients were again therefore just as answerable to the Justices of the Jews as to the creditors themselves. All these payments refer to transgressions committed in relation to the proceedings of the Justices of the Jews, and settlements made under the authority of the Jewish Exchequer.

During Edward's reign such payments commenced with the period January to February 1277.[112] The first roll records payments made by three Jews and two Christians. In an entry for Oxfordshire, Joya the wife of Sweteman of Burford paid £1 13s 4d for a fine; in an entry for Leicestershire, a knight, Thomas de Clinton, paid £2 13s 4d 'from debts

[108] Gross 1887, pp. 192–4, 205.   [109] PRO E/401/1574–1610.
[110] Jenkinson 1918, pp. 31–7.   [111] Lipman 1966, pp. 53–5.   [112] PRO E/401/1574.

owing to Jacob of Oxford', and 13s 4d, 'on behalf of Manser'. Moses fil Leo paid 6s 8d on his own behalf and for his guarantor, who had stood bail for him because Moses did not appear when the Justices of the Jews required him to. Moses of Warwick paid 2s od for the same reason. In an entry for Somerset, Richard Byssop paid £2 18s 4d, 'from the debts of' John fil Robert de Bradeleye, 'on behalf of' Moses Babelard. The whole roll only totals £8 7s od. The next roll records payments made between September 1277 and Easter 1278.[113] Payments for the total value of £24 0s 1½d originated in eleven counties. A further roll lists payments made to the Jewish Exchequer between May and July 1278 during which period £51 2s 2d was received.[114] Another similar roll records only two payments made between 6 and 18 May 1278.[115] In an entry for Norfolk, Colum, who was the wife of Isaac of Warwick, a Jew of Norwich, paid 1s 8d 'for a fine'. In an entry for Yorkshire, Henna, who was the wife of Aaron of York, paid 6s 8d 'for a fine'. Thus, from the evidence of these four rolls, it is clear that between 13 January 1277 and 18 May 1278 the Crown received a mere £84 7s 7½d from this particular source of revenue.

Regrettably, a gap appears in the records until 1281, when there are three rolls which record similar types of payment.[116] The first of these rolls covers the period from September 1281 to January 1282 and clearly demonstrates that on occasion local officials like Thomas de Bray, sheriff of Buckinghamshire and Bedfordshire, made lump payments of monies (received locally) to the central Jewish Exchequer. Strikingly, amongst the names of the individuals who made payments on this particular roll, Jews do not feature very much. In fact only three are responsible for generating payments. Thus the contributors at this time are predominantly Christians. Contributions from Kent reveal thirteen Christians who paid £2 17s od. Four of them paid sums ranging from 5s od to 1s 8d because they did not manage to bring the person in front of officials. John de Bylsinton, a clerk, paid 3s 6d, 'because he was absent from a hearing'. Five others paid fines for not having the felon in front of the Justices, and William Godfrey paid 2s od for making a false claim. John de Wyleston paid £1 towards the debts that he owed Jacob of Oxford; and the heirs of Daniel Bagge paid 6s 8d for debts to Jews. Similarly, the entries for Herefordshire which yielded a total of £9 6s 8d show payments made predominantly by Christians. Walter fil Walter de la Mare paid £1 6s 8d 'from debts owing to Isaac fil Abraham'; Nicholas of Wormelow paid 6s 8d for his debts to Isaac of Southwark. Roger

---

[113] PRO E/401/1575.   [114] PRO E/401/1576.   [115] PRO E/401/1577.
[116] PRO E/401/1578, E/401/1579, E/401/1580.

Ketel, Milo de la Mare, Moses fil Abraham and Isaac de Campeden paid
sums because they did not have the person in attendance. William de
Sholle paid 4s 0d for being absent. Walter de Balun paid £2 for making
a false claim and £3 3s 4d for compensation for an unjust detention.
The tenants of John, son of Randolph of Kings Caple, paid 13s 4d of
the debts their overlord owed Jacob fil Jacob. Payments from Lincolnshire reveal that William le Provost of Rowell and John fil Randolph
paid 4s 0d because they did not have the person in attendance. The total
value of payments from the shires was £67 17s 3½d.[117]

Another roll records payments made between April and July 1281.[118]
Again the payments from over a dozen shires were predominantly made
by Christians. In fact there was only one payment made by a Jewess. The
total of the payments on this particular roll is £67 9s 7d. The last roll,
which covers the period 1281–2, again records payments made by
Christians rather than Jews.[119] The entries for Herefordshire total £3 18s
4d which was paid by thirty-six Christians and three Jews: Moses of
Gloucester, Leon of Worcester and Elias le Ardre, who each paid 3s 6d,
'because they did not manage to produce the person'. Hector of
Bredwardine and Hugh the Frenchman paid 1s 0d for the escape of a
certain Walter de Baskivill, and William de Sholle paid 2s 0d, 'for many
defaults', but the majority of the Herefordshire payments were made by
one or more people because the person they stood surety for did not
appear. Again the payments show that Christians paid partial instalments
towards debts that they owed Jews. The Lincolnshire entry records that
Randolph de Ingoldesby paid 13s 4d towards the debts of Abraham of
Kent. The entries for Kent as a county show that the heirs of Daniel Bagge
paid 6s 8d 'of debts'. The total of payments on this roll is £46 11s 7½d.

Once again there is a gap in the records, but a further three rolls have
survived for the period 1285–6. The total of payments made between
April and July 1285 was £92 3s 7½d.[120] The next roll records payments
for the period from September 1285 to early 1286.[121] The entries for
Kent include two lump payments made by the sheriff, Hamo de Gatton,
totalling £12 17s 1d. Only one Jew, Hagin le Eveske, appears to have
paid 5s 0d, because he was not able to produce the person he had stood
pledge for. The Kent payments totalled £19 15s 11d. The records for
Herefordshire include two entries: one for £8 13s 4d, the other for £4
13s 4d paid for various transgressions, by Roger de Burghill, the sheriff
of Hereford. In this case further details of Roger de Burghill's accounts
of his payments to the Jewish Exchequer have survived in a separate

[117] PRO E/401/1578.   [118] PRO E/401/1579.
[119] PRO E/401/1580; Stacey 1988, pp. 140–1, 145–6.   [120] PRO E/401/1581.
[121] PRO E/401/1582.

document.[122] It also contains payments for the same reasons, for non-attendance, for not producing the person and for various debts to Jews. However, over and above the lump payments by this sheriff, the Receipt Roll also reveals payments from Wenthliana de Kings Caple, who paid 11s 11d, 'from the debts of' Jacob fil Jacob. Miles Pichard, a well-known Jewish debtor, paid £3 6s 8d towards debts owing to Isaac fil Aaron, a Jew of Bristol. The Herefordshire payments totalled £17 5s 3d. The Lincolnshire entries only total £2 8s 4d. The total sum of all the entries received from 14 January to late February 1286 was £69 6s 2d and the final total of the whole roll was £156 13s ½d. The last of the rolls for this period records payments from September 1286 to February 1287 which totalled £306 0s 1d.

The two rolls which recorded payments for late 1287 and early 1288 have already been referred to above because they also recorded payment of the tallage.[123] They represent a total payment of £1,059 2s 8d which does not include the vast tallage payment of £3,302 14s 6d. There are three other rolls which begin before November 1290. These last rolls cover the period from September 1289 to September 1290. The first of these records a total collection of £60 12s 2½d.[124] The second records payments for £90 2s 10d, and the final roll which records payments from Easter 1290 until late July shows a total of £163 17s 8½d.

The Expulsion of the Jews in November 1290 did not mean the end of payments to the Exchequer of the Jews. The king went on receiving money even after the Jews had departed and the *archae* had been called in to Westminster for the last time. Another ten rolls recording payments made by Christians mainly in relation to debts contracted with the now exiled Jews are extant. The rolls cover the period from September 1290 until Easter 1295, when they terminate.[125] These rolls reveal that, for their debts in the Jewry, John le Botiller, the heirs of Benjamin Brunning and the heirs of Daniel Bagge continued to pay in Kent for at least another few years.[126] In Herefordshire the sheriff continued to make his lump payments as did Jewish debtors like Walter Payn and Miles Pichard.[127] In Lincolnshire Robert le Venour, now the

---

[122] PRO E/101/249/25 and E/101/249/26; E/401/1583.

[123] PRO E/401/1584, E/401/1585.   [124] PRO E/401/1586, E/401/1587, E/401/1588.

[125] PRO E/401/1589–1610. Some of these are in fact duplicates. Just over £546 was raised between September 1290 and April 1295: Mundill 1987, p. 105.

[126] John le Botiller made payments on PRO E/401/1588, E/401/1590, E/401/1591 and E/401/1593. The heirs of Daniel Bagge made payments on PRO E/401/1590 and E/401/1591. The heirs of Benjamin Brunning made payments on PRO E/401/1590.

[127] Roger de Burghill made payments on PRO E/401/1588 and E/401/1591. Walter Payn made payments on PRO E/401/1588 and E/401/1591. Miles Pichard made payments on PRO E/401/1591.

Table 2 *Miscellaneous sums received from Jews on the Receipt Rolls, 1277–91*

	£ s d
1277–8	£ 84 7s 7½d
1281–2	£ 181 18s 6d
1285–6	£ 248 16s 8d
1286–7	£ 306 0s 1d
1287–8	£1,059 2s 8d*
1289	£ 60 12s 2½d
1290–1	£ 384 14s 6d
	£2,325 12s 3d

* This does not include tallage payments of £3,302 8s 9d made during this period.
Source: PRO E/401/1574–90.

custodian of the city of Lincoln, continued to collect payments for debts to Jews; and John de Brauncewell and Thomas de Lek and his associates also continued to pay the Crown's pound of flesh.[128]

Thus payments resulting from proceedings before the Justices of the Jews made up another source of revenue for the Crown. From the surviving rolls, the total amount yielded by this type of revenue between 1277 and 1290 can be determined (Table 2). Therefore it is clear that during the period 1277 to 1291 Edward received a further £2,325 12s 3d from the Exchequer of the Jews. As can be observed, the payments received remain well under £100 per annum until 1285, increase dramatically in 1286, 1287 and 1288, decrease in 1289, and increase from 1290 to 1291. Regrettably a fairly complete run of these rolls has survived only for the period 1277–95. The amounts seem relatively insignificant when compared with the tallage returns or the monies taken from the Jews during 1278–9. Charles Gross correctly claimed that this particular revenue was hardly of any great financial significance to the Crown's annual finances.[129] It is admittedly an insignificant amount but it again raises the question of who actually paid it. By having to pay up on their debts, many Christian debtors were put

[128] Robert le Venour made a payment on PRO E/401/1590. John de Brauncewell made payments on PRO E/401/1590, E/401/1593, E/401/1594, E/401/1597 and E/401/1602. Thomas de Lek and his associates made payments on PRO E/401/1588, E/401/1590, E/401/1591, E/401/1593, E/401/1594, E/401/1597, E/401/1599 and E/401/1601.
[129] Gross 1887, p. 194.

under financial pressure because of their previous dealings with the Jews. Similarly those Jews who paid such amercements were also under financial pressure, particularly during the years 1287–8. These receipts might not have yielded much for the Crown but they were certainly of great inconvenience to those who had to pay.

In this examination of Crown revenue from the Jews it is now time to consider the third category of the fiscal operations of the Jewish Exchequer. Charles Gross offered only one definition for what he termed 'reliefs': the death duty of one-third payable by Jews on the estates of the deceased.[130] The main evidence for the estates of deceased Jews is the Jewish Plea Rolls. Although the Jews themselves were the property of the Crown they were allowed to leave their possessions and property to their heirs. Generally, after the king's third had been paid, the beneficiaries of the dead Jew were allowed to have administration of the estate. A Jewish estate was important to the Crown not merely because it enlarged the royal coffers but because it gave an opportunity to scrutinise all the individual Jew's clients and dealings. The opportunity to compile a record of a Jew's finances was particularly important because when a Jew died the natural tendency of his clients would be to try and destroy his bonds and deny that he ever lent any money, possibly claiming that the bond in the *archa* was false. Jewish relatives might also take into their own possession any objects of value. The Crown therefore had to act quickly and thoroughly once a Jew had died. Once the mandate to investigate an estate had gone out from the Justices of the Jews, the sheriff, chirographers and, if necessary, Jews and Christian townspeople would be consulted and a report of the estate would be sent to Westminster.

Clearly Jewish estates did not create a regular, stable income for the Crown and are obviously by their nature difficult to quantify. An examination of evidence for 1274 reveals that the Crown received over £155 6s 2d from its third part of four different Jewish estates.[131] In that year it was discovered at Northampton that the estate of Sadekyn of Northampton had been incorrectly administered and a jury of Christians and Jews was set up to investigate the affair. It was found that Sadekyn

---

[130] Gross 1887, p. 192; Mundill 1987, pp. 88–92.

[131] *PREJ*2, pp. 174, 175, 179–80, 183–4. The available material for 1274 shows the estate of Sadekyn of Northampton which was £30. He had died intestate and it would seem that in this case the Crown claimed the whole estate. For its part the Crown confiscated bonds to the value of £63 6s 8d from Leo of Norwich. Meyr of Oxford had an estate worth £10. Apparently no relief had been paid so the Crown confiscated the whole £10. Saulot Mutun's estate was unknown but the Crown received fines worth £1 19s 6d from various people. Abraham fil Vives' estate was worth £80. This gives a final figure of £155 6s 2d from those estates which can be identified.

had died intestate. They also testified that on the day of his death he had £20 in coin and £10 worth of moveables: brooches, rings, earrings and the like. Gywa, his wife, took the cash and the chattels and soon married Leo of Norwich. Leo and Gywa were found, arrested and imprisoned in London. A few days after they had been imprisoned Leo was found walking at ease in Westminster Hall without a warder. Eventually, after the constable had been rebuked and Leo threatened with a long spell of imprisonment, he was coerced to produce the payment of £30 in full. The chirographers of Bedford produced four charters worth a total of £63 6s 8d which Leo had contracted with Christians and the charters were placed in a pyx in the king's treasury.[132] In Oxford in the same year the Justices of the Jews discovered that Meyr fil *Magister* Meyr had died a long while ago and no relief had been paid for his chattels, which had been concealed. An inquest was held and six local Jews testified that Meyr had died in 1270 and that when he fell ill he had only £10 in gold which his wife, Rose, had taken. The sheriff of Oxford was immediately ordered to levy £10 from Rose's goods.[133] In both these cases the whole estate was forfeited because of maladministration. At Cambridge, in 1274, it was discovered that three Christians, including the prior of Royston, and Abraham l'Eveske and Muriel, the widow of Saulot Mutun, had received the chattels of the late Saulot against the law. At first the sheriff could only track down the prior of Royston. Finally he located the other Christians, but the two Jews had disappeared. Eventually the Christians paid £1 19s 6d into the Receipt.[134] Again, in 1274, in London, Antera, the widow of Abraham fil Vives, paid a relief to the king for her late husband's chattels of £80, which represented a third part of the estate.[135]

An examination of the Plea Roll for 1275 shows that the Crown acquired approximately £53 3s 6½d in that year from its portion of the third on all Jewish estates.[136] The sum of the moveable and immoveable chattels of Leo of Burford, deceased, was £3 18s 4d, of which the king's third was £1 6s 1½d; Leo's widow Antera was to make a payment for his chattels. The scribe duly noted that Antera came to the Receipt and paid it.[137] The constable of the Tower produced £1 in cash, which was

---

[132] *PREJ2*, pp. 174–5.   [133] *Ibid.*, p. 175.   [134] *Ibid.*, pp. 179–80.   [135] *Ibid.*, pp. 183–4.
[136] The figures for 1275 show that Leo of Burford's estate was worth 78s 4d. The Crown took £1 6s 1½d. Moses Babelard's effects were worth £1 16s 2d; the Crown took the whole of it. Isaac Crespin's estate was worth £3 6s 8d; the Crown took £1 2s 3d. Isaac Gabbay's estate was worth £136 17s 0d; the Crown took £45 12s 4d. Ermina the widow's estate was worth £10; the Crown took £3 6s 8d. Thus the total revenue from known Jewish estates in 1275 was £53 3s 6½d: Mundill 1987, pp. 88–92.
[137] *PREJ2*, p. 241.

the money found upon the corpse of Moses Babelard. It was duly delivered to Nigel, the sergeant of the Jewish Exchequer. The constable also produced one silver spoon, one gold ring which was sold for 1s 8d and a brooch which was sold to him for 6s 6d; he also delivered a horse which was later sold for 8s 0d. All of this particular estate went straight to the royal coffers.[138] Later in the year the sum of the chattels of Isaac Crespin was found to be £3 6s 8d, of which the king's third was £1 2s 3d. Upon inquiry it was found that he had nothing in any of the *archae*. The deceased's son, Germin, guaranteed to pay the king's third on pain of a fine of £2.[139] In Lincoln, in 1275, the sum of the chattels of Isaac Gabbay, a Jew of Lincoln, 'moveables and unmoveables as well within the chest as without', was £136 17s 0d, of which the king's part was £45 12s 4d. On closer inspection it was found that Isaac Gabbay had had twenty bonds in the Lincoln *archa*, worth a face value of £313 12s 8d, but it was proved that some were quit and that some had been bought by a Christian, Master Thomas of Wainfleet.[140] Isaac Gabbay also had another bond worth £13 which was outside the chest and in the hands of his brother, Josce Gabbay. The king took his payment of a third in bonds and commanded that the latter should be delivered by the sheriff of Lincoln. If the bonds were not delivered, the money was to be levied on the lands and property of Josce fil Aaron of Colchester and Rose, his wife, who was Isaac's daughter, and Isaac fil Isaac de Provyns and Floria, his wife, another of Isaac's daughters.[141] Again, in 1275, the sum of the chattels of Ermina, a widow who died in London, was £10 and it was found she had nothing in the *archae*; the king's third payable by the heirs was £3 6s 8d.[142]

Clearly the amount that the Crown received from reliefs on the estates of dead Jews varied from year to year. Some of these payments were paid in instalments. The Jewish Receipt Rolls show that Belassez, the wife of Elias of Doncaster, paid a total of £5 15s 0d in instalments between 1285 and 1287 for her right to inherit her late husband's estate which was probably worth about £17.[143] A death in a Jewish family could mean great hardship. When Lumbard of Cricklade died in 1277, he left an estate worth in excess of £100. His wife subsequently had financial difficulties, because the majority of the estate was in fact

---

[138] *Ibid.*, p. 239.   [139] *Ibid.*, p. 250.
[140] It is known that both of Isaac's debts which were owed to him by Richard le Bret, the son of John le Bret, of Wrangle, were in fact sold to Thomas of Wainfleet: *CPR 1272–1281*, p. 83. It is also known from other sources that Thomas of Wainfleet dabbled in moneylending. Richard le Bret of Wrangle can be identified: Mundill 1987, p. 301 notes 105–6 and appendix Table VII; WAM nos. 9027, 9087, 9094, 9132, 9170; *PREJ4*, pp. 66–7.
[141] *PREJ2*, pp. 266–9; Bischoff 1975, pp. 113–15.   [142] *PREJ2*, p. 269.
[143] PRO E/401/1581, E/401/1582, E/401/1583.

invested in loans to Christians who had evidently been avoiding repayment or who had died without paying off the loans. Lumbard's widow was eventually helped by another Jew to make her payment for relief to the Crown.[144] The largest estate that fell into Edward I's pocket must have been that of Rabbi Elias Menahem.[145] In June 1284, the inquiry into his estate was conducted before the Treasurer and the Barons and Chancellor of the Exchequer as well as the Justices of the Jews. It was found that he left personal property to the value of £260 13s 4d, a dwelling house in which he lived, together with an annual rental value of £5, and other real estate worth £19 16s 0d yearly, as well as credits worth £185. However, in 1285, his widow, Floria, was fined £1,000 for concealing the true value of her husband's estate.[146] Jews of Elias Menahem's wealth did not die every day, but the Crown enjoyed another slow trickle of cash, bonds and chattels from the death duty on smaller Jewish estates. It is unlikely that the total amount which the Crown received from Jewish death duties will ever be known. However, this type of income was another financial levy which the Edwardian Jews were forced to pay.

In any examination of what the Jewish community rendered to their royal master it is important to include another category which, regrettably, Charles Gross did not consider. This was another 'overhead' payable by the Jewish community although it was not in fact collected by the Jewish Exchequer. A poll tax or chevage was often collected from the Jewish community by converted Jews. This levy was imposed on the Jews of England for the upkeep of a *Domus Conversorum* or House for Converted Jews in both London and Oxford. Although the chevage was not designed to fill the Crown's coffers but was for the Jews' own spiritual welfare and salvation, it was still another overhead. Until 1280, all the property of Jews who converted to Christianity was forfeited to the Crown. It seems likely that the Crown used this income to make grants to the *Domus*. The *Domus* in turn granted the *conversi* the king's bounty of 1½d a day for men and 8d a week for women.[147] Although it is difficult to assess how many Jews converted to Christianity in Edward's reign, it is known that between 1280 and 1308 there were only thirty-five ex-Jewish inmates of the London *Domus*. It is

---

[144] Mundill 1991b, pp. 141, 165–6.   [145] Roth 1946, pp. 25, 38 and 59; Mundill 1997.
[146] Roth 1946, pp. 25, 38 and 59; Rigg, pp. 131–2; PRO E/9/44. It is clear that Elias Menahem's credits were worth much more than Roth estimated. He had ninety-five bonds in his possession of which forty were owed to him and the others had been acquired presumably from other Jews. The bonds range in date from 1236 to 1276. The majority were contracted between 1269 and 1272. The total face value of the bonds was over £2,000; Mundill 1997, pp. 183–7.
[147] Adler 1939, pp. 279–80, 291–2; Roth 1978, p. 98; Stacey 1992a.

probable, however, that there were more *conversi* in the abbeys and cathedrals of England.[148] Even with these extra *conversi* scattered around the country it is not likely that the number of estates and chattels forfeited to the Crown for the upkeep of Jewish converts was very great.

The estates of converted Jews were not the only source for the maintenance of Edwardian Jewish converts. A few months before his death, Henry III, the founder of the *Domus Conversorum*, sent an order to the mayor and sheriffs of London calling for a full report on the conditions of the institution. The report came back that privileges were being abused and that the finances were in an extremely precarious state.[149] In 1275, Edward I gave his consent to the chapel being enlarged. New houses were built for the converts and £100 was granted towards these works as a special royal favour.[150] It was probably in connection with these reforming measures that, in the same year, Edward imposed a poll tax of 3d per annum per head to be levied on all Jews and Jewesses above the age of twelve. Edward even included the chevage as a separate clause in the Statute of the Jewry of October that year.[151] Records have not survived for the collections of 1276 and 1277. Returns from a chevage for 1278 have survived and show a yield of £11 3s 9d for 895 Jews; however, this collection did not include Jews of Canterbury or London.[152] It seems likely that the chevage was uncollected for a few years: after all, it was not very significant compared with the collection of tallage and other receipts. In the mid and late 1270s, the importance of the *Domus Conversorum* and the need for efficient collection of the chevage was probably put to the back of Edward's mind as he had to deal with the Welsh wars and the coinage and coin-clipping investigations, as well as the works at Westminster Abbey, the Tower of London and provincial castles.

However, in 1280, in pious mood, Edward issued a decree to John de Sancto Dionisio, the keeper of the *Domus*, which outlined further improvements. This decree reflects a more urgent concern for the conversion of the Jews, whereby Edward granted four new sources of revenue for the *Domus* for the period 1280–7. He now allowed converts to keep a moiety of their goods.[153] The *Domus* was allowed to have the property of Jews who had been condemned to death for crime. The House was also granted the 'king's alms called deodands' and once again a chevage was imposed on the king's Jews of England.[154] Of these new

---

[148] Adler 1939, pp. 280–1, 341–7, 350–2; Greatrex 1992.
[149] Adler 1939, p. 299; Stacey 1992a, pp. 274–5.   [150] *CCR 1272–1279*, p. 207.
[151] *Statutes*, pp. 220–1.   [152] Rigg, p. 113.   [153] *CPR 1272–1281*, p. 372.   [154] *Ibid.*

sources of income for the *Domus*, the most important in assessing taxation on the Jews was clearly the chevage itself. The mechanism for collection had been established in 1275, although it was not used in the 1270s. The tax was to be collected by converted chaplains who were to receive the help of the sheriffs and bailiffs of the shires. Collection does not seem to have happened annually; in February 1290 the chevage for 1289 had certainly not been collected. The 'Jewish poll tax' was clearly very unpopular with the king's Jewish subjects. In 1290, the Jews of Oxford refused to pay and even assaulted the unfortunate tax-collector, William le Convers.[155]

The totals of the chevage collected in 1280–3 are known because of the survival of a single roll which was kept by John de Sancto Dionisio.[156] In 1280, the income of the *Domus* was £50 19s 5d. This was made up by the chevage and various other takings and sales of goods presumably received from the possessions of condemned Jews. The chevage that year amounted to £14 14s 9d and represented a poll tax on 1,179 Jews of England. In the following year the income of the *Domus* was £146 5s 8d. This was composed of £21 12s 11d of receipts from deodands in Lincolnshire and £24 2s 0d of receipts from deodands in Devonshire. In addition 12s was raised from the sale of a horse which had been bought and used to collect the chevage itself. The chevage produced £14 8s 3d from 1,154 Jews, and the rest of the total was made up from other sources. The chevage for 1282 was £14 5s 0½d, representing contributions by 1,135 Jews. In 1283, the income from the chevage dropped to £13 19s 11d from 1,151 Jews. In 1284, the last recorded chevage shows that the latter was now farmed out; the *Domus* received a fixed income from this source of £11 per annum. The chevage, although small, was yet another of the fiscal afflictions that the Jews of England had to suffer.[157]

There were of course many other financial pressures on the Jewish community. Some can be categorised as a collective levy, others were local taxes or odd payments for various reasons. Charles Gross had difficulty in defining such payments and indeed classed fines for false charters and for crucifying children as one of his categories.[158] Although a history of such payments can be established throughout the thirteenth century, such payments are extremely difficult to quantify. Examples of both of Gross' specific categories do exist but the general confiscations which took place are clearly much more important than the single instances which Gross cited. Among the latter were the incidents arising

---

[155] *CPR 1281–1301*, p. 398; Roth 1951, p. 162; Stacey 1992a, p. 280.
[156] PRO E/101/249/24.   [157] PRO E/101/249/24; Adler 1939, pp. 302–3; 1968, pp. 64–5.
[158] Gross 1887, pp. 193–4.

Table 3 Domus Conversorum *income and chevage, 1278–84*

Year	Income	Chevage	Number of Jewish contributors
1278		£11 3s 9d	895
1280	£ 50 19s 5d	£14 14s 9d	1,179
1281	£146 5s 8d	£14 8s 3d	1,154
1282		£14 5s ½d	1,135
1283		£13 19s 11d	1,151

Tax farming was introduced in 1284 when the chevage was assessed at £11 0s 0d per annum.
Source: PRO E/101/249/24.

from the alleged ritual murder of Christian children: for example, at Lincoln in 1255 when many Jews were either imprisoned or fined. There were also many instances of the alleged fraudulent use of charters or other financial agreements; and here again Jews were fined for particular crimes.[159] However, such isolated fines, as well as other arbitrary confiscations, are naturally impossible to enumerate in full. Many are mentioned in the Plea Rolls, yet some appear on other governmental records. The ever-present threat of confiscation of his goods and chattels was one which hung over every Jew's life, his family and his business transactions.

In order to give some impression of the types of confiscations and fines which were imposed upon outlawed or condemned Jews a single example may be briefly considered. On 16 March 1276, two officials were empowered to seize a sum of money which belonged to Diey of Holme, a Lincolnshire Jew.[160] In April 1276, Diey was charged with the murder of Brother Richard of the priory of St Michael at Stamford, and it was further alleged that he had also killed a groom in the earl of Warwick's wood outside Stratton.[161] He was officially indicted for murder and receiving from thieves. His body was 'attached' and his goods within the town of Stamford and elsewhere were seized. Amongst these was a sum of money that had been concealed within the walls of his house, which was seized as treasure trove and delivered to Luke de Lucca, the king's merchant.[162] Generally, if a Jew committed any action which was in any sense on the wrong side of the law, the confiscation and wholesale seizure of all his property would ensue. The Crown only needed the slightest excuse.

Types of confiscations which Charles Gross failed to cite are

[159] *PREJ5*, pp. 104–5.   [160] *CPR 1272–1281*, p. 137.   [161] *Ibid.*   [162] Ibid.

exemplified by the major purges connected with the coin-clipping allegations of 1278–9. The full extent of these confiscations has only fairly recently been established by Dr Zefira Rokeah. They are of great importance if any realistic index of Jewish wealth at the time of the Expulsion is to be made.[163] In 1278 and 1279, the Jews were caught up in Edward's campaign against the state of the currency and were in many cases, undeservingly, cast as the villains in the affair.[164] Although the facts of the charges need careful analysis in their own right, it is the actual financial result which must be emphasised here.[165] During these two years the sale of goods of condemned Jews, the sequestration of Jews' property and the confiscations by royal officials which accompanied the accusations brought in a total of over £11,000 for the Crown.[166] This amount was extracted from Jews who had been accused and condemned: those who were not accused presumably (but one can hardly be certain) did not lose any of their wealth.

It was very suddenly in November 1278, overnight it seems, that many Jews were arrested for having allegedly clipped the coin. John of Oxnead and many other chroniclers recorded this attack on the Jews as one of the critical events of the Jews' history during Edward's reign. Oxnead commented that all the Jews of England, whatever their status, age or sex, were suddenly seized and were imprisoned in various castles throughout England with specially appointed guards. A thorough search of their houses was made; in some cases the tools used for coin-clipping were found and in others coinage which had been clipped was found.[167] Another chronicler noted the speed with which the Jews were arrested, because the operation was carried out in a single night. He noted that some Jews were hanged, but also that on another night all the goldsmiths were also imprisoned because of hostile public opinion.[168] That many Jews were hanged in London now needs little confirmation and, as Zefira Rokeah has pointed out, at least 600 were imprisoned in the Tower.[169] There is evidence all over the country which points to very many Jewish *suspensi* or *damnati*.[170] The pogrom was finally stemmed in May 1279 when Edward ordered a sort of general amnesty for the Jews. He claimed that all Jews who had been

---

[163] This total can be arrived at from the various accounts of property of condemned Jews. Rokeah 1973; 1974; 1975. Further amounts can be added from other sources: Adler 1935b.

[164] Rokeah 1990, pp. 94–9.   [165] Mundill 1987, pp. 98–9.   [166] Rokeah 1990, p. 86.

[167] *Chronica Johannis de Oxenedes*, p. 252. Other chronicle references are J. Capgrave, *Liber de Illustribus Henricis*, p. 164 which incorrectly dates the event as 1274. Walsingham, *Historia Anglicana*, p. 172.

[168] Batholomew de Cotton, *Historia Anglicana*, p. 172.   [169] Rokeah 1990, pp. 96–7.

[170] PRO c/47/9/50; Lipman 1967, pp. 168–71; Lincoln Public Library, The Ross Collection, vol. III, pp. 219, 252; *CPR 1272–1281*, pp. 360, 443.

charged, indicted, and convicted of clipping the coinage had now been punished with death. Those who were still imprisoned or who were accused of clipping after 1 May could appease the royal justice and save their lives by paying fines.[171]

After the arrests, confiscations and hangings of 1278–9, the king appointed the officials who had conducted the inquiries to collect and sell off all Jewish chattels and property that had become sequestrated to the Crown.[172] The accounts, for the period 1278–9, of some of these officials have survived.[173] They prove that, as the chroniclers had noted, it was a national investigation. Hugh of Kendal was responsible for investigating and confiscating Jewish chattels in Northamptonshire, Rutland, Warwickshire, Leicestershire, Nottinghamshire and Derbyshire, Lincolnshire and Yorkshire.[174] John le Falconer was the official receiver for Jewish chattels in Gloucestershire, Southampton and Wiltshire.[175] Philip de Willoughby was responsible for chattels in London, Kent, Essex, Norfolk, Suffolk, Cambridgeshire, Bedfordshire and Oxfordshire. A slightly later account of William Gerberd has survived for the Jews of Exeter.[176] Another account of monies raised by the sale of ex-Jewish property in Norwich, Ipswich, Canterbury, London, Bedford and Oxford is also extant.[177] It seems that the receivers itemised the chattels and then sold them off as best they could. At least one 'broker', Henry of Winchester, himself a converted Jew, bought goods *en bloc* and received a special licence to resell them in England and France.[178] It seems that articles of a specifically Hebrew nature were sold back to the Jews.[179] From the seizure and sale of Jewish chattels it appears that Hugh of Kendal accounted for £2,252 12s 1d and also paid in Jewish gold worth £3 11s 4d.[180] John le Falconer realised £736 13s 2½d.[181] The largest sum was paid in by Philip de Willoughby, whose confiscations amounted to £7,500 paid into the Treasury.[182] William Gerberd paid £365 7s 8½d and Walter de Helyun, who sold off former Jewish properties, collected £38 1s 4d.[183]

There was considerable difficulty in collecting the chattels and possessions of the condemned Jews of 1278–9. The royal officials were not the only ones who took the opportunity to seize ex-Jewish chattels. Many local Christians were also fined in the following years for

---

[171] *CCR 1272–1279*, p. 529.
[172] *CCR 1279–1288*, pp. 5, 6, 12, 19, 28, 41; *CPR 1272–1281*, pp. 317, 323, 352, 364.
[173] Rokeah 1973; 1974; 1975; Adler 1935b.
[174] Rokeah 1973, pp. 21–2, 25–42; 1974, pp. 59–64.   [175] Rokeah 1974, pp. 65–80.
[176] Rokeah 1974, pp. 80–2; 1975; Adler 1935b.   [177] PRO c/47/9/50.
[178] *CPR 1272–1281*, pp. 320, 328; Adler 1939, p. 292; Stacey 1992a, pp. 276–7.
[179] Rokeah 1973, pp. 21–3.   [180] *Ibid.*, 1973, p. 21.   [181] *Ibid.*, p. 22.
[182] *Ibid.*, pp. 23–4.   [183] *Ibid.*, p. 25; PRO c/47/9/50.

possessing and receiving ex-Jewish goods. Naturally the Crown pursued a relentless campaign of fining these smaller entrepreneurs. Two rolls of such fines from the period 1283–9 have survived. Although one of them is badly fragmented and neither gives a complete picture of all the fines, it is possible to assert that, in the six-year period that the rolls cover, the Crown was able to add at least another £2,026 6s 8d to its coffers.[184] That many Jews died and that the Crown received much Jewish wealth is clear. Historians have been prone to point to the Statute of the Jewry of 1275 as being the cause of the decline of Jewish wealth; but they should perhaps place more emphasis on the wholesale confiscations of 1278–9 as well as the misery and disruption the whole affair caused. It decimated families, dislocated businesses and shattered financial relationships. Yet perhaps one of the surprising aspects of this catastrophe is the fact that Edward himself seems to have put a stop to it.[185]

Having given consideration to all of the so-called 'cogs' of the 'Engine of Extortion' and to many other ways in which Jewish wealth was channelled into the government's coffers, it is possible to come to several general conclusions about Jewish wealth during Edward's reign. First, it would seem that a somewhat exaggerated picture of the financial importance of the Jew to the English Crown's revenues may have been suggested by various historians.[186] The surviving evidence for tallage collection for the reign indicates that approximately £9,300 was actually collected rather than the £31,333 worth of tallage which was assessed upon the Jews.[187] The surviving evidence for the amounts brought in from small amercements and for transgressions and payments for concessions that are recorded on the non-tallage Receipt Rolls of the Jewish Exchequer suggests a figure of £2,325 for the whole reign.[188] It must also be borne firmly in mind that some of these payments were in fact paid by Christians as the Jews' debtors and that a total evaluation of Jewish wealth excluding investment out on loan is thus impossible to reach.

The examination of income from death duties on Jewish estates for 1274 (£155) and 1275 (£53) also indicates that in the early years of Edward's reign this type of income did not provide very much.

---

[184] PRO E/101/119/12, E/101/119/20.

[185] *CCR 1272–1279*, pp. 522, 529. 'The king learns that many Christians through hatred of the Jews by reason of the discrepancy of the Christian faith and the rite of the Jews and by reason of divers grievances heretofore inflicted upon Christians by Jews endeavour from day to day to accuse and indict certain Jews not yet charged...'

[186] Elman 1936; 1938a, pp. 146–7, 150, 153–4; Roth 1978, pp. 272–3; Mundill 1987, p. 59.

[187] PRO E/401/1567, E/101/249/16, E/401/1568–73, E/401/1584, E/401/1585; Elman 1938a, pp. 146, 154.

[188] PRO E/401/1574–90

Admittedly the occasional windfall of a rich Jew's estate, like that of Master Elias Menahem in 1284 (approximately £1,000), would clearly increase the revenue from such sources.[189] At a very liberal estimate the chevage, which in any case did not enter the Crown coffers but went towards the upkeep of the *Domus Conversorum*, does not seem to have produced more than £15 per annum from 1278 onwards. The largest single amount of 'Jewish revenue' that did provide money for the Crown has until recently been relatively ignored by historians. The results of the confiscations for coin-clipping in 1278–9 brought in approximately £11,000 at a single point in time. However, when considered as a whole, all these different levies upon the Jews seem only to equal the total amount of tallage *assessed* on the Jews during Edward's reign.[190]

It is clear that by the late 1280s Edward I had probably collected just over £22,000 from his Jewish subjects. This in itself is a substantial sum and certainly put the Jewish community under immense financial pressure. However it is not so significant when Edward I's own expenditure is considered. According to Professor Prestwich an income of £27,000 per annum would scarcely have been sufficient for Edward in peace time; the first Welsh war in 1277 cost approximately £23,000. The lay fifteenth of 1275 had yielded in excess of £81,000. Edward's personal overheads and expenditure increased dramatically as his reign went on.[191] Although financially squeezed, imprisoned and fined for alleged charges against them the Jewish community were, even at the start of Edward's reign, of no great financial significance for the Crown revenues. The actual fiscal capacity of the Edwardian Jew has probably been overstated whilst the impact on Jewish wealth of the wholesale confiscations of 1278–9 has been slightly underestimated. Finally the age-old association of the Jew with wealth may have coloured the historian's view of the Jew's financial significance to the Crown and for many perhaps it still does so.[192] It is now time to examine the involvement of the Jews in moneylending and to assess whether Jewish business affairs prospered or not, both before and after the Statute of 1275 which is seen by so many as the crucial turning point in the decline of Jewish wealth and accordingly the preliminary for the Expulsion of 1290.

---

[189] PRO E9/44; Rigg, pp. 131–2; Mundill 1997, pp. 161–87.

[190] Elman 1938a, pp. 146, 154; Roth 1978, pp. 272–3, 84. Roth states that the annual average tallage during the reign of Edward I was £700. Actual figures received intimate a figure nearer £515.

[191] Prestwich 1988, pp. 182, 237, 569–70.   [192] See above, pp. 72–3; Stacey 1987b, pp. 67–8.

Chapter 5

THE ATTEMPTED PROHIBITION OF USURY AND THE EDWARDIAN EXPERIMENT

'He who practiseth usury goeth to hell, and he who practiseth it not tendeth to destitution.' Thus wrote Benevenuto da Imola in the fourteenth-century when completing his commentary on Dante's *Divine Comedy*.[1] His sardonic comment was clearly pertinent for the Anglo-Jew during Edward I's reign. It is now important to discover what kind of usurious practices earned the Anglo-Jew the universal envy and hatred which was heaped upon him.[2] This chapter will consider the way in which the Jewish business man conducted his affairs during what Vivian Lipman dubbed the 'Edwardian Experiment'.[3] It should thus become possible to assess the impact of Edward's programme for the reform of Jewish and Christian business practice and also his own general attitude towards usury. It should also help to establish whether the ravages of taxation and forfeits had an effect on Jewish business and whether on the eve of the Expulsion the Jewish community was so poor as to be financially insignificant.[4] Only after these central issues have been faced will the subsequent chapters consider the mechanics of Jewish moneylending on a local level and the effect of Edward's legislation. Thereafter attention will be turned to the varying fortunes of the principal Jewish communities, to the Jews' clientele both before and after the *Statutum de Judeismo* of 1275 and finally to the several Jewish entrepreneurs who seem to have survived the 'Edwardian Experiment'.

Naturally the moneylending profession and its context within the world of business and commerce must be given some thought. It has always been difficult to establish what constitutes a loan or an investment. All types of trade must strive to bring a profit. The principal objective of any moneylender is to emerge from a purely financial

---

[1] Lacaita 1887, vol. I, p. 579. [2] Menache 1985; Moore 1992.
[3] Lipman 1967, pp. 162–85. [4] Stacey 1987b, pp. 66–7 and note 65; see above, chapter 4.

transaction with pecuniary gain. In order to be a successful trader or lender in any age one must, of course, charge some sort of interest or handling charge. It was the handling charge for speculation or risk which constituted profit and at times caused problems for the debtor. To the medieval world, as to our own society, there were varying degrees of profit that were acceptable, and some that were less so. Gain, profit, interest and usury were all results of successful loans or business transactions. The provision of credit played an ever-increasing part in Edwardian England. Although the problem of usury in the thirteenth century was not solely connected with the Jews it is important to consider the general attitudes to usury as well as those of the late thirteenth-century Jewish business men.

In their very basic forms, the views of the medieval Church and the medieval Synagogue on usurious moneylending were akin: they both deplored it. The Church's view was inherent in the *Decretum* of Gratian which condemned the receiving of more than the sum lent not only of money but of wheat, wine and oil as usurious. It saw any excess demanded by a creditor, though it be only a small gift, as usury.[5] This typified the Church's view: any gain or profit on a loan was usury. There were, however, some exceptions, as when Ambrose declared that usury might be exacted from whomever one might rightfully injure in warfare. The rule of 'where there is the right of war, there is also the right of usury' was a commonly quoted justification for taking profit, deriving from Deuteronomy XXIII:20.[6] The problem of such a generally inflexible stance on moneylending has been pointed out by Raymond de Roover in his masterful study of moneylending in late medieval Bruges:

The social need for credit was not realized by the Church. The Church's doctrine on usury was inadequate, based on a few theological concepts, legal principles, and maxims drawn from classical pagan authors and obscure biblical quotation. It overlooked the real economic and social conditions that allowed usury to exist. The fundamental truth is that people in need of financial help had to depend on the money-lender either because they had not been able to find a Christian soul willing to lend without interest or because they preferred to keep their troubles concealed from relatives and friends.[7]

However, despite the difficulties and equivocation that its stance presented, the Church waged an active campaign against usury, a campaign which began at the Third Lateran Council in 1179 and was to reach its fullest development at the Council of Lyons in 1274 and the

---

[5] McLaughlin 1939, pp. 95–6; Kirschenbaum 1985.
[6] Baldwin 1970, vol. I, p. 279: *Ubi ius belli ibi ius usure.*   [7] Roover 1948, p. 149.

Council of Vienne in 1312.[8] In a last effort to conquer usury, the Council of Vienne identified it with heresy and even went on to suppress the Templars because of it.[9] The campaign had been thorough. The Third Lateran Council condemned usury because it claimed that many people were deserting other occupations to become money-lenders. The Fourth Lateran Council was more specific and launched an attack upon the Jewish moneylender. It claimed that by taking usury the Jews were gradually acquiring all the property in Christendom. Natu-rally, the Church also had a vested interest in liquid capital. If there was a lack of cash in the economy, then as a result the Church became impoverished because tithes and oblations were no longer being paid.[10] It is therefore not surprising that in general the continental councils of the twelfth and thirteenth centuries were all committed to the destruc-tion of usury. It was to be exterminated in all forms whether manifest or concealed, and measures were to be taken to put a stop to fraudulent transactions. The councils declared that anyone who engaged in buying and selling on credit was to be judged a usurer and those who practised usury under pretence of sale were to be punished in this world and the next. The Council of Narbonne in 1227 enacted a canon which provided *Ne Judaei a Christianis immoderatis usuris accipiant* which was clearly inspired by the earlier Fourth Lateran Council, and echoed at Beziers in 1246. The Council of Sens (1269) and the Council of Lyons (1274) even forbade anyone to lease a house to a moneylender and declared that moneylenders' wills should be invalid. Such rulings also reached Britain. Councils held in Scotland in 1225 and in Worcester in 1240 issued decrees against usury. Perhaps more significantly, the Council of Exeter in 1287 pronounced perpetual suspension from office for a cleric involved as either a creditor or a debtor in usurious transactions.[11]

At the same time the representatives of the Church knew that they were fighting a losing battle, largely because of the impracticality of their attitudes. Archbishop Stephen Langton, for example, with a comparatively worldly view, had made important distinctions by claiming that it was a greater sin to seek credit from a novice usurer than from an established one, just as it was more wicked to frequent a young rather than a seasoned prostitute.[12] But the Church's view was rooted in a contradiction. Chaucer's Pardoner might later well decry

[8] Baldwin 1970, vol. I, pp. 296–311; Tawney 1937, p. 58.
[9] Parkes 1938, p. 289; Barber 1978, pp. 39–42.
[10] Synan 1965, pp. 103–4; Marcus 1960, pp. 137–8.
[11] Parkes 1938, p. 283; *Concilia*, vol. I, p. 155; Helmholz 1986.
[12] Baldwin 1970, vol. I, p. 273.

money, but he himself was out to make it. In the Vulgate, even Christ appeared to be ambiguous on this issue: in St Luke VI: 35 he was happy to pronounce, 'But love ye your enemies and do good and lend hoping for nothing there from (*nihil inde sperantes*)', but in St Luke XIX: 14–26 he related the parable about the talents and the servant who was chastised by his master for not making a profit (*cum usuris*) without adverse comment.[13] The laity were quick to turn not only to such biblical precedents but also to other justifications based on civil law. The Justinianic law allowed interest, albeit under certain restrictions. Its principle of *inter-est* allowed the creditor to take 'that which was between' his position when he made a loan and when it was paid back.[14]

In such a situation it was unavoidable that the attitudes of the Christian state should become as ambiguous as the attitudes of the Christian Church. To a medieval king the exploitation of credit systems was a necessary way of life; and yet other pressures made it necessary for him to confiscate the property of a dead usurer (supposedly for it to be distributed to the poor), to see the usurer excluded from communion, the usurers' alms rejected, and a Christian burial refused to the covetous sinner. The usurer was ranked with witches, robbers, fornicators and adulterers. The sin of usury and love of avarice came to be classed as equally as serious as homicide, sacrilege, perjury, incest and homosexuality.[15] The usurer himself was to be an outcast. With such prevailing views it was little wonder that medieval credit operations were always practised in a somewhat secret, surreptitious manner that left few records.[16]

To avoid the stigma of usury and its subsequent penalties, as well as to maintain at all times a respectable Christian façade, many methods of usury evasion became common. The earliest method, used by many monasteries during the twelfth century, was the simple loan on security.[17] In this transaction the creditor enjoyed the use of something

---

[13] *Biblia sacra*, Luke VI: 35 and 19: 14–26; Geoffrey Chaucer, *The Pardoner's Tale*, ed. Robinson, 1957, p. 148, The Prologue to the Pardoner's Tale: 'My theme is alwey oon and ever was/*Radix malorum est cupiditas*', Timothy 6: 10; Parkes 1938, p. 276.

[14] Parkes 1938, pp. 294, 300–1.   [15] *Ibid.*, pp. 283–8.

[16] Langland, *Piers the Ploughman*, pp. 68–9. When asked by Repentance, 'Have you ever in your life practised usury?', the crafty old codger Covetousness is quick to deny it and replies: 'No certainly not except in my younger days. I did pick up a thing or two then, I admit, chiefly from Jews and Lombards. They showed me how to weigh coins with a balance and clip the heavier ones, and then to lend them all out, all for the love of the Cross – the one on the back of the gold piece!!!! The borrower would give me a pledge he was almost certain to lose and that was worth more to me than the clipped coins. And you should have seen the agreements I used to draw up in case my debtors didn't pay on the nail. I've acquired far more properties through arrears of debt, than I ever could have got by showing kindness and lending.'

[17] Parkes 1938, p. 308; McLaughlin 1939, pp. 113–14.

tangible like land, a horse, a carpet, a suit of armour until the loan had been repaid. From this the *mort gage* and the *vif gage* developed. The *mort gage* or *mortuum vadium* was a contract where the creditor got the possession of the land and any profits he could make from it other than the rents, until the debt was paid off by the debtor. The *vif gage* or *vivium vadium* existed where the object or land was made the creditor's possession but the rents and profits of it were allowed to the debtor and could be used to pay off his debts.[18]

Another method of avoiding usury was made possible by extending the concept of interest to include payments which were intended to act as guarantees to the creditor. Payments of this kind were of two basic types: *damnum emergens* and *lucrum cessans*. In the case of *damnum emergens* interest was charged on the understanding that the loss was actually sustained by the creditor by the debtor's default. *Lucrum cessans* meant that interest could be charged when the loan had failed to be repaid.[19] Out of this wide acceptance of such concepts of interest, the legal device of penalty or *lucrum* became common. It also became common procedure in the Middle Ages to attach penal clauses involving monetary fines in order to encourage the fulfilment of contractual agreement.[20] The penal clause did not necessarily go to either of the two parties involved in the agreement: it could be payable to an altar, a shrine, an abbot, the king or a guild.[21] It could also, however, be used to cover the usurious element of moneylending. A further method was to deal in commodities or mixtures of commodities and money. Transactions which involve the changeover of money for goods or commodities were dubbed by Professor Postan as 'sale credits'.[22] According to Gregory's *Decretals*, a loan which was made in coin and repaid in crops worth more than the original capital layout was usurious: unless the lender took a chance that the crops might bring in less than the sum loaned.[23] Thus, whether sale credits were judged to be usurious or not was conveniently in doubt.

There were many other variations and contrivances that were open to Christ's and Moses' faithful so that they could remain within the

---

[18] Baldwin 1970, vol. I, pp. 275–8; Barton 1967; Parke 1938, pp. 308–9; *SCBM*, vol. II, pp. lxiii–lxiv.

[19] Baldwin 1970, vol. I, pp. 282–6; McLaughlin 1939, pp. 145–7; Parkes 1938, pp. 294–5.

[20] Simpson 1966, pp. 392–422; Jones 1989, pp. 5, 10–1.

[21] WAM no. 6859 is a partial transfer of a bond from a Jew to another Jew. If the debt arrangements were not honoured then there was to be a penalty payable to both Henry III and Earl Richard. WAM nos. 6783 and 6784 are other examples of partial transfers of bonds with a similar monetary penalty to be paid to the king and 'to our Lady the Queen' in case of default.

[22] Postan 1928, pp. 238–44. [23] Parkes 1938, pp. 275–6.

bounds of the anti-usury laws.[24] Many would lend money indirectly through an intermediary of another religion or an established money-lender so that the *onus* of usury would fall elsewhere: both creditor and debtor could therefore maintain a clear conscience, which was based on the popular belief that a particular creditor like a Jew might make usury without committing a mortal sin.[25] Annuities were considered lawful because the giver did not know how long the receiver would live.[26] It seems that moneylending could be developed to allow certain forms of blatant usury to be turned into allowable gain. The Reverend James Parkes summed up G. G. Coulton's view of the tacit acceptance of gain: 'Only when the lending of money involved also sharing in the risks undertaken by the borrower was it not reckoned to be usury and allowed to be profit.'[27]

Ironically, the view of the Synagogue on moneylending was similar in tone to that of the Church. Yet it was more realistic in its application. In its basic tenets, the law of the Synagogue was against usury. However, Jewish law had been tempered by the adversities and the needs of its people and was prepared to modify its teachings on usury if necessary. The Torah gave rise to certain laws whilst the Talmud interpreted the laws concerning moneylending in its own way. The Torah could therefore prohibit interest in the terms of Deuteronomy XXIII: 20–1, whilst Maimonides, in his *Book of Civil Laws*, which incorporated civil and religious teachings, could define advanced (*neshekh*) or delayed (*tarbit* or *marbit*) interest as nothing more than quasi-usury:

Advance or delayed interest is prohibited. How is this to be understood? If a man set his mind upon obtaining a loan from another and sent him gifts in order to induce him to make the loan it is advance interest. If a man borrowed money, repaid it, and then sent gifts to the lender on account of the money that was idle it is delayed interest. He who transgresses the prohibition is guilty of quasi-usury.[28]

---

[24] *Cambium* or money-changing was another method. Baldwin 1970, vol. 1, pp. 291–5; Elman 1939, pp. 95–6.

[25] This was prevented in the Diocese of Worcester in 1240 by Bishop Cantilupe, cf. *Concilia*, vol. 1, p. 675. It does seem that Jews often had Christian attorneys working on their behalf: *PREJ3*, pp. 182–5, where Simon de Craye claimed that he was acting for a Jew. Walter of Cnolton, a Christian, was attorney for Aaron fil Vives: *CCR 1272–1279*, p. 306. See also *Annales Theukesberia*, p. 137, where the earl of Gloucester who needed money in 1248 to go on crusade got the monks of Tewkesbury to act as intermediaries. See also WAM no. 6869 where an inter-Jewish bond uses a Gentile as intermediary.

[26] Parkes 1938, p. 293.   [27] Coulton 1921; Parkes 1938, p. 293.

[28] Parkes 1938, p. 340; *Encyclopaedia Judaica*, vol. XVI, pp. 27–8, 'Usury'; Deuteronomy XXIII: 20–1:

You shall not lend on interest to your brother, interest of food or money or anything on which interest can be charged. You may charge interest to a foreigner but not to your brother that the

Thus, although under Jewish law certain types of usury were punishable by public flogging, this did not deter Jews from practising usury by other methods such as annuities, mortgages, commodity bonding and advance sale credits.[29] By the time Maimonides wrote his treatise in the twelfth century, the *odaita*, or bond, was already hundreds of years old.[30] The Jews were well accustomed to the writing of agreements, the enrolment of business transactions and the problem of taking a profit legally long before the rise of western Christendom. The Synagogue had reached a compromise in that even though the Talmud and the rabbinical Responsa forbade Jews to take excessive interest the local rabbi was empowered to decide the 'proper' rate of interest that was to be allowed.[31] The concept of 'where there was the right of war there was also the right of usury' was also inherent in Jewish teachings and attitudes. The *Mishnah* laid down that 'one may borrow from and lend to Gentiles on interest or to an alien resident'.[32] The Wezika Talmud allowed this only under certain conditions: 'a man shall not lend to Gentiles for interest when he is able to get a livelihood in any other way'.[33] Rabbi Eleizar of Mainz echoed this in his code, the *Sepher ha Rokeah*: 'by this we understand that in the present time when Jews own no fields or vineyards whereby they could live, lending money to non-Jews for their livelihood is necessary and therefore permitted'.[34]

Jacob ben Meir Tam, Rashi's grandson, in his *Sepher ha Yashar*, written at Troyes in the late twelfth century, even spoke out in favour of moneylending:

Today people usually lend money on interest to Gentiles . . . because we have to pay taxes to the Kings and Princes and everything serves to sustain ourselves. We live among the nations and it is impossible for us to earn a living unless we deal with them. It is therefore no more forbidden to lend at interest because 'one might learn from their deeds' than it is to engage in any other business.[35]

Similarly Menahem ben Solomon Meiri gives a matter-of-fact account of the position in thirteenth-century Provence:

In our days nobody cares about refraining from business dealings with and loans to Gentiles, even on their feast days not a *gaon* (leader of the community), not a rabbi, not a scholar, not a pupil, not a *hasid*, and not one who pretends to

---

Lord your God may bless you in all you put your hand to in the land into which you are going to possess it.

Rabinowitz 1949, pp. 88–93, 95–6; 1956, p. 251.
[29] Rabinowitz 1949, p. 85.
[30] *Encyclopaedia Judaica*, vol. XII, pp. 243–56; vol. XVI, pp. 27–8; Rabinowitz 1956, pp. 257–63.
[31] Rosten 1968, p. 530–2.   [32] Parkes 1938, p. 340.   [33] *Ibid.*
[34] *Ibid.*, p. 341.   [35] *Encyclopaedia Judaica*, vol. XII, p. 248.

be a *hasid*. All these laws refer only to idolaters and their images, but all transactions with Christians are perfectly legal.[36]

Thus, despite similar views, it seems that usury was accepted as commonplace in thirteenth-century society whilst at the same time universally deplored. It would seem that Benevenuto da Imola was correct.[37] Medieval Hell, whether Jewish or Christian, must have been well populated and very rich in bonds, coins and shady transactions.

Although both Church and Synagogue frowned on usurious activity, they both had to accept it. In England, one of the main reasons for this reluctant acceptance was the Crown's support for the practice of money-lending at interest. This support had been formally expressed by the introduction of the *archae* system in 1194, so that the Crown could test the pulse of Jewish moneylending; until the mid-thirteenth century the Jews had been explicitly allowed by the Crown to take usury, give loans on pledges, grant mortgages and buy and sell their debts quite freely and openly.[38] By the end of Henry III's reign, however, this tide had turned, and Edward's *Statutum de Judeismo* was also to change attitudes to usurious activities dramatically. Dr Sarah Cohen put it succinctly:

The combined enactments of 1269, the restriction of rents of 1271 and the restriction of lapsed securities, the limitation of the sale of debts, in 1275 the prohibition of interest and the restriction of the recovery of the principal to a moiety of the debtor's lands, these formed a background to the last twenty years sojourn of the Jews in England.[39]

These restrictions meant that in the last third of the thirteenth century Jewish moneylending became more and more involved with the use of only two devices: the simple bond and the simple pawn. Evidence for the latter is scarce because pawnbroking did not necessitate keeping records; however some evidence of pawnbroking does remain and the types of securities it produced have already been considered in relation to the confiscations of 1279.[40] It is of more immediate importance here to examine the way Jews were accustomed to making bonds.

In the thirteenth century promissory agreements were given a variety of Latin descriptions. They could take on different forms such as tallies, recognisances or simply bonds. In practice, the arrangements these *instrumenta* represented were essentially of three different types.[41] The

---

[36] *Ibid.*   [37] Lacaita 1887, vol. I, p. 579.   [38] Scott 1950.
[39] Cohen 1951, p. xlviii.   [40] Adler 1935b; Rokeah 1973; 1974; 1975.
[41] *Obligaciones, carta, chirographus, instrumentum*. The rolls of details of extant bonds in 1290 are all headed *Obligaciones et carta de Comitatu X*, PRO E/101/250/2–12; see also WAM no. 6724; Simpson 1966, pp. 394–5.

'simple bond' recorded that 'A' would pay 'B' a sum of money on a certain date and also recorded the date the agreement was made. The 'conditional bond' recorded that 'A' would pay 'B' a certain sum of money or goods (or a mixture of the two), or whatever 'B' desired at the time of payment; the payment was to be made either by fixed instalments or all of it on a certain date. Finally, the 'penal bond' recorded that 'A' would pay 'B' a certain sum on a certain date and that if he did not do so he would pay *lucrum* on the money at a specified agreed rate until the bond had been paid off.[42] Examples of all three kinds of bonds, and bonds which represent different combinations of different types, are multifarious before 1275. It is important to note that in all three cases the actual written transactions rarely contained the amount or quantity of what the creditor actually lent to the debtor. Thus the task confronting the modern historian in interpreting the medieval bond is made exceptionally and frustratingly difficult.

In any discussion of Jewish financial activity it is of course vital to try to consider how much profit and usury the individual Jewish money-lender could make from a single transaction. This is virtually an impossible task for Edward's reign.[43] Generally, as few actual transactions survive, historians are condemned to working from the scribal extracts of the details contained in different agreements. These recorded extracts do not give enough information to come to any firm conclusions about the transaction or the profit margin; essentially they remain simple records of debt. Because of the fear of accusations of usury they do not stipulate the sum lent, the amount of interest or the securities offered by the debtor. However, it can be assumed that these transactions were not entirely free from profit. Presumably the actual terms were agreed verbally between creditor and debtor and might never be known.

Before Edward I's reforms of Jewish moneylending, there were two methods of making a profit on a loan. The first was generally achieved by writing the usury or profit together with the loan as the amount which was the stipulated repayment. The second was an interest or penalty charge, generally known to contemporaries as *lucrum*, which was made on the debtor's default and was generally charged at a rate of 43.3 per cent per annum. This penalty charge was rarely used in Edward's reign. There is therefore no easily identifiable interest rate available for Edwardian Jewish lending. The basis of Jewish money-lending, as Reverend James Parkes correctly observed, 'was usury that is a charge for the loan beginning from the day on which the loan was

---

[42] Postan 1930; Simpson 1966, pp. 392–422.   [43] Mundill 1987, pp. 127–31.

made, calculated in the bond usually as a fixed sum due on the day appointed for repayment'.[44]

Bishop Grosseteste, on his deathbed in 1253, implied that usury evasion was possible and even commonly practised and demonstrated that no one would ever really know what was actually written into a contract:

For instance I borrow a hundred marks [£66 13s 4d] for a hundred pounds (which I am to pay at the end of the term); I am compelled to execute and sign a deed wherein I confess that I have received a loan of a hundred pounds which I will repay at the end of the year. And if by chance thou wilt pay the Papal Usurer the principal of the money which thou hast now in possession within a month or less of the day of borrowing he will not accept it unless thou pay him the whole hundred pounds. This is worse than a Jew's conditions; for the Jew will receive the principal courteously whensoever thou shalt return it with only so much interest as is proportionate to the time for which thou hast it in hand.[45]

Grosseteste and other contemporaries also implied that the Jew was not the worst offender amongst the usurers who operated in thirteenth-century England. The Lombards, the Cahorsins and the Italians, acting sometimes with the full knowledge of Crown and papacy, were all ignoring the smell of sulphur and brimstone and employing what even the Jews referred to as the 'biting dust' of usury. Jewish and Christian historians have been far too ready to state that the Jew became a moneylender because it was an occupation forbidden to Christians by canon law. This is simplistic, naive and unsupportable.[46] As Vivian Lipman observed, such a view is like stating that no archbishop of Canterbury ever had a mistress![47] It must never be forgotten that the Jews were never without rivals in their pursuit of moneylending or usurious transactions. Their business was not the monopoly that historians sometimes intimate. Usury was not just the domain of unpopular aliens; there was, in fact, a strong presence of Christian English moneylenders.[48]

For evidence of the methods used by such Christian English money-

[44] Parkes 1938, p. 305.   [45] Matthew Paris, *Chronica Majora*, vol. v, p. 405.

[46] *Ibid.*, vol. III, p. 328; Jenkinson 1913. Mate 1973, pp. 187–8, 194–5 shows that Canterbury Cathedral Priory was borrowing from the Italians and the Jews throughout the second half of the thirteenth century. It also shows that they borrowed from the Archdeacon of Canterbury, the Archbishop of Armagh, Bartholomew de Castello in 1279, Gregory de Rokesle in 1279 and 1283 when he was an ex-mayor of London, the Archdeacon of Bath, Roger de Northwood in 1278 and Catherine Lovel; Pugh 1968; Butler 1952.

[47] V. D. Lipman at a meeting of the JHSE in November 1989.

[48] Mundill 1987, pp. 134–45; Mundill 1990a, pp. 2–4; 1993, pp. 28–9; McIntosh 1988; Bowers 1983a; Kaeuper 1973; Whitwell 1903, pp. 175–229; Jenkinson 1913.

lenders there is no need to look far. The means which they used to repay their debts was a distant cousin of the Jewish money bond, the recognizance. Professor Michael Postan adequately defined this financial instrument when he described it as being:

the formal acknowledgement of the obligation of the debtor before a judicial tribunal. The recognizance so acknowledged and recorded upon the court rolls was not merely an enrolled obligation, it was equivalent to a judgement. By recognizing the obligation before the court the debtor conceded to the creditor in advance the right to proceed with the execution (against the security of his lands, goods and person) as soon as he defaulted.[49]

Once again the recognizance was just as open to usury evasion and manipulation. Recognizances are plentiful during the thirteenth century, enrolled as they are in urban Letter Books, cartularies and the Rolls of Chancery. From the London Letter Books of 1276–84, it seems that the number of English recognizances increased significantly between these dates.[50] From the Close Rolls for the period 1272–9, almost five hundred instances of these acknowledgements of debt can be found.[51] It is impossible to believe that these debts do not contain a profit for the creditor. If the hypothesis that these are some species of loan is correct, then many of these Christian creditors flouted the usury prohibitions and risked damnation in order to take a profit.

There were several social categories in thirteenth-century England that had access to large amounts of capital and might be expected to be involved in moneylending: the secular clergy, the merchants, the tax-collectors, the Crown, civil servants and the royal household, and foreign merchants, as well as many local officials.[52] Almost all these categories would seem to have been deeply involved in the lending of money in some way or other, be it disguised or otherwise. It was these groups, as well as the alien moneylenders, papal usurers and Jews, that Edward had in mind when, early in his reign, he started a campaign against usury.

Soon after his return from his crusade in August 1274, Edward I, although himself some £30,000 in debt to the Luccans, set about solving the problems that had been caused by debts and usury, and acted, in 1275, against both Christian and Jewish usurers.[53] In January of that year, he gave orders to his Treasurer, Prior Joseph de Chauncy, and others to inquire:

cautiously whether any merchant-usurers are found in the City of London or elsewhere in the realm and to cause their bodies and goods and chattels of any

[49] Postan 1930, p. 36.   [50] Childs 1978, p. 16; Beardwood 1955.
[51] Mundill 1987, pp. 134–45   [52] *Ibid.*   [53] Prestwich 1980, pp. 8–10.

such to be arrested and kept safely until otherwise ordered . . . as the King lately caused proclamation to be made that all merchant-usurers dwelling within the city and realm should quit the realm before the day now past under pain of grievous forfeiture and the King learns that some of them dwell in the city and elsewhere in the realm contrary to the inhibition.[54]

The attitude towards Christian usurers could not have been made more explicit. Edward's policy towards Jewish usurers was to emerge from a parliament which on 25 April 1275 was summoned to Westminster. It was summed up by the Rochester chronicler as: 'and it was particularly forbidden for the Jews to practise unrestrained usury. And so that the King was able to keep them apart from Christians he ordered that they should wear the tablets of the Law in length and width as a sign on the outside of their outer garments.'[55] John of Oxnead gives further details of the parliament's deliberations:

It was forbidden for Jews throughout the whole of the kingdom of England to give their own money to anyone else at usury, but they were to live from the profits of their own merchandise, having the same laws of the Christian merchants for buying and selling and that any of them anywhere of whatever age, standing or sex should give to the king annually three pennies per head.[56]

Such policies were later embodied in the *Statutum de Judeismo* of 1275 which placed both financial and social restrictions upon the Jews and in the end diverted them towards a new role. It was through this legislation that Edward tried to re-align the 'perfidious', 'usury-tainted' Jew with the rest of Christian society. It is now time to consider in more detail Edward's campaign against usury and the ramifications it had for both Jewish and Christian lending.

On the financial side, the preamble to the *Statutum de Judeismo* of 1275 blamed usury for 'disheriting the good men of this land' and then banned it.[57] It ruled that 'henceforth no Jew shall lend any thing at usury, either upon land, or upon rents, or upon any other thing'. It restricted past usuries, and stated 'that no usuries shall run in time coming from the Feast of St Edward last past'. It also seems to have outlawed pawnbroking: 'but all those who owe debts to Jews upon pledges of movables, shall acquit them between this and Easter'. However it does not seem to have forbidden covenants of a non-usurious nature because it limited the amount that bankrupt debtors could be forced to pay towards their debts and allowed them to keep

---

[54] *CCR 1272–1279*, p. 144; Rokeah 1997.
[55] B Cotton MS Nero D II, folio 179. [56] *Chronica Johannis de Oxenedes*, p. 247.
[57] *Statutes*, vol. I, pp. 220–1. For full text and translation see Appendix II, lines 1–2, 7–9, 9–10, 12–14, 21–3.

enough money to maintain themselves; it also decreed that debts could not be claimed from tenants or heirs. Clearly a situation was envisaged in which Christians could still become indebted to Jews. The Statute was, however, designed to ensure that the Jews did not profit from such debts by usury or unduly oppress the Christians to whom they offered credit facilities.

As is well known, the Statute imposed social restrictions on the Jews.[58] It re-established the wearing of the *tabula* and introduced a new poll tax on each Jew or Jewess over twelve years of age. It prevented a Jew from enfeoffing either a Jew or a Christian with rents, houses and tenements and from acquitting any Christian of his debts without the express permission of the Crown by royal licence. In granting the Jews the Crown's protection, it even clarified their constitutional position by stating that they had no legal right to plead a case or be brought to trial in any court except the king's court 'whose bond-men they are' (*serfs*). Finally, it confined all Jews to live in the *archae* towns, where they were to be exempt from taxes because they were answerable to the king for taxes.

Having placed financial and social restrictions on the Jews, two clauses of the Statute went on to define the most important change in the social role of the Jew envisaged by Edward: 'and the king granteth unto them that they may gain their living by lawful merchandise and their labour; and that they may have intercourse with Christians, in order to carry on lawful trade by selling and buying'. The Jews who became traders were granted the right to buy the houses in which they lived to be held in chief of the king. Those Jews who were to live off the land were allowed to buy their farms for terms of ten years or less, without homage and fealty for the next fifteen years.[59]

The basic message of the *Statutum de Judeismo* was that the Jew was to earn his living by competing in Christian society like a Christian whilst at the same time being disadvantaged by discrimination.[60] The Jewish reaction to this piece of legislation was recorded in a letter addressed to the king and his counsellors written by the Jewish community in 1276.[61] In respectful terms, the community begged for mercy and wished to have rulings on several points. They expressed their concern that it was unjust that they could only claim their debts against part of a debtor's security (in order to allow them enough to live off). The Jewish community asked what security the Jewish creditor was to have

---

[58] Roth 1978, pp. 70–3; Appendix II, lines 40–8, 61–2, 72–84.
[59] Roth 1978, pp. 70–3; Lipman 1967, p. 163. [60] Roth 1978, pp. 72–5.
[61] PRO sc/8/54/2655; the letter is also printed in *Select Cases in the Court of the King's Bench under Edward I*, vol. III, p. cxiv.

for his debts if a debtor only had one house in which he lived. They also queried the situation in which the purchaser of the land of a debtor who had died without heir might recover a pledge in lands and rents without paying off the debt connected with the pledge. In such a case they felt the creditor should be allowed to have possession of the property until the debt was paid off. Their letter also recorded their fears about the emphasis placed on their future involvement in trade. They pointed out that some Jews who did not have the means to live by merchandise would have to sell their houses or their rents to richer Jews but that the poorer Jews were unable to do this without express royal permission. They also made the point that they could not compete with Christian merchants because they had to buy dearer and could not manage to sell dearer. They complained that Christian merchants could take their goods far and wide but if the Jews took their merchandise out of the *archa* town they would be robbed. In conclusion, the Jewish community begged to be allowed to live as it had done under Edward's ancestors since the Conquest.[62]

It is not clear that the king or his government took any action on this particular plea.[63] The letter is, however, good evidence of the fact that the Jews were well aware of the Statute's implications and were worried by the prospect of having to make their traditional financial practices non-usurious and by the obvious difficulties which would be involved in moving into a more straightforwardly commercial kind of business. They realised that they were being ordered to act in ways in which society expected a Christian to act and knew that they would have to do this from a weaker position than their Christian competitors.

More evidence of Edward's desire to make the provision of credit facilities by Jews and Christians more streamlined comes from the Statute of Acton Burnell issued in 1283 which established a new system (clearly modelled on Jewish lines) for the formal registration of debts to Christians and for the speedier recovery of those debts.[64] Before 1283 one of the major problems facing a Christian creditor was proving and enforcing the repayment of his debt. The official recognizance certainly recorded a debt but it did not ensure that the debt was paid. The *Statutum de Mercatoribus* laments this fact, 'forasmuch as Merchants, which heretofore have lent their Goods to divers persons, be greatly

---

[62] Richardson 1960, pp. 109–11.

[63] In practice at least orders were given for officials to allow Jews to have distresses for debts and to take moieties of debtors' possessions as securities: *CCR 1272–1279*, pp. 287, 306, 395, 496.

[64] *Statutes*, vol. I, pp. 53, 54, 100 (for the 1285 re-enactment). For the Statute in action see *CCR 1279–1288*, p. 297; Salzman 1931, pp. 101–3; Plucknett 1949, pp. 139–48; Rabinowitz 1956, pp. 257–63. See Appendix II.

impoverished, because there is no speedy Law provided for them to have Recovery of their Debts at the Day of Payment assigned'.[65] It then established that in future the creditor and debtor were to acknowledge the debt and the day of payment in front of royally appointed officials. The recognizance was to be entered onto a roll and a clerk was to make a letter of obligation with his own hand. This was to be sealed by the debtor and would also be affixed by the royal seal. If the debt was not paid then the creditor who retained the 'bill obligatory' was to appear in front of the officials and the mayor of the town and they would then take appropriate action against the debtor. If the debt could not be paid off by securities then the debtor was to be imprisoned and sustained on bread and water at the expense of the creditor until the debt had been paid off.[66] Thus, from 1283, the certificate of Statute Staple or Statute Merchant was officially recognised in a manner which closely resembled the Jewish chirograph and it had a system of registration which was clearly modelled on the Jewish *archa* system.[67] The *Statutum de Mercatoribus* attempted to stimulate commerce and legalised sale credits issued by Christians. However, there was little help for the Jew. The last clause exempted Jews, 'to whom this statute extendeth not'.[68] A system which had been originally designed to assist the Jew was now being placed at the disposal of Christian creditors who were being given means of implementation not available to Jews.

By 1283, Edward had issued two statutes which had weakened the ability of the Jew to compete with his Christian equivalent in the provision of credit facilities. It is, however, possible that sometime in the 1280s Edward decided that he had perhaps gone too far in the restrictions he had imposed on Jewish creditors. Historians are divided over whether the extant draft of the *Chapitles Tuchaunz le Gewerie* were ever formally issued.[69] B. L. Abrahams commented that the purpose of this 'legislation' was a partial revocation of the *Statutum de Judeismo* of

---

[65] *Statutes*, vol. 1, p. 53: 'Pur ceo qu Marchauntz, qi avaunt ces houres unt preste lur aver a diverse genz, sunt cheuz en poverte pur ceo qe il ni aveit pas si redde ley purvewe, par la quele il poeient lur dettes hastivement recoverir al jor asis de paye.'

[66] The certificates of Statute Staple for Edward's reign can be found in the PRO. They run from PRO c/241/1 to c/241/54. If a debt could not be settled locally then the certificate was delivered to Chancery where further action would be taken. The certificates which remain in the PRO are examples of debtors not paying up and action being necessitated; Nightingale 1990, p. 565.

[67] Plucknett 1949, pp. 140–5.

[68] *Statutes*, vol. 1, p. 53: 'Cest ordeinement e establisement veut le Rei qe desoremes seit tenu, par tut sur reaume de Engleterre, entre quel gent, qe ceus seient, qe de lur ein degre voderunt tele reconisaunce fere, farpris Jews, asquels cest establisement ne se estent pas.'

[69] Rigg, pp. liv–lxi; BL Additional MS 32,085, fos. 120–1; Appendix iii; Stacey, 1997; Brand forthcoming shows that the draft Statute dates from a decade earlier.

1275 and again allowed some moneylending and pawnbroking, albeit under stricter conditions. He dated the *Chapitles* to the year 1283 when the *nova cista* at Hereford was opened.[70] Peter Elman even supposed that after 1284 these regulations concerning the Jews permitted the taking of usury within certain limits.[71] Cecil Roth, on the other hand, did not believe that the *Chapitles* were ever issued and in this was followed by Vivian Lipman.[72] More recently Dr Paul Brand has highlighted the problems of interpreting the *Chapitles*. Whether or not they were actually issued, it can, however, be easily demonstrated that the Jews, although for a time bound by the *Statutum de Judeismo* of 1275, were able to register money bonds and lend money once again from the mid-1280s onwards.[73]

Although the *Chapitles* must be treated with caution the preamble explains what Edward had tried to achieve by his legislation in 1275. They outline Edward's acknowledgement that his ancestors profited from Jewish lending and show his desire, led on by piety, to outlaw the Jews' 'vicious' usury. They clearly state his wish that the Jews should live and sustain themselves by 'other business and licensed trading . . . especially since by favour of Holy Church they are suffered to abide and live with Christians'.[74] They then explain how the Jews had abused his legislation by a 'new and wicked device, under colour of trading and good contracts and covenants'. They were accused of making bonds in which they stipulated their repayments should be 'twice, thrice or four times as much as they part with'. It was also claimed that they avoided the use of the term usury by using penalties.[75] In order to solve this situation it was proposed that the lending of money should be allowed once more, but under stricter regulations than those in force before 1275. A proposed interest rate was even established: for a loan of £1 no more than half a mark (valued in the document as 8s 8d) a year and for £2 no more than one mark (valued at 17s 4d) and for more more and for less less. It seems this was considered to be a fair rate and the profit was referred to as '*purvenue*' by way of rent of contract and debt.[76]

The *Chapitles* were so detailed that they even proposed and redefined the method for making a bond and employed a similar formula to that used in recognizances. A time limit was set on a contract: a bond was to be valid for three years from the date of the actual making. After the

---

[70] Abrahams 1894a, p. 140   [71] Elman 1939, p. 99.
[72] Roth 1978, pp. 81, 275; Lipman 1967, p. 163.
[73] Brand forthcoming; Mundill 1990a, pp. 3–6.
[74] See Appendix III, lines 32–42 for translation; Rigg, pp. liv–lxi.
[75] Rigg, pp. liv–lxi; see Appendix III, lines 42–52.
[76] Rigg, pp. liv–lxi; see Appendix III, lines 57–60.

term had passed the Jew was to be able to claim the principal debt and what had arisen from it during the three years. A year of grace was then to be given to the debtor if he or she could not pay. Other regulations stipulated that only one Jew and one Christian were to make a bond in their own names, that a Jew could not lend money to a Jew to then lend to a Christian and that a Jew could not sell his debts without royal permission. It was also stipulated that any lending on gages (forbidden in 1275) worth more than £1 was to be witnessed and recorded by a chirographer and a clerk. The text of the *Chapitles* eventually broke off with the clause, 'it now remains to speak of writings obligatory that remain with the Jews in their custody'.[77] It is of course impossible to tell which of the particular recommendations embodied in the *Chapitles* played a significant part in defining Jewish practice or even if they remained draft proposals; perhaps the return to moneylending in the late 1280s is some indication that they were implemented.

Having clearly established that both Jewish and Christian debts and transactions were of great concern to the Crown in the early part of Edward's reign and that the king himself tried to combat quasi-usurious activities with the legislation which has been examined above, it is now time to consider how this legislation was and has been interpreted and what effect it had on contemporary Jewish credit broking. Cecil Roth summed up what his disciple Vivian Lipman later dubbed 'Edwardian Experiment': 'Yet to do him justice Edward I seems to have felt blunderingly and gropingly towards a less drastic attempt to solve the Jewish problem by economic re-direction which unfortunately was not accompanied by social re-adjustment.'[78] Others have considered the Edwardian Experiment in greater detail. Both Peter Elman and Vivian Lipman came to similar conclusions about the effect of the 1275 legislation. After his consideration of the extant bonds of 1290, Peter Elman stated: 'There is some doubtful evidence that as a result of the prohibition of usury in 1275 the Jews began to grant sale credits on corn and wool. But the paucity of the evidence and the frequent vagueness of its import must forbid arguing from it that the English Jews were important traders.'[79] Dr Vivian Lipman, who had examined the Norwich Jewish community and their surviving bonds of 1290 in great detail, similarly concluded: 'After 1275 when moneylending was virtually forbidden the contracts concerning Jewish trading in corn and wool are camouflaged moneylending contracts.'[80]

Neither historian believed that the Jews' transactions after 1275 reveal

---

[77] Rigg, pp. liv–lxi; see Appendix III, lines 159–60.   [78] Roth 1949, p. 4.
[79] Elman 1939, p. 104; 1938a, p. 148.   [80] Lipman 1968, pp. 72–3.

a genuine trade in commodities. Their view was that the Jews remained primarily moneylenders and the Edwardian Experiment had failed. In their eyes the *Statutum de Judeismo* had failed to encourage the Jews to make a living by trade and agriculture, and had forced them to become clandestine creditors who cunningly camouflaged their bonds in the guise of sale credits. This naturally coloured their own interpretations of the Expulsion. For both Elman and Lipman it was the Jews' failure to succeed under the new legislation, coupled with the heavy burden of tallage, that led to impoverishment and eventually to expulsion.[81]

To see the full effect of the Edwardian Experiment on the business practices of the Jewry it is vital to consider the evidence that the Jewish entrepreneurs themselves have left behind. Such evidence has been preserved in the *Valor Judaismus*, a survey of the full value of Jewish wealth at the Expulsion in 1290. The *Valor* included a survey of all Jewish-owned properties and a survey of the bonds that were left deposited in the *archae* in 1290.[82] Of more immediate interest are the Jewish credit transactions themselves. In 1290 the *archae* from twenty-one towns were delivered to Westminster and their contents recorded.[83] The lists of bonds from eleven provincial towns have survived and preserve the contents of fourteen *archae*. These lists provide details of 1,106 transactions made at various dates before the Expulsion. The approximate value of these transactions which passed into the Crown's hands was £9,100: bonds to the value of £4,000 were expressed in terms of money, bonds to the value of £2,700 were expressed in terms of cereal, and bonds to the value of about £2,400 were expressed in terms of wool.[84] The distribution of these transactions is best explained by Tables 4 and 5 which show the contents of eleven 'new chests' and three 'old chests'.

The forty surviving membranes, alas, only contain abbreviated records of the transactions. The Exchequer scribes recorded the name of the creditor, the name of the debtor, the amount owed and the date the agreement was made; the details of the actual transactions, from which they took their information, have long since been destroyed. The lists also recorded some details of tallies which were treated in the same way, preserving the name of creditor, debtor, the amount owed and in some cases the date the transaction was made. Thus, to refer to these rolls as lists of 'extant bonds' is technically wrong, although it will remain convenient to use such terminology.[85]

---

[81] Elman 1938a, pp. 145–54; Richardson 1960, p. 108; Miller 1962; Stacey 1987b, pp. 67–8.
[82] Mundill 1987, p. 7; PRO E/101/249/27, E/101/249/29, E/101/250/2–12.
[83] PRO E/101/249/29.   [84] Mundill 1990a, pp. 3–5; PRO E/101/250/2–12.
[85] Elman 1939, p. 97.

Table 4 *Bonds and tallies in the* novae archae *in 1290*

Town Date range of bonds	Money bonds	Cereal bonds	Wool bonds	Tallies (money)	Mixed repayment	Total of bonds
Bristol						
1284–7	2	9	0	8	0	19
Cambridge						
1268–86	31	1	3	0	1	36
Canterbury						
1280–90	0	94	1	0	0	95
Devizes						
1282–90	2	15	0	12	0	29
Exeter						
1284–90	0	21	0	24	0	45
Hereford						
1283–90	30	34	4	3	6	77
Lincoln						
1278–90	40	73	136	0	1	252
Norwich						
1280–90	2	41	17	0	0	60
Nottingham						
1284–90	48	7	3	2	0	60
Oxford						
1274–90	0	30	8	9	0	47
Winchester						
1281–90	0	8	1	0	1	10

There are two transactions in the Lincoln *archa* which do not conform but have been included in the table. There are two duplicates listed in the Canterbury *archa*.

Sources: PRO E/101/250/2, E/101/240/3, E/101/250/4, E/101/250/5, E/101/250/6, E/101/250/7, E/101/250/8, E/101/250/9, E/101/250/10, E/101/250/11, E/101/250/12.

These lists have previously been presented and utilised by B. L. Abrahams and Peter Elman.[86] The former produced information concerning the names of the Jewish creditors and the amounts they were owed, whilst the latter, in the 1950s, was the first to try to interpret this valuable evidence. Yet neither examined the stated dates of contraction of the bonds. Elman assumed that the term 'new chest' covered all debts made after 1280, and that the term 'old chest' covered all debts made before 1276, and noted that all the 'old chest' debts were repayable in

[86] Abrahams 1894a; 1896; 1894b; Elman 1936; 1938a; 1939; 1952.

Table 5 *Bonds and tallies in the* veteres archae *in 1290*

Town Date range of bonds	Money bonds	Cereal bonds	Wool bonds	Tallies (money)	Mixed repayment	Total of bonds
Devizes 1258–75	28	0	0	0	0	28
Exeter 1237–75	143	0	0	0	0	143
Hereford 1259–76	172	0	0	0	33	205

The total number of bonds revealed by the *archae* in 1290 is 1,106. Of these, 1,106 bonds only twenty-eight do not bear the date of contract.
Sources: PRO E/101/250/2, E/101/250/5, E/101/250/11.

money.[87] Closer examination of the dates at which the bonds were contracted shows that the division of 'old chest' and 'new chest' bonds at 1276 and 1280 is not correct.[88] For example, the Cambridge *archa* was designated by the scribes as a *nova cista*, but contained, in the main, bonds made before 1275 when the Jews were expelled from the town. However, there were four bonds which dated from the 1280s.[89] Similarly, the Oxford *archa* which was designated as a *nova cista* had bonds in it which dated from 1274.[90] The Lincoln *archa* was described as a *vetus cista*, but had bonds which ranged in date from 1278 to 1290.[91] Thus, the terms *vetus* and *novus* meant little when taken out of their purely local context and no great emphasis could or should be placed on their connotations.

Closer examination of the lists of bonds gives a much fuller and more detailed picture of these dealings. Tables 4 and 5 show that there were fifty-eight tallies in what can be termed *novae archae*. These tallies varied in value from 1s 6d to as much as a tally in the Devizes *nova cista* dated 1282 which was for £10 10s 7½d.[92] There were 730 'new chest' debts. Of these, there were (as observed above) fifty-eight tallies, as well as

---

[87] Elman 1939, p. 97.   [88] *Ibid.*   [89] PRO E/101/250/3.
[90] PRO E/101/250/9.   [91] PRO E/101/250/12.
[92] PRO E/101/250/11. The tallies in the *novae archae* are in the following *archae*: eight in the Bristol *archa*: PRO E/101/250/4; twelve in the Devizes *archa*: PRO E/101/250/11; twenty-four in the Exeter *archa*: PRO E/101/250/2; three in the Hereford *archa*: PRO E/101/250/5; two in the Nottingham *archa*: PRO E/101/250/8; nine in the Oxford *archa*: PRO E/101/250/9.

eight bonds in which there were repayments which stipulated return in a mixture of money and commodities. There were two such bonds in the Lincoln and Cambridge *archae*.[93] There were six bonds which stipulated return in commodities and money in the Hereford *nova cista*.[94] A single bond recorded on the Winchester roll, dated October 1284, showed that John Chelebalton owed Lumbard of Winchester forty quarters of wheat and two sacks of wool.[95] The 'new chests' contained details of 157 money bonds, 331 cereal bonds and 173 wool bonds. Thus there were 504 commodity bonds, just under half of the total number of bonds represented in the lists, all of which were made sometime after 1275.[96]

From these transactions it is possible to see the effect of Edward's legislation. The bonds before and after 1275 are different and it is easy to detect the change. The Devizes 'old chest' contained twenty-eight money bonds; however, the 'new chest' had only two for money, fifteen for cereal and twelve tallies (for money).[97] The Exeter 'old chest' contained 143 money bonds and the 'new chest' twenty-one cereal bonds and twenty-four tallies.[98] The Hereford 'old chest' and 'new chest' differ once again.[99] The details of the bonds in each of the 'new chests' clearly illustrate the shift towards commodities. Peter Elman highlighted this change when he concluded that 'the post 1275 transactions were abnormal and a direct result of the cessation forced or otherwise of the "normal" Jewish moneylending'.[100] He admitted the possibility that 'these figures would seem to point to a very considerable trade in the goods mentioned were it not that a closer analysis of the rolls raises a number of serious complications all of which cannot be completely and satisfactorily unravelled'.[101] It is clearly impossible to unravel these complications without examining the transactions with some regard to the communities and areas in which they were made. Each town was answerable to different chirographers and to different local authorities, and had local clients with different needs. The bonds themselves will be examined carefully and at length in the following chapter, but before doing this it is important to consider Peter Elman's

---

[93] See Tables 4 and 5. PRO E/101/250/3, E/101/250/5, E/101/250/8, E/101/250/10, E/101/250/12.

[94] PRO E/101/250/5. There are thirty-three bonds in the Hereford *vetus cista* and it can only be assumed that this is what Elman was mistakenly referring to. In the *nova cista* at Hereford there are six bonds which stipulate mixed commodity repayments; Abrahams 1894a, pp. 144–58 allowed for forty-one mixed commodity repayments in his reckoning in both the *vetus cista* and the *nova cista* instead of thirty-nine; Hillaby 1990c, pp. 456–61.

[95] PRO E/101/250/10.   [96] See Tables 4 and 5; Mundill 1987, pp. 112–14.

[97] PRO E/101/249/11.   [98] PRO E/101/250/2.   [99] PRO E/101/250/5.

[100] Elman 1952, p. 89.   [101] Elman 1939, p. 96.

hypothesis and the implications of further, fuller, research carried out by Vivian Lipman on the Norwich community.[102]

Before examining what kind of effect the Edwardian Experiment had on the Jewish community it is important to consider the reservations held by Peter Elman, Vivian Lipman and others. Peter Elman's argument against Jewish involvement in trade was fivefold. First, he argued that there was little evidence that there were any Jews involved in external trade. Secondly, and similarly, he asserted that there were no Jews mentioned in the wool export licences. Thirdly, he claimed that the evidence of the proximity of Jewish domiciles to areas of mercantile importance did not necessarily indicate trading interests. Fourthly, he stated that, if there was any Jewish trade worthy of mention, then it was confined to articles of luxury and was specifically inter-Jewish. Finally, he pointed out that all of the prices of cereal and wool recorded in bonds were expressed in round figures and most of the bonds recorded were two years old, facts which he asserted were indicative of the artificiality of the commodity agreements in the bonds.[103] To these arguments, Vivian Lipman added his own anxieties about the 'suspiciously regular prices' quoted in the bonds; he voiced new suspicions about the way in which the bonds specified that deliveries or repayments of commodities should be made at times of the year such as Easter and Christmas and was also concerned about the lack of detail in the wool bonds when they were compared with their Christian counterparts.[104]

These different arguments need to be considered in turn. Peter Elman's first argument was a statement of fact and little discussion of it is necessary. He claimed that there was no evidence that the Jews were involved in external trade.[105] More recently Patricia Allin has shown how it might have been possible for Jews to trade via Christian intermediaries.[106] In any case the argument has little relevance to Jews actually turning from moneylending to trade in general.[107] The argument that no Jew was mentioned in the wool export licences which were granted by the Crown to merchants who wished to export wool is, in effect, the same point as the first. It is, in any event, unlikely that the Jews, who were always regarded as the king's men, would have been granted 'Gentile' licences through the normal channels. The topographical evidence which shows Jews inhabiting the main mercantile areas of towns is overwhelming. The London

---

[102] Lipman 1967, pp. 162–85.
[103] Elman 1939, pp. 92–104; Stacey forthcoming; Brand forthcoming.
[104] Lipman 1967, pp. 164–8; Hillaby 1990c, pp. 456–61. [105] Elman 1939, p. 92.
[106] Elman 1939, p. 92; Allin 1972, p. 94. [107] Mundill 1990a.

Jewry was situated near the Cheap and the Cambridge Jewry, as Peter Elman pointed out, was near the market centre of the town. The Bristol Jewry was situated near the top of Broad Street close to both the quay and the Guildhall.[108] In Colchester, Jews had property in Stockwellstreet, Colverlane and even the market.[109] Two of the four Jewish domiciles in Exeter which appear in contemporary records were in the High Street.[110] The Norwich Jewry was close to the Haymarket, the sheep market and the wheat market.[111] The Nottingham Jewry appears to have been situated in the south-west corner of the town, within 250 yards of the Great Saturday Market and even closer to the weekday market.[112] The Oxford Jewry was situated on Fish Street near *La Boucherie* and Carfax.[113] In Southampton, Jewish residences seem to have been near the quay.[114] The Winchester Jewry appears to have been in Scowrtenestreet or Shoemaker's Street, the present day Jewry Street, situated just off the High Street.[115] The York Jewry was in Coney Street, one of the city's principal streets, and in nearby Micklegate.[116] The Jewry in Canterbury was close to the High Street and not far from the Guildhall and Mercery Lane.[117] In Hereford, the Jews again lived near the High Street, in Widemarsh and Maliere Streets, within easy distance of the High Cross, the town hall and the market.[118] In Lincoln, the Jewry dominated the parish of St Michael on the Hill and was close to the corn and skin markets. It was situated in a fork at the top of the High Street.[119] Throughout England, the Jews had settled in or near the main mercantile centres of towns.

Such locations clearly do not prove that Jews were involved in trade. They do not, however, exclude the possibility. In fact, in the *Valor Judaismus* of 1290, there is evidence which creates closer links between Jewish property and commercial activity. There are references to *shoppae* mentioned in this valuation and in other records.[120] In 1290, Sancte, a Jew, had a tenement in Colchester with three shops adjoining it. In the same town, at the same time, another Jew, Elias, had a shop actually in the market, worth an annual value of 6s 0d, which he had

---

[108] Adler 1928, pp. 119–24, 172–3.
[109] WAM nos. 9074, 9076; Abrahams 1896, p. 90; Stephenson 1984, p. 50.
[110] Adler 1931, p. 222; Exeter Cathedral Muniments: Medieval Deeds nos. 3 and 4.
[111] Lipman 1967, pp. 113–37.
[112] Nottingham RO MS M24/182: the Lassman Papers; Walker 1963.
[113] Roth 1951, map, p. 195.   [114] Allin 1972, pp. 92–3.   [115] Turner 1954.
[116] Dobson 1979, p. 47; Brunskill 1964.   [117] Mundill 1987, pp. 177–8.
[118] *Ibid.*, pp. 240–1.   [119] *Ibid.*, pp. 295–6.
[120] PRO E/9/39 mentions *shoppae* in London and Oxford; WAM no. 6796 mentions *shoppae* in Norwich.

just rented to a Christian in 1289. Dulrie, a Jewess, and her son, Pigge, even had a stall in Colchester worth an annual value of 7s 0d in 1290.[121] In Norwich, in 1269, Roger son of Eustace the Baker granted Abraham fil Deulecresse a stall in the drapers' quarter in the market place.[122] In Oxford, in 1290, Bonefey of Cricklade, Vives le Petit, Sarah le Eveske, Pya and Moses of London all owned *shoppae*.[123] Some *shoppae* possessed by Jews were rented out to Christians but some Jews clearly used shops for their own trading activities. There is evidence for both these situations. On the one hand, Robert de Elmham, a Colchester merchant, rented a shop from Elias of Colchester, but, on the other hand, Abraham fil Deulecresse rented a stall in the drapers' quarter of Norwich. Overwhelmingly, the evidence from most of the major towns indicates that the Jews were in a reasonable position to become *legales mercatores*. Elman's argument that 'no significant evidence for trade can be derived from the proximity of Jewish houses and shops to mercantile areas' can at least be nullified, if not unequivocally reversed.[124]

In considering the other arguments against Jewish involvement in trade, it is necessary to return to the extant bonds of 1290 and to consider local conditions. Consideration of Tables 4 and 5 shows that the post 1275 transactions were difficult, as Peter Elman pointed out.[125] Vivian Lipman also correctly observed that 'the contracts entered into after the Statute of the Jewry of 1275 are very different'.[126] The changes that the Experiment brought about can be easily illustrated by reference to the bonds in the surviving *archae* of Canterbury, Hereford and Lincoln. If the surviving pre-1275 bonds in these local *archae* are considered, it is clear that they almost all stipulated repayments in cash. After the *Statutum*, the bonds in the local *archae* show a clear swing towards payments in terms of commodities. This change can also be seen, for example, in the old and new *archae* at Exeter and Devizes.[127] It is, therefore, clear that between 1275 and the mid-1280s repayments to be made in money disappear while bonds requiring commodity repayments become the vogue. Peter Elman, however, was unconvinced that the bonds which specified commodity repayments really represented a change in Jewish business practice. He interpreted the commodity bonds as fictitious sales: 'For evidence of fictitious sales there is no need to seek far. The lists of 1290 are obviously full of these,

---

[121] Abrahams 1896, p. 90; WAM no. 6709.   [122] WAM no. 6709.
[123] Abrahams 1896, p. 101.   [124] Elman 1938a, p. 148; 1939, pp. 92, 93, 104.
[125] Elman 1939, p. 97.   [126] Lipman 1967, p. 164.
[127] PRO E/101/250/2, E/101/250/11; Mundill 1990a, p. 11.

bearing in mind the fact that all have the prices of corn and wool in round figures.'[128]

Vivian Lipman was also apprehensive about the suspiciously regular prices which were cited in the contracts. He illustrated this point by examining in detail the bonds of Isaac fil Deulecresse of Norwich. Isaac made fifteen bonds between 1278 and 1288 which recorded that he was owed 50 quarters of cereal (just over 5½ tons). All of these fifteen bonds were priced at 6s 8d per quarter. The remaining Norwich evidence reveals a further thirty-eight bonds: and only ten of these varied in price from the price of 6s 8d per quarter. More recently Joe Hillaby has expressed his concern about the standard price of 6s 8d per quarter quoted in many Hereford transactions. He sees this price as a penalty in case of non-delivery. He also finds it difficult to accept such a standard penalty clause when the grain market was 'characterised by a high degree of volatility'.[129] Both Vivian Lipman and Joe Hillaby were correct to look for price variation. It is well known that the price of medieval cereals fluctuated from year to year and from month to month. There is no need to look far for evidence of these types of fluctuation. In the Norfolk manor of Caistor, barley was sold at varying prices during 1299: at 4s 0d, 6s 0d and 8s 0d a quarter. At one point during the year, it dropped as low as 2s 8d per quarter. Professor Britnell has recently drawn attention to the fact that in Hampshire in 1288 the price of wheat was 3s 6d; in 1289 it went up to 4s 0d; in 1290 it increased to 6s 0d; and in 1291 it hit 8s 0d per quarter. Yet he also observed that thirteenth-century farmers were less responsive to prices than modern farmers.[130] Variations in the standard of the coinage, the quality and quantity of the harvest, wage-rates and the level of demand are just some of the many factors which would have led to price fluctuations.

Closer examination of the prices quoted in the extant 1290 contracts is clearly necessary. It was the volatility of the cereal market which made it important to include an agreed price in any transaction which involved grain. When a Jew was lending money expecting repayment in grain, he would have had only the most general indication of what was likely to be the market price of the grain when it was time for his debtor to repay the loan. It was, therefore, logical for him to use a round figure rather than a radically high or low figure in order to make the contract operable. When a Jew had it recorded in a bond that he required repayment of 'x' amount of cereal or wool at 'y' price, he was

---

[128] Elman 1939, p. 97; Hillaby 1990a, pp. 456–61; Stacey 1997; Brand forthcoming.
[129] Lipman 1967, pp. 164–8; Hillaby 1990a, p. 457.
[130] Farmer 1957, p. 210; Hillaby 1990a, pp. 456–7; Britnell 1993, p. 117.

doing two things. He was creating a situation in which all parties to the contract were aware of the value of what the Jew expected to be repaid, information which would be particularly valuable if there was ever the possibility of the debt being liquidated through a cash repayment; and he was also creating a situation in which, if there were any serious variations in market price from the round figure recorded, such variations could be taken into account when a final commodity payment was made. In some cases, the stipulated price could probably have been an indication of the quality of produce that the Jew wished to receive as repayment. Therefore, the existence of a large number of round figures in bonds is much less suspect than one might suppose. At the point of repayment, adjustments could be made in quantity and quality to ensure an appropriate repayment. In fact regular prices might even be expected.

As well as such arguments in explanation of the existence of a large number of round figures in the bonds, there is also another point which has to be raised. There is a considerable variation in the price levels quoted in the bonds. Even in the Norwich *archa*, which Vivian Lipman studied, there were creditors like Cresse fil Sampson of York, who, in 1289, made two bonds repayable in cereals not at 6s 8d per quarter but at 3s 4d and 1s 3d per quarter. Another Norwich Jew, Solomon fil Deulecresse, also contracted for 3s 4d per quarter.[131] At Lincoln, the bonds of the large cereal broker, Jacob of Brancegate, reveal that his price per quarter of *frumentum* fluctuated. In 1284, he was making contracts for 6s 8d per quarter. In 1285, he contracted for bonds which varied in the quoted price between 5s 0d and 6s 0d per quarter. In 1286, the price of his bonds seems to have returned to 6s 8d per quarter. By 1287, they varied between 6s 8d and 4s 0d and even go as low as 3s 6d. In 1289, he made one contract which stipulated that the price per quarter was to be 3s 0d.[132] Other provincial *archae* show even greater fluctuation in price levels both within particular years and between particular years. In 1286, the price per quarter quoted in bonds in the Bristol *archa* rose as high as 8s 0d a quarter in April and dropped to 4s 0d a quarter in May.[133] Again, in 1286, at Nottingham, the price was 5s 0d in August but 4s 0d in September.[134] Price fluctuation can be seen on a more general scale if, in those *archae* with enough surviving material, the mean average price per quarter of *frumentum* for each year is considered. Table 6 demonstrates such fluctuation.

It has, therefore, been possible to show that the suspicions voiced

---

[131] Lipman 1967, p. 165; PRO E/101/250/7.
[132] PRO E/101/250/12. [133] PRO E/101/250/4. [134] PRO E/101/250/8.

Table 6 *Mean price per quarter of corn recorded in provincial archae 1284–7*

	1284	1285	1286	1287
Bristol	6s 8d	6s 8d	6s 8d	6s 8d
Canterbury	5s 3d	5s 5d	5s 11½d	–
Exeter	6s 8d	6s 8d	7s ¼d	6s 8d
Hereford	–	–	6s 8d	–
Lincoln	6s 8d	5s 7d	6s 0d	5s 1½d
Norwich	5s 0d	6s 3d	5s 11d	5s 10d
Nottingham	–	5s 0d	4s 8d	–
Oxford	6s 1d	6s 8d	–	6s 8d
Winchester	6s 0d	6s 8d	–	–

Sources: PRO E/101/250/2; E/101/250/4–10; E/101/250/12.

about the regular prices quoted in commodity bonds are unfounded. The nature of Jewish business practice in commodity bonds was that such bonds were advance sale credits. This, in itself, explains why prices tended to be more regular than they would have been in simple contracts of sale, and there is, in any case, clear evidence of more short-term and long-term price variation than had formerly been recognised. Having produced a detailed response to the anxieties over the regular prices included in the transactions, it is now possible to deal with the other concerns about the nature of the commodity bonds in a more concise fashion.

It is difficult to understand why Peter Elman was concerned about the fact that some of the commodity bonds were only two years old; this only indicates that some contracts had not been honoured by debtors.[135] Given the nature of the 1290 evidence, it is, of course, the case that no one has any idea of what proportion of the commodity bonds contracted is represented by these bad debts. Vivian Lipman queried the time at which the commodities were supposed to be delivered to the creditor. He claimed that several of the commodity bonds enrolled on the Plea Roll of the *Scaccarium Judaeorum* envisaged deliveries to be made at Christmas and Easter. He regarded the use of these two festivals as settlement dates as suspicious and claimed that they were times of the year which were inappropriate to the cereal and wool trades. His doubts, however, appear to be groundless. The grain and wool trades were active throughout the year and these two festivals

---

[135] Elman 1939, p. 97.

were, in fact, normal dates of delivery and account for many medieval transactions, including those involving cereals and wool.[136]

It is, at last, possible to deal with the final argument which Vivian Lipman raised to argue for the artificiality of the commodity bonds. His view was that the Jewish wool contracts were, suspiciously, not as detailed as the *arras* of the larger Gentile merchants.[137] Such a difference can be easily explained by the fact that the vast majority of the evidence for Jewish wool contracts comes not from actual bonds but from the scribal extracts from bonds made up for governmental purposes. This will be demonstrated to be the case when a genuine recognizance for wool is considered in the next chapter. Yet Lipman accepted that some London Jews, who had easy access to legalise their transactions, made official genuine transactions. If this is the case then why should provincial Jewry and their transactions come under such suspicion?

Many of the commodity bonds recorded on the Jewish Plea Roll contain elements of detail which would not have been necessary if such transactions were spurious. One such example is a transaction which was witnessed by the Justices of the Jews in 1277. In late March of that year, Master Adam de Filby, canon of St Martin le Grand, bound himself to deliver twelve sacks of wool to Cresse fil Magister Elias of London. The contract stated that the wool was to be 'good wool, clean and well washed, without cot or any cheap fleece'. It was also clearly stipulated that two sacks were to come from Maldon in Essex, two from Denham in Buckinghamshire, four from Hertfordshire and four from Staffordshire. The sacks were to be delivered to Cresse or his attorney at his house in London, 'in full tale', before Lammas (1 August) 1277. The contract was guaranteed by Ralph Burell of Norfolk and witnessed by both Hamo Hauteyn and Robert de Ludham.[138] There can be little doubt about the genuineness of this particular transaction. Indeed it can be accepted that transactions such as this are genuine and do represent a real exchange of commodities as well as an element of profit.

Having dealt with all the counter-arguments which have led to the accepted view that Jewish commodity bonds were generally concealed money transactions, it is now time to produce the evidence which can be used to indicate that there was indeed a trade in commodities which these bonds reflect and which represents a shift in Jewish business practice after the *Statutum de Judeismo* of 1275. The first point which must be made on this more positive side of the argument is that all of the bonds which make up the evidence were made in front of *archa*

---

[136] Lipman 1967, pp. 166–8; Britnell 1993, p. 122.   [137] Lipman 1967, p. 167.
[138] Rigg, p. 94.

officials. Such officers kept a list of the bonds and, at times, debtors were distrained by local sheriffs or officials of the *Scaccarium Judaeorum* upon the evidence of the bonds made before these same officials. It is difficult to understand why all of these different sorts of officials would have co-operated with the Jews if they considered the bonds to be a circumvention of Edward's statute. It is even more difficult to believe that such officials would have been so ill informed as to have been fooled by the cunning camouflaging of Jewish moneylenders. After all, Edward did not destroy the *archa* system. By 1283, he had even set up a similar system for Christian merchants in which they were to register their debts and recognizances. If Edward had doubted the honesty or the acumen of his various officials, he could have closed the *archae* down. He did not. If Edward and his officials had been prepared to turn a blind eye to 'camouflaged money transactions', then it is very strange that in different *archae* different kinds of connivance with supposed money transactions were taking place in the mid and late 1280s. In *archae* like those at Lincoln and Nottingham there were straightforward money bonds being deposited alongside commodity bonds.[139] If such commodity bonds were indeed camouflaged money bonds, then it is difficult to imagine why, in a situation in which officials were prepared to oversee straightforward money bonds, they felt the need to maintain the pretence of concealing certain transactions by creating artificial commodity bonds. The Elman/Lipman view is therefore dependent upon an interpretation of the actions of royal officials which is difficult to accept. If such a view is to be sustained, contemporary officials have to be seen not only as either stupid or dishonest but also as inexplicably inconsistent.

The second point that can be raised in support of a large measure of real commodity bonding taking place after the *Statutum de Judeismo* lies in the evidence for known commodity exchanges between the Jews and their clients in the thirteenth century. It has long been admitted that there were small commodity payments which were made before the *Statutum de Judeismo*. Vivian Lipman cited some fifty cases from the 'Norwich Day Book' of the 1220s which stipulated small cereal repayments.[140] There are many other examples of debtors who owed small amounts of commodities during Henry III's reign, such as six loads of oats and two cartloads of hay, firewood, and three soams of wheat and even a cask of cider.[141] It is clear that bonds of this kind must

[139] PRO E/101/250/8, E/101/250/12; see Tables 4 and 5.
[140] Elman 1939, pp. 99–100; Lipman 1967, p. 64; Levy 1902b.
[141] WAM nos. 9158, 9123, 9124, 9127, 9170; PRO E/101/249/4, E/101/250/5, E/101/149/10; *PREJ3*, pp. 230–8; Davis 1881, p. 192.

be taken as genuine in the light of evidence such as the agreement reached in the *Scaccarium Judaeorum*, in 1274, between Deulecres fil Solomon of Stamford and William le Moyne in order to liquidate a debt. William was to give Deulecres £2 immediately and was still expected to give him the quarter of corn and quarter of barley at the assigned terms which the original contract had stipulated.[142] The Plea Roll of the *Scaccarium Judaeorum* also reveals a few examples before 1275 of Jews receiving small amounts of goods, nearly always in cereal, in return for what can only have been a cash advance. In all of these cases in which small amounts of produce are to be repaid, it is always expressed as an addition to a main cash payment. Vivian Lipman accepted such trifling commodity repayments as real and concluded: 'It was thus presumably arranged as a matter of convenience between creditor and debtor since the latter living in an agricultural community would find it convenient to meet part of his obligation in produce. Nor would there be any reason at this period to camouflage a usurious transaction.'[143]

Small commodity repayments paid to a Jewish creditor were easily explained, presumably because they could be dismissed as being primarily for personal consumption. But many genuine commodity bonds exist on the Jewish Plea Rolls and the other central governmental records which were recognizances of advance sale credits. A trade in large amounts of commodities did exist between Jew and Christian. There are several examples of genuine significant cereal transactions. These examples generally involve London Jews but they do also refer to the smaller provincial operator dealing in cereal.[144] In 1276, Jacob of Oxford released Lucas de Vyene from a debt for £16 and 20 quarters of corn. In the same year, Robert de Preston of Erle in Buckinghamshire promised to repay Manser fil Aaron 25 quarters of wheat on 28 March 1277.[145] Again in the same year, Simon, the son of Richard of

---

[142] *PREJ2*, p. 126.   [143] *PREJ2*, p. 22, 126 198 199, 265; Lipman 1967, p. 164.

[144] The examples cited are all from the period 1276–8. Cohen 1951, pp. lxxii–xciv provided an analysis of commodity bonds recorded on the Plea Rolls. She pointed out that the larger operators, Aaron fil Vives and Master Elias fil Magister Moses had a special royal licence (p. xcvi). Commodity bonds continue to be recorded on the Plea Rolls during the period 1282–7; PRO E/9/44 reveals Aaron fil Vives being owed large amounts of cereal from debtors in Essex, Lincolnshire, Surrey, Norfolk and Suffolk, Hertford and London, and at least thirty sacks of wool from Lincolnshire. It also revealed commodity debts to other Jews such as Elias fil Cresse, Aaron fil Isaac of Exeter, both described as Jews of London, Leon fil Moses of Clare, Jew of Stamford, Benedict Bateman fil Cresse and Cresse fil Cresse, Isaac le Evesk, Leon fil Jacob and Gamaliel of Oxford. PRO E/9/39 and E/9/40 also reveal more debts to Aaron fil Vives. PRO E/9/39 reveals a wool bond to Josce fil Saulot and cereal bonds which are owed to Cok Hagin and Manser fil Aaron. Both Elman and Lipman seem to have accepted these transactions as genuine.

[145] *PREJ3*, p. 203.

Dunmow in Essex, a *miles*, issued letters patent promising to repay the same Manser fil Aaron of London 40 quarters of 'good, dry, pure, clean and better wheat and without evil moisture'. Simon also promised to deliver the wheat to London at his own expense and cost.[146] It is not likely that any creditor contemplating a concealed monetary repayment would have bothered to include this stipulation and Lipman and Elman recognised this fact. In 1277, Robert son of Otho acknowledged that he owed Abraham fil Isaac of Gloucester 20 quarters of 'good, clean, wheat' which were to be delivered in two instalments, one at Christmas 1278 and the other the following Easter.[147] It is also evident that, in 1277, a London Jew, Master Elias, was contracting for wheat. Robert Springhald and Bartholomew le Cryur, his son, were in debt to Master Elias for 70 quarters of 'good, dry and pure wheat' which were payable to any merchant according to the measurement of the queen's bushel. The delivery or consignment of grain was to be made to Elias or his attorney at his house in London. Master Elias was owed a further 120 quarters of 'good, dry, clean and pure' wheat by Lady Alice de Bellocampo of Schipeton.[148] Payments to Jews in wheat were acknowledged by debtors from further afield. John de Crek of Norfolk acknowledged that he owed Aaron fil Vives 144 quarters of wheat in late September 1277.[149] Robert de Morteyng of Nottinghamshire also owed Aaron 100 quarters of wheat in November 1277.[150] In the same month, Aaron was to receive 200 soams of wheat from Robert de Acorne of Derbyshire or else Robert was to pay the cash value of the wheat. It is known that this debt was paid off, as William de Hamelton paid it on Robert's behalf and it was clearly recorded on the Plea Roll as 'paid'. The entry states that William de Hamelton had 'satisfied him [Aaron] for the two hundred quarters of wheat', although it is not known whether it was paid in cash or commodity.[151] Master Elias and Aaron fil Vives were also owed jointly 200 quarters of cereal by John de Meriette and John de Wacton of Somerset.[152]

Examples of Jews making genuine contracts for wool also survive on the Jewish Plea Rolls.[153] The case already referred to involving Master Adam de Filby and Cresse fil Magister Elias of London is a typical case of such a contract. It was transactions such as this that led Cecil Roth to observe that 'a number of wealthier financiers were able to turn to the wholesale trade in corn and wool'.[154] But, if the post-1275 commodity

---

[146] *PREJ3*, pp. 200.   [147] *PREJ3*, p. 292.
[148] '*Secundum mensuram ripe reginae*'; *PREJ3*, pp. 309–10; Mundill 1997.
[149] *PREJ3*, p. 278.   [150] *PREJ3*, p. 278.   [151] *Ibid.*
[152] *Ibid.*   [153] Lipman 1967, p. 166; Elman 1939, pp. 99–100.
[154] Abrahams 1894b, p. 250; Roth 1978, p. 73.

bonds for wool and cereal which were enrolled on the Plea Roll of the *Scaccarium Judaeorum* are accepted as genuine, then it remains difficult to understand why the commodity bonds in the provincial *archae* cannot also be accepted as real.

Another indication of the reality of the commodity bonds can be derived from an analysis of the dates at which cereal and wool bonds were contracted, according to the evidence of the 1290 *archa*. It is significant that such dates tend to fall into the specific periods of the wool and cereal calendar. In Canterbury, in 1284, the months in which the most cereal bonds were contracted were April and October. In 1285, the months were March and October; in 1286, September and October.[155] The Lincoln cereal bonds show that, in 1284, the month in which the most bonds were contracted was September. In 1285, most bonds were contracted in August. In 1286, the months were August and November. In 1287, most bonds were contracted in August.[156] From the evidence of the cereal bonds in these *archae*, it can be established that generally the months in which most of the cereal bonds were contracted were August, September and October. Evidence from the Lincoln *archa* demonstrates that the busiest period for the contracting of wool bonds was between April and June.[157] In the analysis of such a pattern, the first thing to be remembered is that the information used is confined to unpaid debts. This fact makes it difficult to interpret the pattern itself. It is, however, clear that the commodity bonds for which information is available tended to be made in the period of or immediately after the harvest, or of or after the clip. Such a situation may be the result of Jews bonding with individuals whose medium of repayment, such as wool or grain, was subject to annual production. The situation may also be explained by the fact that the debts which were most likely to remain unpaid were those debts contracted by individuals at the furthest point in time away from the next harvest or clip. There may be other reasons which explain this pattern. However, it is sufficient to indicate that, for whatever reason, the chronology of wool and cereal bonding closely follows the chronology of the agricultural year as it relates to those specific commodities.[158]

A further indication of the reality of the commodity bonds could come from an analysis of the geographical distribution of the clients who chose to bond with the Jews in specific commodities. Such an analysis will be made in chapter 7. However, it is not only the types of

---

[155] PRO E/101/250/6.   [156] PRO E/101/250/12.   [157] *Ibid.*
[158] Lloyd 1973, pp. 2–3. The wool season ran roughly from 24 June to 3 August.

clients involved in commodity bonds that indicate the general nature of such bonds, for similar patterns can be detected in the ways in which individual Jewish creditors developed an interest in a particular commodity. This will be examined in more detail below. However this divergence can be seen in general terms by examining the interests of Jewish communities. Thus, the Canterbury *archa* concentrates on cereal bonds whilst the Lincoln *archa* has an understandable predominance of wool bonds. As well as these general interests of particular communities, individual Jewish preferences can also be seen at a local level. Hence, despite Lincoln's general preference for wool, some Lincoln Jews quite clearly chose to concentrate their activities upon the corn market which would obviously have been as active in Lincoln as in any other town. Others specialised in securing an interest in the particularly expansive Lincoln wool market.[159] One specific example of the sort of connections which individual Jews developed in the trades in which they chose to concentrate their activities comes from a bond in the Norwich *archa* which shows that a certain unnamed Norwich Jew was owed, in 1286, 20 quarters of wheat priced at 8s 0d per quarter by Thomas Galewynde, Thomas *capellanus* of Forhoe Carleton and a certain Geoffrey of Ely who is interestingly described as 'wheat merchant staying in' Forhoe Carleton.[160]

It has already proved necessary to look closely at the price levels quoted in commodity bonds in order to respond to suggestions of excessive price regularity. There are, however, other elements in the pricing policy of Jews which give further indications of the reality of the commodity bonds. Although, in the wool trade, the price per sack of wool could fluctuate within any given year, it is likely that it fluctuated much less than cereal prices. In the wool trade, there was clearly a much more predictable level of supply. In this context, it is therefore even more impressive that Lincoln wool bonds do show price fluctuation, although it is of course possible that such variation was the result of demand for wools of different quality. It is interesting to consider the prices paid by Jews who made contracts for wool in Lincoln between 1288 and 1290. Figure 1 clearly shows that over this period there was an element of price fluctuation during the year. The higher and the lower prices quoted in the Lincoln bonds are both generally above T. H. Lloyd's national average.[161] This is a particularly interesting fact which may demonstrate that Jewish wool brokers were operating with an idea of a high price level. It may have been that they intended to secure good-quality wool

[159] Power 1941, pp. 22–3; Ryder 1981, pp. 16–29; PRO E/101/250/9.
[160] '*bladi mercator manens in*'; PRO E/101/250/7.   [161] Lloyd 1973, p. 38.

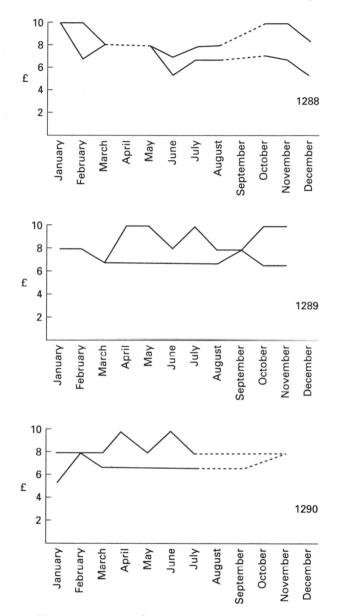

Figure 1 Variation in price of wool bonds contracted in the Lincoln *archa*,
1288–90. *Source:* PRO E/101/250/12.

or the price might have been set to cope with short-term fluctuations in wool prices. Either way it is likely that the price was set in order to make a profit.[162]

It is now time to consider the details of commodity trading, namely the granting of advance sale credits, in a little more detail. All of the indications of the genuine nature of the commodity bonds discussed above suggest that the Jews, as a result of the *Statutum de Judeismo*, responded to the latter's economic sanctions by attempting to find a place within the wool and cereal trades. Jews found different places within the commercial hierarchy. A few may, indeed, have become important merchants in a specific field or in a variety of commercial activities. Many Jews, however, found a role as reasonably small operators. In the wool trade such a role probably involved buying and selling *lana collecta*. The purchasing of *lana collecta* was open to anyone who had capital to invest and somewhere to store the wool. Such wool would then be sold off to larger contractors who might, for a variety of reasons, have had difficulties from time to time in fulfilling their pre-arranged *arras*. It is abundantly clear that many of the provincial Jewish wool contracts were for small amounts of wool. Such was the case with the sack of wool which Hugh of Kendal found amongst the possessions of some condemned Northampton Jews in 1281. The sack, which was priced at £9 6s 8d, was found to belong to Peytevin fil Sampson, a Jew of London. The king ordered that it should be sold and that some of the clearer debts in the treasury should be given to Peytevin as compensation.[163] Such transactions involving small amounts of wool were informal and their sale would not have left any record.

Less is known of the cereal trade than the wool trade in the thirteenth century. It is, however, easy to see how Jews might have acquired cereals from the sorts of producers who lived in rural areas and who had always been their clients. After the lord's harvest had been completed, many smaller producers reaped their own harvests or helped others to bring in harvests from their land. Cereal in some quantity could therefore find its way into the hands of both bond and freeman. It could be acquired as a crop reaped from a small strip of land or even as a reward for taking in someone else's harvest. By the thirteenth century, the custom of rewarding harvest labour with sheaves of corn was both old and widespread. Sheaves were given for each half acre reaped or for a complete day's work. Grain was also acquired as a reward for binding, carting, stacking, threshing and even milling.[164] Cereal was also,

[162] PRO E/101/250/12.   [163] Power 1941, pp. 44–5; *CCR 1279–1288*, p. 95.
[164] Jones 1977, pp. 2–14, 98–107.

understandably, ever present in urban communities. Inventories taken in Colchester in 1295 and 1300 show that nearly every house possessed some quantity of grain of various kinds.[165] Small transactions in cereal were, like wool transactions, also often informal and left no record behind them.[166] In the light of such evidence, there seems no reason why debtors should not have been repaying their creditors in cereals. Indeed in February 1279 John de Gornay appeared at the Norwich *archa* with £5, 1 quarter of wheat and 2 quarters of oats to repay an agreement made with Abraham fil Deulecresse. John was making such a payment because in return Abraham had agreed to release him of all his debts.[167] Jews who received cereal in return for such transactions or loans might well have passed it on at a profit to larger operators within the grain trade. Thus, there was clearly a place in both the cereal and the wool trade for Jewish involvement at the levels evidenced by the commodity bonds. The evidence produced above clearly indicates that certain Jews had, by 1290, begun to play a role in these trades.

There is some evidence to show that Jews had wool and grain in their possession. It is also clear that Christians used such commodities as a medium of exchange. Alice Beardwood has shown that some of the repayments of Bishop Langton's recognizances (1295–1307) were made in wool or grain.[168] In this respect, it is particularly striking that the transactions recorded in the Jewish *archae* were not so very different from Gentile transactions made in accordance with the Statute of Merchants of 1283. It has been intimated above that the Jewish bond was in fact a 'relative' of the Christian recognizance and indeed it was a very similar transaction.[169] A comparison of the bonds of William of Hepham, a Lincolnshire merchant, with those of a Lincolnshire Jew, Ursellus Levi, is particularly revealing. In 1284, William registered four loans in Lincoln which were to be repaid in wool. These loans show that John and Stephen Ducket owed him one sack of wool priced at £9 6s 8d, Suspiro of Bayou owed him one sack at the same price, Richard of Thoresby owed him half a sack priced at £5 and Richard Rudde of Barton (who is also known to have had dealings with Lincolnshire Jews) owed him two sacks of wool priced at £9 6s 8d. In February 1287, John, the parson of the church at Chedde, owed Ursellus one sack of

---

[165] Cutts 1888, pp. 104–9.   [166] Britnell 1993, p. 98.

[167] Rokeah, forthcoming, entry 974–5: although the case was dated 1285 it was stated that John had paid the grain and that the accepted price for the wheat per quarter in 1279 had been 5s 0d and for the oats 2s 0d.

[168] Beardwood 1955, p. 56

[169] *Statutes*, vol. I, pp. 53–4, 100; *CCR 1279–1288*, p. 297; Salzman 1931, pp. 101–3; Plucknett 1949, pp. 139–48; Rabinowitz 1956, pp. 257–63; Nightingale 1990, pp. 564–65. The certificates of Statute Staple for Edward's reign run from PRO c/241 to c/241/54.

wool priced at £6 13s 4d. In July 1288, Geoffrey of Funtaynes owed Ursellus and his brother Jacob six sacks of wool priced at £6 13s 4d per sack. In May 1290, Thomas of Poynton owed Ursellus half a sack priced at £4. In June 1290, Thomas fil Peter of Lincoln owed Ursellus one sack priced at £10 and, in July 1290, William de Brettevill of Houton owed Ursellus half a sack priced at £4.[170] Thus, it is clear that a Christian merchant was operating at the same level in the market and contracting in the same manner as a Jew: both were behaving as *legales mercatores* and making genuine transactions.

It accordingly seems highly unlikely that the commodity bonds in the *archae* in 1290 were not genuine agreements. It seems more probable that they, in fact, represent advance sale credits in wool and cereal which would have involved the Jews, at some point, in a significant amount of trading activity. Certainly some Jews, it seems, therefore obeyed the *Statutum de Judeismo* and tempered their moneylending concerns with increased trading interests. It is now necessary to ask to what degree the Jews were successful in maintaining their social and economic status through this change in their activities. Because of its nature, the evidence of the surviving details of pre- and post-1275 bonds is very difficult to use in this context.[171] The survival of a large number of bonds in an *archa* may, after all, be an indication either of a large amount of unpaid debt or of a large amount of bonding activity or of both. The situation is further complicated by the fact that an *archa* sealed at a specific point in time is always likely to contain a proportionately higher ratio of unpaid debts from the recent as opposed to the distant past. Nevertheless, there are perhaps some indications in the surviving evidence that will make it possible to gauge the economic impact on the Jews of the transfer to trading activities which the *Statutum* inspired.

Bonds remaining in the *archae* in 1290 would, all things being equal, have inevitably become more numerous in the years approaching 1290 (see Figure 2), but the date range of bonds and tallies in the *novae archae* shows that there was a significant rise in the number of bonds made per annum during the period which commenced in 1284 in comparison with the period before that date. This seems to provide evidence that the *Statutum de Judeismo* initially had had a depressive effect upon Jewish business until what was probably some sort of revival in the early 1280s. It also, incidentally, seems that the pattern of surviving Jewish bonds

---

[170] Bischoff 1975, pp. 244–8; PRO E/101/250/12.
[171] PRO E/101/250/2–12; Mundill 1987, p. 111.

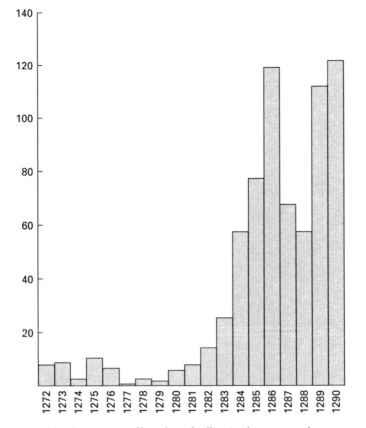

Figure 2   The date range of bonds and tallies in the *novae archae*, 1272–90. The graph represents the vast majority of bonds deposited in the *novae archae*. Twenty-eight bonds and tallies deposited in *novae archae* are undated. Four bonds contracted in 1261 and 1267 and two in 1271 and deposited in the Cambridge *archa* have been omitted. *Source:* PRO E/101/250/2–12.

had more to do with the level of Jewish activity than with the level of Christian default on debts. However, this can only be borne out by examining the varying economic fortunes of provincial Jewry on a local level.

Chapter 6

THE ECONOMIC FORTUNES OF PROVINCIAL JEWRIES UNDER EDWARD I

In order to assess the effects of Edward I's experiment it is now time to turn to an examination of several Jewish communities and to see how they fared during the closing decades of Jewish presence in England.[1] Such a study will consider the social structure and financial resources of particular Jewries and the ability of their financiers to continue to provide credit for Christians. As has been shown, Edward I drew on the financial resources of his Jewish subjects, but he apparently did not consider them to be as financially important as had earlier kings: for instance although he taxed them he never mortgaged his Jewries.[2] Edward placed different financial pressures on his Jews. An examination of what the Jewries rendered to the Crown *in toto*, especially during 1278 and 1279, has already shown how the Anglo-Jewish community suffered financially and was forced to pay a massive individual fine as a result of the coin-clipping allegations.[3] It cannot therefore be denied that the Edwardian Jewries were generally in decline and under much economic and social pressure. Yet some seem to have fared better than others. Indeed the impact of Edward I's reforms of the Jewry are best illustrated on a local level. Such an examination will naturally confirm the view that Edward I's reign was very clearly a time of changing fortunes for the English Jew.

Most obviously perhaps, the Jews experienced major structural changes and upheavals as Edward I's own specific legislation

---

[1] See above chapters 1 and 3 and Appendix 1.

[2] Denholm-Young 1947, p. 80 shows that in 1254 Henry III 'sold' the Jewry to Richard of Cornwall; Prestwich 1988, p. 38 shows that Henry III mortgaged the Jewry to Prince Edward on 4 June 1262; *CPR 1258–1266*, p. 233; PRO E/101/249/10; Pearl 1990, p. 90; Denholm-Young 1947, p. 120 shows that in 1263 when Prince Edward had received the Jewry he granted them to the Beraldi of Cahors; Roth 1978, p. 67 shows that one of Henry III's last deeds was to entrust the Jews to Edmund of Almain.

[3] See above, chapter 4; Salzman 1968, pp. 57–8; Roth 1978, pp. 75–6; Prestwich 1988, p. 245; Rokeah 1973; 1974; 1975; 1990; 1993.

concerning their financial practices and position in society was implemented.[4] One of the harbingers of the new policies was the total exclusion of Jews from certain of the queen mother's dower towns early in 1275.[5] However, as we have seen, the main thrust of Edward I's Jewish policy, the so-called 'Edwardian Experiment', was directed at making the Jews conduct business affairs in a way which Christian society could tolerate.[6] Ironically Edward did not close down the *archa* system or even banish his Jewish subjects in 1275. Instead he encouraged them to trade and clearly expected them to use the existing *archa* system for their business. Many subsequent historians have seen the Statute of 1275 as the final blow for his Jewish subjects and have claimed that Edward thereafter imposed impossible demands upon them.[7] It is indeed apparent that during his reign most Jewish families were probably in financial decline: many suffered from the physical pogroms of 1278 and 1279; many had to move from their towns of residence; many, like the 'poor Jews of Northampton', found their private capital exhausted by the Edwardian tallages.[8] However, the proof for wider claims about the failure of Edward's Jewish policy and the financial decline of the Jewries has to be sought in an examination of the actual financial dealings of the English Jewry after 1275. Were their transactions fewer in number? Were the transactions less valuable? Were they in accordance with the spirit of the law? Such questions can only be answered by considering the local evidence in full.

Attention has already been drawn to the changes in Jewish economic activity which were brought about by the new policies. After 1275 few possibilities of utilising their capital were open to Jews.[9] Jewish financial dealings were redirected towards using the more easily palatable recognizance or certificate of Staple. Edward, however, did grant a few special licences to trade; and Jews who carried out business according to the tenor of the law were still allowed to have the protection of the king's justice and the Court of the Jewish

---

[4] Cohen 1951, p. xlviii. Specific Jewish legislation issued prior to Edward's reign such as the mandate of 1253, the Provisions of the Jewry of 1269, the mandate of 1271 as well as the Statute of the Jewry issued in April of 1275 (Easter, 14 April 1275) were probably only starting to take effect by late 1275. See chapter 5 and Appendix II.

[5] Mundill 1993, p. 48; Roth 1978, p. 82; Dobson 1993, pp. 17–18.

[6] Appendix II lines 71–4; Roth 1978, pp. 70–3; *Chronica Johannis de Oxenedes*, p. 247.

[7] Elman 1938a; Stacey 1987b, pp. 67–8 suggested that the economic explanation for the Expulsion should be reviewed; Pearl 1990, pp. 112–13 examined the views of Lord Justice Coke and William Prynne via those of Tovey; Roth 1949, p. 4; 1978, pp. 72–3. Belloc 1928, pp. 218–19; Atkinson 1912, p. 16.

[8] See above, chapter 4; PRO E/401/1567.

[9] See above, chapter 5; Hatcher and Miller 1995, p. 386.

Table 7 *The values of the surviving Jewish financial transactions, 1262–90*

Cambridge				Norwich			
1240	£1,833	6s	8d	1227	£1,433	6s	8d
1262	£ 183	6s	8d	1262	£ 280	0s	0d
1290	£ 283	6s	8d	1290	£ 646	13s	4d
Lincoln				**Hereford**			
1240	£4,000	0s	0d	1262	£ 100	0s	0d
1262	£ 426	13s	4d	1275	£ 440	0s	0d
1290	£2,600	0s	0d	1290	£2,000	0s	0d
Nottingham				**Devizes**			
1262	£ 52	6s	8d	1275	£ 265	4s	8d
1290	£ 518	4s	4d	1290	£ 126	16s	8½d
Exeter				**Oxford**			
1262	£ 38	9s	4d	1262	£ 80	18s	2d
1275	£1,023	19s	8d	1275	£ 397	0s	0d
1290	£ 211	3s	0d	1290	£ 452	4s	8d

Elman used approximations for several of his figures. My own research shows the figures for 1262 to be generally less. PRO E/101/249/10 reveals that the Cambridge total was £156 18s 0d, Norwich was £227 2s 10d, Lincoln was £405 14s 2d and Hereford was £104 0s 4d. Similarly the 1290 figures are slightly incorrect. For further discussion of the figures for 1290 for Cambridge see Dobson 1993, p. 19; Norwich see Lipman 1967, pp. 178–80; Hereford see Mundill 1987, pp. 223–35 and Hillaby 1990c; Lincoln see Mundill 1987, pp. 284–91. The figures for Nottingham, Devizes, Exeter and Oxford are taken from PRO E/101/249/10, E/101/250/8, E/101/250/11, E/101/250/2, E/101/249/31, E/101/249/32 and E/101/250/9.
Sources: Elman 1936, p. 85 (Cambridge, Norwich, Lincoln, Hereford); PRO E/101/249/10, E/101/250/8, E/101/250/11, E/101/250/2, E/101/249/31, E/101/249/32, E/101/250/9 (Nottingham, Devizes, Exeter, Oxford).

Exchequer.[10] Before turning to the studies of these separate communities, it must be emphasised once again that Edward's reign was indeed a watershed for the Anglo-Jewish community.[11] It was a community which was numerically in decline, frightened and intimidated by new legislation and directives, fearful that one day local officials would enforce the new laws to the final letter.[12] The evidence of how Jewish capital was utilised in the leading provincial Jewish communities will now be considered in detail.

---

[10] Mundill 1990a, pp. 2–3.
[11] Elman 1936, pp. 83–5; Stacey 1985, p. 205; Dobson 1979, p. 36.
[12] See above, chapter 2 and Rokeah 1990, pp. 96–7; Lipman 1967, pp. 65, 76–7, 168–71.

As Table 7 illustrates, Peter Elman has already demonstrated the comparative decline in the fortunes of several different Jewries. He took as his evidence the total value of the various transactions which were recorded in the *archae* and tabulated the more readily available evidence for Cambridge, Lincoln, Norwich and Hereford.[13] Elman's straightforward comparison of values before and after 1250 formed the basis for his general hypothesis that the value of business in the provincial *archae* declined in late thirteenth-century England.[14] It is certainly true, as Professors Dobson and Stacey have demonstrated, that compared with the first half of the thirteenth century Jewish business was no longer as profitable as it had been; but the question of economic decline is still one which needs some qualification.[15] For example the Hereford figures would seem to indicate a rise in the value of business between 1262 and 1290. A similar picture is also true of the Oxford community. Such comparisons accordingly require much careful qualification. For example the evidence for Norwich in 1224–7 was taken from a distinctive source, the Norwich Day Book, essentially a list of bonds.[16] However, the figures for 1240 from Lincoln and Cambridge were taken from full *archae* scrutinies and are probably as representative as any evidence can be of the total value of business in the *archae* at that time. It must be remembered too that 1240 saw the only tallage of the thirteenth century to be collected in full.[17] The 1262 evidence, which gives a view of Jewish financial activity before the civil war, also needs some careful qualification before it can be accepted as a useful indicator.[18] These 1262 samples will be discussed below and will become the basis for the detailed attempt at comparing the values of provincial *archae* to be carried out later in this chapter. The 1275 evidence similarly also needs some thoughtful qualification.[19] For obvious reasons, the *archae*

---

[13] Elman 1936, p. 85.

[14] Elman 1936, p. 1. Developed further in Elman 1938a, pp. 147, 152.

[15] Elman 1936, pp. 83–5; Stacey 1988; Dobson 1979, p. 36.

[16] PRO E/101/249/10 membrane 5, E/101/250/5; *PREJ3*, pp. 230–8; Mundill 1987, pp. 204–44; PRO E/101/249/10 membrane 7, E/101/249/32, E/101/250/9; Levy 1902b; Lipman 1967, pp. 84–6 and 187–225; WAM nos. 6686, 6687, 6693, 9012.

[17] PRO E/101/249/3, E/101/249/4; Stacey 1985, particularly pp. 183, 200; 1988, p. 139.

[18] PRO E/101/249/10.

[19] Canterbury: WAM nos. 9015, 9019, 9020, 9021, 9022, 9025, 9026, 9028, 9034, 9036, 9039, 9042, 9043, 9046, 9047, 9057, 9058, 9086, 9088, 9089, 9090, 9091, 9103, 9104, 9105, 9116, 9118, 9119, 9120, 9121, 9123, 9124, 9125, 9126, 9127, 9139, 9156, 9157, 9158, 9159, 9172, 9173, 9174, 9175, 9176; Exeter: PRO E/101/249/31, E/101/250/2; Hereford: *PREJ3*, pp. 230–8, PRO E/101/250/5; Lincoln: WAM nos 9014, 9027, 9032, 9054, 9087, 9092, 9093, 9094, 9095, 9097, 9098, 9100, 9117, 9130, 9131, 9132, 9135, 9137, 9140, 9142, 9143, 9144, 9145, 9146, 9147, 9148, 9150, 9160, 9161, 9162, 9163, 9164, 9165, 9167, 9168, 9169, 9170; Oxford: PRO E/101/249/32; York: PRO C/47/9/49; Colchester: PRO C/47/9/48; Devizes: PRO E/101/250/11; Northampton: PRO E/101/249/33.

evidence for 1290 in Table 7 can be taken as being a fairly true reflection of Jewish business which had been registered in the *archae* on the eve of the Expulsion: this issue too will be discussed below.

The evidence for Jewish financial dealings during the thirty years before the Expulsion is therefore somewhat fragmentary and piecemeal. It depends on the survival of documents such as bonds and *archa* scrutinies which naturally will not give a full record of all transactions. Indeed, it is fair to say that such evidence will only show the tip of the iceberg for at times it depends on the chance selection of individual bonds for tallage purposes. Moreover, it also relies on whether the bonds were actually placed in the various *archae* or not, and of course it finally depends on the vagaries of survival. The evidence does not show, for instance, whether the Jews became involved in illegal transactions which were withheld from the *archae*: certainly no such transaction has survived. However the evidence can reveal how many Jews were still involved in making financial transactions and whether their dealings were becoming worth more or less. The evidence can also help to indicate the social structure of the individual Jewish community. When considering the extant bonds which were taken into the king's hand in 1291, B. L. Abrahams observed that Jewish social structure seemed to be that of a plutocracy.[20] This is not unexpected. There had, as many subsequent studies have shown, always been outstandingly rich Jewish business men whose transactions reflected their status and wealth.[21] Yet there were also several smaller lenders or traders; and it could be expected that many of these would not have survived the Edwardian Experiment.[22] Naturally there were also some Jews who had perhaps hazarded only a few loans as well as those who have left no record of lending behind them.[23]

Thus the surviving evidence for the financial dealings of the various different Jewish communities permits a fleeting estimate to be made of the social structure and comparative wealth of several communities at different times. Table 8 shows a complete picture of the survival of financial transactions for the different provincial Jewries. The paucity of evidence for the London and York communities is regrettable. Admittedly evidence of bonds made within twenty communities survives in a survey made in 1262. This particular record naturally reflects the type of business being conducted in Henry III's reign on the eve of the baronial

---

[20] Abrahams 1896, p. 82.

[21] Aaron of Lincoln: Jacobs 1899; Aaron of York: Adler 1933; Benedict of Lincoln: Roth 1948; Elias Menahem: Roth 1946 and Mundill 1997; Hamo of Hereford: Mundill 1987, pp. 211–18 and Hillaby 1990b; Aaron le Blund: Mundill 1987, pp. 235–40 and Hillaby 1990c.

[22] Mundill 1987, chapters IV, V and VI.   [23] Roth 1962, pp. 21–33; Rokeah 1993.

Table 8 *Surviving evidence of Jewish financial transactions, 1262–90*[a]

1262	1275/1276	1290
Canterbury (102)	Canterbury bonds (45)[b]	Canterbury (95)[m]
Exeter (15)	Exeter (136)[c]	Exeter (45)[n]
	Exeter Old Chest (143)[d]	
Hereford (44)	Hereford (79)[e]	Hereford (77)[o]
	Hereford Old Chest (205)[f]	
Lincoln (151)	Lincoln bonds (37)[g]	Lincoln (252)[p]
Oxford (45)	Oxford (95)[h]	Oxford (47)[q]
York (24)	York (26)[i]	York (lost)
Colchester (20)	Colchester (44)[j]	Colchester (lost)
	Devizes (lost)	
	Devizes Old Chest (28)[k]	Devizes (29)[r]
Norwich (46)	Norwich (lost)	Norwich (60)[s]
Nottingham (12)		Nottingham (60)[t]
Bristol (9)	Bristol (lost)	Bristol (19)[u]
Cambridge (56)		Cambridge (36)[v]
Winchester (39)	Winchester (lost)	Winchester (10)[w]
Marlborough (6)		
Stamford (26)		
Worcester (22)		
Gloucester (7)	Gloucester (lost)	
Bedford (18)		Bedford (lost)
Wilton (23)	Wilston (lost)	
London (254)		London (lost)
	Sudbury (lost)	
	Northampton[l]	Northampton (lost)
		Huntingdon (lost)
		Ipswich (lost)
		Coventry/Warwick (lost)

The numbers in brackets indicate the number of bonds included in each sample

[a] 1262 tallage payments are all on PRO E/101/249/10. In some cases the number of bonds is an approximation owing to the fact that there are lacunae on the document and some are illegible because of this. The source for the towns in which scrutinies were to be carried out is *Calendar of the Close Rolls* 1276 pp. 126–263. The arrivals of the various *archae* at Westminster in 1290 are recorded on PRO E/101/249/29.

[b] The Canterbury bonds which this sample comprises are WAM nos. 9015, 9019, 9020, 9021, 9022, 9025, 9026, 9028, 9024, 9036, 9039, 9042, 9043, 9046, 9047, 9057, 9058, 9086, 9088, 9089, 9090, 9091, 9103, 9104, 9105, 9116, 9118, 9119, 9120, 9121, 9123, 9124, 9125, 9126, 9127, 9139, 9156, 9157, 9158, 9159, 9172, 9173, 9174, 9175, 9176.

[c] The Exeter Scrutiny is PRO E/101/249/31.

[d] The Exeter Old Chest is PRO E/101/250/2.

[e] The Hereford Scrutiny is recorded on *PREJ3*, pp. 230–8.

Table 8 (*cont.*)

f The Hereford Old Chest is PRO E/101/250/5.

g The Lincoln bonds which this sample comprises are WAM nos. 9014, 9027, 9032, 9054, 9087, 9092, 9093, 9094, 9095, 9097, 9098, 9100, 9117, 9130, 9131, 9132, 9135, 9137, 9140, 9142, 9143, 9144, 9145, 9146, 9147, 9148, 9150, 9160, 9161, 9162, 9163, 9164, 9165, 9167, 9168, 9169, 9170.

h The Oxford Scrutiny is PRO E/101/249/32.

i The York Scrutiny is PRO C/147/9/49.

j The Colchester Scrutiny is PRO C/147/9/48.

k The Devizes Old Chest is PRO E/101/250/11.

l The Northampton Scrutiny is E/101/249/33.

m PRO E/101/250/6.   n PRO E/101/250/2.

o PRO E/101/250/5.   p PRO E/101/250/12.

q PRO E/101/250/9.   r PRO E/101/250/11.

s PRO E/101/250/7.   t PRO E/101/250/8.

u PRO E/101/250/4.   v PRO E/101/250/3.

w PRO E/101/250/10.

wars. However, this source remains merely a list of the bonds granted to the Crown by the Jewish communities, possibly in connection with tallage in 1262. It is not a full *archae* scrutiny and thus naturally gives a distorted view of the total value of Jewish business.

Some fragmentary evidence survives from early in Edward I's reign. Much of it was probably recorded for tallage purposes. Walter of Helyun's scrutiny of the Hereford *archa*, dating from December 1275, has survived intact.[24] A scrutiny made in Colchester on the feast of St Thomas the Martyr (29 December) 1275 by the abbot of St John's, Colchester, and Walter of Essex in front of the Jewish and Christian chirographers of Colchester has also survived intact and forms one of the few records of the Colchester Jewry's dealings. It lists forty-four separate bonds belonging to eleven Jews. The value of the bonds was £584 3s 4d and they all demanded payment in cash.[25] Six of the actual bonds mentioned in the roll of this scrutiny have also themselves survived, presumably passing from the royal treasury to Westminster Abbey where they are now housed.[26] A similar scrutiny for York made by John de Stapleton and the abbot of St Mary's, dated early January 1276, has also survived.[27] A scrutiny for Northampton has survived in a very fragmentary form and records the debts of five Jews.[28] The scrutiny for Exeter made by John Wyger and Robert de Evesham on 14 February 1276 has also survived and runs to four membranes recording the debts to ten Jews who hold 136 bonds.[29] The scrutiny of the

[24] *PREJ3*, pp. 230–8.   [25] PRO C/47/9/48; Mundill 1987, pp. 72–3.
[26] WAM nos. 6698, 9017, 9031, 9052, 9056, 9059.   [27] PRO C/47/9/49.
[28] PRO E/101/249/33.   [29] PRO E/101/249/31.

Oxford *archa* is similarly extant but is in bad condition; it records details of approximately ninety-five debts of the Jews worth a face value of £397.[30]

Two collections of actual bonds can be added to these different scrutinies. These surviving bonds, in the Westminster Abbey muniments, reflect Jewish financial practice in Canterbury and Lincoln just before the 1275 Statute. There are some eighty documents which relate to the Canterbury Jewish community and forty which relate to the Lincoln community.[31] As discussed in the previous chapter, there is also the evidence of what are described as 'Old Chests'. This type of evidence remains for Devizes, Exeter and Hereford and these bonds were collected in 1290 with the contents of the other provincial *archae*.[32]

Surviving evidence for Jewish financial dealings at the end of Edward's reign is more complete and straightforward, but again there are some major gaps. As has already been observed, *archae* were brought in from twenty towns in 1290, but complete lists of their contents have survived for only eleven towns, namely Bristol, Cambridge, Canterbury, Devizes, Exeter, Hereford, Lincoln, Norwich, Nottingham, Oxford, and Winchester.[33]

Clearly it is only possible here to concentrate on those provincial Jewries which have the fullest evidence for the period of Edward's reign. Such centres include, above all, the Jewish communities of Canterbury, Hereford and Lincoln. Fairly complete sequences of evidence also survive for Oxford and Exeter, and more sparse evidence for Devizes and Nottingham. The Norwich community has already been discussed in great detail by Vivian Lipman.[34] The communities of Bristol, Gloucester and Winchester do not have enough records to merit full discussion.[35] Before proceeding to a survey of the Canterbury, Devizes, Exeter, Hereford, Lincoln, Nottingham and Oxford

---

[30] PRO E/101/249/32.
[31] The Canterbury bonds are WAM nos. 9015, 9019, 9020, 9021, 9022, 9025, 9026, 9028, 9034, 9036, 9039, 9042, 9043, 9046, 9047, 9057, 9058, 9086, 9088, 9089, 9090, 9091, 9103, 9104, 9105, 9116, 9118, 9119, 9120, 9121, 9123, 9124, 9125, 9126, 9127, 9139, 9156, 9157, 9158, 9159, 9172, 9173, 9174, 9175, 9176; the Lincoln bonds are WAM nos. 9014, 9027, 9032, 9054, 9087, 9092, 9093, 9094, 9095, 9097, 9098, 9100, 9117, 9130, 9131, 9132, 9135, 9137, 9140, 9142, 9143, 9144, 9145, 9146, 9147, 9148, 9150, 9160, 9161, 9162, 9163, 9164, 9165, 9167, 9168, 9169, 9170.
[32] PRO E/101/250/11, E/101/250/2, E/101/250/5. [33] PRO E/101/249/29.
[34] Lipman 1967.
[35] Bristol: PRO E/101/249/10 membrane 4 records nine bonds owing to Bristol Jews; PRO E/1011/250/4 records the details of nineteen bonds owing to Bristol Jews; Adler 1928 gives wide coverage of the history of the Bristol community; Gloucester: PRO E/101/249/10 membrane 10 records details of seven transactions; the history of the Gloucester community is being compiled by Hillaby; Winchester: PRO E/101/249/10 membrane 13 records thirty-nine

England's Jewish Solution

communities during the last few decades of Jewish presence, it must be stressed that the fortunes of each community are obviously different. They were subject to variable geographical, social and economic influences. They were also subject to the economic success of the town, the richness of its hinterland, even the seasonal vagaries of the local harvests. Many other local factors must include the extent to which the inhabitants of those towns made use of Jewish finance and even how much the Christian townsmen resented the Jewish community. It is most revealing if tantalising to consider the rather sparse evidence for the dealings of the London and York communities before examining the other communities.

LONDON

The study of the London Jewish community poses many problems, above all because of the lack of surviving evidence. It also seems that there were several places in which a London Jew might have recorded his or her transactions. He might for instance have deposited his bonds for safe keeping with the constable of the Tower of London or in the London *archa*, or he could have enrolled his dealings as recognizances on the great governmental records at Westminster such as the Close Rolls or even the Jewish Plea Rolls themselves.[36] Such opportunities were open to all Jews but in the case of the latter alternative, not many London Jews seem to have taken advantage of their proximity to Westminster, with the possible exception of the richer London financiers such as Aaron fil Vives and Master Elias Menahem.[37] Despite all these possibilities for the legal registration of their transactions, there are only two surviving samples of business carried out by London's Jews which are worth consideration. One comes from the tallage which they gave in 1240 and the other from the bonds which were given to the

---

transactions owed to Winchester Jews; Turner 1954 deals briefly with the Winchester Jewry; Adler 1942 deals specifically with Benedict of Winchester.

[36] PRO E/101/249/10 membranes 1–3, 14; E/101/249/29; it seems likely that Benedict of Winchester used the contemporary Close Roll to register some of his transactions when he was in London: *CCR 1272–1279*, pp. 417, 296 and 303. PRO E/9/40 and E/9/44 have some of Aaron fil Vives' transactions on them; Corcos 1903, p. 210, 212. Stokes 1925, p. xi records a debt on the Close Roll made in January 1290 and repaid to Aaron fil Vives; interestingly Bonamy of York recorded the debt of £233 6s 8d which was owed to him by Fountains Abbey on the Close Roll: *CCR 1272–1279*, p. 444; Lipman 1984, pp. 5–8 discusses the relationship of the constable of the Tower with the Jews of London; see also Lipman 1984, note 58; the fact that many important documents concerning the Jewry, and presumably the London Jewry in particular, were kept in the house of Master Elias is indicated by Sayles 1936, pp. clv–clix. It may well be that Master Elias acted as a chirographer: Mundill1997.

[37] PRO E/9/40 and E/9/44 bear many transactions of Aaron fil Vives and Master Elias.

154

king, Henry III, in 1262.[38] No *archa* scrutiny for London has survived for Edward I's reign.[39] In addition to these more communal records, details of the separate dealings of the plutocratic Master Elias have survived; these indicate that he was still able to continue his widescale business virtually unhindered until his death in 1284.[40]

Joe Hillaby has recently extended our knowledge of the London community by considering the topography of the Jewry and the tallage contributions made by the London community in 1221, 1223, 1239 and 1241, and in particular by analysing the great London magnate families: the Crespins, the Eveskes, the le Blunds.[41] However, the most complete record of the tallages paid by London Jewry is that of 1262. Whilst the 1241 tallage identified approximately thirty-six Jews, the 1262 sample identified 108.[42] Many of the contributors to these mid-century tallages are the same, perhaps indicative of businesses that had survived for a period of twenty years. The contributions made by the community in 1262 are therefore worth some consideration.

The details of the bonds given to the king in 1262 add to Hillaby's survey and also provide the last financial and social evidence for the London Jewish community of the thirteenth century. The debts which were surrendered to the Crown in 1262 are represented in two different lists. The first is a list of 181 bonds worth a face value of £888 15s 1d owed to 108 different Jews. The second is a list of tallies owing to the London community, recording details of some seventy-three tallies worth £125 1s 8½d.[43] There is no surprise that these contributions were headed by Master Elias Menahem, son of Master Moses, who gave ten bonds, worth a face value of £148 13s 4d. His brother Hagin, the Archpresbyter of the Jews of England, gave three bonds worth £37 6s 8d; another brother, Deulecresse, gave six bonds which demanded repayments of £29 13s 4d and one quarter of corn. The second highest contributor was Cresse fil Gente who gave eleven bonds worth £68 13s 4d, just under half of Master Elias' major contribution of almost one-sixth of the total value. Only three Jews made individual contributions of more than £50. Nine Jews made contributions of over £20, ranging

---

[38] Stacey 1985; PRO E/101/249/10.

[39] PRO E/101/249/29 notes that the sheriff of London and two chirographers brought in a sealed chest of new debts with two keys and that a small chest with some bonds was also delivered.

[40] PRO E/9/44; Mundill 1997.

[41] Hillaby 1993a, pp. 110–18, 120–50 gives sketches of the main magnate families and the following totals for the London contributions to tallage: in 1221, £80 10s 6½d; in 1223, £214 19s 1d; in 1239 £831 10s 3d; in 1241 £1,485 10s 11½d. To this can be added the total of £1,013 16s 9½d (£888 15s 1d in bonds and £125 1s 8½d in tallies) for 1262: PRO E/101/249/10 membranes 1–3 and 14.

[42] Stacey 1985, pp. 181, 210–49; PRO E/101/249/10 membranes 1–3 and 14.

[43] PRO E/101/249/10 membranes 1–3 and 14.

from Aaron fil Abraham's seven bonds (worth £40 11s 8d) to Benedict Crespin's four bonds (worth £22 16s 8d). Seven Jews owed amounts worth over £10, whilst twenty Jews gave bonds worth £5 or more. Forty-seven creditors gave bonds valued under £5 but worth more than £1, whilst twenty gave bonds ranging from Samuel fil Josce of Northampton's bond worth 19s 0d to Moses of Nottingham's 5s 0d.

The great London magnate families like the Crespins clearly dominated the business of the time. Moses fil Jacob Crespin gave four bonds worth £30 9s 8d, Benedict Crespin gave four bonds worth £22 12s 0d, Jacob Crespin gave five bonds worth £11 2s 0d and half a soam (horse load) of corn, and Moses Crespin and Isaac his brother gave single bonds worth £10. Some of the family gave bonds which were shared between them. Even Jud, the sister of Benedict Crespin, gave a single bond worth 13s 4d. The le Blund family was represented by Elias who gave two bonds worth £4 13s 4d and Moses his son who gave two bonds worth £4 and half a soam of corn. Amongst the London business community there were also Jews like Isaac of Southwark and Leon of Milk Street who were clearly London-based Jews of more moderate means than the great plutocratic families. There is also evidence of Jews who may have come from the provincial centres. Perhaps they came to London on regular business or family visits; perhaps they had settled there.[44] It is of interest that amongst the stipulated repayments on the bonds there were a few commodities mentioned. These were clearly genuine small commodity payments such as the odd soam and quarter of corn, the odd soam or half a soam of oats. At this time there was even a Jewish creditor who was owed a robe and another who was owed £8 as well as a thousand herrings.[45]

Intriguingly, the 1262 record reveals a second list of debts. It records details of seventy-three tallies which were owed to the London community. These debts were worth a face value of £125 1s 8½d. The largest creditor was Benedict Crespin who was owed for seven tallies and who shared one debt with another Jew. He was owed a total of

---

[44] Jews who may not have had firm London connections but who certainly would have visited London number amongst them Bonefey fil Moses of Wallingford, Pictavin of Winchester, Anet the daughter of Deulecresse of Norwich, Isaac of Warwick, Jacob fil Leon of Warwick, Deudon of Calais, Isaac of Oxford, Pictavin of Stamford, Aaron the son of Aaron of Kingston, Isaac fil Diay of Colchester, Avegaye sister of Elias of Lincoln, Jacob fil Leon of Warwick, Abraham of Winchester and Moses of Nottingham: PRO E/101/249/10 membranes 1–3.

[45] Deulecresse fil Magister Moses was owed 1 qtr, Leon fil Isaac was owed ½ soam, Jacob Crespin was also owed ½ soam, Bonefey fil Isaac was owed a soam, Leon of Milk Street was owed ½ soam, Deudon fil Isaac was owed a robe, Moses fil Elias le Blund was owed ½ soam, Abraham fil Sal was also owed a robe, and Deulecresse fil Moses and Isaac fil Deulecresse were each owed 1 soam of oats: PRO E/101/249/10 membranes 1–3. I am particularly grateful to Dr Rokeah for confirming her reading of the manuscript with me.

£12 18s 2½d. Most of the tallies were for comparatively small amounts; they generally ranged from under £10 to as little as 4s 8d. Understandably the London-based Jews again dominated the contributors, notably Benedict and Jacob Crespin, Isaac of Southwark, Abraham of London, Leon Blund and Samuel of London. But again there were indications of provincial Jews who had used the London *archa*, such as Deuleben of Rochester, Sal of Kingston and Deulebeneye of Doncaster. Thus the 1262 record of the London community's financial affairs revealed a plutocracy of communal leaders and leading families, a probable collection of London-based Jews who were negotiating loans, and the probability of other provincially based Jews seeking or making business agreements when they came to London for either private or business purposes.

YORK

In his recent study of the London Jewry in the thirteenth century Joe Hillaby also considered the relative importance of the York Jewry for which, alas, there is also a paucity of records.[46] Professor Barrie Dobson has examined the York evidence, almost in its entirety.[47] The unique history of the York community is a good example of how local events could influence business and the life of the community at large. It seems that, having recovered from the massacre of 1190, it never altogether revived from the massive tallage payment of over £5,000 in 1240. However some Jews certainly remained in business, among them the rich plutocrat Bonamy of York who survived as a fairly successful financier until 1290.[48] A surviving 1262 list identified seventeen York Jews who held bonds worth a total of £91 12s 0d. Apparently at the forefront of the York community at this date was Aaron fil Josce who gave six bonds worth a face value of £52 3s 4d as well as additional repayments of 30 quarters of oats, 15 quarters of corn and 15 quarters of barley. This single creditor provided over 50 per cent of the value of the York community's payment in 1262. Second in importance was Josce fil Master Aaron, who gave a single bond worth £6 13s 4d. Most of the York community contributed single bonds worth below £5, and the large majority gave bonds worth less than £2. Yet again this sample indicates that Jewish creditors from outside the city were depositing bonds in the York *archa*: thus two bonds belonging to Manasser and his son Brunne of Knaresborough were recorded there in 1262. Elias of

---

[46] Hillaby 1993a, pp. 104–6.
[47] Dobson 1974, pp. 1–50; 1979; Addyman 1984; Adler 1933; Brunskill 1964; Davies 1875.
[48] Dobson 1979, p. 46.

Kent and Benet fil Benedict of Namtes (Nantes) would also appear to have visited York at this period.[49]

This surviving and seemingly complete record can be compared with the less comprehensive surviving scrutiny of the York *archa* in 1276, made some fourteen years later. At that period, from an incomplete and slightly illegible record, some fourteen Jews can be identified, who were owed twenty-six bonds, worth a face value of £527 14s 8d *in toto*. What is particularly surprising about this list is that it seems to have been dominated by Jews with London connections. The Crespin family seem to have poured much capital into transactions in the York area. Benedict Crespin had six bonds in the York *archa* worth a face value of £233 17s 4d. Deudone Crespin had a single bond worth £100, while Sarra, Benedict Crespin's daughter, was owed a single bond for as little as 4s 0d. Other London Jews seem to have followed suit. Josce fil Jacob of London possessed a single bond worth £30, Master Elias Menahem also had a bond worth £20, while another of his relatives also had a bond in the *archa*.[50] Regrettably a full picture of the transactions in the York *archa* will never be complete. An *archa* was removed from York to Westminster in 1290 but details have not survived.[51] Yet once again the financial transactions were clearly dominated by a handful of plutocratic Jews; some of them were London based and others clearly came from outside the city itself.

CANTERBURY

By the 1260s Canterbury was probably one of the oldest and best-established Jewries. The town's proximity to the Channel ports and Watling Street makes it likely that the first medieval Jewish settlers at least passed through it on their way to London.[52] Certainly a small community was established by the close of the twelfth century. In the town relations between Jews and Christians seem to have been comparatively peaceful. The Canterbury Jewry were spared from the massacres of 1190 and later ritual murder allegations.[53] They found

---

[49] PRO E/101/249/10 membrane 5.

[50] PRO c/47/9/49; Mundill 1987, pp. 72–3; Mundill 1997, p. 166.

[51] PRO E/101/249/29.

[52] Mundill 1987, pp. 163–5 does much to set the geographical scene in Kent. (I was mistaken by a reference to Jewish presence in Canterbury in 1160 which was in fact Cambridge.) Adler, 1914, pp. 19–22 examines the early references to the Canterbury Jewry and notes that they paid a large amount to the Northampton *donum* of 1194. Richardson 1960, pp. 162–3 refers to Kentish Jews who owed for the Guildford tallage of 1186. Streit 1993 considers the expansion of the Jewish community in the reign of King Stephen but makes little mention of the Canterbury community.

[53] Cohn-Sherbok 1979, pp. 24–31.

clients in the hinterland and, as has been seen above, lived as a community under the protection and control of the sheriff. The type of business which the Canterbury Jews conducted just before the baronial wars can be seen most clearly from their bonds listed in 1262. Although there are specific caveats which apply to the Kentish entries on the 1262 list because of the latter's condition, it is still a useful indicator of the type of business they were conducting.[54]

The 1262 list identifies some fifty-two Jews who gave 102 bonds worth £210 2s 11d.[55] From an analysis of the numerical distribution of bonds owed to each individual Jew, the ability of certain financiers to lend money both more frequently and to a wider clientele emerges. Thus Leon fil Moses, who had twelve bonds owing to him worth a total value of £26 7s 4d, and the Jewess, Milkana filia Deubeneye, who had eight bonds worth £13 16s 2d, may have been among the more enterprising members of the community. Comparisons between the values of transactions themselves can also be made. The four bonds of Miriam, the widow of Samson, were worth only £3 13s 0d; while Isaac fil Benedict's four bonds were worth £7 11s 3d. There were ten Jews at this time with only two bonds each. These ranged in value from Diey fil Benedict's which were worth £33 6s 8d and Jacob Crespyn's worth £25 to Jacob fil Fluria's bonds worth £1 10s 2d, and Bonamy's valued at 17s 0d. Thirty-three Jews each had a single bond. The values of these single loans varied enormously from Vinard fil Isaac's worth £10 to Moses Presbyter's worth 3s 6d. Even from such a brief examination a clear picture of a hierarchy of plutocratic Jews who clearly dominated the financial market emerges. Yet it is also clear that at this time Jewish financiers were making very small loans indeed and that probably virtually every Jewish family might have had the capacity to act as moneylender. Pictavin fil Isaac had debts owing to him totalling as little as £1 18s 0d from no less than five very small transactions: no less than twenty individuals were involved in transactions worth less than £1.[56]

The evidence can also be used to examine the different amounts of capital which Jews were prepared to risk in single transactions. The distribution of the value of the individual bonds reveals that 31.3 per cent were worth a face value of less than 10s 0d each; 28.4 per cent were worth between 10s 0d and £1; 19.6 per cent were worth between £1 and £2, and 17.6 per cent were worth between £2 and £10. Only 2.9 per cent were worth more than £10; the largest was for £20. Thus, the

---

[54] PRO E/101/249/10 membranes 8 and 9. Apart from the fact that it has several lacunae it is almost illegible at points. There is also a distinct possibility that some Canterbury Jews' bonds have also been recorded amongst those of the Norwich community on membranes 15 and 16.
[55] *Ibid.*   [56] *Ibid.*; Mundill 1987, pp. 184–7.

vast majority of the bonds at this time were worth less than £10; and indeed 77 per cent were worth less than £2. The mean average value of a bond from this sample was £2 1s 2d and it is clear that most Jews held individual bonds worth well below this. Even bearing in mind the pitfalls of using such a list, it would seem that a picture emerges from these transactions that, in 1262, many Jews were involved in the making of comparatively small bonds. There were also some debts which involved partial repayment in commodities. In addition to his monetary repayment, Leon fil Moses was owed one soam of oats in a transaction he had concluded with William de Egerdinden; Amendaunt fil Josce was owed one soam of corn by Stephen de Mewell; Pictavin fil Isaac was owed another quarter of corn by Stephen de la Wan. However, these extra repayments are unusual at this time. In 1262, most Canterbury Jews noticeably favoured the cash transaction rather than the commodity. They clearly lent money and expected to be paid back in specie.[57]

Further evidence for the business practices of the Canterbury Jews can be gleaned from forty-five surviving bonds which were contracted between 1261 and 1276.[58] These identify thirty-two Jews as active moneylenders who had contracted bonds worth a face value of £183 6s 8d. It is possible that these surviving bonds represent only a fraction of an *archa* which was brought into Westminster, possibly in 1275 or 1276. Naturally it has to be recognised that their evidence is both different and fragmentary.[59] However, such original contracts can provide a useful basis for making further conclusions about Jewish lending practices. Again it is possible to trace the number of loans that individual Jews were prepared to make at any one time. For example, Hagin fil Leon le Eveske had five bonds owing to him, whilst Vives of Winchester, Isaac fil Abraham and Moses fil Rabbi Aaron had three; Aaron fil Cresse, Abba fil Aaron and Floria filia Elias of Northampton were owed for two bonds. Such individuals obviously stand out above the twenty-five other Jews who only had single bonds.

A brief examination of the distribution of the value of the individual bonds reveals that six of the bonds were worth less than 10s 0d, seven were worth between 10s 0d and £1, ten were valued at between £1 and £2, five between £2 and £3, six between £3 and £4 and eight

---

[57] PRO E/101/249/10 membranes 8 and 9.

[58] WAM nos. 9015, 9019, 9020, 9021, 9022, 9025, 9026, 9028, 9034, 9036, 9039, 9042, 9043, 9046, 9047, 9057, 9058, 9086, 9088, 9089, 9090, 9091, 9103, 9104, 9105, 9116, 9118, 9119, 9120, 9121, 9123, 9124, 9125, 9126, 9127, 9139, 9156, 9157, 9158, 9159, 9172, 9173, 9174, 9175, 9176.

[59] Mundill 1987, p. 187.

between £4 and £10. There were only three bonds worth more than £10, one for £15, another for £20 and another worth £33 6s 8d. Thus, once again, the majority of the individual bonds were worth less than £10 each and indeed 51 per cent were worth less than £2 each. The mean average value of a bond in this sample was £4 1s 4d, almost double the equivalent for the 1262 bonds.[60] Thus, the bonds of this period were seemingly larger than those given to the king in 1262. Nevertheless it would seem that, as in 1262, most of the bonds were concerned with fairly small amounts, although 24 per cent were worth more than the mean value of the bond. This collection reveals a slightly higher percentage of higher value bonds than was found in the 1262 sample.

Once again it is clear that certain Jews lent more money than others. Whilst Abba fil Aaron held two bonds worth £36 13s 4d and Cohke Hagin fil Cresse held one worth £20, other Jews held smaller debts like those of Aaron fil Samuel and Salle fil Abraham, who were both owed £3 6s 8d, and those of Jacob fil Cresse and Cresse fil Jacob, who were both owed 9s 0d. Eight Jews had single bonds worth no more than £2. It therefore seems that at this period (just prior to the Statute of 1275) Jews with little capital could still involve themselves in moneylending, although it is perhaps significant that there were fewer small bonds at this period.

Again amongst these bonds there were transactions which demanded repayment in a combination of money and commodity. Moses fil Salle had a bond which was endorsed to the effect that Master John de Wayhope who owed him £10 had also promised to pay half a bushel of corn; Hagin fil Leon le Eveske and Mynne fil Benedict were also owed one bushel of wheat. More interestingly, Leon fil Jacob had lent 10s to Hamo of Hoath and was to be repaid with the money as well as one cart load of wood.[61]

The evidence of the Westminster Abbey bonds is largely complemented by the register of extant Jewish bonds in 1290.[62] The Canterbury *archa* and other documents pertaining to the Jewish community were taken to Westminster early in 1291.[63] By 1292 the bonds had been

---

[60] The mean average value derived from the 1262 sample was £2 1s 2d; see Table 9.
[61] WAM nos. 9123, 9124, 9127, 9158.   [62] PRO E/101/250/6.
[63] PRO E/101/249/29 shows that early in 1291, the sheriff of Kent and the two Christian chirographers for Canterbury brought *unam archam de novis debitis* to Westminster. The officials also brought two keys for the chest which they duly deposited in the bag which held all the keys for the other Jewish *archae*. At the same time other officials from Canterbury arrived and deposited a small chest, *unam pixidem*, a starr under the names of John fil Solomon of Kennington and Moses le Petit, and two other small chests (*pixides*) full of documents pertaining to the Jews of Canterbury.

examined and enrolled by the Exchequer scribes under the supervision
of William de Marchia. The bonds ranged in date from 25 September
1280 to 26 March 1290. What is of course especially valuable about this
particular list is that it is a complete reflection of the state of Jewish
business at Canterbury during the last decade before the Expulsion.[64]
This list identifies sixteen Jews who held ninety-five bonds worth £523
3s 8d.

Once again it is possible to appreciate how different Jews had made
different numbers of contracts. Moses le Petit had sixteen bonds still
owing to him. Josce fil Ursellus of York, who was described as a Jew
manens in Canterbury, and Aaron fil Benedict of Winchester both had
eleven bonds outstanding. Moses fil Salle and Leo fil Master Elie had
nine each. Vives of Winchester and Cok fil Benedict of Winchester had
eight. Aron fil Cresse had made six different transactions whilst Aron fil
Petevyn and Hagin fil Cresse were each owed four debts. Belia of
Stamford was owed three and Elie fil Hagin two. Unusually, there were
only four Jews who were involved in single transactions: Belaset filia
Benedict, Josce Gilberd fil Aaron of Canterbury, Popelina and Hagin her
son. Of greater importance is the fact that the majority of the bonds
expected repayment in grain. Closer analysis of these transactions also
reveals a degree of fluctuation in the prices quoted in the agreements.
Given that the Canterbury Jewry had made the greatest number of cereal
bonds in 1290 this is not surprising. For instance, in Canterbury, different
prices per quarter were quoted in the same month in February, October
and December of 1284. In 1285, the price per quarter in October varied
between 6s 8d and 5s 0d. In 1286, there is a clear difference in price per
quarter quoted in different bonds contracted in March and April and in
every month between July and December. Such fluctuation could be a
major indicator that these transactions were genuine.[65]

The distribution of the cash value of the individual transactions
reveals that there was none worth less than 10s 0d. At the lower end of
the market there were three bonds worth between 10s 0d and £1; six
bonds worth between £1 and £1 10s 0d; ten bonds worth between £1
10s 0d and £2; eleven bonds worth between £2 and £2 10s 0d; twenty
bonds worth between £2 10s 0d and £5; twenty-five bonds worth
between £5 and £10; and twenty individual bonds (21 per cent) worth
more than £10. Of these slightly higher-value bonds seven were worth
between £10 and £10 10s 0d; one between £10 10s 0d and £11; four
between £11 and £13; two between £13 and £15; and six between
£15 and £20 10s 0d. Thus, 79 per cent of the bonds were worth less

[64] Mundill 1987, pp. 189–93, 395–8.   [65] *Ibid.*, pp. 388–9.

than £10 but only 20 per cent were worth less than £2, compared with 77 per cent worth less than £2 in 1262 and 51 per cent worth less than £2 in the Westminster sample. The mean average value for an individual bond at this period was £5 9s 3d.[66] It would seem from these transactions that during the 1280s the Canterbury Jews were becoming involved in considerably higher-valued loans. However there were fewer Jews operating at the lower end of the market.

The 1290 evidence reveals, on the one hand, large-scale financiers like Leo fil Magister Elias who was owed for nine bonds worth a total value of £84 9s 4d and Moses Le Petit who was owed sixteen bonds worth a face value of £83 3s 4d. There were also several Jews whose debts were larger than £40: Aaron fil Benedict of Winchester, Josce fil Ursellus and Cok fil Benedict. On the other hand there were smaller financiers like Popelina, Josce Gileberd, Hagin fil Popelina and Belaset filia Benedict who were all owed single debts worth less than £4. Such figures suggest a mean average Jewish outlay of £32 8s 11d in the late 1280s, which again is considerably higher than the equivalent for the Westminster sample (£5 14s 6d) and also the 1262 debts (£4 9s 0d). While this difference could have been due to the fact that the 1290 transactions were simply a much fuller representation of Jewish lending practice at the time, it is still a strikingly impressive difference.[67]

In terms of the differences between cash and commodity bonds that have been identified in earlier samples, the Canterbury 1290 bonds are quite exceptional in that all but one of them are expressed in terms of repayment in cereal. Since that one exception is defined in terms of wool there are no transactions which stipulate repayment in specie within this sample.[68] On the face of it the Canterbury Jews had been induced to lend money in return for commodities.[69] The fact that it was money that was lent out in advance is evidenced from the details of a bond made on 6 June 1281, which also provides some insight into how post-1275 transactions actually worked.[70] This particular bond would appear to be a genuine bill of promissory sale. According to the bond, Bartholomew of Pymesdene owed Popelina, a Jewess, 14 quarters of wheat, 'for six marks already received'. In this case advance payment had been made to the debtor.[71] Unfortunately, in this instance, the

---

[66] See Table 9.   [67] *Ibid.*; Mundill 1987, pp. 187–93.
[68] Mundill 1990a, pp. 5–8; see Table 4.
[69] Adler 1914, pp. 55–6; Abrahams 1896, pp. 88–9; Mundill 1990a, pp. 5–8.
[70] PRO E/101/250/6.
[71] *Ibid.* The full entry reads: 'Bartholomew filius Thomas de Pymesdene debet Popeline Judee Cantuarie relicte Abraham Parvi de Bedeford xiiii quarteria frumenti pro vi marcis receptis per unam obligacionem cuius data est die veneris proxima ante festum Sancte Trinitatis Anno Regni Regis Edwardi ix.'

price per quarter of the cereal that Bartholomew was to return to Popelina was not stipulated. According to the late Dr D. L. Farmer's figures, however, the price per quarter would have been something like 6s 3¼d and therefore the amount of wheat owed to the financier would probably have had a face value somewhere in the region of £4 7s 9½d on the open market.[72] Popelina had paid £4 in advance for the wheat and may well have been looking for her profit as time wore on. This price level has an element which suggests that it represents a realistic appreciation of what gain had to be achieved in order to make a profit in the grain markets. There is little reason to suspect the genuineness of this commodity bond as anything else than an advance sale credit.[73]

It is also noticeable that the 1290 scrutiny reveals only sixteen Jews who held bonds in the *archa* compared with thirty-two identified by the Westminster bonds and fifty-two by the 1262 roll. Clearly comparisons of this nature are difficult to explain without accepting the probability that there was a shrinkage in the Jewish population involved in the provision of credit facilities in this period. It is also possible, when comparing the Westminster sample with the 1290 sample, to notice significant differences in the evidence they provide as to the total outlay of individual Jews. It is not surprising that the mean Jewish outlay in the case of the two samples is very different, for the Westminster bonds were probably an incomplete sample. It is, however, worthy of note that the proportion of individual Jews whose total outlay is below the mean outlay in both samples is also very dissimilar. It is highly unlikely that the missing bonds from the Westminster collection would alter the picture in relation to this difference. Thus, a comparison of these two samples points very strongly to the conclusion that there was a significantly smaller proportion of Jews in 1290 who had total outlays below the mean than there was in the period covered by the Westminster bonds. Given that the total number of Jewish creditors identified by the 1290 evidence was smaller, it is possible to conclude that there was a significantly smaller number of Jews operating as small-scale creditors in Canterbury in the late 1280s. The final conclusion to emerge from a comparison of the three samples is that there was a significant shift from a preference for cash repayments to a preference for commodity repayments. Given the other differences which have been perceived between the last two samples, it is possible that this change was the basic reason for the decrease in the total number of Jewish creditors and the reduction in small-scale operators.

Therefore from the late 1270s and increasingly in the 1280s it seems

---

[72] Farmer 1957, p. 212.   [73] Postan 1928, pp. 238–44; Mundill 1990a.

that the Canterbury Jews began to make bonds for commodities either in an attempt to remain within the letter of the law or possibly because the speculation against the harvest offered a better investment. By such means it seems that the Canterbury Jews who were expelled in 1290 had survived the business depression of the 1260s and 1270s. However, it was apparently only the richer Jews who had survived: there were fewer small loans in the *archa* of 1290 than in previous registers. It seems that business and commodity bonding was for certain Jews an important and potentially profitable occupation when the order for expulsion came. Thus, it may well have been that in Canterbury, the plutocracy identified by B. L. Abrahams was able to survive the Edwardian Experiment at the expense of fellow Jews with fewer financial resources.[74]

DEVIZES

An examination of the Devizes Jews and their businesses presents slightly different problems. Although the oldest bond in the Devizes *vetus cista* dates from 1258 there is little evidence of much financial activity in the town until the 1260s. Certainly, it was probably the town's geographical location and the fact that there was a castle there which prompted Jews to start depositing bonds in the Devizes *archa*.[75] The Devizes Jewry made no contribution to the 1262 tallage whereas the neighbouring communities of Wilton and Marlborough did. In 1262, seven Marlborough Jews gave six bonds worth a face value of £38 9s 4d. All of these were single bonds which ranged in value from £6 to as little as 10s 0d.[76] Thirteen of the Wilton Jewish community gave a total of £43 13s 10d in 1262. The latter clearly included Jews who had some sort of connections with Dorchester, Oxford and Marlborough. One Jew, Josce fil Saulot, had seven bonds worth a total of £6 9s 0d as well as promises from his debtors of various repayments of 1¼ quarters of corn. The majority of Jews who contributed from the Wilton community had only single transactions.[77] It seems that before Edward's reign the Jews of the west country were less well established in any one centre than elsewhere. Little in fact is known of the Wilton community, although it had clearly existed in the 1220s and must have been founded sometime before this date.[78] As Professor Powicke observed, it suffered badly during the baronial wars.[79] It seems to have been a community which must have declined long before 1290.

---

[74] Abrahams 1896, p. 82.   [75] PRO E/101/250/11; Stone 1920, pp. 161–3.
[76] PRO E/101/249/10 membrane 7.   [77] PRO E/101/249/10 membrane 13.
[78] Hillaby 1984, p. 380.   [79] Powicke 1947, p. 516.

There are however indications that Jews who had connections with Chippenham, Hereford and Cricklade were using the Marlborough *archa* during Henry III's reign.[80] The earliest reference to payments from Marlborough Jews was in 1253 when they gave a total of £8 15s 9d.[81] The Jews of Marlborough do not seem ever to have been a particularly thriving community. Marlborough was a fairly small, perhaps even embryonic, Jewish centre. Certainly by Edward I's reign Jews had been settled there for some time. By 1272, their tallage capability had increased to £35 7s 1½d.[82] In 1281 several properties held by seven Jews who had formerly lived there were sold off.[83] Yet, Marlborough was still clearly a recognised Jewry at the start of Edward's reign whereas Devizes does not seem to have been so. In February 1273, Thomas le Esperun was commanded to make a scrutiny of the *archae* at Winchester, Oxford and Marlborough.[84] However in January 1275 the Marlborough *archa* ceased to exist when Edward gave his mother permission to expel the Jews from her dower towns. The Marlborough Jews were to take their *archa* to Devizes and to reside there.[85] On 24 November 1275 another order for a general scrutiny was made and this time Robert de Ludham and William Gerebert were ordered to scrutinise the *archae* at Winchester, Wilton, Oxford and this time Devizes.[86] Clearly, in late February 1280, when Edward himself travelled through Marlborough he would have been reminded that the Jews had departed five years before; and this might have prompted him in March 1281 to give permission for the queen mother to dispose of their houses.[87] Similarly when he visited Devizes in early April 1282 Edward must also have been well aware of the town's Jewish inhabitants and their plight.[88]

The decline of the Marlborough community clearly facilitated the ascendancy of the Devizes community. While in 1262 Jews from Devizes appear to have escaped paying the tallage, by 1274 they were paying more than the Marlborough community. In 1274, when the prior of Ogbourne accounted for the tallage at the New Temple, only two Marlborough Jews provided £7 1s 0½d while the Devizes community contributed £32 0s 6½d.[89] The subsequent westward migration of the Jews of Marlborough, partly caused at the instigation of the queen mother in early 1275, must have meant that Christians around the town

[80] PRO E/101/249/10 membrane 7. [81] PRO E/401/20. [82] PRO E/101/249/16.
[83] Mundill 1993, p. 71. [84] *Ibid.*, p. 46. [85] Rigg, p. 85. [86] Mundill 1993, p. 52.
[87] *Ibid.*, p. 71. Jospin, Lumbard of Petersfield and Sweteman each had a single messuage; Salomon had two messuages; Benedict had a tenement with a garden; Lumbard fil Salomon a messuage with gardens, curtilages and other appurtenances; Lumbard fil Lumbard a house; Cok fil Aaron a messuage with a curtilage in Andover.
[88] *Ibid.*, p. 67. [89] *PREJ4*, p. 33.

now found it difficult to obtain credit. For the Jewish financiers in the west country their areas of operation were contracting. Jews would have been most unlikely to return whence they had been expelled. This situation worsened in 1275 when their residence was limited by the *Statutum de Judeismo* to a recognised *archa* town. However, some still seem to have ventured into the surrounding countryside in search of debtors. Interestingly, just as the centre of Jewish habitation shifted so too there was a noticeable change in the geographical provenance of their debtors. Such a shift has been illustrated by the business of Lumbard and Bonefey of Cricklade and elsewhere.[90] From the early years of Edward I's reign the Devizes Jewish community was augmented by refugee Jewish families from the surrounding areas.

Regrettably the scrutiny of the Devizes *archa* which was to have been taken in 1276 has been lost.[91] The remaining evidence for the transactions of the Devizes Jews comes solely from the *Valor Judaismus*. In 1291, the sheriff and John de Leye his clerk, together with Geoffrey Buthard and John le Teyntrer, the chirographers, arrived in Westminster and deposited one *archa* of new debts from the town of Devizes along with one strong box of new debts under the seal of the two previous sheriffs. They also brought one *archa* of old debts owing to the Jews sealed under the seal of John de Weton and Adam de Wootton.[92]

Although it is not exactly clear when the Devizes *vetus cista* was closed, it would seem to have been at about the time of the Statute. The chest of old debts contained transactions dating from 1258 to 1275. Thirteen different Jews were recorded as having registered transactions in the *archa*, worth a face value of £265 4s 8d. Again one Jew, Sweteman fil Licoricia, clearly dominated the community's transactions. He had made three transactions worth a total of £140. Many of those Jews who had registered bonds before the Statute seem to have had some sort of connection, if only nominal, with towns in the hinterland. Jews who had used the *vetus cista* were described as of Marlborough, Newbury, Calne, Fairford, Chippenham and Cricklade.[93] It is known that Jews had frequented these areas earlier in the century because of references then to the Jews of Dorset and Wiltshire.[94] Even before Jewish residence was restricted, Devizes must have provided some focus for numbers of Jews from surrounding places. In 1260 Lumbard of Cricklade, a Jew who came from Cricklade but travelled the west country quite widely, had used the old chest at Devizes to deposit a

---

[90] Mundill 1991b. [91] See Table 8. [92] PRO E/101/249/29. [93] PRO E/101/250/11.
[94] There are arrangements for the collection of tallage for Wilton and Marlborough in 1240 on PRO E/101/249/12; see Stacey 1985, 239–49; Solomon of Wilton and Isaac and Solomon of Marlborough were behind with tallage payments in 1244: *PREJi*, p. 73.

bond made with a Christian who lived quite close to Cricklade. It could be that Devizes was the place at which Jews deposited their bonds in the region, perhaps as they travelled to other communities such as Oxford and Bristol. The chronological range of the bonds is also of interest as it shows that many Marlborough Jews were already depositing their bonds in Devizes even before they were forced to move there after 1275. Thirteen of the nineteen creditors had single bonds. The smallest bond was for only 8s od. The mean value of a bond deposited in the Devizes *vetus cista* was £9 9s 5d. All of the bonds which were registered at this period were to be repaid in cash.

The new debts which the royal officials had brought into Westminster in 1291 referred to bonds which had been deposited in the Devizes *archa* from 1282 to 1290. Thus there is a good clear indication of what Jewish financial practice was like in Devizes in the immediate years before the Expulsion. It shows that there were fewer Jews actually recording their transactions, that some Jews seem to have settled in Devizes itself and clearly those from nearby Marlborough had now quite definitely moved to Devizes. The evidence also, once again, shows a change in the medium of repayment. Seven Jewish creditors were owed 285 quarters of cereal and two bonds to be repaid in money, as well as various tallies worth a face value of £126 16s 8½d. Fewer Jews identified by this sample seem to have been making loans which involved more outlay and to have made loans which were to have been repaid in cereal. Salomon and Colette his daughter dominated the group of Jews in question. Salomon was owed 221 quarters (worth a face value of £82 6s 8d) while his daughter and four other Jews had made single cereal transactions. The sample also shows a clear change in Jewish personnel. The only Jew to have transactions recorded in both the *vetus* and *nova cistae* was Josce of Newbury, who might well have been travelling between Jewries in the course of seeking business: he also used the Oxford *archa* for some of his transactions in 1274, 1279 and 1282.[95] Some Jews were owed debts which were recorded on tallies. Colette, the daughter of Cok of Devizes, Josce, Lumbard fil Josce of Marlborough as well as several Jews who were described as unknown were owed a total of £19 10s 0½d by tally. The twelve tallies were mainly for sums of about £1 but Colette was owed £10 10s 7½d by a tally made in June 1282.[96]

[95] PRO E/101/250/11, E/101/250/9.
[96] PRO E/101/250/11: Colette, daughter of Cok of Devizes, was owed £10 10s 7½d in June 1282 by Thomas Martin of Winterbourne Monachorum of Glastonbury; an unknown debtor owed Cok le Riche of Devizes 13s 4d in April 1285; Josce fil Josce was owed £1 in September 1285 by Peter Cotele of Ore in Wiltshire; an unknown Jew was owed £1 0s 0d in December 1285 by

Although the Devizes Jewish community seems to have been fairly thinly established by the turn of the thirteenth century it clearly expanded to accommodate those Jews who were forced to move there from Marlborough and other places. It had an *archa* with chirographers and some form of protection from royal officials as well as a castle. However it seems that the town was never more than a fairly temporary settlement for the Jews of the west country and was probably never settled by more than a handful of Jewish families. The debts in the *vetus cista* (1258–75) show that it was used by Jews who possibly came from other communities and that they still quite clearly made bonds which demanded repayment in money. In stark contrast were the debts which were registered in the *nova cista* of 1282–90 which show a transfer towards repayments in commodities as well as the wider use of tallies. By the last decade of Jewish presence in Devizes it seems that there were fewer Jews involved in lending and that they were struggling to maintain their business. The mean average value of a bond from the *vetus cista* was £9 9s 5d compared with that of the *nova cista* which was £4 7s 5d. Certainly at Devizes the overall picture is one of a community in decline. More evidence exists for actual Jewish settlement in Marlborough, where Jews held some nine properties, than there was for settlement in the town of Devizes itself. In 1290 only two Jews had rented houses there on relatively short-term agreements: Solomon fil Simon and Josce fil Salomon of Marlborough.[97] In the main the business recorded in the Devizes *archae* between 1258 to 1290 probably represents that of Jewish business men who came to the town in order to use the *archa* facilities, rather than the well-established business of Jewish financiers who belonged to more settled and organised communities such as Canterbury, York or London. Yet the transactions of this small community clearly illustrate a change in business interests after 1275.

EXETER

Although Exeter was a comparatively remote place for a Jewish colony it was first settled by 1181. Rabbi Bernard Susser recently established

Michael Speriur; Lumbard fil Josce, Jew of Marlborough, was owed 15s 0d in 1286 by Willliam of Holebrook; Colette, daughter of Cok of Devizes was owed a further £1 in 1287 by Thomas Martin of Winterbourne Monachorum of Glastonbury; an unknown Jew was also owed 8s 0d in 1287 by Thomas Martin; Koc was owed 13s 11d in 1287 by Walter le Dreu; another unknown Jew was owed 10s 0d in 1287 by Michael Lesper of Cote; another, £1 0s 0d in March 1287 by William de Ringeburn; a further unknown, £1 0s 0d in March 1287 by Robert de Ringeburn; and Josce of Marlborough was owed £1 in August 1289 by William de Holebrok.

[97] See note 87 above; PRO E/101/249/30 membrane 3.

that by 1188 there were enough Jews to form a distinct community and to set up a *Beth din* (Jewish Court of Law). Yet only one Exeter Jew paid a relatively small amount to the Northampton *Donum* of 1194.[98] There is a little evidence (other than tradition) to connect the Jews to the workings of the tin trade and the Stannaries in the late twelfth century and this may have encouraged them to settle in the areas around Exeter. Moreover in 1218 the sheriff of Devon was given express instructions to protect the Jewish community in Exeter.[99] The majority of the evidence for the Exeter Jewry is extremely puzzling. Although intensive research has helped to unravel some of the problems posed by the four surviving lists of bonds, there are still some questions which have not been answered.[100] H. G. Richardson observed that there were only two Jews actively engaged in moneylending in Exeter in 1276. He correctly pointed to the fact that the *Valor Judaismus* only reported a single Jewish household in Exeter, that of Comtesse, a Jewess. He acknowledged that there were two *archae* which were brought in to Westminster in 1290, an old chest for bonds executed before 1275 and a new chest which held bonds from 1283 onwards. He accordingly claimed that 'there was hardly a shadow of a community there and there was certainly no synagogue'.[101]

These observations require some qualification. At one time at least during the thirteenth century Jews must have been tolerated in Exeter. A custumal written in Anglo-Norman, and thus written for use in the town, quite expressly makes reference to how pleas involving Jews should be heard. A plea of a Christian against a Jew was not to be heard without the presence of a Jew and a Christian, neither was a plea of a Jew against a Christian to be heard without Christian and Jew. It also stated that a Jew must give 'wage and pledge' that he would pursue his plea, and that the Christian should 'stand to the law', and if he could find a pledge, the Christian should be bailed on his solemn promise.[102] This single entry, perhaps not unusual among town regulations, presumes that there was once a sizeable and reasonably respected Jewish community in Exeter.[103]

Some idea of the size of the Exeter community can be gained from the bonds which were taken for payment in 1262. It was apparently a

[98] Susser 1977, pp. 9–11; Adler 1931, p. 222; Abrahams 1925, p. lxvii; Susser 1993, pp. 5, 8.
[99] *PREJ1*, p. 18; Adler 1931, p. 225; Susser 1993, pp. 1–2, 22; Lewis 1965, p. 212; Jacobs 1893a, pp. 186–8; Mundill forthcoming.
[100] PRO E/101/249/10 membrane 10, E/101/249/31, E/101/250/2; see Table 8; Susser 1993, pp. 8–19.
[101] Richardson 1960, pp. 18–19; Hillaby 1993b, pp. 186–7.
[102] Schopp and Easterling 1925, p. 37 and plate IV; Susser 1993, p. 14.
[103] Adler 1931, pp. 230–1; Richardson 1960, pp. 18–19.

very small community at that time. The evidence records only nine Jews, who were owed £38 9s 4d and half a quarter of wheat between them. The community included Jews who probably had connections with Dorset, Wilton, Marlborough and Warwick. At the top of the hierarchy one Jew, David fil Jacob, gave a bond worth £10. Another Jew described as Isaac de fil Deodata gave seven bonds totalling £9 10s 8d as well as a promise of half a quarter of wheat. The other creditors were owed single bonds which ranged in value from £8 13s 4d to as little as 2s od.[104]

The 1276 scrutiny for Exeter has been discovered since H. G. Richardson first made his comments on the Exeter Jewry.[105] It reveals the transactions of at least ten Jews who held 133 bonds. The actual document is difficult to read and has many *lacunae*. However some of the membranes have been recovered from other collections within the last twenty years.[106] A close analysis shows that this incomplete list records many of the bonds and transactions which were also contained in the *vetus cista* in 1290. It confirms that at least thirteen Jews were using the Exeter *archa* at this time. It reveals that at least one of those Jews, Moses fil Josce, was dead when the scrutiny was taken. Because of the overlap of information with that of the Exeter *vetus cista* it is easier to use the later evidence of the Exeter *vetus cista* to obtain a clearer view of business and Jewish social structure in Exeter between 1237 and 1275.[107]

In 1291, two Exeter *archae* were delivered to Westminster. The sheriff of Devon and Mathew fil John did not accompany the chests but sent one of the chirographers of the old chest, John Ploth and the chirographers of the new chest, John Hamelyn and Roger Demyn. The *archae* had been separately sealed in Exeter, the *vetus cista* by Martin Durling, formerly mayor of Exeter, and Master Roger de Enerham and the *nova archa* sealed by John de Assele, Waresius Martine, knight, and Brother John Peter of the Friars of Exeter. From these two chests further evidence of the Exeter community can be derived. The record of the *vetus cista* detailed the transactions of twenty-two Jews who had made 143 bonds which specified repayment in terms of money worth £1,023 19s 8d. The bonds ranged in date from 1237 to 1275. Although a good many of the bonds were made in Henry III's reign the majority were made in Edward's reign in 1275 and 1276. These transaction are more representative of the type of business which went on just before

---

[104] PRO E/101/249/10 membrane 10.   [105] Richardson 1960, pp. 18–19.
[106] PRO E/101/249/31. The scrutiny was taken on 14 February 1276 by John Wyger and Robert de Evesham; Susser 1993, p. 15.
[107] PRO E/101/250/2.

and after the Statute and in the years preceding the 1276 scrutiny. Five Jews had amassed debts worth over £50. At this time Jewish business in Exeter seemed to be dominated by Jacob Copin and Amite the widow of Samuel. The *capellanus* of the community, Deulecresse, was also amongst the leading five lenders. Four Jews, Aaron of Caerleon, Salomon fil Salomon, Salomon fil Aaron and Isaac fil Salomon, were owed for debts worth over £20. The rest of the community, some thirteen creditors, were all owed sums which varied from £16 10s 0d to £1. Once again the pattern of a few very rich Jews dominating the market with some Jews making more modest dealings and others only the occasional single loan, seems to emerge.[108]

Much is known of Jacob Copin of Exeter and especially of his transactions as they appear in the *vetus cista*. Jacob was the Jewish chirographer of the Exeter chest for a period of fourteen years from 1266 to 1280.[109] It is clear that he regularly ventured outside Exeter. In 1270, while in Newton Abbot (12 miles south-south-west of Exeter) he was assaulted by Robert of Bole Hill, Christiana his wife and William le Layte. As a result, Jacob took legal action but the Christians absconded.[110] Interestingly, it seems likely that William le Layte was the guardian of a certain Hugh Fychet of Paxton in Somerset (5 miles west of Bridgwater) who was later to accuse Jacob of making false charters.[111] In 1273, Jacob made a tallage payment in Somerset and Dorset.[112] In 1274, as chirographer to the Exeter *archa*, he and his colleague Jacob Crespin became involved in a case concerning a false charter. It was alleged that a charter which had been made between Salamon fil Salamon of Ilchester in Somerset and Robert Fychet of Paxton for £80 had been placed in the *archa* after the former's death. The Christian chirographers, Richard Bullock and David Taylor, had apparently allowed this deposit; the Jewish chirographers' sole defence was that they could not get access to the *archa* without the Christian chirographers.[113] The case appears to have dragged on but was eventually proved in front of a jury which included eight Jews. The Christian clerk, Adam, confirmed that he had in fact written the charter. One of the twelve witnesses verified that the charter had been made because he actually saw Robert Fychet in Exeter and drank with him after the transaction had been completed.[114]

In 1275, the Exchequer of the Jews investigated the debts which William of Middleton owed in the Jewry. They had ordered an inquiry

---

[108] PRO E/101/250/2, E/101/249/29. [109] Susser 1977, p. 14; 1993, pp. 14–5.
[110] Susser 1977, pp. 25–6; *PREJ1*, p. 242; Susser 1993, p. 269.
[111] Susser 1977, p. 26; *PREJ2*, p. 140. [112] *PREJ2*, pp. 13, 52.
[113] *PREJ2*, p. 137. [114] *PREJ2*, p. 194.

to be made in both Latin and Hebrew.[115] The constable of the Tower of London replied that Jacob Copin had a claim against William in the counties of Somerset and Dorset.[116] This can be verified by a contract for £40 made between Jacob Copin and William in July 1274 which was deposited in the *vetus archa*.[117] It seems that this debt was paid or at least acquitted: in 1277, Jacob acknowledged by his starr that William de Middleton and his heirs and assigns were quit in respect of himself and his heirs of a debt of £2 and of all other debts in which the said William was ever bound to Jacob from 'the creation of the world to Easter three weeks in the fifth year of King Edward'. Jacob also acknowledged that William was quit of a debt of £40 from the creation to the end of the world.[118]

Again in 1275, Hugh de la Lade appeared in a plea of debt against Jacob Copin and Salomon fil Aaron of Somerton in Somerset (4½ miles east-north-east of Langport).[119] The list of bonds in the *vetus cista* confirms the fact that a William fil William de la Lade of the county of Somerset was indebted to Salomon fil Aaron for £20 by a bond made in December 1272.[120] It seems clear that Jacob made loans in Somerset as well as Devon. In 1276 Jacob pardoned a Henry of Aluerncote of Somerset of all claim that Jacob might have had on the manor of Bosemeston by reason of a debt made under the names of Richard fil Bernard or John fil Bernard, 'from the creation of the world till the feast of Michaelmas 1276'. This debt can be confirmed by a transaction which was made in September 1274 and deposited in the *vetus cista* which recorded that John fil Bernard owed Jacob Copin £30.[121] A further legal case heard in the Exchequer of the Jews also showed Jacob trying to claim back one of his bonds which had been deposited in the *vetus cista* at Exeter. In September 1276 Roger de Molyns, a Devonshire clerk, acknowledged that he owed Jacob £8: this remained unpaid until 1278.[122]

Jacob was imprisoned in the Tower of London sometime during the period 1275–8; he and Cresse the Chaplain were fined 4s 0d for non-payment of tallage.[123] His detention in London might account for the fact that in 1276 when a case to reclaim a debt was brought against one Henry Bikel, Jacob was represented by Sampson of Wilecestr. The Jews were attempting to reclaim part of the debt owed by Roger de Molyns to Jacob; they claimed that Henry Bikel, who was now a tenant on the late Roger de Molyn's land, was also responsible for the debt.[124] At first

[115] *PREJ2*, p. 277. [116] *PREJ3*, p. 279. [117] PRO E/101/250/2.
[118] *PREJ3*, p. 279. [119] *PREJ3*, p. 1. [120] PRO E/101/250/2.
[121] *PREJ3*, p. 141; PRO E/101/250/2. [122] *PREJ3*, p. 173. [123] *PREJ4*, p. 157.
[124] PRO E/101/250/2; *PREJ3*, pp. 151, 173.

Henry Bikel, probably quite wisely, did not appear. However Jacob was persistent and in 1277 again took Henry Bikel to court for a judgment. This time Henry was present and asked for time to consider the demands of £2 13s 4d of debt and £5 6s 8d of interest.[125] Again, in 1277, Jacob pressed his case but to no avail. Later in the year Sampson fil Isaac appeared in the Exchequer of the Jews and stated that he had lost one part of a bond for £8 in the names of Roger de Molyns and Jacob Copin, of which the other part (with a seal attached) was in the chirographer's chest at Exeter, where in fact it remained until 1290.[126] However eventually Jacob managed to get some money for his debt; in 1278, Henry Bikel was distrained for one carucate of land with an annual value of £1 and six oxen worth £2.[127]

Another of Jacob's debts which was in the *vetus cista* gave rise to further legal wrangles. In June 1274, Henry of Dunesmor owed Jacob £6. In 1277, Jacob brought a case against Tyffonia, the wife of Henry of Dunesmor.[128] Jacob actually produced his copy of the bond for £8 13s 4d which was payable on 3 May 1275 and had been made on 25 March 1275 and demanded £6 13s 4d. The two sides could not agree and the sheriff was ordered to make inquiries in full county court.[129] In 1277, Jacob's attorney managed to secure some sort of judgment from the sheriff. The sheriff had distrained Tyffonia and had found that she had one carucate of land worth £1 and eight oxen (four of them steers) worth £1. Tyffonia did not appear.[130]

During the coin-clipping allegations of 1278–9 the Exeter Jewry suffered badly. Ten Jews and one Christian were arrested. They included Blakeman son of Jacob Copin, Aaron of Caerleon, Deulecresse le Chapleyn, Benedict of Wilton, Aaron of Dorchester and Jorin son of Ursell.[131] They were all allowed bail.[132] Dr Zefira Rokeah has recently shown that Jacob and his son were also accused of the death of a Christian in 1278 and that Jacob was hanged soon after.[133] Yet the imprisonment of these Exeter Jews and the demise of Jacob Copin were not the end of Jewish dealings and business in Exeter. A new generation had survived which was to continue credit dealings until the Expulsion.

This last generation of lenders worked against a background of deep suspicion and mounting difficulties. They apparently began to deal in cereals and to make use of tallies rather than written bonds. The last

---

[125] *PREJ3*, p. 242.   [126] PRO E/101/250/2; *PREJ3*, pp. 108, 122.
[127] *PREJ5*, p. 111.   [128] PRO E/101/250/2; *PREJ3*, p. 243.
[129] PRO E/101/250/2; *PREJ3*, p. 243; PRO E/101/249/31 reveals that Henry of Dunesmor owed Jacob Copin for two different debts, one for £6 and the other for £8 13s 4d.
[130] *PREJ4*, p. 108.
[131] Susser 1977, pp. 28–9; Adler 1931, pp. 233–4; Susser 1993, pp. 16–17.
[132] Susser 1977, p. 29.   [133] Rokeah 1993, p. 194.

evidence for the dealings of the Exeter Jews is the record of transactions deposited in the *nova cista* between 1284 to 1290. Amongst these transactions were twenty-four tallies for sums ranging between £13 16s 8d and 2s 0d. Many of them were undated but the ones which were date from 1286–9. By the very fact that business continued during this final period it seems that H. G. Richardson's conclusions about the Exeter community in the latter years were unduly melancholy. The Exeter Jewry's transactions at this late period also reflect a distinct change in preference from money to commodity bonds. There were twenty-one cereal bonds owed to twelve Jews. One was contracted in 1284, four in 1285, nine in 1286, three in 1287, two in 1288 and two in 1290. The last bond to be contracted was in either August or October 1290 and was owed by William of Cableford to Jacob le ffre Peres.[134] At the head of the financiers was Abraham, who was owed 190 quarters worth approximately £58 6s 8d. The smallest transaction was for a bond which was owed to Abraham and Cok for 20 quarters (worth £6 13s 4d). Jewish women also featured in the Exeter business transactions of this period. Cuntasse, Amite and Aunterre were all owed sums worth more than £10. There was also evidence that certain Jews were entering into partnerships.[135] In total, the Jewish creditors had lent on the strength of promises of repayment of 542 quarters of cereal, worth a face value of £175 13s 4d.[136]

The state of the Exeter Jewry must have been frequently and closely scrutinised. Edward I actually stayed in Exeter from December 1285 to January 1286; and Bishop Peter Quivil held the Synod of Exeter in 1287 which concerned itself with anti-Jewish sentiment.[137] Yet the transactions from this period clearly show that business had continued, although the new chest dealings do seem to drop off towards 1290. What became of the later generation of Exeter Jewry is unclear. The fact that, as H. G. Richardson pointed out, the dwellings of the Exeter Jews were difficult to trace perhaps only suggests that in 1290 the townspeople were quick to move in and take over Jewish dwellings.[138] It may also suggest that the bailiffs were ignorant or did not want royal officials at Westminster to know the local situation. Yet without doubt

---

[131] PRO E/101/250/2.

[135] PRO E/101/250/2 shows that Symme fil Lombard and Josce fil Isaac as well as Abraham and Cok were involved in shared cereal bonds, whilst Cok, Auntetot and Abraham, and Auntetot and Abraham were owed for tallies.

[136] PRO E/101/250/2: Isaac fil Josce 20 qtrs; Jacob le Frere Peres 20 qtrs; Auntere 30 qtrs; Isaac 20 qtrs; Syme fil Lombard and Josce fil Isaac 60 qtrs; Abraham and Cok 20 qtrs; Cok Moses 22 qtrs; Amite 60 qtrs; Cuntasse 100 qtrs; Abraham 190 qtrs.

[137] Mundill 1993, p. 81; Oliver 1861, p. 70; Adler 1931, p. 235; Susser 1977, p. 34.

[138] Richardson 1960, pp. 18–19.

the Jewish community in Exeter carried on business until the final months before the Expulsion and also seems to have moved towards lending money in return for grain.

The plentiful evidence for the Hereford Jewish community is now well known. Thanks to the researches of Joe Hillaby the entire history of that community between 1179 and 1290 has been written. The Jewish community of thirteenth-century Hereford was dominated first by one extremely rich Jew, Hamo, and then later by Aaron le Blund.[139] The financial domination by the le Blund family in the late thirteenth century at times almost obscures the transactions of the other Jewish creditors whose lives were also affected by Edward I's policies. Four main pieces of evidence document the financial practices of the Jewish community between 1262 and 1290. The first item is the list of bonds which were granted for the tallage of 1262.[140] The second piece of evidence is an *archa* scrutiny made in December 1275.[141] Later evidence can be derived from the *Valor Judaismus*. The *Valor* provides two scrutinies of bonds deposited in the *vetus cista* from 1259 to 1276 and the transactions of the *nova cista* which date from 1283 to 1290.[142]

In 1262, thirty-six Hereford Jews contributed £104 0s 4d in bonds towards tallage payment. This contribution was represented by forty-four debts.[143] It is immediately striking that most of these loans are single transactions. Only seven Jews (19 per cent of the total) gave more than one bond to the tallage contribution. These ranged from the three tallies worth £6 18s 4d owed to Blanch, a Jewess, and the three bonds owed to Meyr of Stamford worth £3 6s 8d to the two bonds owed to Meyr fil Solomon: an extremely large bond for £20 and a small one for 7s 0d. It was noted that part of Meyr's large debt was also owed to Master Samuel de Radenor who then actually held the Christian debtor's lands.[144] Jews like Abraham fil Sampson, who gave transactions worth £2 11s 4d, had used various methods to record their debts: a bond for £1 13s 4d, and a tally for 18s 0d and one quarter of corn. The rest of the debts which were given by the Hereford community were

---

[139] Abrahams, 1894, pp. 136–59; Mundill 1987, pp. 204–44; Hillaby 1984; 1985; 1990b; 1990c.
[140] PRO E/101/249/10 membrane 5.   [141] *PREJ*3, pp. 230–8.   [142] PRO E/101/250/5.
[143] PRO E/101/249/10 membrane 5. The discrepancy of 10s in the total values between Mundill 1987, p. 219 and Hillaby 1990c, p. 433 has been resolved by Rokeah who kindly lent me her reading and transcripts of the original. Meyr son of Solomon was only owed 7s instead of 17s for one of his bonds.
[144] PRO E/101/249/10 membrane 5: *ista carta liberata fuit Magro Sam de Radenor ten terram ipsius John*. Blanch's three tallies recorded debts of £1 9s 0d, 16s 0d and £4 13s 4d.

single bonds. Their values varied enormously from one worth £10 to another worth as little as 6s 8d. A single transaction worth £3 6s 8d was owed to two different Jews, Bonefy fil Elias and Manasser fil Benedict, who clearly worked in partnership. Another was to be repaid to Abraham *genus* Elias in commodities. Abraham also expected to be repaid two loads of corn and three loads of oats. Thus in Hereford in the early 1260s there were several business partnerships, there was some commodity bonding and there were, it seems, several Jews whose financial resources allowed them only to make small bonds.[145]

The second impression of Jewish financial activity in Hereford is provided by a scrutiny of the *archa* which was made by Walter de Helyun and his associate on 27 December 1275.[146] As Hillaby has observed, the scrutiny only recorded details of four Jews who had bonds in the *archa*: Aaron fil Elias, Bonenfaunt fil Aaron, Hagin fil Jacob and Hagin fil Elias. These four had seventy-nine bonds owing to them, worth a total of £459 9s 8d. In 1275, Aaron fil Elias had seventy-three debts due to him which were to be repaid in cash and commodities. He was owed bonds worth a total value of £401 12s 4d which included commodity repayments of 23½ quarters of corn, five geese and one robe. His son Bonenfaunt was owed four debts, worth £50 10s 8d and three soams of cereal. Hagin fil Jacob was owed one debt for £4 and Hagin fil Elias one debt for £3 6s 8d.[147]

Several observations can be made about these financiers and their transactions and several very important questions can be posed. First, the bonds ranged in value from as much as £50 to as little as 6s 8d, both of which sums were owed to Aaron. Secondly, there were, just as there had been earlier, commodity bonds being arranged in Hereford before the Statute of 1275. Thirdly, there were clearly bonds which remained unpaid. Of Aaron fil Elias' seventy-three bonds, a total of sixty-two were, as will be seen, still in the Hereford *vetus cista* in 1291.[148] Thus, by 1290, Aaron only seems to have managed to reclaim eleven of his bonds which were registered in 1275. The bonds made by the other Hereford creditors recorded in the 1275 sample were also still unpaid in 1291.[149] Fourthly, as Hillaby also observes, the Hereford Jews in 1275 expected repayment at times of local fairs. Thirty per cent of the bonds in the 1275 scrutiny were repayable at fairs such as those of St Ethelbert, Hereford, of Ledbury and of Leominster.[150] However the most serious

---

[145] PRO E/101/249/10 membrane 5; Mundill 1987, pp. 219–20; Hillaby, 1990c, pp. 433–5.
[146] *PREJ*3, pp. 230–8; Mundill 1993, p. 52;
[147] *PREJ*3, pp. 230–8; Mundill 1987, pp. 222–4; Hillaby 1990c, pp. 444–6.
[148] Mundill 1987, pp. 222–5; PRO E/101/250/5; Hillaby 1990c, p. 445.
[149] PRO E/101/250/5.   [150] Mundill 1987, pp. 223 and 247 note 91; Hillaby 1990c, p. 445.

question raised by the 1275 Hereford sample is why, in the context of the large number of Jewish creditors in Hereford revealed in the 1262 list of creditors and in the context of other larger lists provided from other towns as a result of the 1275 scrutiny, there are so few Jewish moneylenders recorded as being in business in Hereford in 1275. Hillaby has suggested that the list was possibly meant to have been some sort of evaluation of Aaron le Blund and his family's transactions and that details of the other bonds were picked up by accident. This is possible, as the evidence of the *vetus cista* which contained transactions made between 1259 and 1276 reveals many other Jews who were not represented by the four in the 1275 list.[151] If so, this is another timely warning that lists of transactions deposited in *archae* are not necessarily comprehensive.

The more complete evidence of the Hereford *vetus cista* provides a list of thirty moneylenders who registered their transactions between 1259 and 1276.[152] Naturally these financiers held different numbers of bonds. Only nine had made single bonds, which ranged in value from £1 to £18 and one quarter of cereal. There were seven Jews who had two debts owed to them. Two Jews, Jacob fil Sadekyn and Maunsell fil Josce, had negotiated three separate transactions. Bona filia Elias and Elye fil Aaron had made four bonds. There were three members of the community who were involved in five transactions: Cuntessa filia Mosse, Josce fil Mansel and Aaron fil Isaac, Jew of Worcester. Elye fil Isaac and Sara filia Elias each had six debts outstanding. Sampson, Jew of Winchester, was probably involved in eight different bonds.[153] Benedict fil Elye also had eight bonds whilst Aaron le Blund's son, Bonenfaunt, had ten and Hagin fil Elye had twelve. The *vetus cista* was dominated by Aaron fil Elias le Blund. He was involved in 103 individual transactions. Yet if the transactions of the rest of the community are examined in isolation from Aaron's business then between 1259 and 1276 there were

---

[151] PRO E/101/250/5; Mundill 1987, pp. 224–8; Hillaby 1990c, p. 445–8.

[152] PRO E/101/250/5. Mundill's and Hillaby's totals differ. This is probably due to unspecified prices of commodities and the use of differing values. Hillaby makes the total value £1,114 12s 0d: Hillaby 1990c, p. 447; whilst Mundill makes the total value £1,120 13s 8d: Mundill 1987, pp. 225–6.

[153] Abrahams 1894a, p. 155 first drew attention to the error and reference. Sampson, Jew of 'Winchester' (Wyntonia) may well have been wrongly described and the scribe may well have meant Sampson of Worcester (Wygornia); Mundill, 1987, p. 224 lists him as having eight bonds worth £25 16s 0d. On his table Hillaby has Isaac involved in nine bonds worth a face value of £25 16s 0d: Hillaby 1990c, p. 447. Abrahams also made a mistake in his list over the amount of bonds owing to Sampson of Worcester: Abrahams 1894a. A study of PRO E/101/249/5 makes it quite clear that Isaac of Winchester is owed for a list of seven bonds and lower down the entries Isaac of Worcester for one bond.

still openings for financiers like Elye fil Jacob who entered into a single bond worth £1.

In terms of the average amount of capital involved in individual bonds, there was a clear difference between this sample and the sample for 1262. Even if consideration is given to the isolated transactions recorded in connection with the *vetus cista*, it is clear that an average bond to the value of something between £2 and £2 13s 4d represents a much higher average value than that present in the 1262 sample in which thirteen Jews had debts worth no more than £1. This situation may of course have been the result of the connections between the 1262 list and a tallage.[154] Yet it may also indicate an upturn in business.

The bonds from the *vetus cista* (1259–76) identified thirty different Jews involved in lending money who were owed a total of £1,120 13s 8d. Aaron le Blund himself held over 50 per cent of the bonds and was owed approximately two-thirds of the total face value of the transactions. His son, Bonenfaunt, had ten bonds (4 per cent) worth £79 6s 8d, 7 per cent of the total value. Aaron and his son were followed by Hagin fil Elye who held twelve bonds (5 per cent) worth £35 19s 4d, 3.3 per cent of the total value. Between them these three men held 60 per cent of the debts, worth 77 per cent of the total value in the *vetus cista*.[155] A more 'ordinary' Jewish financier, Sampson fil Isaac, had eight bonds worth £25 16s 0d. His bonds were worth just a fraction more than Benedict fil Elye's eight bonds which had a value of £18 7s 8d. The median value of Sampson fil Isaac's bonds is £2 13s 4d, and that of Benedict fil Elye's is £2 6s 8d. Although a bond valued at between £2 and £3 is small by comparison with, for example, Mirabile filia Isaac's single bond for £18 it is interesting to note that it is still a relatively large bond in comparison with those revealed by the 1262 list. It seems that the value of transactions in the *vetus cista* had increased. Only one Jew, Elye fil Jacob, had a single bond in the *archa* which was worth less than £2. The fact that there are considerably fewer small bonds in 1275 than in 1262 is important.[156]

Perhaps, however, the most significant evidence to be yielded by the *vetus cista* is the extent to which commodity bonding was present in Hereford even before the Statute of 1275. Although there were no pure commodity bonds in the *vetus cista*, there were no fewer than thirty-three bonds which state that debtors were owed returns in both money

---

[154] It may be that the low number of large bonds and the lack of Jews with a large number of bonds in the 1262 record is the result of bonds being given for tallage.

[155] Mundill 1987, p. 226; PRO E/101/250/5; *PREJ3*, p. 230–8; Hillaby 1990c, pp. 446–7; Abrahams 1896, p. 82.

[156] PRO E/101/250/5, E/101/249/10 membrane 5.

and commodities.[157] Interestingly, the details of a single extant bond which dates from this period similarly reflect this trend. In 1275 John de Hethe of the parish of Laysters made a contract with Josce fil Manasser of Hereford. In it, John promised to pay Josce 60 soams (horse loads) of 'good, dry and winnowed corn' or half a mark of silver for each soam. The grain was to be delivered to the Jew or to his attorney at his house in Hereford at Michaelmas 1275. The document was witnessed by the sheriff of Herefordshire and the bailiffs of Hereford. Joe Hillaby has recently claimed that in such bonds there was never any intention of the debt being paid in kind.[158] If this is so the descriptive nature of 'good, dry and winnowed' and other factors seem rather superfluous to the contract. As discussed in detail above, many other arguments point towards some Jewish involvement in the grain trade. Be this as it may, it would appear that this contract was fulfilled by John de Hethe, as it does not appear in any other scrutinies.

The *vetus cista*, as Hillaby verifies, also contained some bonds which demanded small amounts of commodities. Where these were stipulated they tended to be small amounts of cereal. Interestingly, the amounts were often stipulated in the local measure, the truge (two-thirds of a bushel). Aaron le Blund was owed twenty-four 'mixed commodity repayments'. Over and above his large cash debts he was owed a total of 30½ quarters and 6 truges of corn with a face value of approximately £10 4s 10d. Aaron's son Bonenfaunt was also owed two mixed commodity and cash repayments which would have provided him with 2½ quarters of corn. These two larger entrepreneurs were also owed fifteen geese, a robe with a hood and one cartload of hay and two geese respectively. Yet it was not only those who had negotiated many bonds who made such stipulations for commodities. Hagin fil Elye made provision in four of his bonds for repayments of a total of 1 quarter and 7 truges of corn. Mirabile filia Isaac, in her single loan of £18 in cash, had also made arrangements for the payment of 1 quarter of corn. Cuntessa filia Mosse and Elye fil Aaron required smaller commodity repayments: 1 truge and 3 truges respectively. As has been observed in the case of the smaller entrepreneurs, their commodities were probably for personal consumption rather than for resale.[159]

---

[157] PRO E/101/250/5. Mundill 1987, pp. 225–8.

[158] Hereford County RO MS AH81/34. This bond was acquired by the record office in 1981. I first came across it in a bundle of papers in 1983. A photograph of it is in Mundill 1990a, pp. 7–8. Although it could be assumed that this particular bond may have been paid, the same John did not pay a £2 debt that he owed another Jew, Jacob fil Sadekyn, in 1276, because, according to the list of bonds in the *vetus cista*, it was still unpaid in 1291: PRO E/101/250/5; Hillaby 1990c, pp. 456–7.

[159] Hillaby 1990c, pp. 441, 447, 476; again there is a small dicrepancy (£1 5s 0d) between Hillaby's

On the other hand, Aaron le Blund's commodity bonds seem a little large for mere personal consumption. The evidence for Aaron's commodity dealings reveals a continuing trend. According to the 1275 scrutiny, Aaron was already owed one robe with a hood, 23 soams of cereal, 3 truges of cereal and five geese and was therefore from the evidence in the *vetus cista*, now owed a further nine geese, a little more cereal and one cartload of hay. Thus, for Aaron le Blund, commodity bonding on a scale larger than that necessary for personal consumption was already a significant practice well before the Statute of 1275.[160] Aaron was only pursuing what was in Hereford a traditional practice for the richer Jew. For, in the first half of the century, Hamo of Hereford had also been owed 13 quarters of assorted cereal and Ursell, his son, was owed 70 quarters of oats, 27 quarters of mixed grain, 33½ quarters of corn and 7 quarters of pease.[161] These examples, in addition to the evidence of the 1262 sample which showed commodity bonding on a smaller perhaps more personal scale, demonstrate that commodity bonds for both consumption and commerce had a long history in Hereford before Edward I's reign.[162]

The details of transactions lodged in the *nova cista* reveal Jewish business practice in Hereford from 1283 to the Expulsion.[163] The stipulated repayments include money, cereal and wool. It was this return to registering monetary repayments at Hereford which led B. L. Abrahams to date the *Chapitles* to the period just before 1283.[164] The *nova cista* gave details of seventeen Jews who held a total of seventy-seven bonds, worth a face value of £1,065 7s 8d. Many of the more active Jews who were registering bonds at this time were also identified in earlier samples. At the top of the creditors was Aaron le Blund who held almost 30 per cent of the total bonds in the chest. However, his son Bonenfaunt, with twelve bonds, was now put into third place by the eighteen bonds of Josce fil Manser of Hereford.[165] As well as the established lenders there was also evidence of new Jewish creditors appearing at this period. Hagin of Weobley, who also contributed to the sheriff's payment for Herefordshire in 1285, had seven bonds in the *archa*, of which the earliest was dated

figures and my own. Hillaby has Aaron le Blund's bonds valued at £743 3s 8d whilst my valuation showed them to be worth a face value of £744 8s 8d: Mundill 1987, pp. 225–8; PRO E/101/250/5.

[160] *PREJ3*, pp. 230–8; PRO E/101/250/5.
[161] Mundill, 1987, pp. 211–14; Hillaby 1990c, p. 441; 1984, pp. 384–7.
[162] PRO E/101/249/10 membrane 5, E/101/250/5.
[163] PRO E/101/250/5; Mundill 1987, pp. 232–5; Hillaby 1990c, pp. 456–61.
[164] Abrahams 1894a, p. 140.
[165] PRO E/101/250/5; Mundill 1987, pp. 232–5; Hillaby 1990c, pp. 456–61.

1285.[166] Other Jews who had not been previously identified in earlier scrutinies were Ursellus of Gloucester, Isaac fil Hagin of Weobley, Abraham *capellanus* of the Jews of Hereford, Hagin fil Belia de Blanc, Isaac le Eveske of London, Sarra filia Elias of Gloucester and Ursellus fil Hak.[167]

There was a change not only in personnel but also in the actual number of Jewish creditors making loans at this time. The *vetus cista* revealed thirty Jews who had bonds owing to them whilst the *nova cista* revealed seventeen. There was also a great difference in the number of bonds which were recorded. The *vetus cista* recorded 205 bonds whilst the *nova cista* only had details of seventy-seven. It is thus not surprising that a comparison between the two different lists shows a large difference in the mean value of Jewish outlay. In the *vetus cista* it was £37 11s 1d and in the *nova cista* it was £62 13s 4d. Similarly, there was a corresponding difference in the mean value of a bond between the two samples. A mean value transaction in the *vetus cista* was worth £5 9s 11d and a similar transaction in the *nova cista* was worth £13 16s 8d. This change in value was also matched by a noticeable difference in the face value of the smallest bonds. In the *vetus cista* there were eleven bonds with a face value of under £5 and in the *nova cista* there is only one.[168]

All of these differences can probably be explained by the shift of preference to commodity repayments. Of the seventy-seven transactions registered in the *nova cista* there were thirty-eight which stipulated repayment to be made in money, thirty-five which stipulated repayments to be made in commodities, four which involved wool repayments and six which stipulated repayment to be made in money as well as a very small commodity repayment. Interestingly, there were some rather odd commodity repayments to the le Blunds. Aaron was now owed twenty-four cheeses and four wagonloads of hay whilst his son Bonenfaunt was owed a robe 'made in the military fashion'. There seems little reason to doubt the genuineness of these particular commodity repayments.[169]

The bonds which stipulated repayment in money were owed to eleven Jews. Of these, Aaron le Blund, Bonenfaunt le Blund and Josce fil Manser, who have been identified as having previously registered bonds in the Hereford *archa*, head the list with fairly large amounts owing to them. Their transactions show clearly the significant return in lending money for monetary repayment during this period. There were also five Jews with single bonds repayable in money. Their debts ranged

---

[166] PRO E/101/250/5; Hagin also contributed to tallage in the 1280s, PRO E/101/249/26.
[167] Mundill 1987, pp. 232–5.   [168] PRO E/101/250/5.   [169] PRO E/101/250/5.

in value from £10 owed to Hagin fil Hagin to the £1 10s 0d owed to Ursellus of Gloucester.[170]

The debts which stipulated repayment in grain once again graphically illustrate the effect of the *Statutum de Judeismo*. More Jews were demanding cereal repayments which were clearly not of the size which could be explained away by claiming that they were just for personal consumption.[171] Even the cereal bond with the smallest face value of £3 6s 8d, the 10 quarters owed to Sarra of Hereford, is unlikely to have been just for her personal use. Certainly the fact that 60 quarters were owed to Isaac fil Hagin of Weobley in a single transaction cannot just be a case of Isaac's obtaining cereal to feed his family. His father Hagin of Weobley was also owed a further 70 quarters in his own right. The nineteen separate bonds owing to Bonenfaunt and Aaron le Blund show that these two members of the le Blund family were owed 993 quarters between them, probably enough to have fed the entire Hereford Jewish community. In the period 1283–90, ten members of the Hereford Jewish community were owed a total of 1,450 quarters of grain.[172] The Hereford *nova cista*, like the Canterbury evidence, shows a massive shift of emphasis towards bonding for grain.[173]

The change in preference for commodity repayments can also be seen by the transactions of the three Jews who were owed four bonds which were repayable in quantities of wool. Strikingly, it was in this context that Bonenfaunt le Blund becomes styled 'Jew of London'.[174] Similarly, Isaac le Eveske is shown to have London connections. Jews who were dealing in wool would naturally do well to have London contacts. The quantities of wool and their respective values were also clear indications of the fact that these Jews were beginning to be involved in the wool trade in a large way.[175] The details of one of Isaac le Eveske's transactions help to show how such a transaction would be arranged. The scribal extracts from the *nova cista* record that Peter de Grenham, *miles* of Devonshire, owed Isaac le Eveske of London eight sacks of wool priced at 6s 8d a sack. The bond was dated on 15 July 1283 and was made at Shrewsbury despite the fact that it was deposited in the Hereford *archa*.[176]

---

[170] *Ibid.*   [171] Hillaby 1990c, pp. 456–7; Mundill 1990a.

[172] Mundill 1987, pp. 234–5; Hillaby 1990c, pp. 456–7; some estimates indicate that a quarter of cereal would make 400 lbs of bread which would probably feed four people for approximately three weeks.

[173] PRO E/101/250/5, E/101/250/6; Mundill 1990a, p. 5.

[174] PRO E/101/250/5; Mundill 1987, p. 235. Bonenfaunt is styled both 'of Hereford' and 'of London'.

[175] Hillaby 1990c, pp. 459–60; Mundill 1987, pp. 390–2.

[176] PRO E/101/250/5 – *apud Salop.*

The same contract was, however, also recorded on the Plea Roll of the *Scaccarium Judaeorum* which was then sitting at Shrewsbury. The Plea Roll entry is, in essence, a recognizance. Because of this double reference and because of the very fact that the recognizance was made in front of the officials of the *Scaccarium Judaeorum*, there can be little reason to doubt the record of the bond's validity. As would be expected, the information on the Plea Roll is much more detailed than that in the later scribal extract and helps to clarify the transaction. Peter de Grenham owed eight sacks of wool to Isaac le Eveske of London priced at £6 13s 4d per sack. This corrects what can only have been a scribal error over the price of the wool on the list of bonds made in 1290. Half the amount was to be repaid on 13 January 1284 and the other half was to be repaid on 9 April of that year. As security, Peter's lands in Devonshire were to be at risk. The recognizance also recorded that a third part of the debt was owed to Josce fil Manser, a Hereford Jew.[177] This probably explains why the bond was deposited in the Hereford *archa*. Such corroboration of evidence is rare.

Thus an examination of the transactions of the Hereford Jewry between 1262 and 1290 shows a picture of a well-established community who managed to survive the Edwardian Experiment and even to prosper in adverse circumstances. The *vetus cista* with transactions dating from 1259 to 1276 had a face value of just over £1,120, whilst the *nova cista* which contained transactions dating from 1283 to 1290 (only a seven-year period) was worth just over £1,050. At least some of Hereford's Jews remained prosperous to the very eve of the Expulsion.

LINCOLN

Without doubt Lincoln was one of the older and more well-established Jewish communities in medieval England and had also been the centre of the great eleventh-century financier Aaron of Lincoln.[178] In the thirteenth century, according to surviving records, it was probably one of the most populated provincial Jewries in the country. An examination of the list of those Jews who had given bonds in 1262 shows that the city had attracted many Jews from other communities. At that time London Jews were conducting business in the city; according to the evidence the richest Jew in Lincoln was Benedict Crespin of London. Other London Jews such as Moses fil Isaac of Colchester, Abraham Crespin, Samuel fil Ursell and Isaac of Southwark also had bonds

---

[177] PRO E/9/43 membrane 64.
[178] Mundill 1987, pp. 253–5; Davis 1881o; Jacobs, 1899; Hill 1979, p. 33; 1965, pp. 218–21.

deposited in the Lincoln *archa*. The York Jews, Isaac fil Josce of Kent and Benedict *Episcopus*, were also represented. It seems there were Jews from Kent like Vives fil Isaac of Canterbury, Deubeneye of Rochester, Sampson, Benedict fil Hakelm, Magister Aaron of Canterbury, Deule-cresse, the husband of Avigaye of Canterbury, Elias of Kent and Samuel fil Aaron of Canterbury, who had Lincoln connections. Possibly other Jews from places like Exeter, Grimsby, Northampton, Colchester, Hereford, Norwich, Stamford, Winchester, Wilton, Worcester, Luton, Kingston and Warwick had also transacted business in the city in 1262.[179]

Another interesting feature of the 1262 evidence is that there were indications that a little trading in commodities was already in progress.[180] This trade was on a small scale and once again possibly only for personal consumption. Six Jews were owed 1 quarter of cereal over and above their monetary debts. Isaac fil Benedict of Northampton and Josce fil Jacob were also owed a soam of cereal whilst Abraham fil Abraham was owed half a soam and Josce fil Abraham of Bungay was owed 2 soams. Josce *genus* Deulecresse of Norwich was even owed 2 quarters of oats. Leon le Blund was owed a bushel of pease and Moses fil Isaac of Colchester, a London Jew, was owed a cartload of wood worth 2s 0d.[181]

There was clearly a wide range of Jewish creditors operating in Lincoln in 1262. One large operator, Benedict Crespin of London, gave fifteen bonds worth £54 1s 8d as payment towards the tallage; yet most Jewish creditors gave only very small bonds.[182] The mean value of a bond from this particular period was £2 13s 8d, and twenty-two Jews contributed bonds worth less than £1. This low mean value may well be explained by the fact that the pogroms which accompanied the Little St Hugh affair in 1255 had affected Jewish credit.[183] Although some recovery in Jewish business had taken place, the value of Jewish loans in 1262 was not particularly high and Lincoln was seemingly only attracting large investment from Jews with connections outside the city.

Some idea of Jewish credit activity at the start of Edward I's reign comes from the scrutiny of the Lincoln *archa* taken in January 1275. This provided details of ninety-three Jews who lived in Lincoln,

[179] PRO E/101/249/10 membranes 12 and 13. There are also small amounts of commodities recorded on an earlier 1240 roll PRO/E/249/4.
[180] PRO E/101/249/10 membranes 12 and 13.   [181] Mundill 1987, pp. 266–8.
[182] PRO E/101/249/10 membranes 12 and 13.
[183] Jacobs 1893b; Langmuir 1972; Saitz 1960I; Tovey 1738, pp. 136–43; Lincoln Public Library, The Banks Collection fos. 80, 81, 154; *CCR 1255*, pp. 142, 143, 145, 227, 241, 451, 493, 510; *CPR 1247–1258*, pp. 453, 457; Roth 1948, pp. 68–9.

although only fourteen actually had bonds in the *archa* at the time. The clerk who recorded these transactions appears to have believed that there were forty-nine bonds in the *archa*, but he in fact recorded fifty-two transactions. This seeming lack of accuracy in the clerk's arithmetic could have been the result of a few Jews holding shared bonds. Regrettably this evidence gave no clue as to the financial value of the bonds at this particular moment in the history of the Lincoln Jewry.[184] However a series of original bonds which were made in Lincoln between 1270 and 1276 have survived at Westminster Abbey and carry fuller details about the nature of the Jewish communities' business affairs.[185] It is likely that these bonds came from a Lincoln *archa* which was probably examined sometime in early 1276.[186] This date seems likely because the sample contains one of the bonds which were returned to Isaac fil Benedict Gabbay after he had paid his tallage in early 1275.[187] This particular bond must also have been returned to Lincoln after the third due to the Crown from Isaac's estate had been paid in 1275.[188] A similar indication of the date at which these bonds reached Westminster is given by the fact that three of the Westminster bonds recording the transactions of Senior fil Abraham may very well be three of the four bonds which were recorded in his name in the 1275 scrutiny which was discussed above.[189]

The bonds confirm that there were Jews in Lincoln at this period who maintained connections with places outside the city. Benedict of London was again near the top of the hierarchy.[190] His son Hagin and another London Jew, Aaron fil Elias were also transacting business.[191] The great York financier, Bonamy fil Josce had a single bond worth

---

[184] *PREJ4*, pp. 25–6 reveals details of the names of the following Jews who held bonds: Isaac fil Benedict (twenty), Jacob fil Isaac (eight), Senior fil Abraham (four), Abraham of Oakham, Moses fil Moses of Clare, Hagin fil Moses and Abraham fil Dyay of Holme (three each), Benedict fil Manser (two), Elias fil Benedict of London, Moses fil Moses, Sampson fil Benedict, Benedict fil Josce, Yvette filia Bonefy, the wife of Josce Bullak and Josce son-in-law of Josce (one each).

[185] The surviving Lincoln bonds are WAM nos. 9014, 9027, 9032, 9054, 9087, 9092, 9093, 9094, 9095, 9097, 9098, 9100, 9117, 9130, 9131, 9132, 9135, 9137, 9140, 9142, 9143, 9144, 9145, 9146, 9147, 9148, 9150, 9160, 9161, 9162, 9163, 9164, 9165, 9167, 9168, 9169, 9170.

[186] Some of the Westminster bonds for Colchester, WAM nos. 9017, 9031, 9052, 9056 and 9059, match up to the bonds listed on PRO c/47/9/48 which was compiled late in 1275. It would seem likely that the Lincoln bonds were also listed either in 1275 or early 1276 but the detailed list is now lost.

[187] WAM no. 9027 was made on 11 November 1271 and was payable on 24 June 1272. It acknowledged that Richard Bret of Wrangle owed Isaac fil Benedict £10. This could also be the same bond referred to in *PREJ4*, p. 67.

[188] WAM no. 9027; *PREJ2*, p. 268. [189] WAM nos. 9130, 9161, 9165; *PREJ4*, p. 25.

[190] WAM nos. 9032, 9100, 9140, 9150. Roth 1948.

[191] WAM no. 9095 was owed to Hagin; WAM nos. 9087, 9098, 9137, 9142, 9143, 9168, 9169 were owed to Aaron fil Elias 'of London'.

£26 13s 4d.[192] However, a significant presence of native Lincoln Jews can also be observed. Jacob fil Isaac of Brancegate whose business and enterprise must have been in the ascendancy at this period had five bonds in the *archa*.[193] Josce fil Benedict Gabbay had two bonds worth £14 13s 4d.[194] Thirteen other Lincoln Jews had made bonds and expected to be repaid a sum worth just under £60.[195]

The thirty-seven Westminster Abbey bonds were worth a face value of £350 11s 4d. They show that there were Jews in Lincoln at this time who were perhaps able to make bigger individual loans and to commit themselves to a greater total outlay than those Jews who had appeared in the 1262 list. Benedict of London had four bonds worth a total of £168, one quarter of the total value of the 1262 bonds. Aaron fil Elias of London and the local Jew, Jacob of Brancegate, both had bonds worth as much as £35 13s 4d.[196] The total value of debts owing to these Jews was greater than the value of the total outlay of all but one of the Jews who gave bonds in 1262. The mean Jewish outlay from the 1262 transactions was £4 10s 1d whilst the corresponding figure from the Westminster bonds is £18 9s 0d. Similarly the mean value of a bond in 1262 was £2 13s 8d and the corresponding value for 1276 was £9 9s 5d. Even given the differences in the types of evidence used, these are significant indications of a real change in the credit operations of the Lincoln Jews. However the Westminster bonds show that there were Jews who made comparatively small transactions. Jews like Josce fil Deulesant, Samuel fil Abraham and Samuel fil Belia were each owed £1 6s 8d, and were still able to operate in the 1270s alongside the more affluent lenders.[197] The Westminster bonds carry little evidence of commodity repayments. Only one bond mentions such a repayment. It was an additional repayment for 1 quarter of grain which was owed to Jacob of Brancegate, the Lincoln Jew.[198] A sum of this size is not significant and may well have been just for Jacob's personal consumption. Yet intriguingly, by 1290, Jacob of Brancegate was owed a total of 570½ quarters of corn.[199]

The evidence from the Lincoln *archa* in 1290 also revealed a large

---

[192] WAM no. 9014; Dobson 1979, pp. 45–6.　　[193] WAM nos. 9117, 9144, 9160, 9164, 9170.

[194] WAM nos. 9132, 9148.

[195] WAM nos. 9027, 9054, 9092, 9093, 9094, 9097, 9130, 9131, 9135, 9145, 9146, 9147, 9161, 9162, 9163, 9165, 9167.

[196] Benedict: WAM nos. 9032, 9100, 9140, 9150; Aaron fil Elias of London: WAM nos. 9087, 9098, 9137, 9142, 9143, 9168, 9169; Jacob fil Isaac of Brancegate: WAM nos. 9117, 9144, 9160, 9164, 9170.

[197] WAM nos. 9146, 9162, 9167.

[198] WAM no. 9170, contracted in July 1275 and payable on 1 January 1276.

[199] PRO E/101/250/12.

change in the way Jews transacted their business. The Lincoln *archa* contained 252 bonds, some 23 per cent of all known surviving Jewish-owned bonds in England.[200] These bonds were described as *nova debita*. In addition to the bonds in the main *archa* there were ten bonds (all dating from 1290) which were contained in a small sealed chest. The fact that the Lincoln 1290 evidence is so complete means that a picture of Jewish financial dealings covering almost a decade can be formed. A quarter of the bonds were actually contracted in 1290, which might give an indication that business was on the increase in the years immediately before the Expulsion. However any *archa* would normally contain a greater proportion of bonds contracted in the recent as opposed to the distant past. The total face value of the Lincoln bonds was about £2,500.[201] Such evidence clearly shows that, in Lincoln, despite the threat of confiscation of property, the hangings during the coin-clipping allegations and the effects of the *Statutum de Judeismo* of 1275, the Jews were at least able to continue their lending. In some cases individual Jewish financiers were able to amass fairly large fortunes from their business. It is also clear that bonding went on until September 1290. No doubt the Jews who entered into these transactions had no premonition of the forthcoming acts of banishment and confiscation.[202]

Before examining the bonds of the 1290 scrutiny, several issues deserve to be clarified. Amongst the bonds there were four that were repayable to two creditors, Jews or Jewesses who acted in partnership and shared debts.[203] The bonds were made as late as 1288 and 1289. Such debts, owed to partners, had often presented difficulty for the Crown: they were difficult to assess for tallage or to claim as 'death duty' and it was difficult to confirm that they had been paid. Whether or not the *Chapitles* were issued they forbade partnership lending. A second peculiarity was a bond, owed to Jacob of Brancegate, which promised repayment in money and a small amount of grain. In September 1278, Thomas, the son of Master Thomas *dominus* of Bekering in Lincolnshire, owed Jacob of Brancegate £1 10s 0d and half a quarter of corn.[204] A third peculiarity amongst the 252 recorded bonds was that there were two which differed from the accepted norm. They were both undated

[200] PRO E/101/250/12; Abrahams 1896; see Tables 4 and 5.
[201] PRO E/101/250/12; Mundill 1987, pp. 267–93.
[202] Bonds were made in Lincoln in August and September 1290: PRO E/101/250/12.
[203] See Appendix III; PRO E/101/250/12 shows that in July 1288 Jacob fil Sampson Levi and Ursell his son were owed 6 sacks of wool at £6 13s 4d each; in October 1288 Sarra filia Bonne and Chera the widow were owed one sack of wool priced at £10; in November 1288 Meyre fil Bonne and Elye fil Manser were owed one sack of wool priced at £10; in July 1289 Bonne and her son Miles were owed two sacks of wool priced at £10.
[204] PRO E/101/250/12.

and contracted between Richard Foliot, *miles* of Yorkshire, and Hagin fil Magister Benedict of London. They were basically annuities or promises of annual payments with a cash price payable to the Jewish creditor on the debtor's death. Hagin was owed one flying-hawk and, on Richard's death, £50. He was also owed a beast of the chase every year and £66 13s 4d on Richard's death. They may well have been much earlier transactions which had remained in the chest.[205]

The rest of the bonds were dated and the contract dates indicate that the vast majority were made between 1288 and the Expulsion.[206] Thus, the contents of the Lincoln *archa*, with bonds which were dated as early as 1278, reflect the type of business being carried out after the disruptions of 1278 and 1279 as well as illustrating the possible effects of Edward's legislation on Jewish lending. In this light, the most exceptional quality of the Lincoln *archa* is to be found in the amount of evidence which it provides of commodity as well as monetary repayments. Fifteen per cent of the bonds, with a face value of £306 10s od, were for repayments in money. Twenty-nine per cent of the bonds were for repayment mainly in cereal. The repayments represented 2,122½ quarters of cereal with a face value of £552 13s 1od. Almost 56 per cent of the bonds stipulate repayment in wool. The Jews of Lincoln, on the eve of the Expulsion, were owed 208½ sacks and 8 stone of wool with a face value of £1,602 14s 8d. It is this considerable volume of evidence of commodity repayment that makes the Lincoln evidence so exceptional.

It is not only the vast number of bonds but also the large number of creditors that make the evidence worth greater discussion. The sixty-two Jews identified by this evidence represent the largest number of provincial moneylenders identified by the information in all the surviving *archae* of 1290.[207] Nevertheless, it is clear that this figure was significantly less than the figures of 133 and ninety Jews who held bonds in the much earlier 1240 and 1262 Lincoln samples.[208] This suggests that

---

[205] PRO E/101/250/12. The entries read as follows:

Ricus Folyot Miles de Comitatus Eboracum debet Hagin filio Benedicti de London Judo Lincolniae unum spuar muer eidem Hagino in vita cuisdem Rici soluend' et post decessum ipsius Rici in primo anno reddent heredes sui eidem Hagino Quinquaginta libra per unam obligationem...

Idem Ricus Folyot eidem Hagino filio Benedicti unam bestiam de crasso salt' Dannu ut Dania annuatim in tota sua predicto Hagino soluend' et post decessum ipsius Rici in primo ano reddent heredes sui eidem Hagino c marc per unam obligationem.

For fuller discussion see Mundill 1987, p. 279; Roth 1957, pp. 66–7, proves that at least some Jews hunted with Christians.

[206] PRO E/101/250/12.   [207] See Tables 4 and 5; Mundill 1987, pp. 267–93.

[208] Stacey 1988, pp. 107, 225; Davis 1881, p. 192; PRO E/101/249/4, E/101/249/10 membranes 12 and 13, E/101/250/12; Mundill 1987, pp. 261–2, 266–93.

the number of Jews conducting some sort of credit business in Lincoln had declined in the fifty years before the Expulsion. It is of course impossible to suggest whether this decline in the number of Jews conducting business was matched by a similar decline in the total Jewish population of the city, although such a conclusion would seem likely.[209]

Another of the features of the 1290 list is a distinct scarcity of toponymic surnames. It is impossible to determine whether such a lack of toponyms was the result of accident or of the fact that these Jews were especially closely identified with Lincoln itself at this period. There are, however, indications that Jewish business in Lincoln was being conducted, in 1290, by Jews who were more obviously based in the city than had been their predecessors. For example, of the three Jews who are referred to as 'of London', two were also clearly identifiable with Lincoln. Both Moses fil Isaac of London and Hagin fil Benedict of London were also significantly described in the list as 'Jews of Lincoln'. In the case of both Magister Benedict and his son Hagin, there is evidence that the family had come to Lincoln in the late 1240s and had become influential members of the community, in terms not only of business but also of learning.[210]

Other Jews with toponymic surnames which suggest connections outside Lincoln can also be linked with the city. Perhaps Giwe of Canterbury and Trina filia Dulcia of York had married Lincoln Jews.[211] Jacob of Hedon (near Kingston upon Hull) might well have been a relative of Benedict of Heydon whose servant lived in St Cuthbert's parish.[212] Manser of Brodsworth seems to have transacted business in Lincoln.[213] Thus, many creditors with probable outside connections had seemingly become Lincoln-based by 1290. It is, perhaps, also significant that these Jews, even with their external connections, had all been surpassed, in terms of financial influence, by the Lincoln-based creditor, Jacob fil Isaac of Brancegate. Jacob of Brancegate is an example of a professional moneylender who seems to have had no other connection than that with Lincoln.[214] Cecil Roth dubbed Hagin fil Magister Benedict the richest Jew in Lincoln. Yet the dealings of Jacob of Brancegate reveal that his loans were worth almost double those of Hagin.[215]

[209] Mundill 1987, pp. 274–5; Rokeah 1993.
[210] PRO E/101/250/12; Roth 1948, pp. 68, 70–3; Davis 1881, pp. 194–5.
[211] PRO E/101/250/12.
[212] PRO E/101/250/12; Lincoln RO MCD 501 (a copy of PRO C/85/99).
[213] Hunter 1828, p. 314; *SCBM*, vol. II, pp. 206–8; *CPR 1258–1266*, p. 581; WAM no. 9085; PREJ2, pp 8, 87, 190, 299–300; Mundill 1987, pp. 282–3.
[214] PRO E/101/250/12; WAM nos. 9117, 9144, 9160, 9164, 9170.   [215] Roth 1948, p. 70.

The numerical distribution of bonds in 1290 shows that over two-thirds of the Jewish business men held three bonds or less. Twenty-seven either shared or held single bonds, nine held two bonds and nine held three bonds. The average Jewish creditor in 1290 held just over four bonds, although individuals like Jacob of Brancegate and Solomon fil Deulecresse of London held as many as twenty or more. Because of the nature of the 1262 and Westminster evidence it is impossible to make any helpful comparison between the number of bonds held by each Jew in 1290 and at the dates of these previous samples. It is also impossible to come to any firm conclusion about the value of the average bond being contracted at various dates. Yet such comparisons can perhaps be used as a guide to the situation. The mean average value of a bond in 1262 would have been £2 13s 8d compared with £9 9s 5d from the Westminster bonds and £9 16s 11d from the 1290 evidence. These are so different that it is difficult to suggest that all of the difference is a consequence of the 1262 evidence's connections with tallage payment. Thus at Lincoln it would seem possible that the mean value of a bond had increased to roughly 1290 levels by the dates at which the bonds in the Westminster sample were contracted. This is an interestingly different situation from that found in other communities. It is, nevertheless, the case that there are just as many Jews with single bonds recorded, of a value of under £4, in the Westminster sample as in the much larger 1290 evidence. This seems to suggest that at Lincoln by 1290 it was Jewish creditors operating on a small scale who had been squeezed out of the market just as they had been elsewhere.[216]

The diversification and specialisation which the 1290 list reveals concerning the specific preferences of Jewish financiers is striking. Jacob of Brancegate clearly preferred to have his bonds repaid in cereal rather than wool and tended not to enter into money bonds. Solomon of London, on the other hand, preferred bonding for wool but, like Jacob, apparently dabbled in all three commodities. Moses fil Isaac seems only to have been interested in wool bonds. It is possible that he was acting solely as a wool-broker. Cok le fiz Hagin had only one bond in the *archa* which stipulated a monetary repayment. Those who had engaged in single bonds and who expected repayments of between £5 and £10 preferred to have them repaid in wool. The Jews who had made single

---

[216] PRO E/101/250/12, E/101/249/10 membranes 12 and 13; WAM nos. 9014, 9027, 9032, 9054, 9087, 9092, 9093, 9094, 9095, 9097, 9098, 9100, 9117, 9130, 9131, 9132, 9135, 9137, 9140, 9142, 9143, 9144, 9145, 9146, 9147, 9148, 9150, 9160, 9161, 9162, 9163, 9164, 9165, 9167, 9168, 9169, 9170.

bonds which expected repayments for a sum less than £3 preferred to be repaid in corn.[217]

There were a few Jews who only expected monetary repayments for their loans. Cok le fiz Hagin, Belassez filia Solomon and Moses le Evesk were the only Jews who had bonds repayable in cash, whilst the other sixteen Jews who were involved with money bonds had other interests. Cok le fiz Hagin's bond for £80 which was made in 1289 was an extremely large repayment. With the exception of this large bond those lenders who bonded for money were dominated by those who offered large-scale credit facilities in both money and in commodities. Interestingly, the average money bond of 1290 was worth less than the average bond of that date. Most bonds which stipulated repayment in money were therefore for comparatively small sums. In fact, the total of just over £300 worth of bonds is a clear indication that the majority of Lincoln lenders did not favour cash repayments. Thus, it is quite likely that in Lincoln the Statute of 1275 did have the effect of turning Jewish interests towards commodities rather than specie. However, as both the Lincoln and the Nottingham *archae* amply illustrate, it was still possible in the 1280s to make legally binding bonds which demanded repayment in cash.[218] The earliest money bond in Lincoln was dated 1278 and was the mixed commodity bond belonging to Jacob of Brancegate. There were also one dated in 1280, one in 1285 and four in 1287. Thirty-four of the money bonds were contracted in the last three years of Jewish presence in Lincoln. The return to bonding for money is evidenced throughout the 1280s. There was therefore presumably little need to disguise moneylending as camouflaged commodity broking in Lincoln.[219]

A more detailed examination of the cereal bonds not only proves their genuine nature but clearly seems to indicate that some Lincoln Jews had shifted their financial interests and had become brokers for commodities which included cereal. Bonds which stipulated repayment in cereal are no novelty amongst the dealings of the Lincolnshire Jewry. It has long been known that Aaron of Lincoln was making bonds for cereal repayments in the Rutland area in the twelfth century.[220] Myer Domnitz Davis, who was the first to examine the 1240 Lincoln scrutiny, demonstrated that at that time some Jews required small commodity repayments including some in cereal in addition to cash.[221] However, before 1275, these promises of amounts of grain were nearly always found as small payments added on to a much larger cash repayment.

[217] PRO E/101/250/12.　　[218] Mundill 1990a, pp. 4–5; PRO E/101/250/8, E/101/250/12.
[219] PRO E/101/250/12.　　[220] Richardson 1960, pp. 247–53.
[221] Davis 1881, p. 192; PRO E/101/249/4.

The 1262 evidence revealed seven Jews who were all owed 1 quarter of corn in addition to their cash repayments, whilst Josce fil Deulecresse of Norwich was owed 2 quarters of oats.[222] One of the Westminster bonds showed that on 15 July 1275 Richard Rudde of Barton promised to pay Jacob fil Isaac of Brancegate £3 6s 8d and 1 quarter of wheat on 1 January 1276.[223] By comparison with these meagre amounts, in 1290 the Jews of Lincoln were owed over 2,000 quarters of assorted cereals (mainly corn). To accumulate this debt, they had contracted seventy-three bonds which ranged in date from 1278 to 1290. The amounts contracted for in each bond vary in size from as much as 240 quarters of assorted cereals to 2 quarters. The average size of a cereal bond would have been for 20 quarters; there were fourteen of these in the *archa*. These represent fairly large transactions and clearly involved something more than just personal consumption.[224]

There are several features of these cereal bonds which suggest that they were transactions concerned with actual repayment in cereals rather than disguised money transactions. The first of these is the degree of detail incorporated in several of the bonds. In September 1279, Jordan Foliot, *miles* of Norfolk, and Adam of New Market, *miles* of Lincolnshire, made a contract to pay Manser of Brodsworth 80 quarters of corn at 6s 8d a quarter, 80 quarters of barley at 5s 0d a quarter, and 80 quarters of oats at 2s 0d a quarter.[225] In June 1280, Andrew fil Benedict and Henry fil William of Rolleston in Nottinghamshire made a contract with Ursell fil Sampson Levy. The details of the repayment were, once again, quite clear. They were to pay 24 quarters of wheat, 12 quarters of corn, 6 quarters of barley and 6 quarters of oats. The price for each quarter of cereal was not stipulated.[226] In September 1281, Geoffrey of Fountains, a Lincolnshire knight, was to pay Jacob fil Sampson Levi 60 quarters of barley, again at an unspecified price per quarter.[227] If these transactions were merely a disguise for monetary repayments then it is

---

[222] PRO E/101/249/10 membranes 12 and 13.   [223] WAM nos. 9170.

[224] PRO E/101/250/12. The dry weight avoirdupois of 20 quarters of corn would weigh just over 4 tons 4 cwt.

[225] PRO E/101/250/12; Farmer 1957, p. 212 gives the following prices per quarter for 1279:

wheat/corn *frumenti*	5s 3¼d	(priced at 6s 8d in bond)
barley *ordei*	3s 9d	(priced at 5s 0d in bond)
oats *avenae*	2s 1d	(priced at 2s 0d in bond).

[226] PRO E/101/250/12. The size of these cereal repayments must have been considerable:

1 bushel of wheat = 60 lbs > 1 qtr of wheat = 480 lbs (4.2 cwt)
1 bushel of barley = 56 lbs > 1 qtr of barley = 448 lbs (4 cwt)
1 bushel of oats = 42 lbs > 1 qtr of oats = 336 lbs (3 cwt).

[227] PRO E/101/250/12.

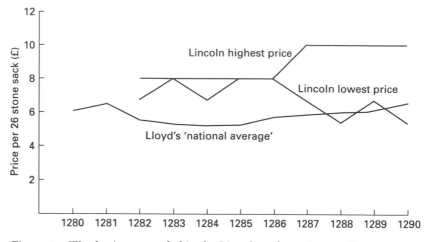

Figure 3   Wool prices recorded in the Lincoln *archa*, 1280–90. *Sources:* PRO
E/101/250/12; Lloyd 1973, p. 38.

inconceivable that such detailed descriptions of the different types of
cereals involved were necessary.

The different price levels for grain referred to in the transactions were
a second feature of the 1290 cereal bonds which suggests that they were
more than disguised money bonds. If they had indeed been intended as
disguised money bonds, there was no reason for the persons contracting
them to create more than artificial price levels to disguise their
clandestine moneylending.[228] And yet, at Lincoln, price variation was
evident. There was a large difference between Bonamy fil Bonamy's
bond for 6 quarters at 2s od a quarter made with Richard fil Gerlon of
Humberstone in late June 1288 and Milo fil Bonne's bond made with
Thomas Spede of Harmston in February 1287, which was priced at 6s
od a quarter. There was also a difference between Benedict fil
Sampson's and Isaac fil Manser's bonds for 20 quarters, with a face value
of £5, and Diay fil Diay's bonds for the same amount of corn worth £5
16s 8d. Another immediate difference in price can be seen in the single
corn transactions of Jacob of Hedon and Benedict fil Jacob.[229] There
were also differences in price levels in bonds which were contracted in
the same month in August 1285, December 1286 and in January,
August and November 1287.[230] Figure 1 indicates price differences not

[228] Lipman 1967, pp. 164–6; Hillaby 1990c, pp. 456–9.   [229] PRO E/101/250/12.
[230] PRO E/101/250/12; Mundill 1987, pp. 379–80.

only within months but also between one month and the next, for example between June and July.

A third feature which helps to prove the authenticity of the cereal transactions is the dates at which bonds expecting cereal repayments were contracted. The bonds recorded in the 1290 sample from the years 1284, 1285, 1286 and 1287 appear to have a seasonal characteristic. Transactions in grain seem to have been more popular in the pre-harvest period, August and September. This sort of evidence, which itself suggests credit facilities being offered on the expectation of the harvest, becomes even more significant when it is compared with the lack of seasonal variation in the dates of the bonds contracted expecting monetary repayment.[231]

Thus the distribution of both large and small debts which stipulated cereal repayments, the difference in the values of the bonds, the variation in price level and the seasonal nature of the bonds are very strong evidence that the Jews of Lincoln had increasingly become involved in the grain trade. Perhaps they acted as middlemen and sold the corn to Christian brokers. They could have done this either at their creditors' manors when the bonds were due for repayment or from their own homes. There can, in any case, be little doubt that a man like Jacob of Brancegate, who had nineteen cereal bonds in the *archa* in 1290 worth over £145, was a significant figure in the Lincoln grain trade. He had quite clearly become one of the *legales mercatores* of pre-Expulsion England.[232]

There were also forty-eight Lincoln Jews who between 1278 and 1290 had registered 136 bonds which demanded repayment in wool. The amounts of wool stipulated in the bonds varied from as much as 8 stone of wool to 12 sacks. The average bond contracted by the Lincoln Jews in the late 1280s required repayment of one sack of wool. The total amount of wool owed to the Lincoln Jewry in 1290 was 208½ sacks and 8 stone of wool. The majority of the wool bonds had been contracted in 1288 and 1290.[233] Thus, at the very least, the Jews of Lincoln were contracting for about 65 sacks of wool per annum in the years immediately before the Expulsion. This was a higher annual figure than the bishop of Winchester could produce on his estates in the south of England at the same

---

[231] PRO E/101/250/12; Mundill 1987, pp. 289–90.

[232] PRO E/101/250/12; Mundill 1990a, pp. 1–21; Hillaby 1990a, pp. 456–9.

[233] PRO E/101/250/12; there was a single bond for 8 stone of wool, thirty-six bonds were for ½ sack, fifty-five were for 1 sack, one bond was for 1½ sacks, twenty-two were for 2 sacks, ten were for 3 sacks, three were for 4 sacks, four were for 5 sacks, three were for 6 sacks and one was for 12 sacks.

period.[234] It was also more than Isabella de Forz could produce on her Holderness estates at this time.[235] It would probably have been more than any of the monasteries of Lincolnshire could produce.[236] This type of comparison indicates the possibility of a new type of business on the part of some Lincoln Jews.

Further analysis reveals evidence of an active wool business on the part of some Lincoln Jews. Closer examination of the transactions indicates that those Jews who had a single bond out for a single sack of wool were pricing it at levels ranging from £8 to £5 6s 8d. Such price variations would surely not have been necessary if such bonds had been nothing other than disguised money transactions. The variations reflect either the ups and downs of the wool market or differences in the quality of the wool that the Jews expected to receive upon repayment. Similarly, just as in the case of the cereal bonds, there does seem to be some sort of pattern in the dates at which wool bonds were contracted. While money bonds were contracted throughout the year, wool bonds show some seasonal variation in that bonding seems to have been most frequent, from the evidence of the 1288–90 bonds, in the period between April and June. This was the period immediately prior to the clip.[237] As has been observed above, a cursory glance at Figure 1 reveals variations in the price of wool within and between months as was the case in April, May, October and November of 1289. Figure 3 also shows price variation for the period 1282–90 and shows that, in the main, the wool was priced just above the level of Lloyd's national average.[238] Hence, just as the Jews were prepared to speculate on the harvest by making cereal bonds in August, so they were prepared to speculate on the clip by making wool bonds in spring.

Those Jews who entered transactions for wool were naturally those who had a fairly large amount of capital. In 1290 in Lincoln there were six Jews, Solomon of London, Jacob of Brancegate, Moses fil Isaac of London, Elias Gubbay, Diay fil Diay and Hagin fil Deulecresse, who were owed fairly large quantities of wool. Three of these larger entrepreneurs had known connections with London. They had all

---

[234] Lloyd 1973, p. 15; the bishop of Winchester's estates produced 93½ sacks in 1273, 79 sacks in 1278, 33 sacks in 1283 and 28 sacks in 1289.

[235] Mate 1980, pp. 327–8; in 1271 Isabella de Forz's Holderness estates produced 38 sacks and in 1277 37½ sacks.

[236] Lloyd 1973, pp. 52–62; in 1294 the Italians bought the following amounts from monasteries in Lincolnshire: 60 sacks from Kirkstead, 10 sacks from Bullington and 10¼ sacks from St Katherine's, Lincoln.

[237] PRO E/101/250/12; Lloyd 1973, pp. 2–3. The wool market like the cereal harvest was seasonal and ran from approximately 24 June to 3 August.

[238] PRO E/101/250/12.

contracted bonds for wool which were worth over £100. These six Jews were owed 104½ sacks of wool with a face value of £800 6s 8d on the open market. They had control of over half the wool which was apparently owed to the Lincoln Jewry at this time.[239] The Lincoln wool transactions also showed a section of Jewish financiers who could be regarded as creditors and may have been wool merchants of more ordinary proportions. This group could be compared to Christian wool merchants like Stephen of Stanham and William of Hepham who operated in Lincoln in the 1280s.[240] Fourteen Jews had bonds worth over £20 and accounted for 67 sacks worth a total of £571 6s 8d at the market value. Ten Jews were owed wool worth over £10 but less than £20 and accounted for 21½ sacks worth a total market value of £154. These twenty-four Jews tended to make smaller contracts for one sack or half a sack at a time from each client. There was, perhaps, an easy market in Lincoln for the odd sack of wool. It could be sold either to the larger wool merchants who inhabited the town or to the merchants who normally came in by river and tied up at Thorngate or to those who had barges in Brayford Pool which were bound for Boston or some other fair.

There were also eighteen Jews who had contracted bonds which demanded repayments in wool at a lower level than this. They were owed bonds worth a value of under £10. They were each owed one sack of wool or less. In total this group was owed 14½ sacks and 8 stone of wool, worth a total market value of approximately £112 14s 8d. There were probably many ways of disposing of small quantities of raw wool in Lincoln. The Newport fair, which normally took place between 17 and 29 June, only 400 yards from the Bail, was a possible outlet for any quantity of wool. It also always took place at about the time of the wool clip.[241] The wool market in Lincoln was in the southeast corner of the town. Dr J. P. Bischoff estimated that, in the years 1292–3, 1,033 sacks of wool passed through the Lincoln wool markets alone.[242] It would seem that between the years 1288 and 1290 the Jews had begun to have some influence on the wool market as, from their bonds, they would appear to have cornered at least 6 per cent of that market. Thus, the wool bonds recorded in the Lincoln *archa* in 1290 revealed Jews, the volume of whose credit activities would have given them recognisable places within what is known of the wool trade of

---

[239] *Ibid.*

[240] Bischoff 1975, pp. 244–8 shows that Stanham even owned his own boat at Boston; Mundill 1987, pp. 291–2, 304. It seems that in the 1250s William of Hepham had Deulecresse the Jew as a next-door neighbour: Lincoln RO D&C II 80/3/25. Hepham had also rented other properties to Jews: Abrahams 1896, p. 96.

[241] Hill 1965, p. 170.   [242] Bischoff 1975, p. 263.

Lincoln. This is further circumstantial evidence to suggest that such Jews were indeed involved in part of that trade. Thus at Lincoln many Jews survived the change in direction and the ravages of the late 1270s; it seems that business, on a new basis, was thriving.

NOTTINGHAM

Apart from some studies by local historians, the community of Jews at Nottingham has tended to be ignored. Admittedly it was never a large Jewry but it was clearly a well-established one which lasted for over a century.[243] Nottingham was probably first colonised by Jews from York or Lincoln in the late twelfth century.[244] As with other colonies, Jews were probably attracted by the castle and the trade along the Trent. The community had an established synagogue and there were clearly Jewish families who lived there for their entire lives. Yet Nottingham never appears to have had a burial ground. Dead Jews were transported for burial via Rufford and Ollerton to Le Jewbury at York. It is clear that in the twelfth century York, Lincoln and Nottingham Jews supplied credit to the citizens of Newark.[245] The topography of Nottingham itself reveals a Jew Lane which led off Castle Gate and kept its name for nine centuries. However, Jewish settlement within the town seems to have been quite widely spread.[246] The evidence for Jewish business at Nottingham consists of details of approximately seventy-two transactions.[247] In 1262, there were only six Jews who gave bonds for the tallage; they rendered up twelve bonds worth a face value of £52 6s 8d. The mean Jewish outlay at this time was £3 and the mean value of a Jewish bond in Nottingham was £2. One Jew, Jacob fil Jacob, actually contributed eight bonds. Jacob was also owed a small quantity of cereal: he had made some loans which promised small repayments of half a quarter and half a bushel of grain.[248]

In late 1290, it was recorded that the sheriff, William de Behadesworth, had not made the long journey to Westminster. The two Christian chirographers, Mewale le Brian and John son of Alan le Panmer, accompanied the Nottingham *archa* to the treasury at Westminster. The Nottingham *archa* contained bonds which had been contracted between 1284 and 1290. When the chest arrived at

---

[243] Potter-Briscoe 1908, pp. 19–25; Stevenson 1882, p. 3; Orange 1840, pp. 814–15.

[244] The Lassman Papers, Nottingham RO M 24/182–8. According to Lassman the village churches of Selston and Normanton were aided with the help of Aaron of Lincoln's money.

[245] Nottingham RO M 24/182–8; Brown 1904, p. 47.

[246] Walker 1963, pp. 37–8; Nottingham RO M 24/182–8; WAM nos. 6734, 6717, 6821, 6799.

[247] PRO E/101/249/10 membrane 6, E/101/250/8.

[248] PRO E/101/249/10 membrane 6.

Westminster it was still sealed, as it had been in Nottingham, with the seal of John de Annesly who was a former sheriff, John de Leke and Robert de Mequinz, a local knight. The chirographers duly deposited two keys to the chest in the appointed strong box in the treasury at Westminster and left to return home to Nottingham.[249]

As is the case with other Jewish communities, the picture of financial practice which emerges from the 1290 bonds is very different from that of 1262. Twenty-two Jews are identified, who had not contributed or had not featured in the 1262 evidence. They were owed bonds worth a face value of £518 4s 4d. On the face of it these creditors seem to have survived the Edwardian Experiment and were still conducting fairly lucrative business in the town. The bonds showed that two of them were owed three bonds which demanded repayment in wool which had a face value of £36 13s 4d. They also revealed six Jews who were owed 126 quarters of cereal with a face value of £31 10s 0d. However, most of the creditors at this time were owed cash repayments. A total of £450 1s 0d was owed to Nottingham Jews who had decided that their loans would be repaid in money. There were also Jews who apparently had connections outside Nottingham. Five of the twenty-two Jews seem to have had links with Sudbury, one with London and two with Lincoln. The average value of a Jewish bond in the Nottingham *archa* by 1290 was approximately £8 12s 8d. When compared with the equivalent value for 1262 this clearly represents a significant increase: an increase which is difficult to explain. It seems most unlikely that the Jewish community of Nottingham in 1262 had been able to defraud the tallage collection of that date. Thus the increase in value can be seen as genuine. The fact that new personnel were using the Nottingham *archa* also demonstrates that some Jews had managed to survive Edward's new legislation. Thus the evidence appears to show that during the 1280s business in Nottingham was on the increase. Over half the contracts in the *archa* were made in 1289 or 1290. Two were made in 1284, one in 1285, ten in 1286, five in 1287, five in 1288, twenty in 1289 and seventeen in 1290. Seven bonds were actually of very recent date and were contracted as late as June 1290.[250]

Out of the Jewish creditors three main entrepreneurs appear: Leo fil Mansell, Moses of Sudbury and Hagin fil Bateman. Hagin fil Bateman transacted a total of eleven loans in the period 1286–90. He was owed a total of £36 13s 0d, 50 quarters of cereal worth £12 and 11 sacks of wool worth £23 6s 8d. Leo fil Mansell made nine contracts between 1288 and 1290 and was owed a total of £129 6s 8d. Moses of Sudbury

---

[249] PRO E/101/249/29. [250] PRO E/101/250/8.

made nine contracts between 1289 and 1290 and was owed a total of £62 1s 4d in cash repayments. Three other families or associations also appeared at this time. Bateman fil Cress of Stamford and his three sons Pictavin, Ursell and Hagin were actively using the Nottingham *archa*. Isaac de *Provincia* (of Provence) was owed money, as was his daughter Floria. The last family, that of Moses of Sudbury, included his sons Isaac and Gente as well as his oldest son Moses who all used the Nottingham *archa*. Thus, in Nottingham, family consortia or associations were responsible for over half the bonds which were recorded as still being outstanding in 1290. The other bonds appear to belong to individual smaller lenders who perhaps had a little surplus cash to lend now and then. These were represented by Jews like Vives of Sudbury, Bonamy, Abraham de Powell and Deudon Crespyn. Once again business was dominated by a pattern of large capitalist operators but there were also opportunities for the individual creditor to make transactions.[251] In the late 1280s Nottingham seems to have been an attractive place for Jews to transact business. This could be because of the way they were treated by the local officials or possibly because there was much scope for lending in the surrounding areas. The connection with Sudbury also has a local significance. B. L. Abrahams was under the impression that this reference to Sudbury meant Sudbury in Suffolk and went on to identify Moses de Sudbur with Moses of Clare who held a messuage in Ipswich at this time. He even identified Vives of Sudbury as having come from Suffolk. This seems unlikely because there was a Sudbury 24 miles to the south-west of Nottingham.[252]

The Nottingham Jewry also provides a further piece of evidence which serves to illustrate business practice in the mid-1280s. On the list of unpaid bonds which were due to the Jews of Nottingham in 1290 an extract of a particular transaction was recorded. Because of chance survival of further evidence this extract can be matched with the original bond. According to the scribe responsible for listing the extant Nottingham bonds in 1291, Hugh the Palmer of Costock in the County of Nottinghamshire owed Hagin fil Bateman 40 quarters of wheat priced at 5s 0d a quarter by an obligation made on 18 August 1286.[253] The actual bond naturally bears more details of this transaction than the scribal extract.[254]

Fuller details show that Hugh the Palmer of Costock, Nottinghamshire, admitted that he was bound to Hagin the son of Bateman, a Jew of Nottingham, for 40 quarters of wheat, 'well dried to the touch and

[251] *Ibid.*   [252] Abrahams 1896, p. 100.   [253] PRO E/101/250/8.
[254] PRO c/146/1360; Richardson 1960, pp. 106–7.

according to good worldly fashion' and 'which I have sold to the aforesaid Jew for a fixed price'. Hugh was to repay the wheat, 'well measured or for each quarter five shillings per quarter'. The debt was to be paid 'to the Jew or his proper attorney at the house of the Jew on 11 November 1286'. If Hugh failed to pay he bound himself and his heirs and all his lands, goods and chattels, wherever, and officially allowed himself to be distrained by the sheriff, the constable or the bailiffs of Nottingham. He renounced all other sworn oaths and placed his seal to the agreement on 18 August 1286. The document was witnessed by three named witnesses and others.[255] This recognizance not only helps to corroborate the scribal extracts on the list made in 1291 but proves that the Nottingham Jews were making bonds for commodities. The Nottingham Jewry's transactions also show that once again in some areas the Jewish business man had survived the Edwardian Experiment successfully. Perhaps even more significant is the apparent return to bonding for monetary repayments in Nottingham.[256]

OXFORD

The last community for which significant evidence survives is Oxford. By Edward I's reign Oxford clearly had an old, well-established and thriving Jewry.[257] Cecil Roth drew a very full picture of communal life in a medieval provincial town in his masterful study of the Oxford community.[258] However, he did not utilise all the surviving evidence available to him. Roth was not aware, for example, of the existence of the 1275 scrutiny which provides an interesting contrast with the final *archa* scrutiny of 1290.[259] Neither did he make much use of the list of bonds which were used for tallage payment in 1262.[260]

This 1262 evidence reveals thirty-seven Jews who had been party to forty-five bonds and tallies with a face value of £80 18s 2d. Only nine Jews had transactions which were worth over £2. Abraham *genus* Jacob had a single bond worth £18. Abraham fil Abraham of Berkhamstead had three bonds which were worth a face value of £8 16s 8d and was also owed a small quantity of cereal from two of the transactions.[261] The names of the creditors at this time reflect, once again, the fact that Jews from other places were pursuing their business interests in Oxford. Financiers such as Moses of Wycombe, Bonefey fil Moses of

---

[255] William of Herdeby, William of Lenton, Hugh the clerk and others: PRO c/146/1360. For a photograph of the bond see Mundill 1990a, p. 10.
[256] See Table 4; PRO e/101/250/8.   [257] Stokes 1921; Cohen 1932; Roth 1957.
[258] Roth 1951.   [259] PRO e/101/249/32.
[260] PRO e/101/249/10 membrane 7.   [261] *Ibid.*

Wallingford and Ansell of Wycombe made transactions at Oxford at this period. Creditors who may have come from further afield numbered Copin and Crespin of Worcester, Bonamy of Hereford, Bonenvye of Bristol, Benedict of Lincoln, the brother of Jacob fil Master Moses (who was described as of London but who had many dealings and actually lived in Oxford) and Sancte of Stamford. Many of the contributions were for very small amounts. Some twenty Jews offered bonds with a value of less than £1; Abraham fil Samuel even gave a bond worth as little as 1s 0d. As with the other 1262 evidence it is possible to identify some Jews who had been promised the odd bushel of corn as partial repayments.[262]

The evidence of the 1275 scrutiny gives a picture of business practice some thirteen years later. However it is only Jacob of Oxford who can be identified as still transacting business in the Oxford *archa* at this time. The 1275 scrutiny identified eleven Jews who were depositing transactions in the Oxford *archa*. They held ninety-four bonds with a face value of £397. Business at this time was dominated by an Oxford Jew, Isaac fil Leon de Polet, who was owed a total of £225 8s 4d and half a quarter and 2 bushels of cereal. Yet he faced competition in his business transactions from Lumbard of Cricklade who held twenty-three bonds with a face value of £103 3s 4d.[263] Lumbard's business has been closely analysed elsewhere.[264] The Jews who had deposited bonds in the Oxford *archa* at this period again seem to have connections with places other than Oxford. For instance, Lumbard of Cricklade used the Devizes *archa* as well as the Oxford one in which to deposit his bonds. The Oxford *archa* was used at this time by Diay, a Jew of Burford, Vives fil Bonenfaunt of Gloucester who had four bonds worth £10 and a 'certain Jew' of Lambourne.[265]

As with the other towns after the Expulsion, the Oxford *archa* was brought into Westminster. It was escorted by Richard de Willamestote, the sheriff, accompanied by his *valletus*, William Baret, and Thomas de Mowy, a chirographer. They deposited the chest, which was described as containing 'new debts'. The chest had been sealed in late 1290 by William de Gromyl, Walter de Wyztchal *miles* and Henry Howen, a burgher of Oxford. The Oxford *archa* contained transactions which had been deposited between 1274 and 1290. A closer examination of the contents shows that there were nine tallies in it, six of which were made between 1274 and 1286. The value of these tallies varied from as much as £4 13s 4d to as little as 4s 0d. Besides the tallies there were the

---

[262] *Ibid.*   [263] PRO E/101/249/32.   [264] Mundill 1991, pp. 137–70.
[265] PRO E/101/249/32.

records of thirty-eight commodity bonds. These bonds ranged in date from 1282 to 1290 and once again represent the type of business being conducted in provincial *archae* during the late 1280s.[266]

At the top of the hierarchy of lenders in 1290 was Bonefey, the son of Lumbard of Cricklade. Bonefey had sixteen bonds with a face value of £231 18s 4d.[267] In marked contrast to the earlier debts owed to his father, Bonefey's debts were to be repaid not in money but in two different commodities, cereal and wool. Bonefey had four bonds which stipulated repayments for 12 sacks of wool; their face value was £100 13s 4d. The majority of Bonefey's bonds were repayable in grain. If the debtors had honoured their bonds, Bonefey should have received 395 quarters of grain, worth £131 5s 0d. Closer investigation of Bonefey's transactions provides more evidence for the reality of the commodity bonds. There was variation in the price of the sack of wool which Bonefey demanded. This represented either quality or the expected market price after the clip. As has been observed elsewhere the wool trade always provided a market for the odd sack or half sack of wool of whatever quality. The use of wool as a medium of exchange was common enough and not in the least suspicious. *Lana collecta* was an important lower level in the wool trade. The Oxfordshire region was also a well-known and flourishing wool-producing region by the late thirteenth century.[268] Some Jews of Oxford had, in 1261, even been accused of receiving thirty-one sheep from a thief who came from outside the town.[269] Indeed, the offence of flaying sheep for their wool was not unknown in Wiltshire.[270] Wool was a valuable and viable commodity in which to deal and it is not surprising that some of Bonefey's debtors preferred to be allowed to make their payments in wool rather than in specie.

What is particularly revealing is Bonefey's success in this field. If the outstanding debts are a good measure of his general financial success, then he coped very well with the Edwardian legislation. In the mid-1270s, Lumbard was owed single debts which might be for as much as £20 (a debt for a similar amount was shared between two debtors); by the late 1280s Bonefey was owed a single debt worth £50. The mean value of a bond owed to Lumbard in the late 1270s was between £4 9s 8d and £4 4s 0d. The corresponding value for one of Bonefey's bonds in the late 1280s was £14 9s 10½d. Bonefey's unpaid debts were fewer in number than his father's, yet he was able to make larger transactions. Similarly, his clients were each borrowing a greater amount of capital

[266] PRO E/101/249/29.   [267] PRO E/101/250/9; Mundill 1991b, pp. 146–7.

[268] PRO E/101/250/9; Power 1941, pp. 29–30; Lloyd 1977, p. 53.

[269] Rokeah 1984, p. 111.   [270] Pugh 1978, p. 9.

from one single source than they had previously been prepared to do. For at least one individual Oxford Jewish creditor the Experiment had meant financial success.[271]

CONCLUSION

Having considered the majority of the provincial Jewries of late thirteenth-century England and their business transactions in particular it is now possible to see the effect of Edward's reforms on the business of the Jewish community in a wider context. However it is important to bear in mind the varied nature of the available evidence. The bonds given in 1262 present some problems of interpretation. Nevertheless they show that in general there were at this period more single transactions made by Jewish creditors who did not live near the *archa* in question. They also show a fairly widespread use of *archa* facilities. The series of eighty original bonds from the Westminster muniments, although clearly incomplete, are also useful as examples of local business. The partial survivals from the 1275 and 1276 *archa* scrutinies do not give a complete picture of transactions and many of these lists have suffered damage or have *lacunae*. The 1290 evidence, although the fullest available, is also incomplete. Yet where the 1290 lists have survived, they can be taken as being fairly comprehensive evidence for the transactions of a particular community. Given these caveats and the fuller analyses which have been carried out above, it is possible to make some more general statements about Jewish financial practices between 1262 and 1290.[272]

First, there is clear evidence that prior to Edward's legislation some Jewish creditors were prepared to make transactions which promised repayment in small amounts of commodities. Secondly, the evidence from the surviving 1275 scrutinies and actual bonds shows a distinct and marked preference for more straightforward traditional monetary transactions, with a little commodity repayment here and there; but it also reveals less freedom of movement for the Jewish creditor as restrictions of movement and local expulsions made in 1275 came to bear. The 1290 evidence shows a distinct and understandable change in accordance with Edward's legislation. Of seven provincial Jewries, the mean value of credit transactions in five *archa* towns actually increased towards 1290 rather than declined.[273] From this it seems that although Jewish creditors may have been fewer in number and have made fewer transactions, they were often able to lend larger sums.

---

[271] Mundill 1991b, 163–5.   [272] See Table 8.   [273] See Table 9.

Table 9 *Values and mean values recorded in provincial* archae, *1262–90*

Date of sample	Number of Jews	Number of debts	Number of single debts	Total value of debts in sample	Mean value of debts per Jew	Mean value of Jewish outlay	Mean value of debts
Canterbury							
1262	52	102	33	£ 210 2s 11d	2	£ 4 9s 0d	£ 2 1s 2d
Canterbury							
WAM	32	45	25	£ 183 6s 8d	1.4	£ 5 14s 6d	£ 4 1s 4d
Canterbury							
1290	16	95	4	£ 523 3s 8d	5.9	£ 32 8s 11d	£ 5 9s 3d
Devizes							
vetus cista	19	28	13	£ 265 4s 8d	1.4	£ 13 19s 2d	£ 9 9s 5d
Devizes							
nova cista	7	29[t]	5	£ 126 16s 8½d	4.1	£ 18 2s 4d	£ 4 7s 5d
Exeter							
1262	9	15	8	£ 38 9s 4d	1.6	£ 4 5s 5d	£ 2 11s 3d
Exeter							
vetus cista	22	143	8	£1,023 19s 8d	6.5	£ 46 10s 9d	£ 7 3s 2d
Exeter							
nova cista	16[+]	45[t]	16	£ 211 4s 0d	2.8	£ 13 4s 0d	£ 4 13s 10d
Hereford							
1262	36	44	27	£ 104 0s 4d	1.2	£ 2 17s 9d	£ 2 7s 3d
Hereford							
1275	4	79	2	£ 459 9s 8d	19.75	£114 17s 5d	£ 5 16s 4d
Hereford							
vetus cista	30	205	9	£1,120 13s 8d	6.8	£ 37 11s 1d	£ 5 9s 11d
Hereford							
nova cista	17	77[t]	8	£1,065 7s 8d	4.5	£ 62 13s 4d	£13 16s 8d
Lincoln							
1262	90	151	52	£ 405 14s 2d	1.6	£ 4 10s 1d	£ 2 13s 8d
Lincoln							
WAM	19	37	12	£ 350 11s 4d	1.9	£ 18 9s 0d	£ 9 9s 5d
Lincoln							
1290	62	250	24	£2,461 18s 6d	4	£ 39 14s 2d	£ 9 16s 11d
Nottingham							
1262	6	12	3	£ 52 6s 8d	2.6	£ 8 14s 4d	£ 3 5s 4d
Nottingham							
1290	22	60[t]	12	£ 518 14s 4d	2.7	£ 23 11s 1d	£ 8 12s 8d
Oxford							
1262	38	45	17	£ 80 18s 2d	1.1	£ 2 2s 7d	£ 1 15s 11d
Oxford							
1275	11[+]	94	5	£ 397 0s 0d	8.5	£ 36 1s 9½d	£ 4 4s 5d
Oxford							
1290	19	47	12	£ 452 4s 8d	2.4	£ 23 16s 0d	£ 9 12s 4d

[t] tallies – Devizes *nova cista* 12; Exeter *nova cista* 24; Hereford *nova cista* 3; Nottingham 1290 2; Oxford 1290 9.

[+] The Exeter *nova cista* has many shared transactions plus tallies owed to certain Jews; similarly the Oxford 1275 scrutiny has an unidentified creditor.

Table 9 (*cont.*)

Sources: PRO E/101/249/10; WAM nos. 9015, 9019, 9020, 9021, 9022, 9025, 9026, 9028, 9034, 9036, 9039, 9042, 9043, 9046, 9047, 9057, 9058, 9086, 9088, 9089, 9090, 9091, 9103, 9104, 9105, 9116, 9118, 9119, 9120, 9121, 9123, 9124, 9125, 9126, 9127, 9139, 9156, 9157, 9158, 9159, 9172, 9173, 9174, 9175, 9176; PRO E/101/250/6; E/101/250/11; E/101/250/2; *PREJ*3, pp. 230–8; PRO E/101/250/5; WAM nos. 9014, 9027, 9032, 9054, 9087, 9092, 9093, 9094, 9095, 9097, 9098, 9100, 9117, 9130, 9131, 9132, 9135, 9137, 9140, 9142, 9143, 9144, 9145, 9146, 9147, 9148, 9150, 9160, 9161, 9162, 9163, 9164, 9165, 9167, 9168, 9169, 9170; PRO E/101/250/12, E/101/250/8, E/101/249/32, E/101/250/9.

Other observations can be made about the social structure of the different communities. The 1262 evidence for the London community is a good example of how families of entrepreneurs transacted business together.[274] The Canterbury evidence shows that by 1290 fewer Jewish creditors were making loans of a high value, and that in Canterbury Jewish financiers had started to bond for grain on a large scale. The business community there was dominated by large-scale operators such as Leo fil Master Elias and Moses le Petit.[275] Elsewhere a similar picture emerges. The evidence of the Devizes *vetus cista* (1258–75) shows one plutocratic financier, Sweteman fil Licoricia, dominating the business of the *archa*; but after the Statute of 1275 a new generation of Jews, although fewer in number, were able to extend more credit. The Devizes *nova cista* (1282–90) was dominated by Salomon, who was owed 221 quarters of wheat with a face value of some £82 6s 8d.[276] Although somewhat puzzling, the Exeter evidence also shows that there was a small but thriving community in Exeter right up until the Expulsion. Again the community must have been dominated by the experience and business acumen of Jacob Copin, who was no longer operating in the 1280s when a new generation of credit agents started to lend in accordance with Edward's legislation and to use commodity broking and trading as a means of livelihood.[277] In Hereford the magnate family of Aaron fil Elias le Blund, with his son Bonenfaunt, dominated the financial scene for the whole of Edward's reign. Despite the apparent difficulties that they both suffered in obtaining their repayments they were able to continue in business. Not all such financiers found it easy to survive. Whilst Aaron fil Elias had dominated the transactions in the *vetus cista* (1259–76), having over 50 per cent of the bonds owing to him worth almost two-thirds of the value of the *archa*, in marked contrast the evidence of the Hereford

---

[274] PRO E/101/249/10 membranes 1–3 and 14.

[275] PRO E/101/249/10 membranes 8–9; WAM nos. 9015, 9019, 9020, 9021, 9022, 9025, 9026, 9028, 9034, 9036, 9039, 9042, 9043, 9046, 9047, 9057, 9058, 9086, 9088, 9089, 9090, 9091, 9103, 9104, 9105, 9116, 9118, 9119, 9120, 9121, 9123, 9124, 9125, 9126, 9127, 9139, 9156, 9157, 9158, 9159, 9172, 9173, 9174, 9175, 9176; PRO E/101/250/6.

[276] PRO E/101/250/11. [277] PRO E/101/249/32, E/101/250/2

nova cista (1283–90) shows him holding only 30 per cent of the bonds. The *nova cista* also shows the appearance of financiers such as Hagin of Weobley, who had apparently started his business in the last years of Edward's reign. A comparison of the mean value of a bond and the mean Jewish outlay at Hereford between the time of the *vetus cista* and the *nova cista* underlines the point that not all Jews were impoverished by Edward's legislation.[278]

At Lincoln a picture emerges of quite a thriving community, perhaps indicating the role of local fortunes in the survival of the local Jewish community. Throughout Edward's reign the Lincoln Jewry not only kept up its connections with the great London Jewish families but also had its own local financiers who managed to sustain their business throughout the problems of the time. The Gubbays and Jacob of Brancegate show that it was still possible for local Jews to build financial empires. There was apparently a distinct numerical decline in the community; but there was also an increase in the amount lenders were prepared to hazard as a loan. Moreover financiers like Cok le fiz Hagin still managed to make transactions which stipulated repayments in money. Interestingly, those Jews who held single bonds of a value of between £5 and £10 tended to stipulate repayment in wool, whilst those who were owed £3 or less tended to prefer cereal repayments. In all, the Lincoln Jews were owed over 2,000 quarters of assorted grain, although their preference was for wheat. The wool market was dominated by the rich plutocratic wool brokers such as Salamon of London, Jacob of Brancegate, Elias Gubbay, Moses fil Isaac of London, Diay fil Diay and Hagin fil Deulecresse, who between them were owed 104½ sacks worth £800 6s 8d or half the total value of wool owing to the Jewish community. After 1275 the Lincoln Jewry evidently enjoyed economic success and were obviously prepared to diversify their interests.[279]

The Nottingham community was dominated in 1262 by a single Jew, Jacob fil Jacob, but by 1290 many other Jews such as Hagin fil Bateman, Moses of Sudbury and Leo fil Mansell had appeared who, apparently unperturbed by the Edwardian legislation, stipulated repayment in money. There was still room in Nottingham for large capitalists and smaller lenders.[280] At Oxford the mean value of a transaction also

---

[278] PRO E/101/249/10 membrane 5; *PREJ3*, pp. 230–8; PRO E/101/250/5. See Table 9.

[279] PRO E/101/249/10 membranes 12 and 13; WAM nos. 9014, 9027, 9032, 9054, 9087, 9092, 9093, 9094, 9095, 9097, 9098, 9100, 9117, 9130, 9131, 9132, 9135, 9137, 9140, 9142, 9143, 9144, 9145, 9146, 9147, 9148, 9150, 9160, 9161, 9162, 9163, 9164, 9165, 9167, 9168, 9169, 9170; PRO E/101/250/12.

[280] PRO E/101/249/10 membrane 6, E/101/250/6.

increased towards 1290. Whilst the community was clearly made up in 1262 of quite small lenders from the surrounding countryside and then dominated by Jacob of Oxford with his London connections, it was still possible for a business to expand. There was also a marked and distinct difference in preference for monetary and commodity repayments between the transactions of Lumbard of Cricklade and of his son Bonefey who still dominated the financial dealings of the Oxford community in 1290.[281]

Thus from the evidence of their recorded transactions it is not easy to state firmly that the Edwardian Anglo-Jewry was a business community in decline. Although many Jews had suffered financial and personal disaster during Edward's reign, at least a small number had survived and had managed to ride out the ravages of taxation and oppression. Indeed it is not just those who perhaps inherited capital who had survived, as many new financiers appear in transactions made during the last decade of Jewish presence. Accordingly, the traditional explanations of why Edward I decided to banish the Jews in 1290 may need to be re-examined.[282]

Edward had first come into contact with the Jewish community on a large scale in 1262 when his father had mortgaged the Jewry to him. He had subsequently been involved in all national legislation affecting the Jewry and he had (as he had promised in 1262) left them financially viable. He had not tallaged them so severely as his predecessors, although he had tried to raise money in the Great Tallage and had been party to the mass confiscations of 1278-9. Yet neither the tallages, the confiscations nor the Statute of 1275 and its subsequent modifications were apparently the final blow for the Jewish community. To explain the latter it is necessary to look further than the theory of financial decline. In order to do so, and to prove the partial success of Edward's Jewish Experiment, it is now important to turn to the Jews' Christian clients and debtors and to try to establish who they were and how far they might have been a force in deciding medieval Anglo-Jewry's fate in 1290.

[281] PRO E/101/249/10 membrane 7, E/101/249/32, E/101/250/9; Mundill 1991b, pp. 163-70.
[282] Stacey 1987b, pp. 67-8.

Chapter 7

THE CHRISTIAN DEBTORS

Charles Lamb once observed that the human species was formed of two distinct races: those who borrow and those who lend.[1] It is obviously true that the fate of one of these races must necessarily affect the other: the one is inevitably dependent on the other. It is therefore essential to turn our attention to the late thirteenth-century Jews' clients in more detail and to try to ascertain whether they were genuine beneficiaries of credit facilities or whether they were ensnared, as some contemporaries observed, in financial thraldom.[2] It is also important to determine whether the Christian beneficiaries of Jewish capital were a real force in the decision to expel their creditors in 1290.[3] It is a fair assumption that those using Jewish credit were comparatively few in number; but were they a minority who could have had some influence on the final expulsion? It is possible that those who had borrowed on credit may have had many reasons for wanting the wholesale expulsion of the Jews. Their motives may have ranged from simple resentment fuelled by their indebtedness to strong nationalistic and racial motives. Or might it be argued that they preferred the service or interest charges of their own co-religionists to those of alien Jews?[4]

This chapter will consider the historiography of the work on the Christian debtors of the Jews as well as the methodologies used by previous studies. It will also examine the naming patterns which were used by contemporary scribes to record the financial transactions of the Jews. It is naturally very difficult to unearth, and to come to any firm conclusions about, the names of most Jewish debtors.[5] However for every source which allows us to study how much the Jewish business man lent there is usually also listed the name of his debtor; the latter was

---

[1] Lamb 1903.   [2] *Chronicles of St Augustine's Canterbury*, p. 1,872.
[3] Stacey 1995, pp. 100–1.
[4] Menache 1985; 1987, pp. 223–36; Mundill 1987, pp. 134–45; 1990a, p. 1.
[5] McIntosh 1988, pp. 558–9.

essential for identification and for providing a key to the creditor's financial security. Consideration and use of these names may help to prove the provenance of a large majority of the debtors who frequented Jewish financiers between 1262 and 1290. From other information such as the size of transaction and the use of seals it will be possible to consider the debtors' social status. The borrowers can also be examined in the light of the commodities which they promised to repay their Jewish creditors. Finally an examination of the geographical distribution of Jewish debtors in late thirteenth-century Kent, Herefordshire and Lincolnshire will be made which will help to build up a sounder picture of those who used Jewish finance near those *archa* towns.

Until comparatively recently the study of the Jews' debtors in medieval England has tended to be neglected. Admittedly Joseph Jacobs, in 1893, commented that it was mainly the 'smaller barons' and the monasteries that were in need of Jewish capital in the twelfth century.[6] In 1894 B. L. Abrahams published a list of the Jewish creditors who held bonds in the two Hereford *archae* in 1290 and this revealed that certain well-known Herefordshire families were to be found amongst the debtors of the Hereford Jewry.[7] A more methodical study did not emerge until 1932.[8] In her study of that year Dr Sarah Cohen used law suits recorded in the Jewish Plea Rolls to analyse what type of person was indebted to the Jews. She was able to identify two broad groups, 'those who belonged to ecclesiastical houses and important Oxfordshire families such as the Stockwells, Feteplaces and Kepeharms and the great landowners, tenants-in-chief or sub-tenants of the king in Oxfordshire and of knights holding direct from the manors or houses which lay within the county boundary'. Cohen's study, although based on law suits and not on actual bonds, thus paved the way for future research.[9]

Peter Elman was the first to consider systematically the debit side of the medieval Jewish bonds. In 1936, he utilised the three Cambridge-shire *archae* scrutinies (1240, 1262 and 1290), published by H. P. Stokes, and the list of debts owed to Abraham of Berkhamstead in 1255 to produce a more thorough investigation of the Jews' Christian clients.[10] His results are still impressive. From his conclusions he was able to emphasise that, although the Jew was an urban phenomenon during the thirteenth century, his clientele was primarily rural: 'An examination of the debtors . . . shows clearly that well over seventy per cent of Jewish debtors belonged to the agricultural classes, and particularly to the

---

[6] Jacobs 1893a, p. xiv.   [7] Abrahams 1894a.   [8] Cohen 1932.   [9] *Ibid.*
[10] Elman 1936, pp. 113, 140–7; 1938a; Stokes 1913, appendices 4–6; *CCR 1254–1256*, pp. 170–2.

smaller tenants who formed an important element of the opposition to the policy of the crown.'[11] His sample of 396 debtors was divided into six different categories, of which he found 42 per cent to be 'agricultural', 13 per cent 'urban', 1.75 per cent 'clerical', 0.25 per cent 'noble', 0.25 per cent 'abbatial' and 42 per cent 'unidentifiable'.[12] His method involved attempting to track down the name of each debtor in other records and paying particular attention to the way debtors were described in those records. He also used topographical clues, for instance where the name was qualified by the postscript *in* he took it to denote a landholder at a particular place. He did not however use names which were followed by *de*. His task was obviously simplified when he encountered information about the debtor's occupation or status. The conclusions of his work are still generally acceptable and it is possible to assert that at least 42 per cent of the debtors were indeed what he termed 'agrarian'.[13] Elman's methodology provided a useful cornerstone for further discussion of the Jews' clientele in the late thirteenth century.

Although it is clear that no direct comparison between moneylending in England and southern France in the thirteenth century can be usefully made, the method used by Dr Richard Emery in 1958 to identify the clients of the Jews of Perpignan is also worth considering.[14] From a total of 1,321 'new loans' made by the Jews of Perpignan between 1261 and 1286, he concluded that 65 per cent were owed by 'villagers', 30 per cent by 'townsmen', 2 per cent by 'knights and nobles', 1 per cent by 'clergy', 1 per cent by 'royal officers' and 1 per cent were unidentifiable.[15] Emery's high success rate in classifying the debtors owed much to the fact that the Perpignan notarial registers were far more informative and descriptive than the rolls of extant debts compiled by the English *Scaccarium Judaeorum*. He also, rightly or wrongly, used toponyms to indicate provenance or connections with a particular place in a more liberal way than had Elman.

In 1967 Vivian Lipman made a brief analysis of the debtors of the Norwich Jewry during the 1220s.[16] Dr Lipman's conclusions were that only a very small percentage of the debtors were 'great noblemen' or 'religious houses' and that most of them appeared to be 'members of the rural gentry'. He went on to state that 'the Jews' financial role in medieval England was to provide loans for the "ordinary" Englishman'. Lipman also indicated the possibility that the Jews could subsist in small

---

[11] Elman 1938a, p. 148.   [12] Elman 1936, pp. 112–13.   [13] Elman 1938a, p. 148.
[14] Emery 1959, pp. 39–67.   [15] *Ibid.*, p. 39.
[16] Lipman 1967, pp. 93–4; Levy 1902b. Students of Vivian Lipman will know that he had engaged in further research into debtor/creditor relations.

numbers in relatively small places and survive by lending money.[17] More recently, Joe Hillaby has examined the debtors of the Hereford Jewry.[18] His study of the Herefordshire business of the Hamo family in the first half of the thirteenth century meant that he was able to consider the relationship of four important Herefordshire families and their creditors in some detail. He was able to conclude that these families often actually protected their Jewish creditors and used the loans they received for castle building and self-aggrandisement. This was an important study of some easily recognisable upper-class debtors.[19]

In contrast Joe Hillaby's most recent study of the debtors of the Hereford Jewry during Edward's reign has shown that many local knights, including amongst others William de Bliss, John de Balun of Much Markle and Henry of Pembridge, were indebted to the Jews.[20] The great Hereford financier, Aaron le Blund, also lent to many locals who had held the shrievalty of Herefordshire, such as the Kinnersley, Pembridge, Solers, Pichard, Hakluyt and Chaundos families.[21] He clearly demonstrated that the clients of Aaron le Blund were very different from those of Hamo of Hereford who had dominated the local Jewish business community in the early thirteenth century: 'Aaron . . . was meeting the needs of a wide range of other social groups. Some were townsmen and clerics such as William Mael and Reginald Russell of Hereford, William, the fuller of Leominster . . . Richard, son of Roger, the mercer and John le Amblur, chaplain of Hanley; but predominantly his clients were drawn from the knighthood and peasantry.'[22]

Nevertheless when writing in connection with more general issues, historians have tended to be reticent when considering the many Christian clients of the Jews, let alone their status. In 1970, Dr Paul Hyams, in a discussion of moneylending at village level, hinted that 'Too little attention may have been paid to the existence of village moneylenders. Jewish finance must have affected at least some rural areas.'[23] His suspicion was echoed in 1972 by Professor Michael Postan, who posed a question which still has to be answered: 'The Jews before their Expulsion and the Italians both before and after that date do not appear to have operated in villages or to have found many peasant customers . . . but why should they not have been lending money to

---

[17] Lipman 1967, p. 94.   [18] Hillaby 1990b; 1990c, pp. 447–53.
[19] Hillaby 1985.
[20] Hillaby 1990c, pp. 447–53: others included Henry of Hereford, Henry de Dolers of Dorstone, Roger the son of Stephen de Butterley, Nicholas the heir of Nicholas Lord of Tarrington, Roger son and heir of Richard of Hereford.
[21] Hillaby 1990c, pp. 450–5.   [22] *Ibid.*, pp. 447–8.   [23] Hyams 1970, p. 30.

the peasant freeholders?'[24] Unfortunately, and perhaps inevitably, attention has been more readily paid to Jewish dealings with the gentry and nobility than with the peasantry. In 1974, for instance, Paul Hyams drew attention to the involvement of Jewish financiers in what he termed 'one of the most significant economic movements of thirteenth-century England: a large scale shift of landed wealth from all kinds of declining families towards the newly rich'.[25] Such evidence for the influence of Jewish finance in the thirteenth century, particularly in the area of mortgaging land, is abundant.[26] For example, Professor Mavis Mate has shown that, early in the century, Christ Church, Canterbury was indebted to the Jews; Dr King has asserted that the knights of Peterborough were also in debt and, more recently, in 1975, Peter Coss has used the example of Sir Geoffrey de Langley's dealings with the Jews to re-examine the mid-thirteenth-century 'crisis of the knightly class'.[27]

Further study of the Jews' debtors in the mid-century period would undoubtedly both clarify and amplify the 'knightly crisis'. However, the knights have already received much more attention than the clients of the Edwardian provincial Jews who, as will be seen, were for the most part not knights and who were the recipients of loans no longer secured on mortgage of land but on a more commercial basis. Regrettably such clients remain difficult to identify. In 1983, Dr Sharon Lieberman examined Jewish debtors in the mid-thirteenth century.[28] She found that the lesser gentry were the Jews' chief customers and confirmed Professor Postan's statement that 'the smaller landowners were the chief clients and the chief victims of Jewish finance'.[29] She also made two important conclusions: 'If Elman's figures are correct they raise the possibility that as the century progressed the Jews' clients were of diminishing social status.'[30] She also observed: 'The small number of actual knights who were in debt suggests that the Jews were drawing their clients from a lower social stratum. The evidence suggests that a large proportion of debtors were lesser landholders.'[31]

It is important to try to discover exactly who used Jewish finance during Edward I's reign. Many debtors have remained merely names on documents awaiting examination. If, in the early part of the thirteenth century, provincial Jews were involved in rural land mortgages, it is perhaps not surprising that it was in the same geographical areas that the Edwardian Jew found his clients. The earliest studies of Jews' debtors indicated that the Edwardian Jew's client was 'rural' rather than 'urban'.

[24] Postan 1972, pp. 152–3.   [25] Hyams 1974, p. 291.   [26] See chapter 2 above.
[27] King 1973, pp. 39–40, 44–5; Mate 1973; Coss 1975.   [28] Lieberman 1983.
[29] *Ibid.*, pp. 66–9; Postan 1966, p. 595.   [30] Lieberman 1983, p. 117.
[31] *Ibid.*, p. 116.

It therefore seems likely that, as A. Lassman observed when considering the bonds in the Nottingham *archa*, 'from the way in which the debtors are found grouped together in districts it is very clear that the country districts had been regularly travelled over in search of clients'.[32] Yet it was not just Jews who travelled in search of clients. Christians obviously knew where they could obtain Jewish credit. That potential creditors actually sought Jewish credit agents in market towns can be easily proved; such was the case with Robert Fychet of Paxton who in 1274 went into Exeter to negotiate a loan with a Jew.[33] The points of contact for both creditor and debtor can be comparatively easily dealt with; but the reasons why credit was needed and what type of client used such credit are naturally more difficult to discover. A closer analysis of the surviving transactions is necessary to try to ascertain the sort of clientele with whom the Edwardian Jews dealt.

Before embarking on such an analysis it is worth considering the methods used by the late E. M. Carus-Wilson when she examined a survey of those who held tenements in Stratford on Avon in 1251–2. She found that virtually all those listed were described by a Christian name and a second name (a combination of onomastic, patronymic or cognomen). These second names were subdivided into occupational surnames (descriptive) and what she called place surnames (locatives). Eighty-two burgesses had second names which bore the name of a place. If local toponyms such as *de Bosco* and *de la Warde* were excluded, fifty-seven different place-names occurred, of which forty-seven could be identified with a fair degree of certainty. She was able to conclude that 90 per cent of those who took up Stratford burgages came from villages and hamlets which were within a 16 mile radius.[34] It is possible to use a similar method to identify the debtors of Edwardian Jewry. When considering a similar problem Dr Keith Wrightson pointed out that there must be some caveats concerning 'the point at which inventive use of sources shade over into invention': care should be taken.[35] Susan Reynolds has also stated that such a methodology can be used in a purely local context as an indicator if nothing else.[36]

The naming patterns used by contemporary scribes to record the name of the debtor from the Jewish bonds fall into seventeen broad categories.[37] The categories can be subdivided into three different sections, which for ease of reference can be defined as onomastic, descriptive and locative. Examples of these can be seen in Table 10.

---

[32] Nottingham RO MS M 24/182–8: the Lassman Papers.   [33] *PREJ2*, p. 194.
[34] Carus-Wilson 1965, pp. 52–5.   [35] Wrightson 1978, p. 213.
[36] Reynolds 1977, pp. 69–70.
[37] See Table 10 based on naming patterns on PRO E/101/250/2–12.

Table 10 *Examples of naming patterns used in Jewish transactions*

Onomastic

Forename	**Patronymic (fil)**		
Roger	son of Harry		
Forename	**Patronymic (fil)**	**Cognomen**	
Roger	son of Harry	Strugnell	
Forename	**Cognomen**		
Roger	Strugnell		

Locative

Forename	**Locative**			
Roger	of Liss			
Forename	**Locative (de)**	**Patronymic (fil)**		
Roger	of Liss	son of Harry		
Forename	**Locative (de)**	**Patronymic (fil)**	**Paternal locative**	
Roger	of Liss	son of Harry	of London	
Forename	**Locative (de)**	**Description/occupation**		
Roger	of Liss	the Old/Forester		
Forename	**Locative (de)**	**Present locative (manens in)**		
Roger	of Liss	Staying in Waltham		
Forename	**Patronymic (fil)**	**Locative (de)**		
Roger	son of Harry	of Liss		
Forename	**Description/ occupation**	**Locative (de)**		
Roger	the Old/Forester	of Liss		
Forename	**Description**	**Patronymic**	**Locative**	**County**
Roger	the Old	son of Harry	of Liss	of Hampshire
Forename	**Patronymic (fil)**	**Cognomen**	**Locative (de)**	
Roger	son of Harry	Strugnell	of Liss	
Forename	**Cognomen**	**Locative (de)**		
Roger	Strugnell	of Liss		
Forename	**Cognomen**	**Local description**	**Locative (de)**	
Roger	Strugnell	of Parish of St Faith	of Liss	
Forename	**Cognomen**	**Local description**	**Locative (de)**	
Roger	Strugnell	of the Byre	of Liss	

Descriptive

Forename	**Cognomen**	**Description/occupation**
Roger	Strugnell	the Old/Forester
Forename	**Cognomen**	**Patronmyic (fil)**
Roger	Strugnell	son of Harry

There are many other combinations but these examples serve to represent the majority of occurrences.

Clearly, as Carus-Wilson and others found, pure onomastics, such as 'Roger fil Harry', lack both descriptive and locative qualities and yield very little help for positive identification unless, by chance, the person may be found and identified in other contemporary records. The naming patterns which include descriptive information concerning status or occupation are clearly of more value. At times the actual descriptions written on the bonds and extracts are extremely helpful. Descriptions such as *civis Cantuariae, clericus, faber, vitarius, aurifaber, piscator, carpentarius, miles, bedellus, dominus, civis, capellanus* and *marescall* indicate both social position and occupation.[38] Lengthier descriptions such as 'Thomas, rector of the church of Barton of the county of Lincolnshire', 'Philip of Staunton, rector of the church of Thorefreya of Nottinghamshire' and 'John, the son of Randolph Basset, knight of Leicestershire, parson of the church of Chedde' are also helpful in identifying a debtor.[39] A description such as that of 'William, the son of Randulph, of Stokes of Bubbe Clyne who lives next to the house of William Quntyn in the same town' who made a bond in 1290 in the Devizes *archa* not only can be useful in helping identification but can be absolutely corroborated.[40] Other records show that William Quntyn of Bupton held lands there in 1285 and that, in 1306, William, the son of Randulph de Stokes of Bupton, transferred a messuage in Marlborough.[41] In Devonshire in the 1270s, John Quynel, who is described as the rector of Shobrooke, clearly came from that village. It is interesting to note that other records show that he had inherited a tenement from his father in Exeter, near to where his Jewish creditor lived.[42]

Although those descriptions which state occupation are in a minority they do give an impression of what types of people used Jewish finance. The Jewish bonds given to the Crown in 1262 show that the prior and canons of Bentley, Middlesex, and the priory of Newenham, Bedfordshire, were both indebted to Jewish financiers. Apart from these religious establishments some fourteen knights and clerks can be identified as being users of Jewish finance. However carpenters, smiths, butchers, oxherds, tanners, vintners, dyers, women, widows, millers, butlers, chaplains, goldsmiths, a summoner, a painter, parsons, a former sheriff of Yorkshire, bakers, chamberlains, children of mercers, a cordwainer, a shepherd, masons, a former brother of St Frideswide's, tilers, fishermen, a cutler, a mercer, a marshall, a leather dresser, a priest, a palmer, a frankleyn, a cellarer and a tailor also used Jewish finance at

[38] *Ibid.*   [39] PRO E/101/250/12.   [40] PRO E/101/250/11.
[41] Fry 1908, pp. 152–3, 181; Pugh 1939, p. 24; Mundill 1990a, p. 12.
[42] PRO E/101/250/2; Exeter Cathedral Muniments, Medieval Deeds no. 52.

this period.[43] Other bonds made in Henry III's reign reveal the dealings of both knights and artisans and even show that Alexander, a knight who was steward of the kingdom of Scotland, had borrowed £200 from Deulecresse fil Aaron.[44] The details of the extant bonds in 1290 identify some twenty-three knights, nineteen members of gentry families, fourteen clerks, thirteen women, and over fifty artisans and craftsmen.[45]

Thus the fuller descriptions of occupation, social position or even provenance recorded upon the bonds themselves can offer possible help in identifying the debtors. However such positive identifications are rare. For the most part the transactions only contain the necessary name with which the debtor can be identified and as often as not his or her occupation is not recorded. As Table 10 shows, there are of course many variations not only between what types of person borrowed from the Jewish creditor but also in how they described themselves in front of the chirographer as the contract was actually drawn up. Some may have been well known to both the Jewish creditor and the Christian official who recorded the transaction, so making it unnecessary for further comment. This makes the problem of identification very difficult and is probably why historians have tended to have only a secondary interest in the Jews' clients. Yet a closer consideration of the descriptive element of the many remaining bonds does give some indication as to the origins, occupation and status of the debtors. The most frequent occurrence in the naming patterns of Christian debtors is the locative and it is possible to use these descriptions, as others have shown, to track some of them down.

Before attempting to examine the provenance of such debtors it is vital to make three general observations about those who used Jewish finance. There are some helpful clues which are available in almost every surviving transaction. First, it can be asserted that whoever made a bond with a Jew had a personal seal or had access to someone who possessed one and would lend it to them as guarantor. Secondly, it is likely that whoever entered into a loan would have to have had some security to offer the creditor. Thus, any debtor was likely to have owned something that was worth at least a considerable proportion of

---

[43] PRO E/101/249/10.

[44] *Calendar of Ancient Deeds*, vol. III, pp. 410, 412, 424, 434–5 reveals borrowings by a poulterer, various women, a vicar, a vintner, a chamberlain, a goldsmith, a moneyer, a carpenter, a baker, several clerks and a carter.

[45] PRO E/101/250/2–12 reveals the borrowings of three townsmen, three rectors, two smiths, two beadles, two chaplains, two widows, two bailiffs, a baker, a palmer, a poulterer, various women, a vicar, a vintner, a chamberlain, a goldsmith, a moneyer, a carpenter, a baker, clerks, a carter, a fisherman, a monk, a parson, a lord of a manor, a farrier, a tailor, a parson, a crossbowman, a miller, a quilter, a corn merchant, a butcher and a butler.

the sum lent by the creditor. Thirdly, the actual name of the debtor which was entered on the bond had, as we have established, a special significance. In general, it is reasonable to assume that identification of the debtor was the main purpose of recording the bond in the first place.

The fact that the bonds bore seals may mean that sillography could help in tracing the status of the borrower.[46] All legal transactions with Jewish creditors had to bear the seal of the debtor. Unfortunately, few actual bonds still remain. Of the extant bonds which were once deposited in *archae* at Canterbury and Lincoln only a few still bear the seals of their debtors.[47] However a brief study of these surviving seals may give some indication of status. Amongst the Canterbury bonds, for example, it is perhaps significant that ostensibly insubstantial debtors such as Susan, the widow of Tonge, William the carpenter of Selbire and Letitia, the daughter of William Kemme of Graveney, all had seals.[48] Yet no striking indications of social status emerge from these Kentish seals. The simplistic standard devices (the petal, the star, the foliate cross, the fleur-de-lis or other foliage) predominated. Interestingly, they were personalised, as the seals bear the name of the owner inscribed in the border legend.

In contrast there are greater variations amongst the Lincolnshire seals. Debtors such as Geoffrey, the son of Lawrence of Eresby, Thomas, the son of Belaward of Scopwick, and Alan, the son of Richard de Venella of Hackthorn, tended to have fairly simplistic seals.[49] However, Salmann fil Roger of Stenigot used a bird as his device; Richard Rudde of Barton a rampant lion; Hawis Daubeny of Hiptoft the head of a lady; John Garnel of St Botulph's parish in Lincoln a dragon; and Richard Bret of Wrangle an equestrian device.[50] In the absence of other evidence, it is possible that these more intricate devices might reflect a higher social status. Certainly, in a more heraldic vein, Sir Adam de Newmarket had 'five fusils in fess for Newmarch, a shield suspended from a dragon and dragon supporters'; Hugh Duket, a knight, had 'a bend quarterly' and Jordan Foliot, a knight of Yorkshire, had 'a bend

---

[46] Hereford RO MS AH81/34 still bears the fragments of a seal; *SCBM*, vol. II, pp. cxxiii–cxxx; Rokeah 1971; Jenkinson 1968; Kingsford 1920; Clanchy 1979, pp. 244–57.

[47] Canterbury bonds with surviving seals: WAM nos. 9020, 9021, 9025, 9026, 9028, 9034, 9039, 9042, 9046, 9047, 9057, 9058, 9088, 9090, 9091, 9104, 9105, 9116, 9118, 9119, 9120, 9121, 9123, 9124, 9125, 9127, 9139, 9156, 9157, 9172, 9175, 9176. Lincoln bonds with surviving seals: WAM nos. 9014, 9027, 9032, 9054, 9087, 9092, 9093, 9094, 9097, 9098, 9117, 9130, 9131, 9132, 9137, 9140, 9142, 9143, 9144, 9145, 9146, 9147, 9148, 9150, 9160, 9161, 9162, 9165, 9167, 9168, 9169, 9170.

[48] WAM nos. 9028 (still with a seal), 9036, 9043.   [49] WAM nos. 9162, 9169, 9092.

[50] WAM nos. 9027, 9087, 9094, 9132, 9170.

over all a label of eight points'.[51] These last three devices are clear indicators of the social status of the men to whom they belonged. Thus, sillography might have been a useful guide to the status of the debtors if more seals had survived. As it is, except in individual cases, it can only be firmly established that, to be able to borrow money from the Jews, the debtors needed to possess or have access to a seal.[52]

Secondly, it is evident that in order to secure a loan most potential debtors must have had some security or collateral. The two surviving late Edwardian bonds were secured on lands and chattels.[53] Even after the *Statutum de Judeismo* limited the security for a debt to anything in the possession of the debtor except 'the moiety of his land and chattels for his maintenance as aforesaid and the chief mansion', the creditor would still have required evidence of collateral before making a loan.[54] Thus, the Christian debtor could be considered to be a man or woman of some means, at least equal or nearly equal to the amount of his or her loan. It would therefore seem unlikely that a prospective client would be of servile status. In a case brought in February 1275 in the *Scaccarium Judaeorum*, a jury was summoned at Derby to establish whether Ralph of Ripley was a villein. If Ralph was found to be a *villeinus nativus* of *servilis condicionis* of the abbot of Darley, then the land that he held could not have been used as a security. The findings of the jury are unknown because Ralph never appeared.[55] It can, however, be normally assumed that the majority of the Jews' clients were probably above servile status and held more than 'a moiety for maintenance and their chief mansion' to be able to persuade a creditor to make them a loan.

Finally, the actual name of the debtor inscribed on the bond is obviously the most important key to the identification of the Christian who made the contract with the Jew. After all, the chirographers who drew up the bond received money from both parties for their troubles and there is no reason to believe that they were not diligent in their work of noting who made the transaction.[56] It was important not only for the creditor but also for the officials of the *Scaccarium Judaeorum* to know exactly who owed what to each Jew. The Close Rolls show that mistaken identities could cause problems.[57]

It is also within the context of the very local nature of a list of debts that the names can be used to build up a wider picture. The naming

---

[51] WAM nos. 9014, 9140, 9150.
[52] *Cronica Maiorum*, pp. 237–8; *SCBM*, vol. I, pp. xiv–v; *PREJ1*, p. 311.
[53] Hereford RO MS AH81/34; PRO C/146/1360; Postan 1930, p. 36.
[54] *Statutes*, vol. I, pp. 220–1; *CCR 1272–1279*, pp. 287, 306, 395, 496.
[55] *PREJ4*, p. 19; *CCR 1276–1279*, p. 297. [56] Scott 1950, p. 446.
[57] *CCR 1272–1279*, pp. 161–3, 284–5.

patterns found on details of debt are naturally different from other administrative lists. It is not surprising that of Lumbard of Cricklade's debtors in 1277 93 per cent had locative elements in the name recorded on the bond. Similarly, of the debtors of his son, Bonefey of Cricklade, in 1290, 92 per cent had locative elements in the recorded details.[58] If other lists of names such as the Rolls of the Freemen of Canterbury for 1299–1303 are considered a significantly different picture emerges. Of forty-one men admitted between 1299 and 1300, only 51 per cent have locative elements. In 1303, of 117, only 33 per cent have locative names.[59] More recently Professor Robert Bartlett found that the guild merchants roll for Dublin in about 1200 revealed a rate of around 40 per cent toponymic surnames which mentioned a specific place of origin.[60] Generally the lists of Jewish debtors have much fuller entries whenever a name is recorded than those lists of Freemen or Guildsmen. Ninety per cent of the names of Jewish debtors from both Canterbury samples have a locative description. The Hereford 1276 scrutiny reveals 93 per cent, the *vetus cista* 88 per cent and the *nova archa* 79 per cent. The Lincoln bonds have 84 per cent and the 1290 list of transactions 94 per cent.[61] The abundance of locative descriptions in lists which record indebtedness clearly indicates that both the scribe and the creditor must have had a desire to know where the debtor actually lived. Even given that locative names had perhaps in some cases become heritable, in a situation where they refer to debt in a local context, names such as Roger son of Harry of Liss can, if used cautiously, give a fair impression of provenance.

The names which include the locative description can be divided into two types: names which include highly localised locatives and names with less localised locatives referring, for example, to a village or manor. Examples of the first type are evident in many of the transactions. Thus *de la Dane, at Mede, de la funtayne, atte Broke, atte Water* and *de la parc* appeared on bonds made in Canterbury.[62] Similarly, local

[58] Mundill 1991b, p. 159.
[59] PRO E/101/250/6; Thrupp and Johnson 1964, pp. 173–213. Ironically these rolls were compiled by Reginald Hurell who was himself indebted to a Jew.
[60] Bartlett 1993, p. 181. The roll contained some 2,800 names.
[61] Canterbury: WAM nos. 9015, 9019, 9020, 9021, 9022, 9025, 9026, 9028, 9034, 9036, 9039, 9042, 9043, 9046, 9047, 9057, 9058, 9086, 9088, 9089, 9090, 9091, 9103, 9104, 9105, 9116, 9118, 9119, 9120, 9121, 9123, 9124, 9125, 9126, 9127, 9139, 9156, 9157, 9158, 9159, 9172, 9173, 9174, 9175, 9176; PRO E/101/250/6. Hereford: *PREJ3*, pp. 230–8; PRO E/101/250/5. Lincoln: WAM nos. 9014, 9027, 9032, 9054, 9087, 9092, 9093, 9094, 9095, 9097, 9098, 9100, 9117, 9130, 9131, 9132, 9135, 9137, 9140, 9142, 9143, 9144, 9145, 9146, 9147, 9148, 9150, 9160, 9161, 9162, 9163, 9164, 9165, 9167, 9168, 9169, 9170; PRO E/101/250/12.
[62] WAM nos. 9039, 9057, 9088, 9120, 9172; see PRO E/101/250/6. Other references like *de la forge, de la le, atte wode, de la hill, qui est ad parcum* also appeared.

examples were to be found in the Herefordshire samples, where *de la foresta* (in this case the Forest of Dean), *de la more, atte Wodegate, de la birches, de la pole, de la legh, de Crowenhill* (in the parish of Sutton), *de Hatsend, de Wormhull* (in the parish of Madley), *de la forde* and *de la lome* (again in the parish of Sutton) appeared.[63] The Lincolnshire samples did not have so many examples of local toponyms but they revealed a few highly localised descriptions such as *de montibus* (which, when used in the context of a citizen of Lincoln, more than likely referred to the Steep Hill area of the town), *de Crackpol* (again, another area of Lincoln), *de venella* (in Hackthorn) and, finally, *de la launde*.[64] These highly localised locatives are naturally of limited use in identifying the debtor any further.

The second group of locative descriptions are of much more use. Generally, the debtor is simply identified by a locative preceded by '*de*' and the name of the village or manor. This can be an identifying feature. One such example, 'Robert Kaynel de Yatton' who had a bond in the Devizes *nova cista*, can be more positively identified by connecting him to the village of Yatton Keynell, 13½ miles north-west of Devizes. Even today it is noted on an old board at the back of the parish church that Robert Kaynel was a patron of the church there from 1265 onwards.[65] Such identification is regrettably not possible with all the Jewish clients but it does strengthen the use which such descriptions have. Other evidence can establish the utility of the locative description. Some of the Herefordshire debtors can be seen acting as witnesses to land grants in the Herefordshire valley.[66] Many connections can be made between debtors with locative descriptions and lands in Lincolnshire.

Richard Rudde of Barton in Lincolnshire can be positively identified with that village.[67] In 1282, Richard Rudde was concerned with a land transaction at Barton on Humber.[68] Similarly, Adam fil Randolph of Hemswell, in Lincolnshire, who made bonds repayable in wool in 1287

---

[63] *PREJ3*, pp. 230–8; PRO E/101/250/15 also had other references such as *de la hull, del park, de la feld, de la hethe, de la nope, de furrio, de frene*.

[64] WAM nos. 9032, 9131, 9162; PRO E/101/250/12.

[65] PRO E/101/250/11; Fry 1908, pp. 448–9.

[66] Hereford Cathedral Archives, P. E. Morgan's name index: Pauncefot 353, 444; Hurtesle 139, 240, 851; Maurdin 966, 994, 1034, 336, 660; Penebrug 581, 867; Danyell 1235; Mael 298, 359, 400, 403, 416–18; Solle 18 19, 317, 343, 346, 424, 111, 118, 119, 307, 318, 331, 382, 383, 384, 399; Balun 166; Clehonger 92, 115, 188 199, 288, 289, 290, 384, 404, 443, 527, 529, 584, 590, 591, 593, 595, 655, 680, 690.

[67] WAM no. 9170.

[68] Lincoln RO, Foster Library Transcripts A144; Cohen 1951, pp. 149–50. Richard Rudde gave Robert of Wolinham and Elena his wife 'a sore sparrow hawk' and the promise of a penny rent at Christmas for a toft and a half a bovate of land in Barton on Humber.

and 1289, transferred the advowson of the church of Glentworth (2 miles south-east of Hemswell) to the abbot of Newhouse in return for 'one sore sparrow hawk' in February 1286.[69] Another Lincolnshire debtor, Geoffrey fil Alexander of Hackthorn, can be identified in 1282 as acting as the attorney for the prioress of the house of Stainfield which was situated just 8 miles south-east of Hackthorn.[70] John le Aumoner of Stow St Mary, Lincolnshire, who was indebted to several Jews between 1285 and 1288, can be identified as the man who, in 1301, sold the rights he had to two messuages and one bovate of land in Stow St Mary and Stretton by Stow.[71] An indebted Lincolnshire knight, Robert of Legbourne, can also be identified as having links with Legbourne. In June 1290, on his behalf, Thomas of Lough negotiated an annual rent to be paid to him by Robert de Somercotes. In return for £15 per annum, de Somercotes was to receive rents of £4 os 3d, 2 pounds of pepper, 3 pounds of cummin and 2½ quarters of salt. De Somercotes was also to have Robert of Legbourne's rights to lands which were situated in Somercote, Skidbrooke and Saltfleetby, the last of which was just 6 miles to the north-east of Legbourne.[72]

In Wiltshire, William Laddok of Heytesbury who, in the 1250s, deposited bonds in the Devizes *vetus cista*, can be identified as a man who witnessed several local land deeds and who transferred some of his own land and who had a burgage in Heytesbury some 13 miles south-west of Devizes.[73] Similarly Thomas Bacun of Chesingbury can be associated with the Bacun family of Chesingbury who, in the early fourteenth century, had considerable lands in Uphavene, Chisingbury and Rusteshale.[74] Nicholas Baddebir of Cricklade, who contracted a bond for 3 sacks of wool in 1284, can be identified as having had land in and around Cricklade; certainly in 1263 his widowed mother held one workshop and one burgage in Cricklade.[75] In 1303 his daughter, Alice, transferred one messuage and 20 acres of land and 14 acres of meadow in Cricklade and Great Chelworth.[76] Several of the debtors of Lumbard and Bonefey of Cricklade, who had bonds in the Oxford *archa*, can also

[69] PRO E/101/250/12; Lincoln RO, Foster Library Transcripts A320.

[70] PRO E/101/250/12; Lincoln RO, Foster Library Transcripts A198.

[71] PRO E/101/250/12; Lincoln RO, Foster Library Transcripts A593: John le Aumoner and Alice his wife sold two messuages and one bovate of land to John and Isabella Henry for £6 13s 4d.

[72] PRO E/101/250/12; Lincoln RO, Foster Library Transcripts A393, A394.

[73] PRO E/101/250/11; Wiltshire RO 490/1491, 490/1492, 132/1.

[74] PRO E/101/249/32; Pugh 1939, pp. 60, 81; Salter 1930, p. 199; Mundill 1991b, p. 161. These lands included 3 virgates, 5 acres of meadows, one messuage, 20 acres of feeding for fifteen oxen, nine oxen, 218 sheep and nine pigs.

[75] PRO E/101/250/9; Mundill 1991b, pp. 161–2. In 1303 Nicholas Baddebir's daughter Alice transferred the land.

[76] Mundill 1991b, p. 160.

be identified. One of Lumbard's clients, Ralph de Pinkeny, who was described as of 'Parva Sherston', certainly had lands and tenants in Wiltshire.[77] William Ingelot of Great Tew, who was indebted to Lumbard in 1273, can be identified as William Ingelot of Tew who effectively sold a messuage and a virgate of land in Idbury (8½ miles from Great Tew) in 1268.[78] One of Bonefey's debtors, Philip le But of Cricklade, also paid 2d per annum for a croft in Cricklade between 1271 and 1277.[79]

Even where the record has sometimes distorted the locative description, further identifications can be made if other records have survived. John Malet of Orby, Lincolnshire, who owed £9 6s 8d in July 1289, can probably be identified as the same John Malet who held a tenement consisting of one messuage in Irebby (presumably the same as Orby) for a rent of £2 10s 0d a year.[80] Similarly, in Lincolnshire, Robert Benet of Heneby, as he was identified by the bonds he made in February 1289, is very probably the same Robert Benet, who in April 1291 granted one toft, 8½ acres of meadow and 3 bovates of land situated in Ouneby iuxta Navenby to Walter Bek of Laceby in return for 'one sore sparrow hawk'.[81]

Even the barest evidence of a Christian name and a second name can sometimes make an identification possible. Such a case is that of a Lincolnshire debtor, William le Engleys, who in a bond made in 1285 was only described by his Christian name and cognomen. In this instance, it can be established through other evidence that he had connections with lands to the east of Grantham. In 1282, William le Engleys and Mariota, his wife, both described as of 'Skrevington', granted lands in 'Wylgebby' to Alexander and Hawis of 'Trikyngham' in return for 'one sore sparrow hawk' and one grain of pepper payable at Christmas. The places can be identified as Scredington, Scott Willoughby (now disappeared) and Threekingham, all within 2½ miles of each other and to the east of Grantham. In the same year, William le Engleys and Mariota, his wife, of 'Scretington' granted Ralph fil John of 'Old Lafford' 1 acre, 1 rood, and 5 shillings of rent in 'Kyrkeby, Old Lafford and Leilthorp' in return for £2 and a half a penny payable at Easter. The places can be identified as Scredington, Kirkby la Thorp, Old Sleaford and Laythorpe (now disappeared), all situated within 5 miles of Scredington to the east of Grantham. It is fairly safe to assume, from this other evidence, that, when William made his bond with

---

[77] *Ibid.*, p. 158.   [78] *Ibid.*, p. 160.   [79] *Ibid.*
[80] PRO E/101/250/12; Lincoln RO, Foster Library Transcripts A667.
[81] PRO E/101/250/12; Lincoln RO, Foster Library Transcripts A402.

Hagin fil Benedict in 1285 for £2 13s 4d, he still had some connection with Scredington.[82]

Two other Lincolnshire debtors certainly had local connections, despite the failure of the name recorded on the bond to provide a provenance. Agnes, the widow of Philip de Caltoft, and William de Cressy can both be identified from other sources. Agnes held lands in Toynton after her husband died. In November 1291, John, her son, granted the lands which his mother held as her dower (situated in an area 13 miles north-north-east of Boston) to John Bek in return for 'one sore sparrow hawk'. The actual deed was made at Westminster in Agnes' presence. The lands were to pass to John Bek on Agnes' death.[83] Similarly William de Cressy, whose wife Matilda de Cressy of Great Markham in Nottinghamshire was also indebted to the Jews, can be seen to have some Lincolnshire connections. In 1274, he put in a claim against two final concords which involved lands in Grantham, Gonerby, Manthorpe and Claypole. Thus, William de Cressy did in fact have at least a landed interest in Lincolnshire.[84] A debtor who had bonds in the Exeter *vetus cista* in 1255, John Comyn, can be identified as having connections with Exbridge.[85] Similarly Jacob le Mohun, who had a bond recorded in the Exeter *nova cista*, had control of a broken-down mill in South Milton (34 miles south-west of Exeter) in 1281. Interestingly he had borrowed from Abraham of Exeter in 1286 and was to repay him 20 quarters of wheat.[86] Such useful ancillary information is, however, rare. Naturally identification by means of a clear local reference after the Christian name of the debtor is relatively easy compared with trying to identify the more distorted locative descriptions like those discussed above.

Thus chance survivals in other records show that debtors like Richard Rudde of Barton, William Laddok of Heytesbury and Nicholas Baddebir of Cricklade did in fact have land in those villages and had for some reason turned to the Jews for credit. Such connections also show that it is possible, in the context of creditor and debtor, to put considerable trust in the locative descriptions. The exceptional frequency of the use of the locative element, the indications from other evidence of the genuineness of the toponyms and the proximity of the particular villages referred to in the bonds show that the locative part of the debtor's description can take on a much greater significance.

---

[82] PRO E/101/250/12; Lincoln RO, Foster Library Transcripts A145, A154.
[83] PRO E/101/250/12; Lincoln RO, Foster Library Transcripts A408.
[84] PRO E/101/250/12; Lincoln RO, Foster Library Transcripts A10, A21.
[85] PRO E/101/250/2; Reichel 1912, pp. 286–7.
[86] PRO E/101/250/2; Reichel 1912, pp. 23–4.

Regrettably not much can be gained from a very local locative such as 'at the Park', 'at the Hill' or 'at the Mede'. However, wherever the name of a village or town is indicated by the Christian debtor's full descriptive name, an effort can be made to identify it. As other studies have proved both *de* and *in* can be used to indicate that there was a connection between the person and the place given in the record. Clearly on the odd occasion where the naming pattern was followed by the formula *de parochia de X*, a definite connection can be made: this can naturally be accepted as greater proof of residence. A description such as *manens in* can be taken to represent the place where the debtor lived at the time the bond was contracted.[87]

The large numbers of recorded Christian debtors can therefore be used to demonstrate the effect of Jewish finance in rural areas. Before moving to a more specific study of Jewish clients in late thirteenth-century Kent, Herefordshire and Lincolnshire there are some further observations that should be made about the Jews' borrowers and their status. Naturally, there are some debtors who used credit more frequently than others. There are also some whose debts were particularly large. As has been observed for both types of debtor, it is fair to assume that their securities were either commensurate with their loans or that they presented good propositions for profit. Yet it is possible to use the value of their debts as a reflection of both their social and credit status. In considering the debts and the amounts owed in each transaction it is perhaps useful to have some sort of indication of some real values in thirteenth-century terms. A knight might expect to earn as much as £55 a year in time of war; a horse cost £9 a year.[88] The qualification for taking on knightly status was to have land worth more than £20 per annum.[89] It can become far too easy to consider the value of the debts without giving thought to what they actually meant in real terms at the time.

The surviving Kentish bonds in the Westminster muniments reveal four debtors who owed the richer Jews of Canterbury debts over £10.[90] In November 1270, Adam Daniel of Newchurch owed £33 6s 8d, in 1271, William Ordiner of Romney owed £15, in July 1273, John de Mortun owed £20 and in August 1275, *Magister* John de Wayhope owed £10 and 1 bushel of grain. These four debtors who all owed debts

---

[87] See Table 10; Elman 1936, pp. 113, 140–7; Mundill 1987, pp. 325–6; 1990b, p. 160.

[88] Denholm-Young 1944, p. 115; Prestwich 1988, 'Notes on money'.

[89] Harding 1993, p. 193.

[90] WAM nos. 9015, 9019, 9020, 9021, 9022, 9025, 9026, 9028, 9034, 9036, 9039, 9042, 9043, 9046, 9047, 9057, 9058, 9086, 9088, 9089, 9090, 9091, 9103, 9104, 9105, 9116, 9118, 9119, 9120, 9121, 9123, 9124, 9125, 9126, 9127, 9139, 9156, 9157, 9158, 9159, 9172, 9173, 9174, 9175, 9176.

for single transactions must have had good securities and can be considered to have been of fairly high social and credit status.[91] The bonds also reveal two debtors who owed more than one debt. Richard fil Hamo de la Dane borrowed twice during the period from Aaron fil Cresse. In February 1274, he owed £1 which was not repaid on time in August of that year. In February 1275, he managed to secure another loan and owed a further £4 to be repaid in November of the same year.[92] Ralph fil Robert Renyr of St John's parish in the Isle of Thanet owed Hagin fil Leon le Eveske for three loans during the same period. In April 1273, he owed 13s 4d which he did not repay on 24 June as contracted. On 9 June in the same year, he managed to negotiate a further loan for which he was to pay 14s 0d and 1 bushel of wheat in late September. In October, having failed to pay in September, he received another advance and owed a further £2 13s 4d which brought his total debts for 1273 to a total of £4 0s 8d and 1 bushel of wheat.[93] The activities of these debtors prove that, to the Jewish creditor, it occasionally made business sense to offer to some clients a further series of loans even when debts were not repaid in time. It can be the case either that such debtors must have had good security and were well-known local inhabitants, or that they had a strong relationship with their Jewish creditors.

As well as revealing Christians who went to Jews for loans more than once, the Canterbury bonds show, on some occasions, that more than one member of the same family made use of the credit facilities provided by the Jews. Two brothers, both the sons of William Cokin, who was described as 'a citizen of Canterbury lately deceased', owed two fairly sizeable debts. In March 1272, Stephen Cokin owed Vives of Winchester £4 which was to be repaid in the following November. In July 1275, John Cokin owed Floria filia Elias £6 13s 4d to be repaid in February 1276.[94] Another pair of brothers, the sons of Thomas de Mortun, were also both in debt. In February 1272, Alan de Mortun owed Moses fil Vives of Winchester £8. In July, his brother John de Mortun owed Cohke Hagin fil Cresse £20. It is clear that Alan went on borrowing from the Jews and sank further into debt. In 1278, he was in dispute with Hagin fil Deulecresse in the Exchequer of the Jews on a plea of account.[95]

The bonds which were still in the Canterbury *archa* in 1290 reflect the type of business which was transacted in Kent between 1280 and

---

[91] WAM nos. 9022, 9058, 9126, 9158.   [92] WAM nos. 9098, 9172.
[93] WAM nos. 9104, 9124, 9116.   [94] WAM nos. 9019, 9173.
[95] WAM nos. 9047, 9126 actually witnessed by Alan de Mortun 'the said John's brother'; Cohen 1951, p. 365.

1290.[96] As all the debts were for amounts of cereal, it is possible that the debtors were either purveyors of or even producers of types of cereal or that they had access to grain. The larger debtors such as Robert fil William of Herthanger, Waresius of Valoynes *miles*, John of Northwood, John fil Solomon of Elstuen of the Parish of Selling, and Richard le Jovene of Chilham, who all owed 40 quarters or more, may be considered to be large cereal producers and as such must also have been rural landholders.[97] If they were to repay their debts from a single harvest they would probably have had to have had access to at least 50 or 60 acres of fertile ground. This would place these particular debtors as fairly substantial villagers who had required a loan from their creditor. Professor Harding has recently shown that in 1251 at Doddington, in the Isle of Ely, there were at least fifteen men who held between 10 and 100 acres. Four men held between 50 and 100 whilst only one held over 100 acres. Harding has also shown that the economy of the late thirteenth-century village was producing a 'class of thriving yeomen'.[98] Thus if those who were indebted for larger quantities of grain had access to the land on which it could be produced then they may well have been those who dominated local agriculture.

Those clients like Angotus, the clerk of Sheldwich, Thomas fil Roger, the beadle, Juliana, the widow of William Geynvelde, and Stephen fil Mathew, the fisherman, who all owed 4 quarters to their creditors must also have had access to grain either by being able to buy from a producer or by having a small ground or strip on which it could be grown. These would be more likely to be 'ordinary villagers' who, as Dr Britnell has shown, were numerous in the medieval countryside.[99] They were men and women who might, as Professor Harding inferred, earn £1 10s 0d to £2 annually. In times of dearth or famine, as in the early 1270s, such borrowers may well have been prepared to turn to the only security they had, which was seeded in the ground. Little is known of how ordinary villagers traded and, as Dr Britnell has observed, small grain transactions were often informal. Even less is known about what they may have been able to produce from their smallholdings.[100] It is possible that some Kentish villagers had found that their crops could bring them the advantage of loans from Jewish moneylenders in order to tide themselves over another year.

Our knowledge of the clients of Aaron le Blund in Herefordshire

---

[96] PRO E/101/250/6. [97] *Ibid.*

[98] Arrived at by assuming that 1½ acres might grow 1 quarter of wheat. See Postan 1972, p. 25; Hatcher and Miller 1978, pp. 147–9; Harding 1993, p. 95.

[99] PRO E/101/250/6; Britnell 1981, p. 211.

[100] Harding 1993, p. 100; Britnell 1993, p. 98.

proves that the more easily identifiable debtors were naturally of a high social status.[101] They included men like Henry de Pembridge who owed the largest single debt of £60 as well as others who included John fil Richard Rumel, Richard Pauncefoot (possibly a relative of Adam Botiller Pauncefoot, another client of the Hereford Jews), William de Solle, John Daniel, Robert fil Robert of Weston and his brother or son John fil Robert of Weston and John of Marden. William de Bliss *miles* owed £20 and Richard of Eardisley *miles* owed two bonds contracted in 1274 and 1275 worth £9 and 1 soam of cereal. William Mandut was described as *dominus de Bulley*, a Gloucestershire manor, and was indebted for £11 6s 8d. Most of Aaron's other debtors were described merely by locative names.[102] Aaron's transactions also showed borrowing by members of the same family. In August 1275, John de Balun, the lord of the manor of Much Markle, owed Aaron le Blund £5 and one robe with a hood. It is known that John de Balun, who had previously been indebted for over £70 to Moses fil Hamo of Hereford in 1244, died in 1275. His family was then again indebted to Aaron in 1286.[103]

Other Hereford Jews also lent to easily recognisable local dignitaries like Hugh fil Reginald Moniword, a very prominent Hereford citizen, whose father had been the bailiff of Hereford between 1276 and 1277.[104] They also lent to men such as Peter de Grenham, a Devonshire knight.[105] The details of the Herefordshire transactions of Jewish creditors between 1283 and 1290 again identify several debtors who were of high status. For example, there were five debtors who were described as sons and heirs of lords: Nicholas le Archer of Tarrington, son and heir of Lord Nicholas; John, son and heir of Lord Walter of How Caple; Richard, son of Lord Adam of Elmridge; John de Balun, son of Lord Walter of Much Markle; and Walter Hakelutel, son and

---

[101] *PREJ3*, pp. 230–8, Mundill 1987, pp. 331–6 and appendices 3 and 4; Hillaby 1990c, appendix 1.

[102] Hillaby 1990c, appendix 1 identifies William de Solle as coming from Sholle Court, Yarkhill and John of Marden as of Mawardyn; Abrahams 1894, p. 141 identifies Hurtesle as Eardisley; Hillaby 1990c, pp. 452–3 identifies the Pembridge family.

[103] Humphery-Smith 1976, p. 119; Moor 1930, vol. I, p. 38; *Calendar of Inquisitions Post Mortem – Edward I*, vol. II, p. 79; Hillaby 1990c, pp. 450–1.

[104] PRO E/101/250/5; Hereford RO Bailiffs' accounts 1276–7 – the roll of Reginald Moniword; Hillaby 1990c, pp. 460–1.

[105] PRO E/101/250/5; Peter de Grenham had land in Oburnford in the parish of Halberton (3 miles east of Tiverton) in Devon in 1282. He also had dealings with Jacob Copyn of Exeter, borrowed from a Christian moneylender in 1285 and in December 1285 granted the manor of Oburnford to Sir Adam de Cretting. Moor 1930, vol. II, p. 143; *CCR 1279–1288*, pp. 181–2, 351.

heir of Lord Walter of Hakelutel.[106] Other borrowers of higher social standing were men like Roger of Hereford who was the son of Richard, a clerk of the Royal Exchequer, and the four debtors described as *miles*: Henry of Hereford, Henry de Solers, the Lord of Dorstone, and Roger of Butterley who held lands at Butterley after 1280.[107]

Many of the Jews' clients in Herefordshire who owed debts at this late period had contracted to repay in commodities, mainly in cereal, and can thus possibly be seen as local landholders. It is also significant that some clients had access to different commodities. Nicholas le Archer of Tarrington (in four different bonds) owed a total of £234 13s 4d, to be repaid not only by 200 quarters of cereal but also by 17 sacks of wool. John of Marden owed one bond worth approximately £37 and was to repay 28 quarters of cereal but also twenty-four cheeses and four cartloads of hay. At the lower end of the scale, Brian son of Brontun owed £1 4s 0d and one military over-tunic.[108] Clearly in Herefordshire during the 1280s the nature of the debtor's repayments had changed, probably in accordance with the requirements of the Statute of the Jewry.

Once again it is more difficult to identify those debtors who owed small sums. Little can be discovered about the status of John Freeman of Stoke Lacy who owed 2 quarters or of Hugh Baudewyn of Byford and Nicholas fil Nicholas le Secular who both owed half a quarter in a shared transaction. In the late 1280s in Herefordshire borrowers joined together in single debts. In an unusual transaction made in 1286 as many as eight individuals joined together in a debt to Aaron le Blund for £13. It is difficult to understand why Walter of Frene of Sutton, John de la Lone, Robert Jurdan, William Balle, John Hereberd, William son of John the clerk, Walter son of Hugh, and Richard of Crowenhill of Sutton combined in such a transaction. Men like Richard of Crowenhill of Sutton, Walter of Frene and Stephen le Paumer of Sutton had also joined in a debt owed to Bonenfaunt le Blund for 40 quarters in 1285 and the partnership of Richard of Crowenhill and Stephen le Paumer also owed Benedict le Eveske 30 quarters to be repaid at Leominster Fair in 1285.[109] It is unlikely that anything concerning the status of such debtors will ever be known.

A similar pattern emerges from the Lincolnshire transactions, where

---

[106] PRO E/101/250/5; Moor 1930, vol. II, p. 171: Walter's father, Lord Walter, had received a pardon from the king for the £57 which he owed Aaron le Blund, 'in consideration of his grateful service to the king and of his costs and expenses in newly erecting a house in the Welsh marches and afterwards crenellating it'.

[107] Crook 1980, p. 22 gives further details of Richard of Hereford; Hillaby 1990c, p. 462.

[108] PRO E/101/250/5.   [109] *Ibid.*

local notables can be easily identified. Some debtors were frequently involved in obtaining Jewish credit and can also be identified from other sources. Such was the case of Stephen Malevolel of Rampton in Nottinghamshire, who owed Benedict of London the sum of £94 13s 4d by a bond made on 1 November 1274, and who also owed further debts to other Jews. In Hilary term 1275, Malevolel clearly had problems in meeting his debts. The sheriff of Nottingham was ordered to distrain him for £13 6s 8d which was owing to the king on account of a confiscated bond contracted in February 1275 with Bonamy, the son-in-law of Josce of York. The sheriff responded that Stephen had a writ under the Great Seal and, later in the year, the bond, still unpaid, was returned to the York *archa*.[110] Another frequent client of the Jews was Richard Rudde of Barton, who had made a bond for £3 6s 8d. In 1278, Solomon Bunting sued Richard Rudde, the tenant of the lands formerly belonging to William le Bretun, and claimed £10. Solomon claimed that William owed him two debts contracted in 1276 which were in the London *archa* and that he was trying to obtain the money from the new tenant of William's lands, Richard Rudde. Richard Rudde duly appeared and said that he did not hold the land at the time the chartérs were made and therefore was not liable.[111]

The surviving Lincoln bonds also reveal three *milites*, namely Hugh Duket, Adam of Newmarket and Jordan Foliot. These three can also be proved to be Lincolnshire landholders who had incurred several debts to various creditors. In 1274 and 1275, Hugh Duket *miles* owed Hagin fil Benedict £50.[112] It is clear that Hagin had difficulty in reclaiming his debt as, in 1278, he tried suing Hugh Duket's tenants for the sum.[113] Hugh himself had recourse to borrowing from Christian moneylenders, as, in May 1275, he owed John de Ubbeston, the usher of the king's chamber, £3 6s 8d 'to be levied in default on his lands and chattels in Lincolnshire'.[114] It seems that most of Hugh Duket's lands were to the south of Lincoln. In 1275, he had given over 17 acres in Wellingore to the Knights Templar at Temple Bruer. In 1306, it is clear that he also held lands in Navenby, just 14 miles south of Lincoln.[115]

A history of debt can also be established in the case of Adam of Newmarket, who in 1274 owed Bonamy fil Josce, a York Jew,

---

[110] WAM no. 9100, endorsed 'I Benedict will allow the said Stephen £2 at next Christmas term'; *PREJ2*, pp. 221, 224, 260–2, 292; *PREJ3*, p. 55; *CCR 1272–1279*, pp. 97, 103.

[111] WAM no. 9170; Cohen 1951, pp. 149–50; Lincoln RO, Foster Library Transcripts A120, A144.

[112] WAM nos. 9095, 9140.

[113] Cohen 1951, pp. 1–2, 87, 299, 440, 459; PRO E/9/44 shows that debts owed by Hugh Duket to Hagin and Benedict were sold eventually to Master Henry de Bray; *CPR 1281–1301*, p. 116.

[114] *CCR 1272–1279*, p. 236.   [115] Lincoln RO, Foster Library Transcripts A24, A787.

£26 13s 4d.[116] It is clear that his father, Adam, held lands in Wheateley and Harwell beyond the Trent in Nottinghamshire and had been in the company of John Dayville, John de Vescy and Baldwin Wake, some of the baronial rebels responsible for the sack of the Lincoln Jewry in 1260.[117] Perhaps it was because the Newmarkets had fought on the losing side in the war that they had recourse to borrowing. In May 1273, Adam of Newmarket Junior sent his serjeant, Henry Masy, to arrange for the release of two of his retinue who were prisoners in Newgate for robbery and to acquit Adam of £100 which he owed a certain Jew of London.[118] In November 1274, Adam made a recognizance with Deconicus Guylelmy (a merchant of the queen mother) and Guyettus Bonaventure for £112 and offered as security his land and chattels in Yorkshire. It is known that Newmarket was also in debt to Aaron of York. His son Adam of Newmarket Junior later inherited his father's debts. In 1275, he was to be distrained by the sheriff of York for £50 which had been owed to Hagin by his father.[119] In 1278, the Newmarkets' debts were acquired by the king. However, their indebtedness did not reduce them to total poverty and it is clear that, in November 1285, Adam Junior still had one messuage, with over 60 acres of land, meadow and woods as well as a water mill in Asbern and Mosley in Lincolnshire which he had rented out to John le Barber.[120]

The third Lincolnshire *miles*, Jordan Foliot, was also a man who seems to have been more often in debt than out of it. He was described as the son of Lord Richard Foliot who held lands in Nottinghamshire and Derbyshire and who had dealings with Hagin fil Benedict of Lincoln.[121] The Lincolnshire bonds show that Jordan was indebted to Benedict of London.[122] Other sources reveal that in 1275 he was also indebted to a Christian, Roger de Evesham, and that he used his lands in Norfolk as security. Jordan had further dealings with Benedict of London and with a Christian clerk.[123] In 1277, he made a recognizance

[116] WAM no. 9014.
[117] *CCR 1272–1279*, pp. 151, 190; Moor 1930, vol. III, p. 263; PRO E/9/44 shows that both father and son were indebted to other London Jews by bonds made in 1259 and 1271; Lieberman 1983, p. 124; Coss 1975, p. 31.
[118] *CCR 1272–1279*, p. 46. They were imprisoned in Newgate for robbing merchants between Stamford and Walmesford.
[119] *Ibid.*, p. 222; PREJ4, p. 55.
[120] Cohen 1951, pp. 391–2, 446, 467; Lincoln RO, Foster Library Transcripts A836, A850; *CCR 1272–1279*, p. 458. The Barons of the Exchequer and the Justices of the Jews were commanded to pay Robert Tibbetot in Jewish debts and to 'take of the clearer debts of Hagin in the king's hand either of the debts of Adam of Newmarket or of another to the value of 100 marks'.
[121] Moor 1930, vol. II, pp. 77–8; PRO E/101/250/12 and E/9/44 record a further debt to Benedict of London.
[122] WAM no. 9150; PRO E/9/44 also records that Jordan owed Benedict £40.
[123] *CCR 1272–1279*, p. 248; *CPR 1281–1301*, p. 324; PREJ3, pp. 65, 294; Cohen 1951, p. 397.

with Manser fil Aaron and promised to deliver 4 sacks of wool, 'of worldly and ancient weight', to the Jew's house in London. It is clear that Jordan had some Lincolnshire connections, as in September 1279 a bond was made between him and Adam of Newmarket which promised delivery of 120 quarters of assorted grain. It is likely that when Jordan died the family still experienced financial difficulties as in 1307 his widow Margery and his son and heir Richard were indebted for £410 by a recognizance in favour of Bishop Langton.[124]

The bonds which were recorded as being in the Lincoln *archa* in 1290 reveal the type of business conducted there after 1278.[125] They show repayments which were to be made in three different media of exchange: money, grain and wool. Approximately 10 per cent of the 185 debtors owed debts repayable in combinations of these three commodities, either money and grain, grain and wool, or money and wool or all three. Sixteen per cent of the debtors owed debts repayable in money, the majority of which were contracted in the last three years before the Expulsion. Twenty-six per cent of the debtors owed amounts of cereal which varied from as much as 100 quarters to half a quarter in single transactions. Forty-six per cent of the debtors owed debts repayable in wool which varied from as much as 12 sacks to just 8 stone of wool owed in single transactions.

According to this later evidence the amounts owed to any one Jew range from those debts owed by Randolph Selweyn of Thorpe, a *miles* from Yorkshire, who owed £113 6s 8d to the debt of Randolph Stag of Hackthorn who owed only 10s 0d. A third of the debtors owed debts which were worth over £10; such debtors seem to be a cross-section of local society. Immediately identifiable were twelve *milites*, twelve debtors who were the sons, daughters and wives of *milites* or *domini*, three *clerici*, three other members of the clergy, one *alblaster* or cross-bowman, one individual who might have been a miller and four female debtors.[126] Several members of the same family, like William fil William de Cressy and Matilda de Cressy, were also indebted to Jews.[127] Three members of the de la Launde family had debts which were owed to the same Jew, Diay fil Diay, a Jew of Lincoln. In April 1290, William de la Launde of Ewerby and Richard de la Launde of Blankney agreed to repay Diay half a sack of wool. A third member of

---

[124] *PREJ4*, p. 120; Cohen 1951, pp. 63, 308, 397 reveals further transactions made in 1277 and 1278. PRO E/101/250/12; Benedict eventually pardoned the Foliot family of all their debts, PRO E/9/44; Beardwood 1955, p. 68.

[125] PRO E/101/250/12.   [126] *Ibid.*

[127] PRO E/101/250/12; Moor 1930, vol. I, p. 248; Lincoln RO, Foster Library Transcripts A10, A21.

the family, John de la Launde of Ewerby, was also indebted to Diay for a quantity of wool by a bond which was dated January 1290. It seems likely that John, like William, came from Ewerby, about 6 miles from Blankney. Clearly these members of the same family chose to deal with a specific Jewish financier.[128]

The list of bonds in the Lincoln *archa* in 1290 also reveals transactions made by other members of the Foliot family. Jordan Foliot's bonds made in the early 1270s have been discussed above and Jordan has been identified as a rebel sympathiser who had connections in Lincolnshire and Norfolk. His relative, Richard, who was described as being of Yorkshire, was involved in two unusual annuities which were owed to Hagin fil Benedict of London. The transactions promised annual payment of a beast of the chase and a sparrow hawk, presumably minimal feudal dues. Yet another member of the family, Edmund, a *miles* of Lincolnshire, owed a London Jew a sack of wool by a bond made in October 1289.[129] Edmund held 6 acres of land, 1 acre of pasture, the moiety of an acre of meadow and a quarter of a messuage in Raithby.[130] Although the relationships between these three members of the Foliot family cannot be properly established, it seems that they were all clients of the Jews of Lincoln and elsewhere, for a period which spans at least fifteen years.

The information that can be gleaned from Jewish provincial credit transactions in Edward's reign makes it abundantly clear that a variety of people dealt with the Jews and that often individuals and even families made a habit of obtaining credit. In most areas such individuals and families were often of fairly high social status: several local landholders, including *milites* and *domini*, were clearly in debt to the Jews. From the later Lincolnshire evidence the *milites* as a group owed debts which amounted to just over £400 in value and were worth approximately 17 per cent of the total value of the debts registered in the Lincoln *archa* in 1290. When the debts of the families of Lincolnshire *milites* and *domini* are added to this total, it is possible to conclude that at least a quarter of the value of the Lincolnshire debts in 1290 were owed by men and women of fairly high social status.[131] In general the conclusions from such an examination show that as well as important landholders, there were *clerici*, artisans such as smiths, tailors, carpenters, farriers and

---

[128] PRO E/101/250/12; Lincoln RO, Foster Library Transcripts A145: in September 1291 he was promised a 'sore sparrow hawk' for land in Blankney; Moor 1930, vol. III, p. 25.

[129] PRO E/101/250/12.

[130] Lincoln RO, Foster Library Transcripts A627. Edmund disposed of his land for £20 in 1302.

[131] PRO E/101/250/12; Mundill 1987, appendix XI.

glass-makers, and estate officials (including bailiffs and beadles) as well as local clergymen who all sought finance from the Jews.

Such a list does not, of course, refer to the vast majority of particularly small debtors whose social status is in no way identified from the available evidence. Because many clients of the post-1275 transactions promised to repay their debts in commodities it is very probable that a large proportion of this silent majority were members of the free rural peasantry. Such a conclusion is suggested by what is known of the social status of men such as the beadles, smiths and farriers who have been identified in these samples and by the evidence of the predominantly rural character of the Jews' clientele, which will now be examined in greater detail.[132]

Perhaps as revealing as the social status of the debtors is their geographical provenance. It seems that, as would be expected, many of the Jews' debtors came from areas around the centres in which Jews had settled. A brief comparison of the identifiable debtors who transacted business in the Devizes *vetus cista* and the *nova cista* certainly shows such a pattern. Nine debtors who used Jewish credit between 1258 and 1275 and eight who made transactions between 1282 and 1290 came from within a radius of 20 miles of the *archa* town. Even after the Statute of 1275 the Devizes Jews were still dealing with clients from a similar catchment area.[133] Such was the case elsewhere: the impact of Jewish finance was essentially very local to the relevant *archa* town. Table 11 shows that the vast majority of the debtors of provincial Jewry came from areas which were well within 12 miles of the *archa* town. This is not surprising when, as Dr Britnell has recently observed, the normal minimum short-haul distance for the cereal market might have been just over 6 miles and more probably 10 to 12 miles whilst in years of high prices it could even extend to 20 miles.[134] Accordingly the geographical distribution of Jewish debtors can also be best understood in a more detailed local framework and in relation to the *archa* town. Such a consideration suggests that it is more than likely that the provision of credit and the building up of an accepted clientele was done either by constant travelling or by word of mouth as the Jewish creditor from a particular *archa* town established a network of clients.

An understanding of such a network or social circle may be crucial to a proper understanding of the relationship between creditor and debtor. Regrettably, however, such networks are difficult to perceive as they have left no tangible record behind them. When considering peasant

---

[132] Postan 1972, pp. 152–3; Harding 1993, p. 116; Clapham 1933, pp. 198–9; Britnell 1981, pp. 211, 214.
[133] PRO E/101/250/11; see Table 11.   [134] Britnell 1993, p. 83.

Table 11 *The geographical distribution of the debtors of provincial Jewry, 1258–90*

Sample	Date range	4 miles	8 miles	12 miles	16 miles	20 miles	24 miles
Canterbury	1261–76	4	7	5	3	5	2
Canterbury	1280–90	10	17	29	6	3	1
Hereford	1268–75	5	13	21	12	5	0
Hereford							
Aaron le Blund's clients	1264–75	6	10	23	10	2	1
Hereford	1259–75	3	9	16	13	3	0
Lincoln	1270–6	4	4	2	1	11	2
Lincoln	1278–90	4	19	20	22	15	13
Devizes	1258–75	0	1	2	2	2	2
Devizes	1282–90	1	1	5	1	0	0
Total		42	99	134	82	46	23

Sources: WAM nos. 9015, 9019, 9020, 9021, 9022, 9025, 9026, 9028, 9034, 9036, 9039, 9042, 9043, 9046, 9047, 9057, 9058, 9086, 9088, 9089, 9090, 9091, 9103, 9104, 9105, 9116, 9118, 9119, 9210, 9121, 9123, 9124, 9125, 9126, 9127, 9139, 9156, 9157, 9158, 9159, 9172, 9173, 9174, 9175, 9176; PRO E/101/250/6; *PREJ3*, pp. 230–8; PRO E/101/250/5; WAM nos. 9014, 9027, 9032, 9054, 9087, 9092, 9093, 9094, 9095, 9097, 9098, 9100, 9117, 9130, 9131, 9132, 9135, 9137, 9140, 9142, 9143, 9144, 9145, 9146, 9147, 9148, 9150, 9160, 9161, 9162, 9163, 9164, 9165, 9167, 9168, 9169, 9170; PRO E/101/250/12, E/101/250/11.

moneylending in the late Middle Ages, R. H. Tawney observed: 'the moneylending which concerns nine tenths of the population is spasmodic, irregular, unorganised and a series of individual and sometimes surreptitious transactions between neighbours'.[135] Given that such transactions leave no records and that these problems would naturally have applied equally to Jewish and Christian lending, recreating the 'network' is similarly difficult. Most of the information for such an analysis has to be based on the evidence of toponyms which, as has been established above, can probably in this context be used extensively because of the more precise nature of the evidence of financial records.

It is possible to use the more easily identifiable locative descriptions recorded by the scribes, as the creditor might have done, to identify exactly where his debtors came from. By using such a method, the

[135] Tawney 1925, pp. 21–2; Holderness 1976, pp. 98–9; McIntosh 1988, pp. 558–9.

Kentish samples show that the majority of debtors came from the villages and manors that were situated just off the great arterial roads that the Romans left as their legacy (Figure 4). The actual bonds dating from 1261 to 1276 show that in east Kent there were very few debtors at this period with the exception of those resident in the Isle of Thanet in the north-east.[136] To the west, three debtors can be traced: one from Selling, and two from Newnham iuxta Ospringe.[137] To the north, there were three debtors who appeared to live near the Thames estuary: from Tonge, Graveney and Whitstable.[138] To the south and south-east, there were debtors from the rich agricultural lands around the villages of Bishopsbourne, Petham, Barham, Brabourne and Swingfield.[139] To the south-west, there was a group of debtors who inhabited the small villages on the Romney Marsh. It is interesting to note that, between 1270 and 1275, debtors from the Marsh owed the Jews of Canterbury almost £60 in cash terms or almost a quarter of the value of the bonds revealed by this sample.[140] It also seems that Abba, the Jew of Canterbury, dealt particularly with Marsh debtors. His clients came from Woodchurch and Newchurch.[141] Only one debtor indebted to the Jews at this time came from more than 24 miles away from Canterbury: Geoffrey le Chip of Cobham near Rochester.[142]

Owing to the fact that, with one exception (the single wool bond owed by a Canterbury citizen), all the debts revealed by the 1290 Canterbury list of bonds were repayable in grain, it is of no surprise that the geographical distribution of the debtors shows that once again they were predominantly rural. The majority appear to come from the hinterland of Canterbury in eastern Kent. From the south and west of Canterbury, there are debtors from the villages of Wye, Chilham, Ospringe, Stuppington, Newnham, Sheldwich and Stowting. To the east and the south, there was another group of debtors from the villages of Wingham, Wickhambreaux, Ash, Sandwich and Eastry and from the villages and manors of Frogham, Soles and Harthanger. In the same area, there were also clients from the settlements which straddled the old Roman road from Canterbury to Dover: from Lydden, Alkham, Swingfield, Wootton, Buckland and Dover itself. To the north of

---

[136] WAM nos. 9015, 9019, 9020, 9021, 9022, 9025, 9026, 9028, 9034, 9036, 9039, 9042, 9043, 9046, 9047, 9057, 9058, 9086, 9088, 9089, 9090, 9091, 9103, 9104, 9105, 9116, 9118, 9119, 9120, 9121, 9123, 9124, 9125, 9126, 9127, 9139, 9156, 9157, 9158, 9159, 9172, 9173, 9174, 9175, 9176. Bonds which show debtors from the Isle of Thanet are WAM nos. 9104, 9116, 9121, 9124. See Fig. 4.

[137] WAM nos. 9015, 9103, 9105.   [138] WAM nos. 9028, 9036, 9042.

[139] WAM nos. 9046, 9089, 9125, 9156, 9157.

[140] WAM nos. 9020, 9022, 9039, 9058, 9086, 9090, 9118.   [141] WAM nos. 9039, 9058.

[142] WAM no. 9091.

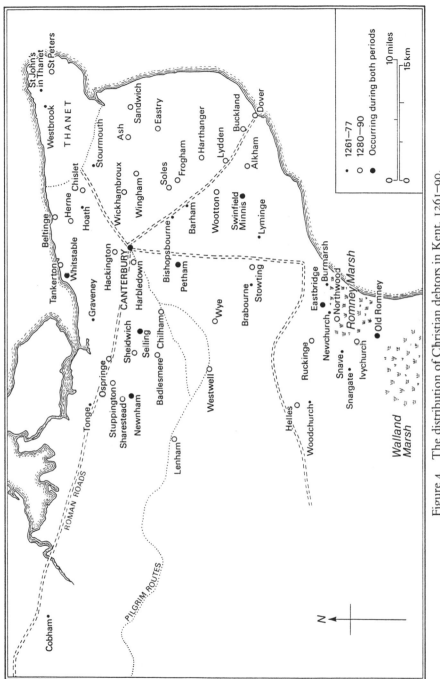

Figure 4   The distribution of Christian debtors in Kent, 1261–90.

Sources: WAM nos. 9015, 9019–22, 9025, 9026, 9028, 9034, 9036, 9039, 9042, 9043, 9046, 9047, 9057, 9058, 9086, 9088–91, 9103, 9104, 9105, 9116, 9118, 9119–21, 9123–7, 9139, 9156, 9157–9, 9172–6; PRO E/101/250/6.

Canterbury, there were debtors who came from Hackington, Herne, Beltinge and Chislet as well as coastal dwellers from Tankerton and Whitstable. In the north-east, there were a few debtors who seem to have had links with the Isle of Thanet which was an extremely fertile region in the medieval period.[143] The Romney Marsh, another fertile region, reveals another group of debtors. There were seven clients from the Marsh who between 1282 and 1290 owed the Jews of Canterbury a total of 170 quarters with a face value of £44 10s 0d.[144] It is striking that, while most of the places where the debtors of this sample lived are easily accessible by either the old Roman roads or tributaries of the Stour, another group of debtors lived quite close to a lower road in Kent: the Pilgrim's Way. This road, which had been well trodden by pilgrims for over a century, ran from west to east from Maidstone through Charing to Canterbury and the royal procession passed this way for Edward's marriage in 1254. It almost intersected Lenham, Westwell and Chilham, the villages where some of the Jews' clients lived.

The Herefordshire debtors came overwhelmingly from a catchment area which could be defined by drawing a circle of a 19 mile radius from Hereford itself into the Herefordshire basin (Figures 5 and 6).[145] This catchment area was neatly bounded in the north by the River Teme, in the west by the Forest of Radnor and the Black Mountains, in the south and south-east by the Forest of Dean, and in the east by the Malvern Hills and the Worcestershire and Gloucestershire boundaries. It is thus possible to identify four different groups of debtors. The first group came from the villages and manors to the west of Hereford, whose main communications with the town must have been by the old Roman roads or by the River Frome. The second group lived in an area that was neatly bounded by the River Wye and the rivers Monnow and Dore to the south-west of the town. A third group occupied the north-west of the county and was situated around the northern banks of the River Wye and further north towards the River Arrow. The last group came from the villages to the north of Hereford, between the town and Leominster along the River Lugg. The bonds which were deposited in the *vetus cista* (1259–75) provide a similar pattern, although the debtors from the villages to the east of the Roman road seem to be replaced by debtors who inhabited villages to the north-west of the River Frome and to the north-east of Hereford: Much Cowarne, Stretton Grandison, Ocle Pychard, Pencumbe, Bromyard and Norton.

[143] du Boulay 1966, p. 245.
[144] Postan 1972, p. 21; Hallam 1981, pp. 77–8, 80, 83; Butcher 1974, p. 18.
[145] *PREJ3*, pp. 230–8; PRO E/101/250/5.

Figure 5   The distribution of Christian debtors in Herefordshire, 1261–90,
excluding clients of Aaron le Blund and other Hereford Jews.
Sources: PREJ3, pp. 230–8; PRO E/101/250/5.

Figure 6   The distribution of Christian debtors in Herefordshire: the clients of
Aaron le Blund, 1263–76, and of other Hereford Jews, 1259–76.
Sources: PREJ3, pp. 230–8; PRO E/101/250/5.

To the north of Leominster, there were also two debtors from Laysters and Eaton. To the north-west of Hereford, Kinnersley, Kings Pyon and Birley seem to have provided clients for the Jews of the city. To the south-west, there were debtors from Snodhill, on the River Dore, and Crasswall, in the foothills of the Black Mountains. To the south natives of Kilpeck, Wormelow Tump and Burton had clearly made some use of the credit facilities provided by the Jews of Hereford.[146]

The bonds deposited in the Hereford *nova cista* (1283–90) make it possible to consider geographical distribution in a slightly different way. These debtors can be considered in the light of the commodities that they owed. One of the two debtors for wool, Peter de Grenham, as has been discussed above, came from as far away as Devonshire.[147] The other, Nicholas le Archer, seems to have come from Tarrington where he was the son of the lord of the manor. Between March and September 1286, he made bonds with two Jews and owed a total of 17 sacks of wool worth £168. It seems likely that his flocks grazed on the manor of Tarrington, 7 miles east of Hereford. He was also indebted for 200 quarters of grain.[148] Those who owed cereal appear to have come from the areas which surrounded Hereford. There were three large grain debtors from the west of Hereford: Henry de Solers, the lord of the manor of Dorstone, William de la More of Staunton on Wye and Philip of Wormhill in the parish of Madley.[149] A partnership between William Kanne of Fawley and Roger de Caple of Upton, both to the south-east of Hereford, promised a repayment of 40 quarters of cereal. Another partnership, of Stephen of Bodenham, a clerk, and Nicholas *cissor* of Vern, promised repayment of 15 quarters and seems to have been based to the north of Hereford. One specific area which made transactions which were to be repaid in both cereal and money stands out. The village of Sutton, situated some 4 miles to the north-east of Hereford, provided debtors who made two shared bonds. Sixteen inhabitants of Sutton made transactions in February 1285 and May 1286 which promised repayment of 130 quarters of cereal and £13. The overall distribution of debtors who owed money is again similar to the general pattern. There were, however, two cash debtors who seem to have come from outside the highly localised catchment area discussed above. One of them appears to have come from Patton in Shropshire on Wenlock Edge and the other from Elmbridge in Worcestershire.[150]

The distribution of debtors revealed by the Lincoln bonds shows that the catchment area they came from was roughly bounded in the north

---

[146] *Ibid.*

[147] PRO E/101/250/5; Moor 1930, vol. II, p. 143; *CCR 1279–1288*, pp. 181–2, 351.

[148] PRO E/101/250/5; Hillaby 1990c, p. 462.   [149] PRO E/101/250/5.   [150] *Ibid.*

by the Humber, in the west by the Trent, in the south by the county boundary and in the east by the seaboard (Figure 7).[151] The majority of the debtors came from a large area within a 30 mile radius of Lincoln itself. Most of them came from villages and manors which were reasonably accessible by either road or river. To the south of Lincoln, the villages situated either side of Ermine Street provided clients for the Lincoln Jews. To the east, some clients seem to have come from the marshy fenlands of Stenigot, Enderby, Eresby and Wrangle on the coast.[152] To the west, at least six debtors had connections with the Nottinghamshire villages of Rampton, Rolleston, Ravenscalf, Blyth and Stratton. One debtor can be identified as coming from across the Humber in Yorkshire. Some places can be shown to have been the homes of several clients of the Jews. There were three debtors from Hackthorn, 8 miles to the north of Lincoln; two from Leadenham, 12 miles to the south; two from Rauceby, 17 miles to the south; and two from Kelby, some 19½ miles to the south.

The different types of repayments found in the 1290 Lincolnshire sample again make it possible to discuss the geographical distribution of the debtors in the light of the commodities they owed. Of the debtors who had promised repayment in money, three came from beyond Lincolnshire: Adam fil Randolph of Normannyl, a *miles* of Yorkshire; another debtor from Lowestoft in Suffolk;[153] and a third from Staunton in Huntingdonshire. Only three of the debtors who owed money appear to have come from more local 'towns': two citizens of Newark and Peter of the Mill from Boston. In the north and east, there were debtors from Driby, Beckering, Orby and Ingoldmells on the coast. In the north-east, there are cash debtors from Hackthorn, Market Rasen, Otby and Swallow. To the north-west of Lincoln, there were two clients from Upton, one from Willingham, one from Stow St Mary and four from beyond the Nottinghamshire border, from Wheateley, East Markham, Skegby and Weston. To the south-west, in the triangle between the Roman roads, there were two debtors from Welbourne and one each from Boothby Graffoe, Coleby and Harmston. To the south-east, there were also clients from Navenby and one each from Blankney, Asgarby, Ropsley and Greatford near Stamford.[154]

---

[151] WAM nos. 9014, 9027, 9032, 9054, 9087, 9092, 9093, 9094, 9095, 9097, 9098, 9100, 9117, 9130, 9131, 9132, 9135, 9137, 9140, 9142, 9144, 9145, 9146, 9147, 9148, 9150, 9160, 9161, 9162, 9163, 9164, 9165, 9167, 9168, 9169, 9170.

[152] WAM nos. 9027, 9092, 9097, 9132.

[153] Normannyl was the King's Escheator beyond the Trent. WAM nos. 9100, 9117, 9130, 9143, 9145, 9146, 9147, 9162, 9163, 9168.

[154] PRO E/101/250/12; Moor 1930, vol. III, p. 269.

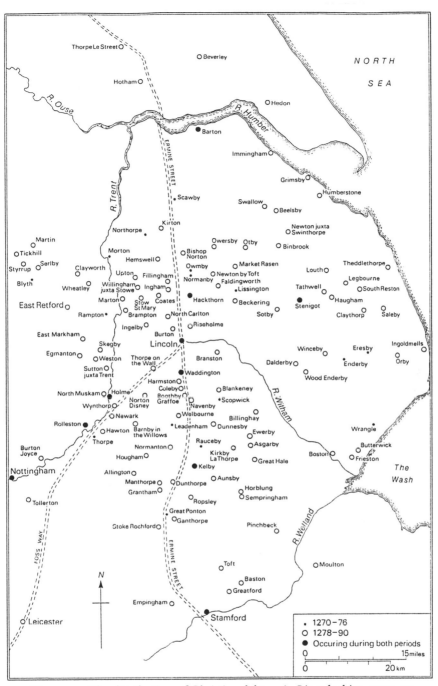

Figure 7   The distribution of Christian debtors in Lincolnshire, 1270–90.
Sources: WAM nos. 9014, 9027, 9032, 9054, 9087, 9092–5, 9097, 9098, 9100,
9117, 9130–2, 9135, 9137, 9140, 9142–8, 9150, 9160–5, 9167–70;
PRO E/101/250/12.

It is presumably significant that the majority of the debtors who had bonded for cereal repayments came from the northern part of Kesteven and the south-western part of Lindsey, bounded by Ermine Street in the west, the River Witham in the south and the Lincoln Wolds in the east. North Kesteven, in medieval times, was studded with small villages built on a good sandy loam which was excellent for growing crops or for pasture.[155] Villages which provided debtors to the south of Lincoln such as Coleby, Harmston and Waddington were all situated in the 'Low Fields', a rather good productive area.[156] To the north of Lincoln, the majority came from villages which lay near the foot of the Lincoln Wolds and are still to this day good arable areas: Hackthorn, Falding-worth and Market Rasen.[157] One debtor seems to have inhabited the marshy coastal strip around Theddlethorpe. To the west of Lincoln, and just over the Nottinghamshire boundary, there were cereal debtors from Claworth, Weston, Sutton on Trent, Barnby in the Willows and other villages of the fertile Trent basin. It is, therefore, noticeable in the Lincolnshire samples, more than any of the others, that the actual geographical areas where those who were to repay in grain lived were also the areas most likely to be able to produce grain in the late thirteenth century.[158]

The debtors who owed payments in wool came from rather different areas. To the extreme south of Kesteven, in the flat lands near the Northamptonshire border just to the west of the Fens, there were debtors from Baston and Greatford. In the south, and slightly nearer Lincoln, there was a group of borrowers from the villages along Ermine Street and from the Grantham area of central Kesteven. To the east of Grantham, there were debtors from Braceby, Aunsby, Kelby and Ganthorpe, situated in the slightly higher 'clay country', and from Horbling on the fen margin. There were a few from Grantham itself and from villages such as Stoke Rochford to the south and from the flat lands around Allington and Hougham. There were also those who had promised repayments in wool from the north-west of Kesteven, an excellent pasture for sheep. There were some from the rich marlstone villages of Waddington and Navenby and a group from Newark itself and Wynthorp.[159] The majority came from an area to the north of Lincoln in Lindsey, from Barton, situated on the Lincoln Edge, Riseholm, Ingleby, Stow St Mary, Upton, Ingham, Fillingham, and Hemswell in western Lindsey. They also inhabited places like Hack-thorn, Faldingworth, Newton by Toft and Middle Rasen which were

[155] Hallam 1981, pp. 40–2, 53; Lloyd 1983, pp. 39–43. [156] Lloyd 1983, pp. 63–5.
[157] *Ibid.*, pp. 191–3. [158] Hallam 1981, pp. 40–2. [159] PRO E/101/250/12.

situated in the central vale of Lindsey at the foot of the Wolds. A further group of debtors came from an area around Louth on the Lincoln Wolds themselves: Newton iuxta Swinhope and Binbrook to the north-west of Louth; Louth itself (the very point where the central Wolds join the marsh) and, to the south-west of Louth, Stenigot (in the Bain valley) and Sotby. To the east of Lincoln, there was a group of debtors situated in the fenland around Horncastle, from Winceby, Wood Enderby and Driby (on the very edges of the fen), all areas ideally suited to grazing sheep. Thus, the Jews' clients who had promised repayments in wool tended to come from areas which were likely to produce that commodity. It is highly significant that the majority of them came from Lindsey, an area which Pegalotti, in the fourteenth century, claimed to be the area which produced the finest wool in all England.[160]

As in the other samples, so in Lincolnshire, the evidence demonstrates that the Jews had a predominantly local clientele. There were, however, a few debtors who came from beyond the Nottinghamshire border: from Nottingham itself, Tollerton far to the south-west of Lincoln, Holbeck, Kirton, Egmanton, East Markham to the west of Lincoln, beyond the Trent, and Styrrup and Clayworth to the north-west of Lincoln. To the far north of Lincoln, there were a few debtors from Hedon, across the Humber, from Grimsby and Immingham on the coast as well as Barton on Humber on the north-east coast. In the far south-east near the Wash, there were clients from Frieston and Boston and more centrally from Billinghay near the Witham and Kirkby Le Thorpe in Kesteven.[161]

Thus it is possible to assert that according to the available evidence the majority of the Jews' clients were not from the *archa* towns themselves but from manors and villages in their hinterland. The Jews' clientele was clearly overwhelmingly rural and for the most part came from an area within 20 miles of the *archae* towns. Such an analysis helps to reinforce Peter Elman's claim that 70 per cent of the Jews' clients were of the agricultural classes.[162] They were certainly dependent on the local economy to repay their debts. Each Jewish community tended to draw its clientele from a surrounding area whose size was dictated both by the size of the *archa* town itself and by the proximity of similar towns. Where the samples of debtors have been big enough to provide a reasonable statistical basis for the analysis of the distribution of the Jews' clients, it has been possible, as was the case with the final Lincoln

[160] Power 1941, pp. 22–3; Ryder 1981, pp. 16–29.
[161] PRO E/101/250/12.   [162] Elman 1938a, p. 148.

example, to demonstrate that those debtors who were obliged to repay in specific commodities were resident in areas which were particularly suited to the production of those commodities. This is further evidence not only of the genuineness of the commodity bonds, but also of the fact that some Jews were probably able to modify their financial dealings so that they could successfully engage in advance sale credits.

The Jewish inhabitants of late Edwardian England can therefore be seen as primarily credit agents for village needs.[163] It seems that on the whole by Edward I's reign they were less concerned with 'high finance' than with extending credit to local men and women who were in need of financial aid either to expand their operations or to cope with financial hardship. Throughout the thirteenth century the Jews must have become well acquainted with their debtors and the places they came from. Accordingly some Jews were able to continue their financial transactions within established networks. There is also some evidence of Jewish creditors acting almost as personal family bankers as well as lending in different geographical areas.[164] It is also clear that, even on the eve of the Expulsion, they were still finding new clients with whom they could do business.[165]

However it seems that between 1275 and 1290 there had been a shift towards more Jewish lending to those of lower social status, a development which perhaps the 'Experiment' had brought about. The fact that 'advance sale credits' were now more acceptable than straightforward usurious monetary loans may also have precipitated such a change in clientele. It could even be that by the 1280s most of the Jews' clients were in fact primarily local wool and grain producers. If this was the case, then it would be more than likely that the latter would especially welcome loans from local Jews on the security of their goods and for an agreed advanced sale. It would seem unlikely too that such debtors, who might indeed have benefited from 'advance sale credits', would have been eager to witness the removal of the Jews. It is perhaps more likely that local Christian merchants could have been concerned about the inroads that Jewish finance was making on their markets; it seems, for example, that at Lincoln a small number of Jewish financiers had made an impressive impact on the local wool market.[166] Despite the post-1275 restrictions and growing anti-Jewish feeling it was still possible that Jewish financiers could continue to do business with their former debtors. Before 1275 the Jews had dealt with the latter in

---

[163] Hyams 1970, p. 30; Postan 1972, pp. 152–3; Mundill 1990a; 1991b.
[164] PRO E/101/250/5, E/101/250/6, E/101/250/12.
[165] The Hereford *nova cista* – PRO E/101/250/5 is a good example. See Table 4.
[166] Mundill 1987, pp. 289–93.

making usurious transactions, thus taking business away from Christian moneylenders. The Statute of Merchants in 1283 and the Statute of Acton Burnell in 1285 were after all protectionist but (as will be remembered) they did not apply to Jews, 'for whom other arrangements will be made'.[167] Christian merchants may have resented having to compete with the Jews who after 1275 were in some cases effectively licensed to become *legales mercatores*.

Throughout the thirteenth century the Jews' clients were naturally of varying status. It is probably easier, as has been shown above, to consider them in their geographical contexts than to try to classify them into social groupings. However, the work of Peter Elman seems to have indicated the correct proportion of urban and clerical debtors (13 per cent urban and 1.75 per cent clerical). He perhaps over-emphasised the involvement of those he termed as 'noble'.[168] In nearly all cases the transactions reveal that there were a few leading local families, sometimes described as *milites*, who were in debt to Jewish financiers. Such debtors may have had influence which was greater than just at a local level. It is naturally more than likely that those who were arguing for the expulsion of the Jews from England were those whose estates had become encumbered or whose debts had grown the most. However, although the Jew had been effectively squeezed out of the land market the local commodity market was still open to him. Men like Adam of Newmarket and Jordan Foliot, whose families had been involved in rebellion during the mid-century and whose finances were poor, may have had their lands saved from being taken over by the sale of a mortgage or a fee debt but they were now indebted to the Jews in their own right.[169] Knights or prominent gentry, like those who were in debt to Rabbi Elias Menahem and other well-established London Jewish creditors, were probably the most likely to be crying out for the removal of their creditors.[170] It was such prominent clients who were forced by the Jewish Exchequer to pay up when a tallage was demanded by the Crown. If there was an anti-Jewish lobby which came from those in debt to the Jews it may have consisted of this small minority of Jewish debtors. In general, however, those who were in debt to Jews in 1290 were numerically too insignificant to have had that much impact on the final decision for expulsion. Some Englishmen may have been grateful for the Expulsion in 1290, some may have feared the fact that their debts now belonged to the Crown but others may have genuinely regretted the loss of capital which the Jewish credit agents had

---

[167] *Statutes*, vol. I, p. 53.   [168] Elman 1938a, p. 148.
[169] Moor 1930, vol. III, p. 263; vol. II, pp. 77–8.   [170] Mundill 1997; PRO E/9/44.

provided.[171] To that extent it seems the 'Edwardian Experiment' had partly succeeded and Jewish credit agents were in some cases making a living and, more importantly, still finding clients who were willing to deal with them. It is now accordingly time to consider the other and more persuasive motives behind the final Expulsion of 1290.

[171] That some Englishmen were concerned about a possible Jewish return after 1290 was kindly communicated to me by Dr Rokeah who let me see her unpublished work on the Memoranda Rolls. In an entry dated 5 July 1293 when discussing a quitclaim from Edmund of Cornwall to the Hospital of St John of Jerusalem of all actions and demands because of the debt between Thomas de Ardern and Aaron fil Vives it mentions: 'should the aforesaid Jews return to England hereafter . . .' Entry no. 1321, p. 447.

Chapter 8

INTERPRETING THE ENGLISH EXPULSION

'Yet still it will remain a question why the Jews were banished at this particular time.' Thus wrote De Bloissiers Tovey in the early eighteenth century when concluding his history of the medieval Anglo-Jew.[1] However, Tovey did not supply an answer to that fundamental question and passed on to discuss the readmission of the Jews to England, 'leaving this mystery of state to more skilful decypherers'.[2] To provide such an answer is still a serious challenge; and ultimately it will always be open to debate. Some of the preconditions which most historians suggest always surround the expulsions of minority groups were certainly present in England in 1290.[3] Many of these were, for instance, similar in nature to those visible at the expulsion and outlawing of the Knights Templar in 1307 and even at the Dissolution of the monasteries in the sixteenth century.[4] They ranged from a deep suspicion and fear of heresy and even magic, to a distinct predilection for listening to rumour about the minority concerned. The background to such events obviously included economic envy, jealousy of the outsider's position within society, and the marshalling of public and theological opinion against the minority.

Clearly there were many factors which had led to the ostracism of the Jewish community of late thirteenth-century England. Dr Gerd Mentgen has recently redrawn attention to the fact that over a century ago B. L. Abrahams discussed the many motives behind the Expulsion.[5] Abrahams pointed out that many of the contemporary chroniclers gave varying explanations for the Expulsion. The latter could be seen as a concession to papal pressure; as the result of the efforts of Queen Eleanor; as a measure of summary punishment against the blasphemy of the Jews taken to give satisfaction to the English clergy; as an answer to

[1] Tovey 1738, pp. 234–5.   [2] *Ibid.*   [3] Menache 1985, p. 351; Stacey 1990, p. 1.
[4] Barber 1978, pp. 19–22, 40–3 193–220; Guy 1983, pp. 118–32.
[5] Mentgen 1997; Abraham 1895.

the complaints made by the magnates of the continued prevalence of usury; as an act of conformity to public opinion; as a reform suggested by the king's independent general inquiry into the administration of the kingdom during his absence; and as Edward's discovery, through the complaints of the Council, of the continued deceits of the Jews.[6] Clearly it would be a difficult task to single any one of these as the major motive for the English Final Solution. However, historians of this century are certainly not venturing on new ground when they start by considering these very varied explanations.[7]

This chapter will commence by examining two of the most recent interpretations of the Expulsion. It will then attempt to make a more precise examination of the procedures of the Expulsion itself and of the subsequent dissolution of the Jewries. Consideration will then be given to the wider explanations and longer-term causes which have already been utilised to explain the Expulsion, be they economic, sociological, political or religious.[8] An attempt will also be made to try to decide what part the host population and the Church played in the banishment of the Jews from England. Finally, the English Expulsion will be put into context alongside other continental expulsions. Only then may Tovey's question be given some form of answer.

As Professor Stacey has suggested, historians are now more able than ever before to understand Edward I's own position both before and during 1290. Edward returned from France to England on 12 August 1289.[9] On 13 October 1289, he started an assault upon the corruptions and mismanagement over which some of his justices and officials had presided in his absence.[10] Many of these men, and Sir Adam de Stratton in particular, had had close connections with the bureaucracy which co-ordinated Jewish affairs.[11] However, it was not just affairs of state that involved Edward during the following months. On 28 April 1290 Edward visited his mother and daughter at the convent they had settled in at Amesbury.[12] From 28 April to 23 June, he stayed in his capital,

<hr/>

[6] Abrahams 1894b, pp. 449–450.
[7] It is not surprising that Abraham's work won a prize in 1895.
[8] Abrahams 1894b; Aronsfeld 1990, pp. 7–9; Elman 1938a; Hyams 1974; Leonard 1891; Lieberman 1983, p. 2, 217–20; Menache 1985; 1987; Ovrut 1977; Prestwich 1988, pp. 345–6; Richardson 1960, pp. 213–33; Richmond 1992; Rigg 1903; Stacey 1990, p. 1–10; 1992b, pp. 1–28; Stow 1992a, pp. 290–5; Watt 1987, pp. 146–7.
[9] Stacey 1997 develops this point and links together the events in a more detailed fashion. The idea of putting the Expulsion into the context of the events of 1290 was reached independently before Professor Stacey's article. See also Prestwich 1988, p. 339.
[10] Tout and Johnstone *State Trials of the Reign of Edward I*, p. xii.
[11] Particularly Sir Adam de Stratton: see Brand 1985, p. 39; Tout and Johnstone 1906, p. xxx–xxxi; Prestwich 1988, p. 341.
[12] Powicke 1962, p. 512; Prestwich 1988, pp. 123, 128.

occupied on both family and state affairs. Edward returned to Westminster specifically for the Easter Parliament on 29 April 1290. A gathering for parliament was also to be a gathering for a royal wedding. His daughter, Joan, was married to Gilbert de Clare on 30 April.

A flurry of legislation and governmental decisions followed the royal wedding and the opening of the first parliament of 1290. Edward did not waste the opportunity of such an assembly and asked parliament for a much needed subsidy. He also put forward new legislation. The Statute of *Quo Warranto* was issued on 21 May. In June, the sheriffs were ordered to send two or three knights from each shire to Westminster by 15 July to give counsel and consent to certain matters. According to most explanations the crucial decision to expel the Jews was taken in secret on 18 June; but as we shall see, Professor Stacey questions this. Edward then retired to Havering-at-Bower, returning to Westminster on 8 July for the marriage of Princess Margaret to John of Brabant.[13] Soon after, the Statute of *Quia Emptores* was issued.[14] On 18 July Edward issued the edict which banished the Jews from his realm. Parliament subsequently voted Edward a subsidy of a fifteenth in late July and later in October the clergy voted him a subsidy of a tenth. By 1 November the Jews were exiled from England.

From his recent examination of the crucial events of 1290 Professor Stacey concludes that the decision to expel the Jews was a short-term political expedient which Edward did not take entirely on his own intiative.[15] He states:

The expulsion came about because the king concluded that in 1290 he could get more out of his Christian subjects through a subsidy than he could get from his Jewish subjects through a tallage . . . they were expelled because their expulsion was useful to him in negotiating with the much wider political nation which had emerged during the thirteenth century.[16]

The Jews had become political pawns which Edward used to bargain with, finally placating his subjects by expelling them. There is clearly much to recommend such an explanation; but as Abrahams and Dr Gerd Mentgen have both indicated, it cannot be the whole answer to Tovey's question.[17] Certainly in 1290 Edward was under many political pressures. As Sir Maurice Powicke observed, both *Quo Warranto* and *Quia Emptores* were promulgated in order to satisfy and please Edward's tenants in chief.[18] Powicke also shrewdly saw that Edward had orchestrated events in order to win favour with

---

[13] Powicke 1962, pp. 512–13; Salzman 1968, pp. 91–7; Prestwich 1988, pp. 344–7.
[14] Powicke 1962, p. 513.   [15] Stacey 1992b, p. 2.   [16] *Ibid.*, pp. 21–2.
[17] Mentgen 1997; Abrahams 1894b, pp. 449–450.   [18] Powicke 1962, p. 513.

parliament: 'moreover the time at which the knights were to arrive coincided with that of the royal edict of 18 July for the Expulsion of the Jews from the kingdom; an act of grace for which the grants in Parliament and later in convocation at Ely were regarded as a thanks offering'.[19] More recently, Professor Michael Prestwich cited contemporary evidence to back the notion of a 'thanks offering' and observed that this parliamentary subsidy was assessed at £116,346 and that the clergy also offered a tax.[20]

Using a more sociological approach, Professor Sophia Menache also drew a picture of a grateful English people giving a fifteenth in return for expelling the Jews; but she specifically identified the factors of centralisation and 'nationalism' as being new long-term causes.[21] She also raised the question of whether *vox populi* was a driving force behind the Expulsion and claimed that such an event could not have been carried out without the co-operation of society at large.[22] Certainly the king's subjects obeyed the royal orders and there were few complaints raised against his decision. Some sources indicate that the people had already asked Edward I to expel the Jews in 1281 in return for a fifth. Yet if there had been unanimous approval, or if it had been a major issue for agrarian society, small landholders, townsmen, guildsmen, clerics, abbots and bishops, then the actual act of expulsion would surely have been a licence for a new pogrom. If, in 1290, the attitudes of the people of England had been the major driving force, it is perhaps surprising that, apart from several small massacres as the Jews left England, there was not a general repetition of the pogroms of 1190, or the violence which accompanied the barons' wars and the coin-clipping allegations.[23] Surely a very grateful people would not have voted such a massive tax without resorting to at least some violence against the departing Jews?

These two recent explanations indicate that the Jews were sacrificed almost as a whim, either to gain favour with parliament or to appease rising nationalism or both. Moreover, the fact that the final decision was taken between 18 June and 18 July is supported by Professor Stacey who believes that the 'secret' orders of 18 June 1290 were, in fact, preparations for yet another tallage; but that sometime during the

---

[19] *Ibid.*   [20] Prestwich 1988, p. 343.
[21] Menache 1985, p. 370, 374; Schwarzfuchs 1967, pp. 488–9; Mentgen 1997.
[22] Menache 1985, p. 351.
[23] For the offer of a fifth in return for expulsion see Tovey 1738, p. 235 and Daniel, *The Collection of the Historie of England*, pp. 160–1. For the massacres of 1190 see Dobson 1974, pp. 1–50; Hemingburgh, *Chronicon*, p. 21–2; Rapin de Thoryas, *Acta Regia*, vol. I, p. 364; Prestwich 1988, p. 346; Rokeah forthcoming, pp. 405, 407 (entries 1236 and 1244); *CCR 1288–1296*, p. 295; see chapter 3 above.

month Edward changed his mind.[24] Even given the indecisiveness of contemporary chroniclers, which Abrahams revealed long ago, this still cannot be the whole explanation.[25] The decision to expel the Jews from England was mooted well before June 1290 and was the result of many other factors. There were other pressures apart from political ones which affected Edward's decision in 1290. As we shall see, papal and ecclesiastical attitudes had changed in the 1280s. Attitudes in Christendom as a whole had also changed as enthusaism for the new crusade began to take hold. Financially, Edward was trying to cope with his steadily mounting personal debts. These had been increased by his expensive wooing of his magnates during the summer of 1290. In the last resort the English Final Solution was Edward's own decision and not that of his people.

That said, there were also social groups who were eager to take advantage of the pomp and ceremony which accompanied the royal marriages in the capital during the summer of 1290. Such an opportunity was not lost by Archbishop Pecham who, already railing against the Jews and the evils of usury, now also actively preached the crusade. Indeed at least one historian has claimed that it was such a revival of crusading enthusiasm which finally prompted Edward to make the edict of expulsion.[26] However, it was important in this instance for Edward to follow the lead of Archbishop Pecham as it was he who had arranged for the diocesan and provincial consideration of a clerical subsidy. Clearly, in the first half of 1290 Edward had pleased the clergy, those present at the weddings and those present at the parliament by righting the evils done by his corrupt officials, by trying to make new laws to protect landholding and possibly by promising the expulsion of the Jews. As a result he had gained financially by the voting of a new tax worth over £100,000.

It is now time to examine the actual procedures of the Expulsion in order to ascertain what direct financial gain Edward actually derived from it. The English Expulsion was accomplished in less than five months between 18 June and 1 November 1290; the subsequent dissolution of the properties of the Jews was carried out within the following five years. The Expulsion and dissolution were highly organised, systematic and thorough procedures which affected the lives of Englishman and Jew alike. As has been observed, there was a necessary prelude to the final official edict of Expulsion; on 18 June 1290 instructions were issued to the sheriffs ordering them to seal the

[24] Stacey 1997; 1990, p. 9; 1992b, p. 21.   [25] Abrahams 1894b, pp. 449–50.
[26] Salzman 1968, p. 94.

archae.[27] The local officials were to be responsible for closing and sealing the *archae* by 28 June. The official edict of Expulsion, now lost, was issued on 18 July 1290. Cecil Roth referred to the irony of this date (the Fast of the Ninth of Ab), as an 'anniversary of manifold disasters for the Jewish people'.[28] On the same day, writs were also officially issued to the sheriffs, which informed them that it had been decreed that all Jews were to leave England by 1 November. The Jews were given 105 days to leave the realm or be outlawed and subject to the wolf's head bounty. On 18 July the king also issued a firm declaration that the Jews were to be allowed to leave the country peaceably and entrusted the sheriffs to carry this order out:

Whereas the King has prefixed to all the Jews of his realm a certain time to pass out of the realm and he wills that they shall not be treated by his ministers or others otherwise than has been customary, he orders the sheriff to cause proclamation to be made throughout his bailiwick prohibiting any one from injuring or wronging the Jews within the said time. He is ordered to cause the Jews to have safe-conduct at their cost when they, with their chattels which the king has granted to them, direct their steps towards London in order to cross the sea, provided that before they leave they restore the pledges of Christians which are in their possession to those whom they belong.[29]

It seems likely that by late July the edict of Expulsion had been read in the synagogues and had become public knowledge to both the Jewish and the general populace. However, it is particularly striking that despite the impending exodus some Jews still continued to lend money and go about their business. At Devizes Solomon of Devizes registered a debt in the *archa* as late as 27 October.[30] There is also evidence from Lincoln that Jews were still registering debts in August and September 1290.[31]

The royal safe conduct was issued again in late July when the bailiffs, barons and sailors of the Cinque Ports were ordered not to molest the Jews.[32] Some influential Jews managed to secure personal safe conducts from the Crown. On 8 August the citizens of the Cinque Ports were ordered to give Moses fil Jacob of Oxford, a Northampton Jew, a 'safe and speedy passage at moderate charges'.[33] On 24 August Bonamy of York, his son Josceus and other York Jews were ready to leave and given the same protection by order of the king.[34] The York community also received the protection of Archbishop John le Romeyn, who wrote to his diocese threatening with excommunication any who

[27] PRO c/255/18 nos. 9–12.   [28] Roth 1978, p. 85.   [29] Stokes 1925, p. 10.
[30] PRO E/101/250/11.   [31] PRO E/101/250/12.   [32] *CPR 1281–1301*, p. 378.
[33] *Ibid.*, p. 381.   [34] *Ibid.*, p. 382.

molested the Jews.[35] Other, more fortunate, Jews who had Christian patrons managed to procure special licences to sell their property. On 28 July Aaron fil Vives, who had held the private property of Edmund the king's brother, managed to secure a licence to sell his houses and rents in London, Canterbury and Oxford. Less than a month later, he also was formally banished.[36]

During the summer of 1290 parties of Jews left their houses, sold off what they could, aided the Rabbi in taking the scrolls of the Law from the ark in the synagogue, and set out for exile. There was no resistance from the Jewish community and few records of any major outbreaks of violence have survived. The protection of the Crown for its Jewish subjects held good while they travelled to the ports of embarkation, although this did not help a party of Jews who were beached and left to drown at Queenborough nor a party of Jews who may well have suffered a similar fate at Burnham, Norfolk.[37] The captain of the vessel at Queenborough, Henry Adrian, later spent two years in Sandwich prison for his murderous deed in the Thames estuary.[38] After the Expulsion, the only Jews to remain in England were those who had become Christians or those who remained as illegal immigrants. The number of converted Jews does not seem to have risen dramatically in 1290; but the records are unhelpful with regard to the Jews who may have remained illegally. Many arrived in France but some may well have fled to Scotland, Wales and even Ireland. It is possible that some families may have got as far as Spain, Savoy, Germany and even Gozo.[39]

On 1 November 1290 all the bonds, financial instruments and chattels that had been left behind, together with the properties that the Jews had possessed, passed into the hands of the king. On 5 November, satisfied that the Jews had left the realm and could no longer destroy their bonds or houses, Edward stated what may well reflect his true reasons for the Expulsion. He claimed that the motive for the latter was the Jews' persistence in practising usury in direct contravention of the *Statutum de Judeismo* of 1275. The Jews were cast as rogues in the affair, 'and the Jews afterwards, maliciously deliberating amongst themselves, changed the kind of usury into a worse which they called "*curialitas*", or courtesy, and depressed the king's people under colour of such by an error double that of the previous one'.[40] Edward now cancelled all

---

[35] *The Register of John Le Romeyn 1286–1296*, p. 109.   [36] *CPR 1281–1301*, pp. 379, 381.

[37] Hemingburgh, *Chronicon*, pp. 21–2; Rapin de Thoryas, *Acta Regia*, vol. I, p. 364; Prestwich 1988, p. 346; Rokeah forthcoming, pp. 405, 407 (entries 1236 and 1244). Burnham is 25 miles north-north-east of King's Lynn.

[38] *CCR 1288–1296*, p. 295.

[39] Adler 1939, p. 306; Stacey 1992a, p. 283; Roth 1978, pp. 87–8; Mundill forthcoming.

[40] *CCR 1288–1296*, p. 99.

usuries, 'willing that nothing shall be exacted from the Christians except the principal debts that they received from the Jews'.[41] Although justifying his decision and attacking Jewish usury, it seems that at this particular moment the king had no intention of losing the financial windfalls which could be gained from the banishment: indeed his organisation of and preparation for the Expulsion was so meticulous that where the Expulsion ended, the dissolution of the Jewries and the sequestration of debts began. However the process of transferring Jewish wealth into the royal coffers was not to be as straightforward as the banishment of approximately 2,000 Jews.

In September 1290 William de Marchia, the treasurer, and a team of royal administrators were appointed by the king to prepare what amounted to a list of the Jews' assets: a *Valor Judaismus*.[42] The officials wished to know exactly what financial debts the Jews were owed and what property they owned or administered. Accordingly, writs were sent out to the local officials of the major towns in which the Jews had been dwelling.[43] These officials and, in particular, the two Christian chirographers or keepers of the *archae* were ordered to make sure that the *archae* were sealed, that all bonds were handed in, and that the *archae* were carried under safe and secure conduct to London by 26 November 1290. The sheriffs, having diligently inquired what houses and tenements had belonged to the Jews, were also to present themselves in Westminster on the same day. The property returns were to stipulate what property the Jews had held in fee, its value per annum and to whom the Jews had owed service. The *archae* were sealed and transported to London with most of the officials, who arrived in Westminster, at the Treasury, on 26 November.[44]

As is now well known, details of the arrival of the twenty-one different *archae* which were brought in were meticulously noted and their keys duly deposited. In late November and early December the Treasury officials set about opening the *archae* and, under close scrutiny, made lists of all the bonds which were now in the king's hands.[45] Although it seemed that Edward originally had every intention of trying to claim these debts for himself, the Close, Patent, Fine and Plea Rolls do not reveal any concerted attempt to do so. This in itself is difficult to

[41] *Ibid.*   [42] Mundill 1993, pp. 25, 43–4.

[43] *CCR 1288–96*, p. 145; the majority of the original writs concerned with property have survived as PRO E/101/249/27.

[44] Details of the arrival of the *archae* from the provinces have survived as PRO E/101/249/29; *archae* came in from Bedford, Bristol, Colchester, Cambridge, Canterbury, Devizes, Exeter, Hereford, Huntingdon, Ipswich, Lincoln, London, Northampton, Norwich, Nottingham, Oxford, Winchester, Worcester and York.

[45] These lists form PRO E/101/250/2–12.

explain and will be discussed below. The Exchequer of the Jews also continued to collect receipts from the Jewry for another five or six years but a concerted effort to claim even the principal debts does not seem to have been made. In 1326, the Crown finally issued a general pardon of all Jewish debts.[46]

Edward proved more able to realise a small profit from the properties that he confiscated from the Jews. Many records of these properties have survived: the original extents which the local officials had sent back to Westminster in reply to the Chancellor's writ of 12 September 1290, the working copies of the local officials who drew up the lists, the Exchequer scribes' lists of the Jewish properties in the various parts of England, an account of the sale of some of the property, and several copies of grants from the king to new owners.[47] The disposal of the Jewish properties was entrusted to another royal official who had had experience in Jewish affairs, Hugh of Kendal. He was appointed on 20 December 1290 to value and sell all the houses, rents and tenements which of late belonged to the Jews.[48] Kendal lost no time in doing so and by 27 December had already drawn up a full list of the values of the properties and had found buyers for many of them. His account lists the value of ex-Jewish properties in sixteen towns. The total value of the property included in his account was £1,835 13s 4d, and he noted that he was to receive a further £15 from the merchants of Lucca, possibly for some property or, more likely, for Jewish chattels.[49]

It is clear that Kendal's account cannot be taken as the total value of all the properties which the Crown confiscated. A house in Devizes and houses at Cambridge and Hereford were not included in the valuation, in the case of the Hereford properties because it was not confirmed that they had belonged to Jews. However, by 27 December, a week after his appointment, Hugh had received £677 19s 4d as payment for ex-Jewish property which was paid into the royal Treasury. As further payments came in, Hugh paid off some royal debts. Just over £100 was immediately spent on King Henry III's tomb at Westminster, for glass windows in the royal palace and for general repairs. It was also noted that various individuals still owed amounts totalling another £941.[50] By

---

[46] *Statutes*, vol. I, p. 255.

[47] PRO E/101/249/27, E/101/249/30, E/101/250/1; BL Additional MS 24,511 fos. 48–9 and Lansdowne MS 826 fos. 28–64; CCA C 1211 and C 1213.

[48] *CPR 1281–1307*, p. 410.   [49] PRO E/101/250/1; BL Additional MS 24,511 fos. 48–9.

[50] BL Additional MS 24,511 fos. 48–9. Master William Torel, the maker of the statue of King Henry, received a part payment of £26 13s 4d; John of Bristol received £64 13s 4d for making glass windows in the Palace of Westminster and £26 13s 4d for repairing and renovating former Jewish houses in London; William de Ideshalle recived two payments amounting to £2 4s 4d for sculpting the tomb of King Henry.

Table 12 *Hugh of Kendal's accounts of the value of properties formerly belonging to the Jews, 27 December 1290*

London	£ 956 6s 8d
York	£ 243 13s 4d
Lincoln	£ 173 0s 0d
Oxford	£ 100 0s 0d
Canterbury	£ 85 13s 4d
Northampton	£ 50 13s 4d
Norwich	£ 47 0s 0d
Winchester	£ 44 0s 0d
Colchester	£ 38 13s 4d
Hereford	£ 26 13s 4d
Cambridge	£ 16 13s 4d
Bedford	£ 14 6s 8d
Nottingham	£ 13 6s 8d
Stamford	£ 13 6s 8d
Ipswich	£ 7 6s 8d
Sudbury	£ 5 0s 0d
Total	£1,835 13s 4d

Source: PRO E/101/250/1; BL Additional Manuscripts 24,511 folios 48–9.

April 1291, twelve of them had made payments direct to the Treasury amounting to £312; and Peter de Appleby had also paid £6 13s 4d for various ex-Jewish tenements in York.[51] Therefore, within six months, Edward had gained almost £1,000 from the sale of former Jewish properties.

There were, of course, difficulties in disposing of all the buildings. Some the Crown retained or could not find buyers for. Grants of properties which formerly belonged to the Jews in Colchester, Coventry and Cambridge were made as late as 1293, 1318 and 1319 respectively.[52] It was also some time before all the payments were received. In July 1291 Hugh of Kendal wrote to the archbishop of Canterbury and reminded him that he still owed £53 6s 8d for his purchases.[53] As late as September 1294, William la Vavassur of Hazelwood still owed £46 13s 4d for property he had bought in York.[54]

Despite these difficulties, the dissolution of the Jewries of England

[51] PRO E/401/115, E/401/117, E/401/119.
[52] *CPR 1281–1301*, p. 18; *Calendar of Fine Rolls 1307–1319*, p. 397.
[53] CCA Eastry Correspondence, IV, 13.   [54] *CCR 1288–1296*, p. 368.

was generally accomplished effectively and speedily. As Professor Dobson has observed, Hugh of Kendal did not experience any difficulty in finding a market for the Jewish houses in York amongst a wide range of social groups.[55] This was probably the case all over the country, for many Jewish properties were situated in the most important towns in the realm, as a glance at Table 12 illustrates. It is also quite clear that, throughout the land, influential local men, royal favourites, churches and churchmen were glad to receive some of the more valuable properties. Between 1291 and 1292 the king made eighty-five separate grants which disposed of the property of 113 Jews. In Cambridge, the mayor received one of the grants; in Northampton, William de Hamilton, the archdeacon of York, received another; in Lincoln, Robert le Venour, recently appointed keeper of the royal city of Lincoln, managed to secure two properties; in London, Isabella de Vescy bought an expensive property in Wood Street; in Canterbury, William de Somfeld, the queen's tailor, received the synagogue. The abbey of Chicksand bought property in London, the abbey of St James bought property in Northampton, the abbey of Newnham was granted property in Bedford, and Christ Church, Canterbury received a grant of the majority of the Jews' property in Canterbury. All of the property which had been confiscated in Oxford was sold to the Chancellor's relative, William Burnell.[56]

Although many notable individuals gained from the redistribution of former Jewish property, it is clear that Edward himself did not make much financial gain from the Expulsion. He had probably received a mere £1,835 or so from the sale of Jewish property.[57] By 1291 he had received bonds, perhaps worth a face value of £20,000, which he never claimed. However, even without actually collecting the debts Edward's own personal situation would naturally be enhanced by the fact that he now held the debts. Fiduciary indebtedness had increasingly become a form of patronage: Edward had been known to pardon Jewish debtors in return for loyal service.[58] Only a few years earlier, Simon de Montfort had used the cancellation of Jewish debts to his own advantage and had managed to convince followers that it was worth rebelling for.[59] Edward was after all a martial king, hoping to embark on crusade,

[55] Dobson 1979, p. 48.
[56] BL Lansdowne MS 826, 4, fos. 28–64; Playford, *Rotulorum*, vol. I, pp. 73–6.
[57] The face value of the bonds in the *archae* for which details survive was just over £9,100. A further £1,835 13s 4d was raised by Hugh of Kendal. The value of the bonds from Bedford, Colchester, Huntingdon, Ipswich, London and Northampton is unknown but other sources indicate that the London *archa* would probably have been the most valuable.
[58] *Calendar of Chancery Warrants 1244–1326*, p. 2; Mundill 1993, p. 39.
[59] Lieberman 1983, pp. 116–17; Maddicott 1994, pp. 315–16.

and he wanted the full support of his subjects rather than a people who opposed him. To be able to pardon debts was not only a method of securing followers but a means of ensuring loyalty. It was a way of countering the breakdown of 'feudal' contracts. Thus, to many townsmen, barons, knights and small landholders the Expulsion of the Jews would have been popular but it was not something which would necessarily have entailed direct financial gain. Financial profit on Edward's behalf is also unlikely to have been a prime motive for the Expulsion, not least because he never claimed the Jews' debts. Perhaps Edward's own justification for the Expulsion, that the Jews had not adhered to the Statute of the Jewry, is the central key to interpreting the Expulsion. Bearing this in mind, a consideration of some of the other explanations behind the Expulsion can now be made.

In reviewing the long-term causes of the Expulsion Professor Stacey divided them into four main categories: the Jews' legal status; their financial debility; the need to find a solution to the 'Jewish problem'; and anti-semitic bigotry.[60] The ongoing thirteenth-century problem of the Jews' legal status has been touched upon in preceding chapters; the Jews literally belonged to and were protected by the Crown. This in itself set them apart but did not provide a tangible reason for expulsion unless the Crown wished to disentangle itself from protecting those of another faith. As regards the more traditional explanation that the Jews had lost their financial *raison d'être*, Professor Stacey has done much to overturn this by discarding Sholom A. Singer's explanation, put forward in 1965, as 'doing little more than repeat the misleading arguments that Peter Elman advanced fifty years ago'.[61] As we have seen, the case for the Jews' financial debility can be exaggerated, particularly if some Jews did start to prosper after the economic restrictions of the Statute of 1275.[62] It is true that long before 1290 the Jewish community had been under enormous financial pressure; but this in itself cannot be used properly as a valid explanation for the Expulsion in 1290 itself.

That the Expulsion was a solution to the 'Jewish problem' and came about as a result of anti-semitic bigotry cannot be wholly denied. Yet some historians like Harold Pollins have warned against using anti-semitism as the sole reason:

A limited, parochial view of the removal of the Jews from England in 1290 has to be avoided . . . It is necessary to look at the relationship between the Jewish and the Christian worlds . . . It is noteworthy that the deterioration in the Jews' condition coincided with the stricter attitude of the Church towards them. But the Expulsion *ought not to be seen as the culmination of two centuries of*

---

[60] Stacey 1992b, p. 2.   [61] Stacey 1987b, pp. 71–2.   [62] See chapters 5 and 6 above.

growing anti-semitism. The explanation for the Expulsion has to be brought in a combination of political and economic circumstances in which anti-Jewish sentiment was only one factor.[63]

Although growing 'Jew hatred' was clearly an important element in the situation, to be discussed below at greater length, it is necessary to strike a balance between the 'lachrymose conception' of Jewish history and the contemporary chroniclers' complete commitment to the classical medieval Christian stereotype of the blaspheming and sacrilegious enemy of Christ.[64] Growing hatred of the Jew can again only be a partial explanation for the final Expulsion. Stacey himself has indicated that there were also other factors which were long term but 'which are less clear'.[65]

Of the many different interpretations of the Expulsion expressed by historians of this century, one of the most important is that of H. G. Richardson. In claiming that historians had misunderstood Edward I as the leading character in the Expulsion, Richardson struck a blow against the insularity of English historians: he reminded us that Edward was 'neither English nor heroic' and that he also had Jewish subjects in Gascony. He also posed the crucial question of whether the Expulsion was a ministerial act performed in the king's name or whether it was the result of Edward I's own personal decision. He then concluded with another, more simplistic 'economic' argument, namely that the Expulsion came about because Edward was in need of ready cash.[66] Edward's direct financial gain from the Expulsion can be discarded, as has been demonstrated above, but some of Richardson's other views remain illuminating.

Richardson's theories have been attacked by Professor Gavin Langmuir on the grounds that he had depended far too heavily on the records and thus had over-emphasised the 'archival perspective in medieval studies'. However, Richardson's arguments are still highly relevant. As far as Professor Langmuir was concerned Richardson had not paid enough attention to the attitudes, emotions, irrationality and prejudice which Langmuir claimed are so essential to understanding the medieval Jewish experience.[67] Professor Stacey also criticised Richardson's account of the Expulsion on the grounds that it had neglected the origins and development of anti-semitism. Anti-semitism was and is an important modern concept; but whether medieval minds could cope with the differences between anti-Judaism and anti-semitism or would

---

[63] Pollins 1982, pp. 20–3.   [64] Langmuir 1990b, p. 48; Dobson 1974, p. 20
[65] Stacey 1987b, p. 68.   [66] Richardson 1960, pp. 213–33.
[67] Langmuir 1963, pp. 183–7; 1971; 1990a, p. 276, 305; 1990b, pp. 301–10; Abulafia 1995, p. 135.

have preferred to admit to pure raw Jew hatred is another matter (which Langmuir himself has debated at length).[68] The English Final Solution was not arrived at just because of Jew hatred as there were other factors at work. Nevertheless, the work of Joshua Trachtenberg and others is obviously crucial to the issues and clearly shows that the prevailing common beliefs concerning the Jews would certainly not have endeared them to the host society.[69] At least one English historian, Dr Paul Hyams, has also drawn inspiration from Gavin Langmuir and used sociological and psychological perspectives in explaining the Expulsion.[70]

As observed above, even more emphasis has been put on the sociological approach by Professor Sophia Menache who examined the link between the stereotypical view of the Jew and the Expulsion. She supports the view that the endemic nature of religious violence is crucial to an understanding of the Expulsion and went on to examine the Judao-Satanic threat. She concluded that 'Blood libels thus functioned as a catalyst in the deterioration of the Jewish situation in England during the thirteenth century. A case can be made, on the grounds of chronological proximity for regarding blood libels as a possible cause of the expulsion of 1290.'[71] There can be little doubt that the blood libel accusation was one of the main causes of Jew hatred and that instances of such accusations had increased throughout the thirteenth century. On the other hand Professor Robert Moore and others have warned that care must be taken with the stereotypical view of the Jew.[72] Dr Joseph Shatzmiller also investigated the medieval Jewish stereotype in detail. He too showed that a stereotype existed and was easily detectable in the invective of church sermons as in various decrees ordering the expulsion of usurers. But he warned that much can be learned about the limitations of medieval stereotypes from closer attention to the realities of everyday life. He emphasised that 'people very much appreciated moneylenders who displayed qualities that made one an honest and righteous man'.[73] Moreover stereotypical/sociological arguments like those based upon a Judao-Satanic link should be approached with extreme caution, as they were originally presented mostly by chroniclers, churchmen or even converts.[74]

Although there are many examples of hatred and persecution of the Jews, there were also some well-attested amicable relationships between Jew and Christians in late thirteenth-century England. In 1286, a Jewish

[68] Stacey 1987b, p. 63, 70; Langmuir 1971, pp. 383–9.   [69] Trachtenberg 1943.
[70] Stacey 1987b, p. 64; Hyams 1974, pp. 280–3.   [71] Menache 1985, p. 357.
[72] Moore 1987, p. 31, 34–9; Dobson; 1974, p. 20.   [73] Shatzmiller 1990, p. 118, 123.
[74] Dobson 1974, p. 20; Langmuir 1972; 1984a, pp. 833–42.

wedding took place in Hereford to which Christians had been invited. This event caused Richard Swinfield, bishop of Hereford, to write to the chancellor of Hereford Cathedral ordering him to forbid all Christians from attending the convivialities of the Jews by a proclamation to be made in all the churches in Hereford. Many Christian townsmen clearly ignored the prohibition. After the event Bishop Swinfield, in more caustic mood, claimed that certain numbers of his flock had attended the 'displays of silk and cloth of gold, horsemanship, equestrian processions, stage-playing and sports and minstrelsy' that had accompanied the Jewish wedding feast. Furthermore, he claimed that his congregation had eaten, drunk, played and jested with the Jews. He warned that all members of the Christian faith who had attended the celebrations should receive absolution within eight days or be excommunicated.[75]

It must not be forgotten that many of the Jews who were expelled in 1290 were probably third- or fourth-generation immigrants and had established some local relationships and ties. Benedict of Winchester, Master Elias Menahem and Aaron fil Vives of London, Aaron le Blund of Hereford and Benedict of Lincoln were probably more influential in the Christian community at large than their predecessors ever had been.[76] By this time some amicable relations had been established. Several Jews rode with Christians, hunted with them, discussed ideals, and, as Dr Rokeah has shown, could even be partners in crime with them. According to a Hebrew source they even drank strong drink with Christians. These relationships in late thirteenth-century England and much of Christendom are also evidenced by the canonical prohibitions and protective legislation concerning Christian wet-nurses and general living conditions. That there were some harmonious relationships between Jew and Christian obviously militates against the theory of a perceived Judao-Satanic threat being the sole factor behind the Expulsion,[77] but naturally caution should be exercised. Occasional instances of good relations do not deny that Jew hatred existed or that many of the population had irrational beliefs about Judaism to add to their private economic jealousies.

Professor Menache has also observed that some contemporary chronicles showed ambivalent attitudes rather than zealous support for the

[75] *Roll of the Household Expenses of Richard de Swinfield*, 1853, pp. 100–1; *Episcopal Registers of Richard de Swinfield* 1909, pp. 120–1.
[76] Mundill 1997; Roth 1946; 1948; Adler 1942; Hillaby 1990c.
[77] Jacobs, 1893a, p. 269; Roth 1957, pp. 66–7; Rokeah 1982b, pp. 348–50; Shatzmiller 1990, pp. 103–18 examines the relationship between Bondavid of Draguignan and his neighbours and clients in early fourteenth-century Marseilles.

Expulsion. As she pointed out, this situation becomes more paradoxical when one bears in mind the attitudes of these chroniclers towards the Jews a few years before their Expulsion.[78] For example, the Annals of Osney described the Jews as 'the enemies of the Cross of Christ' and had much to say about Jewish exploitation of Christians; yet they referred to the Expulsion as 'something most remarkable that should not be passed over in silence', without praising the king's policy. Instead they stressed the resulting financial losses sustained by the royal Exchequer, and the new forms of taxation implemented to refill its coffers. On this subject the Osney annals mourned that 'thus also the Catholics were punished mercilessly just the same as the enemies of the cross of Christ'.[79] Accordingly, those explanations which use only rising anti-semitism, or which develop the more sociological approach by accepting the traditional Jewish stereotype, need considerable qualification.[80]

Other historians such as Barnett D. Ovrut have seen the final decision to expel the Jews as being 'intricately related to the primary political-constitutional issues of the day'.[81] Ovrut's arguments were based less on the centralisation of the English state or in growing nationalism than on the immediate mid-century problems which preceded Edward's reign: 'As the thirteenth century advanced the smaller landowners became very nearly the sole clients and chief victims of Jewish finance while the monasteries and greater barons became as we shall see indirect beneficiaries . . .'[82] He concluded that the Expulsion was:

a conscious act of an aggressive and far-sighted government made in response to a number of political and constitutional factors which were playing an important role in the development of the English state . . . the general banishment of the Jews in 1290 must be seen as part of a conscious policy on the part of the king by which, in seeking to augment his own power and to define more fully his own position as a feudal monarch and overlord he sought to come to the aid of the lesser landowners and to cut down the power of the great lords.[83]

This particular explanation depends on how influential the smaller landowners were and how politically aware Edward himself was. That Edward I decided on expulsion because he was influenced by his lesser supporters seems very unlikely given the fact that the Jewish debts passed from the hands of Jewish creditors into the king's hands.[84]

---

[78] Menache 1987, p. 226.   [79] *Ibid.*, p. 227.
[80] Menache 1985, p. 372 claims: 'The Jewish stereotype . . . expressed the existential confusion of medieval society'. She then quotes Bonfil who in a Hebrew article claimed: 'the Jew both pleases and castigates'.
[81] Ovrut 1977, p. 224.   [82] *Ibid.*, p. 230.   [83] *Ibid.*, p. 224, 235.
[84] PRO E/101/249/29.

Having considered some of the longer-term explanations for the Expulsion, the rise of hatred of the Jews, the various suggestions of chroniclers and some of the opinions of those whom Tovey would have termed 'decypherers', it is necessary to consider the possible motives and influences of Edwardian society at large. Clearly, as has been discussed, late thirteenth-century society had differing views of the Jew. For instance, long ago B. L. Abrahams pointed out that the different towns and their respective attitudes were important factors in the final Expulsion.[85] As the thirteenth century began, many major provincial towns were enhancing their own legal status and gained or bought the right to be largely autonomous self-governing communities. Some towns which failed to tolerate settlement by Jews expelled them long before Edward's reign. One of the earliest was Bury St Edmunds where Abbot Samson induced the king to expel the Jews in 1190.[86] In the first third of the thirteenth century there was a very pronounced series of expulsions which also accompanied a new period of Jewish colonisation. Leicester received a grant from Simon de Montfort to expel the Jews in 1231.[87] Other towns followed suit: Newcastle and Warwick in 1234, High Wycombe in 1235, Southampton in 1236, Berkhamstead in 1242, Newbury and Speenhamland in 1244, Derby in 1261 and Romsey in 1266. Finally in 1245 the Crown itself began to restrict Jewish settlement and Henry III then issued the first decree which limited Jewish residence.[88]

Yet there seem to have been many towns which did not ask for their Jews to be expelled. Perhaps this was because of royal intervention rather than a genuine desire for toleration. Many towns seemed to comply with the royal order that Jewish residence should be allowed and that they should actually protect their Jews. Such was the established norm at Gloucester and Hereford where the burgesses were responsible for the Jews' safety.[89] In the early thirteenth century the sheriffs of

[85] Abrahams 1894b, pp. 87–94.
[86] *Chronica Jocelini de Brakelonda*, pp. 1–2, 4, 33; Haes 1899, p. 19; Scarfe 1986, pp. 81–109.
[87] Levy 1902a, p. 37. The Jews remained in a suburb of Leicester until 1253 because of the intervention of Margaret de Quincy and Bishop Grosseteste of Lincoln: Maddicott 1994, pp. 15–16.
[88] Newcastle, 1234: Guttentag 1977, p. 2; Warwick, 1234: *CCR 1231–1234*, pp. 515–16; Wycombe, 1235: *CCR 1234–1237*, p. 20; Southampton, 1236: Allin 1972, p. 89; to move from Berkhamstead to Wallingford, 1242: Denholm-Young 1947, p. 69; Newbury and Speenhamland, 1243: *CCR 1242–1247*, p. 149; Derby, 1261: *CPR 1258–1266*, p. 153. There are instances of several other local expulsions, namely from Romsey in 1266: *CPR 1258–1266*, p. 613. This is a most unusual example as it was granted by the king to the abbess of Romsey at the instance of Robert Walerand, a royal favourite; Alice his sister was the abbess of Romsey; Winchelsea, 1273: *CCR 1272–1279*, p. 50; Bridgnorth, 1274: *CCR 1272–1279*, p. 130. The entry for 1244 is headed *De judaismo*: *CCR 1242–1247*, p. 275.
[89] *CPR 1216–1225*, p. 157.

Worcester, York, Lincoln, Stamford and Bristol, Northampton and Winchester were charged with the duty of protecting the Jews. It is also clear that there were Jewish bailiffs appointed in Exeter and Hereford.[90] Civic authorities which could see the value of having Jewish settlements tolerated them despite local risings such as those in Norwich in 1234, and in Oxford in 1244 when scholars attacked the Jewry.[91]

In the thirteenth century there was probably a conflict of interests with regard to the Jews in many towns. The very fact that the Jews had the protection of the king might also have led to animosity and local tension as it had at Bury St Edmunds in 1190. The fact that the debts of Jews fell into the king's hands gave the king the right to intervene in town affairs (particularly during the 1279 coin-clipping allegations). This too must have caused local tensions, especially when townsmen were fined for harbouring former Jewish property.[92] Even in those towns which tolerated Jewish settlement there must have been resentment when, as in Canterbury and other towns, the Crown protected its rights over former Jewish residences. Certainly townsmen used the 1278–9 coin-clipping allegations and hangings to gain Jewish properties.[93] There is a fairly strong case for believing that, although towns were resentful of a Jewish presence, in many Jews were tolerated without the violence of 1190 or that seen during the barons' wars of the 1260s.

For evidence that the English baronage had been antagonistic to the Jews during the mid-century there is clearly no need to search far.[94] Yet by the 1240s many magnates had gained power over the Jews and had experience of the problems caused by Jewish finance. In 1244, they demanded the right of appointing one of the two Justices of the Jews.[95] In 1259 the complaints from the lower barons of widespread trafficking in bonds and estates went unheeded and led to the mid-century violence against the Jews.[96] Edward, who has been depicted as 'the sworn friend of the lower baronage', was naturally sympathetic to their pleas and did what he could to help alleviate the situation.[97] His first step, as has been observed above, was to issue the Provisions of the Jewry of 1269 which kept land out of Jewish hands. The attempt to evade the law was made punishable by death.[98] However, these Provisions were a little too late to help those of knightly status whose

[90] *CPR 1216–1225*, p. 157; *PREJ1*, p. 18.   [91] Lipman 1967, pp. 59–64; Roth 1951, p. 127.
[92] PRO E/101/119/12, E/101/119/20. Mundill 1987, p. 99 shows that in addition to the fines collected from the Jews for the coin-clipping allegations of approximately £11,000, Edward collected just over £2,000 from Christians for receiving or harbouring ex-Jewish goods.
[93] Mundill 1987, pp. 180–2.   [94] Roth 1978, p. 59.   [95] *Ibid.*
[96] See chapter 2 above.   [97] Elman 1938a, p. 152.   [98] Rigg, pp. xlix–li.

fathers had unleashed their wrath on the hated Jewish moneylenders during the baronial revolt. Men like Adam of Newmarket, Jordan Foliot, Nicholas of Tarrington, John de Balun and others were still encumbered by their debts in 1290.[99] Those knights, like Sir John de Burg, Bartholomew of Redham, William Mountchesney, Robert Canvil, William Leyburn, Gilbert Peche, Stephen Cheyndut, Norman de Arcy and John de Cameys, who had lost their lands to the queen in 1281 because of their Jewish debts, were also the type of men upon whom Edward relied to fight for him and who were likely to have influence in his early parliaments.[100] Certainly they had much to gain from the expulsion of the Jews; it would have been popular with them even if it meant they had to find alternative finance.

Although the Statute of 1275 had protected those in debt by guaranteeing them 'maintenance of their land', in reality this had not happened.[101] Distraint for Jewish debts continued and encumbered estates and debts were eagerly bought up.[102] Many Christian debtors still had to contribute to Jewish tallage payments and as these continued so did the financial pressures. There was little relief for what Professor Harding has termed 'yeomen' who were under pressure for their debts.[103] The heirs of Daniel Bagge and John le Botiller of Kent continued to pay back their Jewish debts for many years after 1290.[104] An examination of tallage payments and in particular the sheriff of Hereford's accounts shows that in 1280 the tallage was paid by fourteen Christian debtors and two Jews; in 1282 by thirty-four debtors and three Jews; in 1285 by forty-eight debtors and several Jews.[105] A similar pattern prevailed across the country. There can be little doubt that expulsion of the Jews would have been seen as a popular step by those Christians who paid towards Jewish tallages. By the 1280s a Jewish tallage had become almost a mass distraint of Christian debtors. Yet would the latter, of their own volition and initiative, vote such a massive tax when they were paying comparatively paltry sums?

Could others within the royal circle have had influence on Edward? As has been discussed, the queen mother, the queen and other members of the royal family had had many dealings with the Jews. It would seem unlikely that knowing how they could profit from Jewish money-lending they would have moved directly against the Jews. Paradoxically

[99] See chapter 7 above.   [100] Parsons 1995, pp. 120–56, 168, 174, 176–7, 180, 183–5.
[101] Appendix II, lines 20–6.
[102] Rokeah forthcoming, pp. 167–71, 194–8, 233–4, 265–7, 354.
[103] Harding 1993, p. 96.
[104] PRO E/401/1582, E/401/1584–8, E/401/1590–1, E/401/1593.
[105] PRO E/401/1578, E/401/1580, E/401/1582, E/101/249/26.

it seems that by the later 1280s they had openly turned against the Jews. The queen, Eleanor of Castile, had been widely criticised for her dealings and the queen mother, Eleanor of Provence, had taken the veil.[106] In the last few years government had been dogged by the inefficiency of royal officials like Stratton, Hauteyn and Ludham, both within and without the Exchequer. There were officials of the latter who were eager to make amends for their errors which were being revealed by the state trials: perhaps some were only too willing to shift the emphasis of blame onto another agency such as the Jews.[107] Naturally, royal advisers may also have had impact on Edward's thinking. The king's inner circle of advisers, Robert Burnell, Chancellor, John Kirkby, Treasurer, William Leyburn and Otto de Grandison, as well as new officials such as William de Middleton, Hugh de Kendal and William de Marchia, were all men who had experience of how the Jewish Exchequer worked, how unpopular it was with those it distrained and how Jewish moneylending had operated. Indeed some of them had themselves profited both directly and indirectly from the Jews.[108] Although discussion must have taken place between Edward, his family and his officials it still seems unlikely that, as H. G. Richardson and others have intimated, the final decision was a ministerial one.[109]

Thus the final decision for expulsion seems to lie essentially with the king. Edward I had long held a deliberate policy towards both usury and the Jews. He was also driven by his own piety and by his own desire for the Jews' conversion. His 'Jewish policy' is at times difficult to detect. Edward was both impulsive and inconstant: this can be illustrated not only in his legislation but in his own religious convictions.[110] Evidence for Edward's 'Jewish policy' begins in the early 1260s when he was the Prince Edward and tried to combat the alienation of land by stopping mortgaging.[111] The Jews were an obvious target for his campaign against land alienation and later usury. There were many consistent

---

[106] Parsons 1995, pp. 126–30, 139–41, appendix 1 shows that Eleanor of Castile was moving away from involvement with the Jews. Eleanor of Provence had taken the veil and was also distancing herself from involvement with the Jews: Biles 1983, p. 129; Mundill 1993, p. 48.

[107] Certainly this was true of the trial of Hamo Hauteyn and Robert de Ludham in 1286: *Select Cases in the Court of the King's bench under Edward I*, vol. 1, pp. clv–clix; Brand 1985, pp. 31–2.

[108] Mundill 1993, pp. 28–9. Burnell had received two yearly fees from Elias Menahem in 1267: *CPR 1267–1272*, p. 67; he had also profited in 1286 from taking over the lands of the Coleworth family in Essex: *CCR 1279–1288*, p. 387.

[109] Richardson 1960, pp. 213–33.

[110] *Political Songs of England*, p. 93: 'He is a lion by his pride and ferocity; by his inconstancy and changeableness he is a pard, changing his word and his promises, excusing himself with fair speech.' Prestwich 1985.

[111] See chapter 3 above

threads in the Provisions of the Jewry and the Statute of 1275.[112] It is also likely that Edward understood the Jewish communities and the problems associated with their businesses far better than his father had done. It is clear that, like other rulers, Edward held set, firm attitudes towards his Jewish subjects. Yet he could only take action against the Jews, issue legislation and address the Jewish problem when he was in a position to do so.

Edward's reign started whilst he was engaged on a holy crusade from which he returned much in debt and probably very sympathetic towards warriors who had mortgaged and borrowed in order to fight the infidel.[113] On his return to England he was also confronted with many problems in taking full control of the administration of the land. Even so in January 1275 he assented to his mother's desire to expel the Jews from her dower towns; and in April, for the first time, he adopted what might be termed a Jewish 'policy' and promulgated the Statute of the Jewry.[114] It seems no small coincidence that this new step was partially in harmony with discussions at the Council of Lyons of 1274.[115] Edward was no doubt well aware of the findings of this Council as he had passed through much of Europe before reaching home and must have heard the many differing opinions on how Jews should be treated. However, Edward did not exile the Jews at the earliest possible opportunity. It seems that, as far as he was concerned, as long as Jewish interest rates were not high and as long as Jews did not threaten the Christian religion itself they were there to be converted.[116] He clearly remained intent more on conversion and assimilation than on genocide: for it was Edward himself who put a stop to the hangings in 1278–9.

His policy was not totally clarified in 1275. The Statute of the Jewry of that year allowed for actions against the Jew at a later date.[117] Dr Lieberman and others have also questioned the fifteen-year lease of land which Jews were allowed to take up by the Statute, and have showed that after 1275 further legislation was to be expected. It is indeed possible that the 1275 Statute really was an experiment for a period of time which expired in 1290. Yet in 1287 this policy was affected by a sudden change in Edward's own personal and religious attitude towards the Jews. This change of direction sounded the death knell for the presence of Jews in all his domains. The formulation of Edward's final

---

[112] Rigg, pp. xlviii–li; see Appendices II and III.   [113] Prestwich 1980, pp. 8–10.
[114] Mundill 1993, p. 48; see Appendix II.
[115] Baldwin 1970, pp. 296–311; Tawney 1937, p. 58.
[116] Roth 1978, pp. 78–9; Stacey 1992a, p. 274.
[117] See Appendix II, lines 75–84; Lipman 1967, p. 163.

solution, as we shall see, lies between the years 1287 and 1290 and it was probably more than a change which was first fostered by religious conviction and convention rather than by political acumen or necessity. It was in Gascony that Edward's policy of wholesale expulsion of the Jews was first arrived at.[118]

By the late 1280s it was becoming clear that Edward had failed to realise his own religious aims for the Jews; he had not achieved a mass conversion. Although some historians have claimed that 'religion was an inappreciable factor' many others have correctly seen it as an important long-term cause of the Expulsion.[119] In 1891 George H. Leonard claimed: 'The matter is popularly explained on the score of religious bigotry: the people it is said are ignorant fanatics, led on by a less ignorant but more fanatical clergy and the King shares in the fanaticism of his people. This explanation is not untrue but it is not the whole truth.'[120] Leonard also correctly examined the possibility that the expansion of the Franciscans had created a new spiritual climate.[121] As Dr Jeremy Cohen has subsequently shown, the coming of the Friars in the 1220s had brought with it a renewal of spiritual zeal and a new impetus for conversion which was often supported by the Crown.[122] Leonard also pointed to the fact that in Oxford the Dominicans were particularly successful and managed to convert many Jews.[123] It was not just missionary zeal but the very ideals of the mendicants which posed a challenge to the Jewish financier. After all, the Franciscans and the Dominicans preached poverty and frowned on all forms of profit. The mendicant orders not only began to reform the Church but, perhaps more importantly, also actually appeared to the general populace at large. Both these aspects clearly contributed to rising popular disapproval against the Jews and their refusal to assimilate or give up usury.[124]

Such religious influences stirred king and commoners alike. Edward was only too aware of the new spirituality which the mendicants preached. Long ago Professor Tout pointed out that Edward was greatly influenced by the Dominicans.[125] It is well known that the mendicants were responsible for disseminating the official doctrine of the

---

[118] Lieberman 1983, pp. 219–20; Tovey 1738, p. 235; Salzman 1968, p. 85; Richardson 1960, p. 213.
[119] Rigg 1903, p. 18; Ovrut 1977, pp. 228–9; Watt 1987; 1991; Stow 1992a.
[120] Leonard, 1891, p. 103.   [121] *Ibid.*, p. 124.
[122] Cohen 1982, pp. 19–77, 260–4; 1983, pp. 24–7.   [123] Leonard, 1891, p. 125.
[124] Cohen 1982, pp. 19–77; Moore 1987, pp. 107–18; Parsons 1995, pp. 139–42 discusses the influence of the Dominicans on Eleanor of Castile.
[125] Tout 1920, p. 69.

Church.[126] At the same time the vicars of Christ in Rome also had their own ideas about the Jewish problem and the wider problem of usury. B. L. Abrahams considered the papacy as a driving force behind the change in attitude towards the Jews. He pointed to Innocent III's own crusade against the Jews which was summed up in the rulings of the Lateran Council of 1215. He also highlighted the connections between the papacy and the mendicant orders.[127] Cardinal Ugolino, the friend of St Francis, became Gregory IX; the Franciscans Petrus de Tarentagio and Girolamo di Ascoli became Innocent IV and Nicholas IV.[128] Gregory X (1271–6) had visited England in 1265 accompanied by Cardinal Ottoboni. He had also accompanied Edward I on crusade and had been at the Council of Lyons in May 1274.[129]

Under such influences, the papal policy underwent an alteration in attitude towards the Jews. Whilst in the early 1270s the papacy had to an extent previously protected the Jew this was to change. On 7 October 1272, for example, the ritual murder charges were denounced by Gregory X. His bull claimed that there should be no forced conversion of Jews, no one should oppress them, their festivals should not be disturbed and there should be no destruction of Jewish cemeteries.[130] Although a coherent papal policy against the Jews is difficult to discern, particularly when as in 1276 there were three popes, it is clear that later popes were less likely to favour the Jews. They included Innocent V (January–June 1276), the first Dominican pope and friend of Thomas Aquinas, who had helped to prepare and taken a major part in the Council of Lyons. There followed Hadrian V (July–August 1276), formerly Cardinal Ottoboni Fieschi, who had been sent on mission to England in 1265 to preach a crusade, organise Church affairs and resolve the conflict between Henry III and his barons; he was a man who had probably met many leading London Jews.[131] Finally, Nicholas III (November 1277 to August 1280), who was a keen promoter of both the Franciscans and the Dominicans.[132]

A distinct change in papal attitudes became even clearer in the 1280s. For most of the 1280s, Martin IV and Honorius IV wore the papal tiara. The former, by the Bull *Ad fructus uberes* issued on 13 December 1281, granted the mendicants enhanced rights of preaching and hearing

---

[126] Abrahams 1894b, p. 238; Stow 1992a, pp. 259–62; Cohen 1982, pp. 253–8; Watt 1987, pp. 138–9; 1992.

[127] Abrahams 1894b, pp. 236–9, 428–35; Grayzel 1966, pp. 132–43, 307–13.

[128] Abrahams 1894b, p. 238; Kelly 1986, pp. 189–93, 205–6; Grayzel 1966, pp. 178–249, 249–95; Stow 1989, pp. 164–92.

[129] Kelly 1986, pp. 197–8; Stow 1989, pp. 116–34.   [130] Stow 1989, pp. 116–20.

[131] Kelly 1986, pp. 198–200; Roth 1946, p. 38.

[132] Synan 1965, pp. 118–21; Kelly 1986, pp. 201–2; Stow 1989, pp. 137–46.

confessions which exasperated even the secular clergy.[133] Honorius IV was a staunch supporter of the religious orders and confirmed and extended the privileges of the Dominicans and Franciscans. A change in papal policy towards the Jews, as Professor Kenneth Stow has observed, can probably be detected in Honorius' letter of 1286 which was sent to the archbishops of Canterbury and York: 'We have heard that in England the accursed and perfidious Jews have done unspeakable things and horrible acts, to the shame of our Creator and the detriment of the Catholic faith.'[134] Honorius went on to condemn the continuing study of the Talmud, accusing the Jews of seducing converts with gifts, inviting Christians into their synagogues, keeping Christians in their households, using Christian wet-nurses, banqueting and feasting together, publicly abusing and cursing Christians. He also questioned the loyalty of the English clergy by insinuating that they had done nothing about such abuses. When the bull reached England in early 1286, Edward (who, ironically, was himself indebted to Honorius' money-lenders) had already embarked for Gascony.[135] It was left to the archbishop of Canterbury, the former Franciscan John Pecham, to act, which he did at the Council of Exeter in 1287.

The religious campaign against the Jews in England was stepped up as a result of papal intervention and the changes of attitude towards the Jewish communities. Although opposition to Judaism had naturally come from earlier archbishops of Canterbury like Stephen Langton and Boniface of Savoy, it is possible to detect a change of emphasis and a more severe attitude towards the Jew.[136] Pecham's predecessor as archbishop of Canterbury, Robert Kilwardby, a former Provincial Prior of the Dominicans in England, was appointed archbishop on 11 October 1272, just before the beginning of Edward's reign. He certainly did not favour the Jews and must have been acutely aware of their financial role as his own clerk, William de Middleton, had financial dealings with them.[137] He too had attended the Council of Lyons and had also visited many English towns which had Jewish communities such as Worcester, Winchester, Lincoln and Oxford. Yet Kilwardby was more interested in promoting the Dominican order than in directly attacking the Jews. He bought a new site for the Dominicans in London and favoured the conversion of the Jews by theological argument and

---

[133] Kelly 1986, pp. 202–5; Stow 1989, pp. 147–54.
[134] Stow 1989, pp. 155–64; Abrahams 1894b, pp. 440–2.
[135] Prestwich 1988, p. 233, 257; Stow 1989, pp. 155–64; Abrahams 1894b, pp. 440–2.
[136] Leonard, 1891, pp. 125–7.
[137] *PREJ3*, pp. 37–8, 65, 123, 129–30, 159, 182, 214, 273, 278–9.

preaching. Eventually he was appointed cardinal-bishop of Porto and Santa Rufina, resigned from Canterbury and moved to Rome.[138]

In 1278, Edward's Chancellor and favourite, Robert Burnell, was elected archbishop. However, Nicholas III quashed the election and on 25 January 1279 nominated John Pecham as his candidate.[139] As a Franciscan, Pecham had been educated at Lewes and later at Oxford in the 1250s. He had been to Paris and had there met Thomas Aquinas. He advanced the interest of the Franciscans in England and had even been appointed as the 'protector of the privileges of the orders of Minors in England'.[140] Although they did not necessarily always agree neither Pecham nor Edward could afford to incur the papal wrath. The new archbishop became more actively involved in a deliberate campaign against the Jews.[141] In July 1281, he had secret discussions with the bishop of London and tried to stop the building of a new London synagogue.[142] Later that year he railed against some apostate Jews who had 'returned to their vomit'.[143] In August 1282, he ordered the bishop of London to destroy all the synagogues in London except one. As Professor Jack Watt has pointed out, it was also the archbishop who had in 1285 complained in parliament, 'because the royal court does not know how the Jewish evil can be curbed'.[144] Possibly encouraged by the bull of 1286, in December of that year Pecham even tried to remonstrate with the queen and her councillors for acquiring property from the whirlpool of Jewish usuries.[145] In England it was Archbishop Pecham who spearheaded the religious campaign against both usury and the Jews.

Pecham did not need to look far for clerical support. There had always been a large group of ecclesiastics who had, as Matthew Paris pointed out, become 'enmeshed by the usurers'.[146] In the late twelfth century those 'enmeshed' had, amongst others, included the bishop of Hereford, the abbey of Glastonbury, the monastery of St Swithin's, Winchester (which owed several thousand pounds); in the thirteenth century they included Fountains Abbey, the abbey of Stratford and Bridlington Priory.[147] Indebtedness had even been so serious that allegedly the prior of Lewes had to rent out his churches and some

[138] *Dictionary of National Biography*, 1892, vol. XXXI, pp. 120–2 by TFT; Prestwich 1988, p. 249.
[139] Prestwich 1988, p. 249.
[140] *Dictionary of National Biography*, 1895, vol. XLIV, pp. 190–7 by CLK.
[141] Logan 1972, pp. 214–29. [142] Pecham *Epistolae*, vol. I, pp. 212–13.
[143] *Ibid.*, p. 239. [144] Watt 1987, pp. 144–5; Stow 1992a, pp. 285–8, 294.
[145] Pecham *Epistolae*, vol. II, pp. 407–10; vol. III, p. 397.
[146] *Chronica Majora*, vol. III, pp. 188–9, 328.
[147] Abrahams 1894b, 96–8; *PREJ*3, pp. 223, 285–6; Dobson 1979, pp. 45–6; Mundill 1993, p. 60.

churches could not afford a clergyman.[148] When Pecham first went to the see of Canterbury it too was greatly in debt, partly because of Kilwardby's extravagance.[149] Following Pecham's appointment, many other high-ranking clergymen began to take action against the Jews. In 1278, the bishop of Lincoln, Richard de Gravesend, tried to arrest and excommunicate thirteen Christians who were in the employment of Jews in Lincoln. These arrests may have been part of a comprehensive purge of Christian servants working for Jews, because they affected four different areas of Lincoln.[150] Two Christian maids from the Bail were imprisoned. Two nursemaids, two maids and one servant were taken from the parish of St Michael on the Mount. From the Skin Market a male and a female servant as well as a nursemaid were arrested. Three female maids were removed from the parish of St Martin.[151] Other English clergy were also similarly motivated to take action as a result of papal pressure and Pecham's influence.[152]

Edward I was, as Professor Prestwich has noted, becoming more dependent on clerical taxation.[153] Such taxes could be particularly valuable as most early taxes on clergy were assessed on a totally different basis from those on the laity. Clerical taxes were calculated on the rental value of estates, unlike the lay subsidies which were based on levies on moveable property. However, in order to obtain a vote of a tax directly from the clergy he first had to negotiate with them and get papal permission. Edward had first approached the clergy for a grant of taxation in 1275 but was refused on the grounds that they were already paying a tenth to the papacy. In 1279, a request for a fifteenth to meet expenses in Wales was successful. The convocation of Canterbury agreed to pay at this rate for three years. The York convocation granted a tenth in 1280 for two years. Edward tried again in 1283 to get permission to raise a clerical tax but had difficulties. It is perhaps more than coincidental that, in late 1290, after the Expulsion had been ordered, the clergy finally made Edward a new grant.[154]

Edward I and the English clergy became united in the 1280s in their religious attitude towards the Jews. It was not the prelates or the friars alone who started to raise the impetus of the religious campaign against the Jews of England: it was also a campaign aided by Edward himself.[155] Edward had always been very concerned with conversion and apostasy. He had a strong religious conviction that the Jews lived in ignorance

[148] Abrahams 1894b, pp. 96–8.   [149] Pecham *Epistolae*, vol. I, pp. 156–7, 341.
[150] *Concilia*, vol. I, pp. 675, 719.   [151] Lincoln RO, MCD 501; PRO C/85/99.
[152] *Concilia*, vol. II, p. 155; Abrahams 1894b, pp. 440–2; Susser 1993, p. 19.
[153] Prestwich 1972, p. 185–6.   [154] *Ibid.*
[155] Roth 1978, pp. 78–9; Stacey 1992a, p. 274; Mundill 1993, pp. 61, 68–9;

and sin and he was also quick to act whenever the Christian faith was threatened. In 1275, the unthinkable had happened, a Dominican was converted to Judaism.[156] In January 1280, in accordance with the papal bull *Vineam Sorec* of 1278, Edward personally endorsed the Dominicans' wish for the forced attendance of Jewish communities at their religious sermons; and he issued orders to all the sheriffs and bailiffs in England bidding them to do their best to induce all the Jews in the counties and towns under their charge to assemble and hear the word of God as preached by the friars.[157]

Edward also took immediate and harsh action against blasphemy. The prince who had once witnessed the degradation of the Holy Rood in Oxford, as a king set severe penalties for the crime of blasphemy. Proclamation was to be made throughout England that any Jew found guilty of having spoken disrespectfully of Christ, the Virgin Mary or the Catholic faith should be liable to the loss of life or limbs.[158] In 1276 Edward turned an accusation of ritual murder made against the London Jews over to parliament. In 1277, at the request of Archbishop Kilwardby, Edward ordered that a ribald Jew, who had masqueraded as a Franciscan, should perform a penance that had been imposed on him by the archbishop. Sampson, son of Samuel, of Northampton was arrested by the sheriff for having taken the habit of a Friar Minor and for preaching certain things 'in contempt of the Christian faith'. Kilwardby had convicted him and sentenced him to go naked for three days through the midst of the cities of Canterbury, Lincoln, London, Northampton and Oxford carrying in his hands the entrails of a calf; the rest of the calf was to be flayed and placed on his neck. Sampson seems to have escaped the punishment.[159] Yet further similar persecution took place. At Nottingham in 1278 a Jewess was charged with abusing in scandalous terms all the Christian bystanders in the market place.[160] At Norwich in 1279 Abraham fil Deulecresse was actually burned for blasphemy.[161]

Even though sometimes at serious loggerheads with Archbishop Pecham (for political and personal reasons), Edward shared with him a common desire for the conversion of the Jews.[162] At the same time as the *Statutum de Judeismo* was issued, orders were given to enlarge the *Domus Conversorum* in London.[163] On 10 May 1279, Edward decreed that all relapsed converts from Judaism were to be subject to the secular

---

[156] *CPR 1272–1281*, p. 356; Hyams 1974, p. 275.
[157] Abrahams 1894b, p. 438–9; Stacey 1992a, p. 274; Roth 1951, pp. 151–3.
[158] *CCR 1272–1279*, pp. 271–4; Cluse 1995b.   [159] *PREJ3*, pp. 311–12.
[160] Mundill 1993, p. 60.   [161] *Calendar of Charter Rolls 1257–1300*, p. 213.
[162] *CCR 1272–1279*, p. 207; Adler 1939, pp. 300–3;   [163] Adler 1939, pp. 300–3.

arm.[164] In mid-1280 he offered would-be Jewish converts to Christianity an attractive compromise in that, from now on, they would be allowed to keep half the value of their possessions with the other half going to the *Domus Conversorum* instead of all their possessions going into the royal coffers.[165] Edward offered Archbishop Pecham support in his relentless pursuit of thirteen relapsed converts.[166] Yet the mission to the Jews failed. In 1290, the Oxford Jews, in one of the few examples of Jews rioting, rose and attacked a converted Jew who was collecting the poll tax for the *Domus Conversorum*.[167] As late as 1290 the London Jews objected vehemently to the baptism of a Jewish boy in St Clement's Church because they had not given their permission.[168] The more pressure exerted on the Jews to convert, the more their spirit seems to have strengthened. The Jews' refusal to assimilate must have been another factor in Edward's final decision to expel them from England. The Jews of Edwardian England remained true to themselves and their faith: it is perhaps an irony that their memory is preserved not in any *Memorbuch* or martyrology but only in their remaining financial bonds and fines.

Having examined some of the religious influences which might have led to Edward's final decision it is now important to return to contemporary events. Some historians and chroniclers have juxtaposed the Expulsion of the Jews from England with that from Gascony a few years earlier.[169] In particular it was H. G. Richardson, in more recent times, who linked these events.[170] Some historians have claimed that links between the English and European expulsions are on the surface difficult to perceive; yet as we shall see, a closer comparison shows this not to be the case.[171] The Gascon expulsion has not been examined closely enough. When considering the example of Gascony, as Dr Mentgen has correctly pointed out, some historians have even offered a different date for the expulsion there.[172] Yet it is clear that the English Expulsion was inextricably connected to those abroad. Just as Anglo-Jewry had connections with the continent so too links existed between Jewish or rather anti-Jewish policies there. Recently, Dr Nicholas

---

[164] Logan 1972.   [165] Stacey 1992a, p. 280.   [166] Logan 1972, pp. 214–29.
[167] Lipman 1968, p. 64;   [168] *Rotuli Parliamentorum*, vol 1, p. 46 no. 7.
[169] Walsingham, *Historia Anglicana*, p. 31.   [170] Richardson 1960, p. 213.
[171] Stacey 1990, pp. 1–2 sees them as similar but different because of the political situation in France and England. Jordan 1989, p. 182 intimates a link between the expulsion from Anjou and Maine; Stow 1992, pp. 281–3 considers the expulsions in the context of medieval Latin Europe.
[172] Mentgen 1997; Jordan 1989, p. 182 gives 1288; Stow 1992, p. 292 gives 1289; Prestwich 1980, pp. 201–2 gives 1289 but later corrects this, in Prestwich 1988, p. 306 where he accepts 1287; Stacey 1992b, note 34, favours 1287; Trabut-Cussac 1972, p. 85 gives 1287. It is now clear that it was late 1287.

Vincent has shown how, in the 1230s, Peter des Roches was probably influenced by continental actions against the Jews. Similarly Dr John Maddicott has also shown how de Montfort might also have been influenced by French attitudes towards the Jews.[173]

Edward I was a king of international repute, bearing and connection. He was married to a Castilian princess, his father-in-law, Alphonso X, was king of Castile; his mother was a Savoyard and Edward himself was also duke of Aquitaine. These relationships meant that Edward must have been aware of the prevailing European attitude to the 'Jewish problem'. Edward retained strong connections with France and Spain and was also an international crusader.[174] As a king with interests on the continent Edward had to be very much in touch with the European scene and he had to have a strong foreign policy. Two of his daughters were married to continental rulers.[175] Many European princes also had Jews living in their domains and their presence must have been the cause for some discussion and debate at an international level. The policies of one country towards the Jews must have had some influence on the policy of another. In 1180 Philip Augustus imprisoned all Jews and only released them after a heavy ransom. In 1181 he annulled all loans made to Christians by Jews, taking 20 per cent for himself. In 1182 he confiscated all the lands and buildings of the Jews and drove them out of the lands that he directly governed.[176] The Expulsion of the Jews from France clearly overshadowed the events of *Shabbat ha Gadol* in England in 1190.[177] In 1194 Richard I regulated his Jewries and set up the *archa* system: in France Philip Augustus re-admitted the Jews in 1198 and also started to regulate their financial business.[178] It is quite likely that events elsewhere on the continent could have precipitated the English Final Solution.

There are many common threads to most medieval European anti-Jewish legislation. In Austria, the Charter of Frederick the Belligerent, issued in July 1244, encouraged moneylending, gave the Jews ducal protection, allowed them to live and travel free of tolls, and prohibited

---

[173] Vincent 1992, pp. 129–31; 1996, pp. 363–4; Maddicott 1994, p. 15.

[174] Prestwich 1988, preface and pp. 572–5. Edward was in fairly close contact with Margaret of France, the count of Luxembourg, the duke of Slavia and Cassabia, the duchess of Brunswick, the burghers of Douai, Bruges, the mayor of Rochelle, the master of the Hospital of St John in Jerusalem, Magnus of Norway and Alphonso of Castile who even wrote to him in Spanish: Seventh Report of the Deputy Keeper of Public Records, 1846, pp. 264, 267, 270–5; Richardson 1960, p. 213.

[175] Prestwich 1988, pp. 126–9.

[176] Chazan 1973, pp. 64–5 notes that it was Ralph of Diss who recorded the ransom payment of 15,000 marks; Jordan 1989, pp. 30–1.

[177] Dobson 1974, pp. 1–50 is still the best account of the English massacre.

[178] Chazan 1973, pp. 74–7; Jordan 1989, pp. 38–45; Howden, *Chronica*, vol. III, pp. 266–7.

them from taking bloody and wet clothes as pawns. In Austria the Jews had a Judge of the Jews and one of his responsibilities was to protect the Jews.[179] Similarly, in England in the 1230s and 1240s, Henry III issued legislation and insisted that his Jews be submitted to a census to ascertain where they lived.[180] B. L. Abrahams and others have pointed out that in 1253 St Louis, even while in the Holy Land, sent an order that all Jews should leave France except those who became traders and workers with their hands.[181] This conception that Jews should become involved in the land or in occupations other than usury shows that the medieval state was putting into action the injunctions of the Fourth Lateran Council of 1215.[182] In Spain, Edward's father-in-law, Alphonso X of Castile, must have been aware of the Disputation of Barcelona in the summer of 1263. At this major disputation, judged by James I of Aragon, the Dominicans attempted to browbeat the Jewish religion into mass conversion.[183] In 1265 Alphonso X issued *Las siete Partidas*. These anti-Jewish guidelines laid down severe social restrictions on the Jews of Castile. No more synagogues were to be built, Christians who became Jews should be killed, social intercourse between Christian and Jew was forbidden and a distinguishing mark had to be worn.[184] Similar legislation was to follow in England in 1269 and 1275.

In 1274, Christendom's attention was drawn to an anti-usury campaign at the Council at Lyons. Even before this, of course, many attacks in Europe had been made against moneylenders and their trade. However, as a result of the new campaign, it was especially the Italian moneylenders who suffered. In England, the brother of the papal legate, a moneylender, was killed at Oxford. In London, Bishop Roger solemnly excommunicated all the Italian lenders and excluded them from his diocese.[185] Pope Gregory X ordered that no community should permit foreign usurers to hire houses from them or to dwell on

---

[179] Parkes 1938, pp. 178–82, 401–3.   [180] Stacey 1985, pp. 175–96.

[181] Abrahams 1894b, p. 244; Jordan 1989, pp. 148–9; Chazan 1973, p. 121; in 1233 Grosseteste noted that 'they should be made to work in the fields and for the usefulness of the kingdom': Grosseteste, *Epistolae*, pp. 35–6; Thomas Aquinas gave similar advice in the 1260s to a lady of Flanders: Liebeschutz 1962, pp. 71–2; see Appendix II, lines 70–90.

[182] Watt 1987, p. 146.   [183] Chazan 1977, 838–42.

[184] Carpenter 1986, pp. 1–5; Gerber 1992, pp. 94, 104, 111.

[185] Abrahams 1894b, p. 240; Parkes 1938, pp. 286–7; Stow 1989, pp. 122–34; Matthew Paris, *Chronica Majora*, vol. III, pp. 482–3; vol. IV, p. 8. It looks as if the English Church was well represented on 28 March 1274. Permission was given to go 'overseas' to the abbots of Westminster, Osney, Seleby, Shrewsbury, St Peter's, Gloucester, Croyland, Evesham, Malmesbury, Stanes and Abingdon; the treasurer of Salisbury, the prior of St Bartholomew's, London and the prior of Spalding; the bishop of Coventry and Lichfield, the dean of Lincoln, Richard de Mepham, Master Ralph of Freningham, Master Peter de Abendon, master of the House of Scholars at Merton, Oxford and Master Thomas de Cantilupe: *CCR 1272–1279*, pp. 117–18.

their lands but should expel them within three months.[186] It was no doubt examples such as these that led Edward to take his own firm stance against usury on his return from crusade in 1274.[187] Yet it was not just the dogma of canonical legislation which influenced kings and princes. There were other voices which spoke out clearly against the Jews. In the early thirteenth century Grosseteste had voiced the views later expressed by Thomas Aquinas who claimed: 'If rulers think they harm their souls by taking money from usurers, let them remember that they are themselves to blame. They ought to see that the Jews are compelled to labour as they do in some parts of Italy.'[188] Aquinas believed that unrestricted intercourse between Christian and Jew was likely to result in the conversion of Christians to Judaism; thus all intercourse between the two should only be allowed to those Christians who were strong in faith.[189]

Nor is it coincidence that just as Edward passed legislation against the Jews of England in 1275 so in France under Philip III (1270–85) similar measures were taken. In 1275 Edward restricted his Jews to *archa* towns. In April 1276 the Exchequer of Normandy registered a decree expelling the Jews from the villages of France, effectively restricting Jewish habitation to towns.[190] It is clear that Edward discriminated against the Jews in the 1280s; again in France similar restrictive ordinances were passed in 1283. These regulations made it obligatory that the Jews should wear a badge so that Christians should not be allowed to serve them. They prohibited the building or repairing of synagogues, made it necessary for Jews to live in areas of towns, and ordered that all Talmuds were to be burnt.[191] Edward ruled Gascony as a fief of the king of France and must have been well aware of his overlord's attitude to his Jewish subjects.[192]

The Gascon and other such expulsions accordingly deserve more attention as exemplars of what was to happen in England. H. G. Richardson described Edward's expulsion of the Jews from Gascony as callous and premeditated and puts it in the same class as his raid on the Templars in London when he carried off a prize of £10,000.[193] Professor Prestwich also noted the link between the two expulsions and was similarly clear about Edward's premeditation: 'In 1289 (*sic*), the Gascon Jews were expelled, the motive being quite blatantly the

[186] Stow 1989, pp. 131–3. [187] *CCR 1272–1279*, p. 144.
[188] Abrahams 1894b, p. 244. [189] *Ibid.*; Liebeschutz 1962, pp. 61–81.
[190] See Appendix II, lines 41–2; Chazan 1973, p. 156.
[191] See above and Appendix III; Chazan 1973, p. 156.
[192] Wade Labarge 1980, pp. 41–62; for earlier links between events in England and France see Vincent 1992, p. 132.
[193] Richardson 1960, pp. 225–6.

acquisition of their assets by a king hard pressed to raise the funds needed to obtain the release of his cousin, Charles of Salerno, from captivity.'[194] L. F. Salzman also linked the Gascon expulsion and the major wave of arrests of Jews which took place in England in May 1287 but gave a slightly different explanation: 'It is probable . . . that there may be some connection between his convalescent vow of crusade and the arrest by his orders in May 1287 of the Jews of England. Their subsequent release on payment of a fine is good evidence that Edward did not allow religion to interfere with business principles.'[195]

Yet the motives behind the Gascon expulsion, as with the English Expulsion, are difficult to fathom. As with its English counterpart, Edward did not keep the money for himself, perhaps a strange act for a king who was short of finances? In his examination of the Gascon expulsion Professor Trabut-Cussac showed that the motives which led Edward to decide to banish the Jews of the duchy in the spring of 1287 and to seize their wealth are not easy to define.[196] It is certain, however, that Edward I was lying sick at Blanquefort at the start of 1287 and was recovering from an illness.[197] Chroniclers and charters prove that the expulsion of the Jews from Gascony was decided after the recovery of the king and indeed after he had officially taken the cross, which he did at Bordeaux in May 1287.[198] The expulsion and dissolution of the Gascon Jewries was swift. The Jews were arrested, their goods were seized, liquidators headed by Tayllefero de Monte Oseri arranged the sale and the confiscated money was received into the Treasury and the Wardrobe by William de Louth.[199]

Wardrobe receipts from August, October and November 1287 reflect the meticulousness of the work of the liquidators. On 26 November 1287 the total value of the Gascon Jewry's assets, some £1,095 17s 9½d, became apparent and was immediately given to the Friars Minor and Preachers and other mendicants in the duchy of Aquitaine, particularly those at Condom. Any debts which contained usury clauses and were found in the possession of the Jews were cancelled; the remainder went to the profit of the duke, Edward.[200] In 1289, the king wrote to his debt

[194] Prestwich 1972, p. 201.   [195] Salzman 1968, pp. 84–5.
[196] Trabut-Cussac 1972, p. 85.   [197] *Ibid.*; Salzman 1968, p. 85.
[198] Trabut-Cussac 1972, p. 86; Byerly 1986, pp. xii–xiii.
[199] Trabut-Cussac 1972, p. 86, note 254; Byerly 1986, p. xxviii notes that £50 was given to the Dominicans for their building programme and the *Domus Conversorum* in London also received a stipend. That the Dominican House in Condom was in need of rebuilding is apparent from a letter which had been sent to Edward at Easter 1285: *Seventh Report of the Deputy Keeper of the Public Records*, p. 286.
[200] Trabut-Cussac 1972, p. 86; Tovey 1738, p. 235 states that Edward wished to convert his profits from the Expulsion to pious uses.

collectors in Aquitaine asking them to listen to all those who could prove that they had been encumbered by usury and asking them to levy only a moiety of the debt. They were commanded to 'listen to their proof and dismiss as much as they have proved and omit to force payment and levy part of the rest'.[201] Although deeply indebted by the heavy expenditure entailed by his stay in Paris, his journey in crossing France and the negotiations with Aragon, Edward did not make any personal financial gain from the Gascon expulsion.[202] In reality, the majority of the money extorted from the Gascon Jews was converted into alms. The result of the Gascon expulsion was financial gain for the Church and in particular the mendicants.

For geographical reasons the Gascon expulsion was a difficult act to complete and actually overlapped the English Expulsion of 1290. We know a little about the disposal of former Jewish property in Gascony because of a reference to a confiscated synagogue.[203] However the Gascon expulsion was far from a complete ejection of all Edward's Jewish subjects there. On 14 July 1292 Edward wrote, from Berwick on Tweed, to John de Havering, seneschal of Gascony, and Iterius de Engolisma, constable of Bordeaux, concerning a Jew called Boneonus that 'we do not wish that any Jews delay in our duchy or dominions, we enjoin you and entrust you to expel Boneonus from our duchy of Aquitaine, and do not permit him or any other Jews to remain in the aforesaid duchy any longer'.[204] Some Frenchmen took the edict of expulsion as a signal that the killing of Jews was open season and several of Edward's subjects took the law into their own hands. Richard and John of Boulogne were outlawed on 29 June 1294, 'for the recent killing of certain Jews done upon the seas'. They were later pardoned.[205] Other Christians were also guilty of robbery of certain Jews.[206] Some Jews were able to shelter in various areas of the duchy. As late as April 1305 Edward wrote to his seneschal: 'we entrust that all Jews be totally exiled from our duchy when you see these letters. I do not permit them to remain or delay anymore.'[207] In 1306 some Jews paid £1,250 to remain in Bordeaux and Bordelais. As late as 1310 there were still Jews in the province.[208]

There were other problems involved in expelling the Jews from Gascony. A letter from the French king, Philip IV, written on 30

---

[201] *Rôles Gascons 1273–1290*, pp. 329, 358, 457.

[202] Richardson 1960, pp. 225–6; Prestwich 1980, pp. 201–2.

[203] Cuttino 1975, p. 42: in Saintonge the treasurer of Gascony, Peter Tarzati, had appropriated the house which had been the synagogue of the Jews without permission of the king.

[204] *Rôles Gascons 1290–1307*, pp. 43, 55.   [205] *Ibid.*, pp. 187–8, 191.

[206] *Ibid.*, p. 212.   [207] Trabut-Cussac 1972, p. 313; Cuttino 1975, pp. 84–5.

[208] Cuttino 1975, pp. 689–90.

August 1288 in Paris, throws light upon the complications of what was really a large-scale local expulsion. The letter was addressed to Robert Burnell, Edward's Chancellor. In it Philip complained that some of his Jews had been arrested and their goods seized in the recent banishment of the Jews from Edward's jurisdiction. He asked respectfully that Burnell should make an inquiry and report back to him as to what value of goods had been taken. Clearly, Philip wanted restitution.[209] This was still a problem in January 1308, when Thomas Cobham, as English envoy to France, made a request that Philip answer certain petitions concerning the handing over of Jewish goods and 'delinquents'.[210]

It is naturally as difficult to piece together all the motives for the Jewish expulsion from Gascony as indeed it is for the English Expulsion. However, what is clear is that in Gascony the decision to expel the Jews was made by Edward himself. Certainly it must have coloured his view of the Jewish problem in England. What is perhaps also significant is that many of Edward's officials who were with him in Gascony not only had seen expulsion at work but had taken part in it. Both William de Louth and William de Marchia, later to become Treasurer of England in April 1290, travelled with the king while he was in Gascony. The royal cofferer, Walter Langton, was responsible for accounting for the goods confiscated from the Gascon Jewry. William Burnell and the Provincial of the Dominican order in England, Brother William de Hotham, were also there and even carried letters for the wardrobe to John de Reda concerning the monies which had been confiscated from the Gascon Jews.[211]

In the wake of the Gascon expulsion there were two other events in France which might well have had some relevance to Edward's final decision and to anti-Jewish feeling in England. At Troyes, in April 1288, thirteen Jews were put to death by the Inquisition for allegedly having killed a Christian. In 1290 the Jews of Paris were accused of host desecration.[212] Such events must certainly have influenced the rulers of France and might similarly have influenced Charles II, the king of Sicily. In October 1288, after long negotiations and the promise of a large amount of money, secured on the word of Edward I, Charles was finally freed after almost four years of captivity. He immediately visited France and Italy and then returned to discussions with the major lay and ecclesiastical figures in his French counties. Soon after his release Charles II expelled the Jews from his own large counties of Maine and Anjou.[213] Professor Robert Chazan has examined these French

[209] *Ibid.*, pp. 4, 519–20.   [210] *Ibid.*, pp. 367–8.
[211] Byerly 1986, pp. viii–xii.   [212] Chazan 1973, pp. 180–2; Jordan 1989, pp. 190–4.
[213] Powicke 1962, pp. 282–4; Prestwich 1988, pp. 305, 318–26; Chazan 1973, pp. 182–6.

expulsions of 1289 in great detail.[214] Here it seems easier to supply a motive and Chazan himself emphasises 'popular clamour for expulsion and profit'.[215]

Charles II's Edict of Expulsion, issued on 8 December 1289, shows that the final decision to expel his Jews had some popular support and was taken in consultation with 'the bishops and many clerics and also with the faithful counts and princes and with others worthy of faith'.[216] In his edict Charles was quick to point out that he had 'enjoyed extensive temporal benefit' from the Jews but that he naturally would prefer not to 'fill our coffers with the mammon of iniquity'.[217] Yet Charles' coffers did not go empty: in Maine and Anjou a grateful people were to provide a pre-arranged tax in return for the expulsion: 'it has been conceded to us freely and without force that we ought to receive from each hearth three shillings once only and from each wage earner six pence once only, as some recompense for the profit which we lose through the expulsion of the aforesaid Jews'.[218]

Charles insisted that his expulsion was to be complete, utter and irrevocable. Professor Chazan believed that the concept of an expulsion tax was a striking innovation.[219] This idea was immediately taken up by Philip the Fair, and by the early 1290s he had made the same arrangements with the citizens of Saintonge and Poitou. On 20 May 1290 the Jews were expelled from Saint-Pierre sur Dives.[220] If Charles of Anjou could emulate Edward's banishment of the Jews from Gascony and indeed raise a tax in return, then surely Edward I must have been aware of the possibilities of ridding himself of his English Jews. He had already expelled the Jews from Gascony and had not benefited from the proceeds; it would be far easier to expel a community from an island and to hope for a tax to be voted in return.

Therefore the English Expulsion cannot be seen in isolation from smaller expulsions on the continent.[221] It must be regarded as part of a general movement in western Christendom against the Jews by monarchs who knew the views of the Church, the mendicants and the papacy and were aware of what was happening elsewhere. They were also rulers who knew the prospects of enhanced popularity among their subjects at a time when the canonical ideal of the Cross, and of purging internal infidelity, was at a height. Professor Jordan has observed that 'in location after location on the borderlands of France, princes and their

---

[214] Chazan 1973, p. 184; see Appendix III.
[215] See Appendix IV; Chazan 1973, pp. 185; 1980, pp. 314–17.
[216] See Appendix IV; Chazan 1980, pp. 314–17.   [217] *Ibid.*   [218] *Ibid.*
[219] Chazan 1973, p. 186; Jordan 1989, pp. 182–3.   [220] Chazan 1973, pp. 183, 186.
[221] Menache 1985; 1987; Stacey 1990, pp. 1–2;

counsellors were abandoning the policy, dear to St Louis, of attempting to coerce Jews to convert by means of economic and social disabilities and were offering them instead a starker choice: convert or depart'.[222] In France another local expulsion took place, on 14 September 1290, when the bailiff of Cotentin decided that the Jews might not settle in the town of St Pair.[223] While in England, in November 1290, Edward I decreed a total banishment of Jews from his realms, and as one writer, echoing a conciliar decree, has observed, 'these rejected outcasts were doomed to disperse themselves, in different ways, to quit England forever and to perish by eternal misery in other lands until they should be entirely cut off'.[224] On 16 February 1291 Philip IV of France ordered the expulsion of those Jews recently arrived from England.[225] On 1 April 1291 this was followed by Philip's expulsion of all Jews from the villages and small towns of France.[226] This particular expulsion seems to have been due to ecclesiastical pressure on the supposed grounds that the rural populace might easily be seduced by Judaism.[227] However some Jews did stay in France, if only until 1306.[228]

What had been started in Gascony in May 1287 by Edward I out of piety and as a demonstration of his thanks to God for his recovery at Blanquefort was therefore perhaps the real catalyst which led to the Expulsion of the Jews from England.[229] Although there are no letters or agreements between the king of France, Charles of Anjou and Edward concerning expulsion it is quite clear from the overall chronology and the prevailing attitudes of Church and people alike that the answer to de Bloissiers Tovey's question, posed in the eighteenth century, is simply that the time was right.[230] Yet the explanation for the English Expulsion is not monocausal and must be seen in a broader context. As Professor Stow, when considering the motives for European expulsions, has observed, 'Religiosity, social perceptions and political aims had become intertwined.'[231] The reasons for the Expulsion of the Jews from England are undoubtedly multifarious. Edward I clearly and deliberately made the decision which was to lead to the final solution of the Jewish problem in England. The actual Expulsion of the Jews may have been exploited by Edward I, as Professor Robert Stacey and others have observed, to help persuade a grateful people to vote a new form of taxation, just as Charles of Anjou had done almost a year before.

---

[222] Jordan 1989, p. 180. [223] Chazan 1973, p. 183.
[224] *Concilia*, vol. II, p. 180; Lincoln Public Library, Ross Collection.
[225] Chazan 1973, p. 183; Jordan 1989, p. 183. [226] Chazan 1973, p. 183. [227] *Ibid.*
[228] Schwarzfuchs 1967; Brown 1991.
[229] Salzman 1968, pp. 84–5; Trabut-Cussac 1972, p. 85; Prestwich 1988, p. 328.
[230] Jordan 1989, p. 182; Tovey 1738, pp. 133–4. [231] Stow 1992a, p. 290.

However, the English Expulsion was a symbiosis of previous develop-ments, primarily perhaps because of the Jews' own failure to convert and the fact that they still practised usury and the evolution of a distinct change in the prevailing political and religious climate during the preceding decades. The English Expulsion had been conceived at an earlier date than 1290 itself.

Appendix 1

PLACES OF JEWISH SETTLEMENT, 1262–1290

Toponymns in connection with Jewish names obviously present many problems of interpretation. Clearly a Jewess called Floria of Northampton who married Rabbi Elias Menahem of London sometime after 1275 kept her toponymic name when she moved to London. As Professor Barrie Dobson has observed, the toponym which connects Moses and the place of Colton in Yorkshire is very difficult to interpret. Similarly instances of Samuel of Loun/Lohun, Isaac of Caleys, Isaac of Provyns, Isaac fil Jacob of Custances present as many problems as the occurrence of Isaac of Paris or even Josce of Germany! There are many toponyms connected with Jewish names such as Brodsworth, Patripol, Pavely, Doggestrete, Kingston, Senlis and Haverhill which may have indicated residence at one time or another. Places where several Jews took the toponym as part of their name naturally make it more convincing as a probable place of residence.

Where there is proof of a Jew being resident this has been noted in the table. Clearly an *archa* scrutiny denotes settlement. The holding of property may or may not denote settlement. References like the one to Carshalton in Surrey could just indicate the place the particular Jew was travelling through or even fleeing to when he was arrested. In cases such as this, quite obviously, settlement cannot be proved.

Place	Dates	Source
Abergavenny	1275	*PREJ2*, p. 278, resident
Alcester, Warwick	1277	*PREJ3*, p. 270, resident
Andover	1281	*CPR*, pp. 428–9, land in
Arundel	1272	Rigg, p. 69, resident
Basingstoke	1273	*PREJ2*, p. 104, resident
Bedford	1262	*Archa* scrutinies
	1290	
Berkhamstead	1274	*PREJ2*, p. 144, resident

(cont.)

Place	Date	Source
Beverley	1275	*PREJ4*, p. 25, toponym
Bosworth	1279	*PREJ5*, p. 177, 182, toponym
Bottisham	1272	Rigg, p. 68, resident
Bread Street, Gloucestershire	1275	*PREJ2*, p. 278; *PREJ3*, p. 319, resident
Bridgnorth	1274	*CCR*, p. 130, resident
Bridgwater	1276	*PREJ3*, p. 87
Bridport	1265	*CPR*, p. 442, resident
Bristol	1262 1275/6 (lost) 1290	*Archa* scrutinies.
Brodsworth, Yorks.	1278	*PREJ3*, pp. 14, 18, 135; PRO E/101/250/12
Buckingham	1268	*PREJ1*, p. 190, toponym
Burford	1275	PRO E/101/249/32; *PREJ4*, p. 119, toponym
Caerleon	1262	PRO E/101/249/10, toponym
Calne	1278	*PREJ5*, p. 123, toponym
Cambridge	1262–1275	*Archa* scrutinies; local expulsion
Canterbury	1262 1275/6 1290	*Archa* scrutinies
Carshalton, Surrey	1276	*PREJ3*, p. 124
Caversham	1275	*CCR*, p. 260; *PREJ4*, p. 131, resident
Chesterton, near Cambridge	1277	*CCR*, p. 370, resident
Chichester	1272	Rigg, p. 69, resident
Chippenham	1262	PRO E/101/249/10, toponym
Chipping Campden	1262	PRO E/101/249/10; Hillaby 1990a, p. 110, resident
Clare	1277	*PREJ3*, p. 302, toponym
Colchester	1262 1275/6 1290	*Archa* scrutinies
Colton	1275	*PREJ3*, p. 94, toponym
Coventry	1290	*CFR*, 2, p. 388, houses in
Cricklade	1272	Rigg, p. 69, PRO E/101/249/10, E/101/249/32, resident
Dartford	1277	*PREJ4*, p. 177, toponym
Derby	1277	*PREJ3*, p. 315, toponym
Devizes	1275/6 1290	Rigg, p. 69, *Archa* scrutinies, resident
Doncaster	1262	PRO E/101/249/10, E/101/249/16, E/401/1582, toponym
Dorchester	1277	*CCR* p. 382, resident

Appendix I

(*cont.*)

Place	Dates	Source
Dorking	1274	*PREJ2*, p. 209, toponym
Dover	1272–4	Communicated by Dr Rokeah; PRO E/352/67 mem 3
Dunmow	1277	*PREJ4*, p. 152, toponym
Dunwich	1275	*PREJ3*, p. 43, resident
Evesham	1262	PRO E/101/249/10, toponym
Exeter	1262 1275/6 1290	*Archa* scrutinies
Fairford	1275	PRO E/101/250/11, toponym
Farningham, Kent	1274	*PREJ2*, p. 186–87, resident
Faversham	pre-1275	VCH, *Kent*, II, p. 47, resident
Fisherton Anger	1275	Pugh 1978, p. 38, resident
Gloucester	1262 1275/6 (lost)	*Archa* scrutinies
Grantham	1278	PRO E/101/249/4
Grimsby	1276	*PREJ3*, p. 192, toponym
Guildford	1272	Rigg, p. 69; *PREJ4*, p. 157, 180, resident
Handborough	1277	*PREJ5*, p. 19, toponym
Hatcham, near Deptford	1272	Rigg, p. 69, resident
Hedon	1272	WAM no. 6831; *PREJ4*, p. 26, toponym
Hendon	1276	*PREJ3*, p. 94, toponym
Hereford	1262 1275/6 1290	*Archa* scrutinies
Highworth	1277	Mundill 1991, p. 139 resident
High Wycombe	1262 1275	PRO E/101/249/10, resident
Holme, North Lincolnshire	1272	Rigg, p. 68, resident
Honiton	1277	*PREJ5*, p. 24, toponym
Hungerford	1276	*PREJ3*, p. 113, toponym
Huntingdon	1272 1290	Rigg, p. 68; PRO E/101/249/10, resident
Ilchester	1274	*PREJ2*, p. 193, toponym
Ipswich	1277 1290 (lost)	*CCR*, p. 376, *Archa*
Kingston	1262	PRO E/101/249/10, toponym
Kirton	1278	*PREJ5*, p. 33, toponym
Knaresborough	1262	PRO E/101/249/10, toponym
Lambourne	1262 1275	PRO E/101/249/10, E/101/249/32; *PREJ5*, p. 163, toponym
Lewes	1272	Rigg, p. 69, resident
Lincoln	1262 1275/6 1290	*Archa* scrutinies

288

(cont.)

Place	Dates	Source
London	1262	*Archa* scrutinies
	1290 (lost)	
Linton, Cambridgeshire	1279	Clapham 1933, pp. 198–9, resident
Luton	1262	PRO E/101/249/10, toponym
Maldon	1275	*PREJ2*, p. 278, resident
Market Harborough	1273	*CCR*, p. 70, toponym
Marlborough	1262	PRO E/101/249/10, *Archa*
Marlow	1277	*PREJ4*, p. 168, 192, toponym
Much Markle, Herefordshire	1290	PRO Just 1/303, m 65 (63), dorse
Newbury	1276	*PREJ3*, p. 142, toponym
Newmarket	1272	*PREJ1*, p. 279, toponym
Newport	1262	PRO E/101/249/10, toponym
Norwich	1262 1275/6 (lost)	*Archa* scrutinies
	1290	
Northampton	1275/6	*Archa* scrutinies
	1290 (lost)	
Nottingham	1262 1290	*Archa* scrutinies
Oakham	1275	*PREJ4*, p. 25, toponym
Ospringe	1266	*PREJ1*, p. 134, resident
Oxford	1262 1275/6	*Archa* scrutinies
	1290	
Rayleigh	1275	Rigg, p. 82, resident
Retford	1277	*CCR*, p. 389, resident
Rising	1262	PRO E/101/249/10, toponym
Rochester	1262	PRO E/101/249/10;
	1276	*CCR*, p. 260, resident
Romney	1262	PRO E/101/249/10, toponym
Romsey	1266	*CPR*, p. 613, expulsion from
Rotherham	1275	*PREJ4*, p. 17, toponym
Royston	1277	*CCR*, p. 382, resident
Rye	1266	*PREJ1*, p. 136, toponym
Sandwich	1273	*PREJ2*, p. 13, resident
Scarborough	1275	*PREJ4*, p. 17, toponym
Seaford	1272	Rigg, p. 69, resident
Shoreham	1270	*PREJ1*, p. 265, toponym
Sittingbourne	1266	*PREJ1*, p. 134, resident
Somerton, Devon	1275	*PREJ3*, p. 1, toponym
Southampton	1274	*PREJ2*, p. 119;
	1275	*CCR*, p. 259, resident
Southwark	1262	PRO E/101/249/10, toponym
Stamford	1262	*Archa* scrutiny;
	1274	*CCR*, p. 102, synagogue resident
Staundon	1275	*CCR*, p. 213, toponym

(cont.)

Place	Dates	Source
Sudbury	1275	*PREJ3*, p. 302, *Archa*
Tewkesbury	1277	*PREJ3*, p. 319, resident
Thrapston	1275	*CCR*, p. 259, resident
	1277	*PREJ4*, p. 167, 191, toponym
Tickhill	1275	*PREJ3*, p. 15, 67, toponym
Wakefield	1275	*PREJ4*, p. 17, toponym
Wallingford	1262	PRO E/101/249/10, toponym, resident
Warwick	1262 (lost)	*Archa*;
	1275 (lost)	*CCR*, p. 244
	1290 (lost)	
Weobley, Herefordshire	1285	PRO E/101/250/5, toponym
Wilton	1262	*Archa* scrutinies;
	1275 (lost)	*Archa* scrutinies;
	1276 (lost)	*CCR*, p. 341
Winchcombe	1278	*PREJ5*, p. 69, toponym
Winchelsea	1273	*CCR*, p. 50, removal
Winchester	1262	*Archa* scrutiny
	1275/6 (lost)	
	1290	
Windsor	1278	*PREJ5*, p. 61;
	1285	*CCR*, p. 241, expelled
Worcester	1262	*Archa* scrutiny
	1290 (lost)	
York	1262	*Archa* scrutiny
	1275/6	
	1290 (lost)	

THE STATUTE OF THE JEWRY, 1275

Les Estatutz de la Jewerie originally appeared in Anglo-Norman. There are various versions other than this one from Statutes of the Realm. The Statute was probably first mooted at Westminster in the Common Council of the Realm at Easter 1275. It was clearly promulgated by Michaelmas 1275. *Source: Statutes of the Realm*, vol. i, pp. 220–1. Other copies exist in the British Library (BL Additional Manuscripts 15,667, 32,085, 32,085, 38,821).

Forasmuch as the King hath seen that divers Evils, and the disheriting of the good Men of his Land have happened by the Usuries which the Jews have made in Time past, and that divers Sins have followed thereupon; albeit he and his Ancestors have received much benefit from the Jewish People in all Time past; nevertheless for the Honour of God and the common benefit of the People, the King hath ordained and established, That from henceforth no Jew shall lend any Thing at Usury, either upon Land, or upon Rent, or upon other Thing: And that no Usuries shall run in Time coming from the Feast
10 of Saint Edward last past. Notwithstanding, the Covenants before made shall be observed, saving that the Usuries shall cease. But all those who owe Debts to Jews upon Pledges of Moveables, shall acquit them between this and Easter; if not they shall be forfeited. And if any Jew shall lend at Usury contrary to this Ordinance, the King will not lend his Aid, neither by himself nor his Officers, for the recovery of his Loan; but will punish him at his discretion for the Offence, and will do justice to the Christian that he may obtain his Pledge again.

  And that the Distresses for Debts due unto Jews from henceforth
20 shall not be so grievous, but that the Moiety of the Lands and Chattels of the Christians shall remain for their Maintenance; and that

no Distress shall be made for a Jewry Debt; upon the Heir of the Debtor named in the Jew's Deed, nor upon any other Person holding the Land that was the Debtor's, before that the Debt be put in Suit and allowed in Court.

And if the Sheriff or other Bailiff, by the King's Command hath to give Seisin to a Jew, be it one or more, for their Debt, of Chattels or Land to the Value of the Debt, the Chattels shall be valued by the Oaths of good Men, and be delivered to the Jew or Jews, or to their Proxy, to the Amount of the Debt; and if the Chattels be not
30 sufficient, the Lands shall be extended by the same Oath before the Delivery of Seisin to the Jew or Jews, to each in his due Proportion; so that it may be certainly known that the Debt is quit, and the Christian may have his Land again: Saving always to the Christian the Moiety of his Land and Chattels for his maintenance as aforesaid, and the Chief mansion.

And if any Moveables hereafter be found in Possession of a Jew, and any Man shall sue him, the Jew shall be allowed his Warranty, if he may have it; and if not, let him answer therefore: So that he be not herein otherwise privileged than a Christian.

40 AND that all Jews shall dwell in the King's own Cities and Boroughs, where the Chests of Chirographs of Jewry are wont to be: And that each Jew after he shall be Seven Years old, shall wear a Badge on his outer Garment; that is to say, in the Form of Two Tables joined, of yellow Felt, of the Length of Six Inches, and of the Breadth of Three Inches. And that each one, after he shall be Twelve Years old, pay Three pence yearly at Easter of Tax to the King, whose Bond-man he is; and this shall hold place as well for a Woman as a Man.

And that no Jew shall have Power to infeoff another, whether Jew
50 or Christian, of Houses, Rents, or Tenements that he now hath, nor to alien in any other Manner, nor to make Acquittance to any Christian of his Debt, without the especial Licence of the King, until the King shall have otherwise ordained therein.

AND, Forasmuch as it is the will and sufferance of Holy Church, that they may live and be preserved, the King taketh them under his Protection, and granteth them his Peace; and willeth that they be safely preserved and defended by his Sheriffs and other Bailiffs, and by his Liege Men; and commandeth that none shall do them harm, or damage, or wrong, in their Bodies or in their Goods, moveable or
60 immoveable; and that they shall neither plead nor be impleaded in any Court, nor be challenged or troubled in any Court, except in the Court of the King, whose Bond-men they are. And that none shall

owe Obedience, or Service, or Rent, except to the King, or his Bailiffs in his Name; unless it be for their Dwellings which they now hold by paying Rent; saving the Right of Holy Church.

AND the King granteth unto them that they may gain their living by lawful Merchandise and their Labour; and that they may have Intercourse with Christians, in order to carry on lawful Trade by selling and buying. But that no Christian, for this cause or any other,
70 shall dwell among them. And the King willeth that they shall not by reason of their Merchandise be put to Lot or Scot, nor in Taxes with the Men of the Cities or Boroughs where they abide; for that they are taxable to the King as his Bondmen, and to none other but the King.

Moreover the King granteth unto them that they may buy Houses and Curtilages, in the Cities and Boroughs where they abide, so that they hold them in chief of the King; saving unto the Lords of the Fee their Services due and accustomed. And that they may take and buy Farms or Land for the Term of Ten Years or less, without taking
80 Homages or Fealties, or such sort of Obedience from Christians, and without having Advowsons of Churches; and that they may be able to gain their living in the World, if they have not the Means of Trading, or cannot Labour; and this Licence to take Lands to farm shall endure to them only for Fifteen Years from this Time forward.

ARTICLES TOUCHING THE JEWRY

The *Chapitles Tuchaunz la Gyuerie* were first printed in Gross 1887, pp. 219–29. This version is from Rigg 1905, pp. liv–lxi. They were originally copied from BL Additional Manuscripts, 32,085, folios 120–1 which were purchased at Sotheby's in June 1883. In the manuscript they were wrongly dated to 1294. Gross identified the handwriting on the manuscript as dating from the early part of the fourteenth century. He also noted the abrupt termination of the text and thought that despite the final 'explicit' the document was incomplete. In an as yet unpublished paper, Dr Paul Brand claims that the draft statute which follows the articles differs in date from the articles themselves. The articles seem to belong to the late 1270s.

Touching Jews who falsify and clip coins, and receivers who buy from them silver in plates fused from the clippings.

Touching Christians and Jews who give and receive in exchange good money for clipped money.

Touching charters, letters patent or tallies, which though made in favour of Jews are outside the Chest, and charters kept outside the Chest by chirographers for more than ten days.

Touching Jews who receive stolen cloth moist with blood or
10 ornaments of Holy Church.

Touching Jews practising usury since the Statutes made, etc.

Touching Houses of Jews and rents sold by them without license of our Lord the King, etc.

Touching discharge of Jews arrested or kept in prison by sheriffs for trespass against the peace or for coin clipping, without warrant of our Lord the King.

Touching sheriffs and other bailiffs taking amercements from Jews above the sum of 2s., etc.

20   Touching treasure trove underground in houses of Jews, or elsewhere, after the death of Jews.

Touching chattels of Jews concealed after their death, of which the
King has not the third part.

Touching Jews for whose chattels and houses no fine has been
made within a year after their death, etc.

Touching Jews having carnal intercourse with Christian women,
etc.

Touching converts to the Christian Faith who afterwards revert to
the Jewish Law.

Touching Jews outlawed and recieved in the Jewry, etc.

30   Touching Jews who have Christian servants couchant and levant
with them.

Whereas loans at usury by Jews of our realm were wont to be made
and allowed in the time of our ancestors, Kings of England, and our
ancestors had large profits thereby as issues of our Jewry, and We, led
by the love of God and more devoutly mindful of the way of Holy
Church, did ordain that all Jews whosoever of our realm that had
viciously lived by such loans should from that hour no more
mischievously have recourse to usury or usurious loans of any kind
whatever, but should by other business and licensed trading seek their
40   living and have their sustenance, especially since by favour of Holy
Church they are suffered to abide and live with Christians; but they,
nevertheless, did afterwards, blinded by the malice of their hearts,
convert to an evil purpose that which We had enacted with sound
intent, and by a new and wicked device, under colour of trading and
good contracts and covenants, have dealings with Christians by bonds
and divers instruments which remain in the hands of the Jews, and in
which they stipulate for twice, thrice, or four times as much as they
part with to Christians in one and the same transaction of debt or
contract, avoiding the use of the term 'usury' by means of penalties,
50   whence only confusion, and the ruin of a great part of the people,
and the ultimate disherison of many can ensue. We therefore, to the
intent to oust the wicked practices of such Jews thus discovered, and
their pains and usuries likewise discovered, do now, touching grants
and contracts henceforth to be made between Christians and Jews,
ordain on this wise: that is to say, that in future Jews receive from
Christians on a loan of 20s. no more than ½ mark, or 8s. 8d. a year,
and for 40s. 1 mark or 17s. 4d, and for more, more, and for less, less,
as 'purvenue' by way of rent of contract and debt; and that the loan
be made by writing between the contracting parties by the hand of a

60   clerk specially assigned and sworn for the purpose, and to be indented, the part from which the seal is pendent to be placed in the Chirograph-Chest, the middle part to remain with the Jew, and the third part with the Christian, and the tenor in brief to be as follows:- Know all that I, so and so, owe such or such a Jew so much, payable on such and such a day. And if I shall make default, I grant that the amount be made and levied from my goods and chattels, and from the issues of my lands, in whose hands soever they may be. And thereto I bind myself and my heirs. In witness whereof, &c. Given, &c. Which writing is to be placed in the Chirograph-Chest under

70   the keys of three lawful Christian chirographers and two Jews specially sworn for the purpose. And that which is to be recieved, as aforesaid, by the Jews shall be only for the space of three years from the date of the said contract, nor shall the Jew after the said three years be able to demand or claim aught from a Christian, except only the principal debt and what arises from what maybe due in the meantime, i.e. during the said three years of the debt's duration, on account of the loan or contract before authorised; so nevertheless that the Jew may after three years aforesaid demand his debt with all that arises therefrom in the time past, and recover it in full by law;

80   provided that if the Christian be unable, or perchance unwilling, to pay the said debt within the three years aforesaid, then the same Jew may also extend the time of payment of the debt with its exact amount, according to the form and condition of the former contract, for the space of a year next following the period for which the debt runs, and no more. And should it so happen that Jew or Jewess make loan or contract with any against the statutory form aforesaid or against this our Statute, let him or her be at the mercy of our Lord the King touching life and limb, and all of his or her goods and chattels.

90   It is further provided, that no writing of loan or contract be in future made between Christian and Jew save in the names of one Christian and one Jew; so that no Jew may be able to demand or claim aught upon that contract, except that Jew with whom the contract is made and whose name is in the writing aforesaid, and that the Christian who contracts with any for that debt answer only to that Jew whose name is in the writing, or to his heir.

    Also for the future no Jew is allowed to grant or sell his debt to Christian or Jew without special licence of the King.

    Also let no Jew lend money to any other Jew to lend to Christians,

100   unless it so be that our Lord the King may be certified of their chattels; and should they do so, from that hour let the goods and

chattels of such Jews so lending be wholly forfeit to the King, and their bodies none the less be at his mercy.

Also, whereas our Lord has in time past had grievous loss in respect of the recovery of the third part of the goods of deceased Jews and the assessment of talliage upon them; whereas also Christians have lost their gages by reasons of contracts of loan privily made between them and Jews; it is provided, that no Jew or Jewess for the future lend to Christians on any gage more than the sum of 20s., except in presence of a chirographer and a clerk especially assigned and sworn for the purpose, so that the gages and loan aforesaid may be plainly and openly enrolled by a clerk in the view and with the attestation of a chirographer. And let the roll remain in the keeping of the one under the seal of the other. And let the loan made on gage after such secret manner be forfeit, and the penalty have the same extent as aforesaid.

Be it also specially and plainly provided, that the chirographers and their clerks sworn to enrol the gages and loans aforesaid do not deal harshly in discharge of the duties laid upon them in this regard, when and by whomsoever they be required to perform them; and that the Christian chirographers take nothing for entering the writing, but take 3d. on its withdrawal; the Jewish chirographers, however, are to take nothing either on the entry or the withdrawal; and let the clerks take 2d. for penning the three parts aforesaid of the writing

Also, whereas Jews wickedly conceal and deny that they have recieved gages delivered to them privily, no Christian witness being present, and when they are impleaded thereof in the King's Court they, by virtue of the custom hitherto observed, do all purge themselves by their own oath of the said receipt, and depart quit, whereby the Christians have had grievous damage and loss; therefore it is provided, that if there should be plaint or plea in process between Christians and Jews in such case, to wit, touching a loan made before this Statute, and also in future touching a sum less than 20s., the Jew shall not be believed on his own oath; but let inquest be had of the truth of the matter by Christians and Jews, unless the Christian be able lawfully by Christians and Jews to prove the delivery of his gage, for then it shall rest on his proof.

Also, whereas in inquests made or to be made by Christians and Jews of pleas and plaints brought touching debt and trespass laid in the Jewry, the custom has hitherto been to admit as jurors as well Christians as Jews and in equal numbers, who are hardly able to agree, whereby justice is often delayed and damage thence results to the parties; it is provided, that when there is such discord arisen between Christians and Jews placed on the inquest, the matter be tried and adjudged by several lawful Christians of known credit, and also, if need be, by several Jews, according to the discretion and direction of the Justices. And let it rest on the verdict of several or the more part of them.

150 And moreover, whereas the Chirograph-Chests have long been closed and sealed by command of our Lord the King, whereby Christians cannot yet have their charters of which they have had acquittance, it is provided, that these Chests be brought by the chirographers to London on a day and to a place certain, and be there opened and searched, and that the debts therein found be cleared, and the charters which are acquit be delivered to the Christians quit and cancelled, and the other charters which are in the same Chests be placed in a chest by themselves where our Lord the King and his Council shall ordain.

160 It now remains to speak of writings obligatory that remain with the Jews in their custody.

FINIS

Appendix IV

CHARLES OF ANJOU'S EDICT OF
EXPULSION, 1289

Charles of Anjou emphasises the losses which he would suffer as a result of his pious action. He indicates that the deficit will be made up by a set of taxes which the leading men of the country have agreed to. The technique of an 'expulsion tax' is, as Professor Chazan observed, new. Chazan copied the order from Pierre Rangeard, *Histoire de l'université d'Angers*, vol. III, pp. 27–31, Angers, 1877. *Source:* Chazan 1980, pp. 313–17.

Charles II by the grace of God king of Jerusalem, prince of Sicily and of Apulia and of Capua, count of Achea and Anjou and Forcalquier:

We have given notice to all by the contents of the present letter that we have considered the fine words of sacred authority, in which it is warned that a mouse or a viper or a serpent in the lap or a fire in the bosom tend to confer unjust retribution on their hosts. When careful investigation has been made, we readily recognized the condition and situation of the counties of Anjou and Maine, which by divine will are subject to our authority. We have ascertained the
10 state of the aforesaid land and have found that it is subject to many enormities and crimes odious to God and abhorrent to the Christian faith. In many locales of that land, numerous Jews, enemies of the life-giving Cross and of all Christianity, dwelling randomly and publicly among Christians and deviating from the way of truth, subvert perfidiously many of both sexes who are considered adherents of the Christian faith. They seem to subvert all whom they can. They despoil these Christians of their movable and immovable goods by their devious deceits and by the endless abyss of usury, and thus they wickedly force these Christians to beg for alms. What is most horrible
20 to consider, they evilly cohabit with many Christian maidens.
Since it is our responsibility to purge the territories subjected to us

299

of evil men, we, pierced by the arrow of compassion, have consulted about these matters with the reverend father the bishop and with many clerics and with our faithful barons and nobles and with others deserving of trust, sometimes directly and sometimes through our faithful deputies, so that we might have the strength to overcome powerful maladies and to uproot totally the above-examined frauds from those places. Indeed it pleases our majesty, we believe with the assent of God, that we should provide for our aforesaid counties and
30 for those living within the confines of those counties by an expulsion of the aforesaid Jews and of their descendants.

Although we enjoy much temporal profit from the aforesaid Jews, we prefer to provide for the peace of our subjects rather than to fill our coffers with the mammon of iniquity, especially since by the loss of temporal goods spiritual gains are achieved. Therefore, exhibiting zeal for the life-giving Cross, we have, for the honour of God and the peace of the aforesaid areas, expelled and ordered expelled from our aforesaid counties of Anjou and Maine all Jews, male and female, adults and young people, children and infants, of whatever sex or
40 condition they might have been born and raised. We have expelled them from all areas of these counties not only for the present but for all times, both for our time as well as that of our successors upon whom the said counties may happen to devolve.

Thus they are prohibited from residing or living henceforth in the aforesaid places, both those already alive and those yet to be born . . . We shall hold contracts, if they make them, null. Insofar as it pertains to us and relates to our jurisdiction, they shall be prohibited from entering the aforesaid areas or crossing through them. We order all our bailiffs and vicars and officials by the firmest adjuration and under
50 threat of the loss of grace that, after this letter has been seen, should they find any Jew in any of the aforesaid places, they must seize him and expel him immediately. We grant and extend irrevocable authority to all our barons, knights, judges and others exercising high and low jurisdiction in the aforesaid counties that, if, after this, they find any remnant of the Jewish sect, of whatever sex or condition, in any areas of the aforesaid counties subject to them, they shall seize him or her or them, shall despoil them utterly, and shall drive them out. We wish and demand, insofar as it pertains to us and our jurisdiction, that their contracts, drawn up in the said places, shall
60 henceforth be executed. If a common man or a rustic finds a Jew or a Jewess dwelling in the aforementioned places and lacks jurisdiction or authority, we wish and grant and extend nonetheless authority for seizing the aforesaid Jews at any time in the future, for despoiling

them, and for bringing them along with their goods before the local judge. He shall immediately expel these Jews from the said counties, properly beaten without the inflicting of wounds, and shall order and dispose of the said goods with the advice of our official.

In order that the sincerity of our intention show forth more openly and more clearly and lest fraud wickedly be perpetrated on our munificence, we decree and order that the aforesaid expulsion be extended to all Lombards, Cahorsins, and other foreigners who engage in public usury without public contracts and who are properly considered usurers. We expel from the aforesaid places now and forever those persons, both those already living as well as those to be born subsequently. We order that they be expelled in the future both by our successors and by all barons, knights and nobles of the aforesaid counties, with no other permission required of us or of our heirs. Their goods shall be turned over to the lords of those places. If the lords of those places prove negligent or remiss in this regard, we reserve the confiscation of goods to our authority.

Since, according to the prophetic gift of the Holy Spirit, all, from the most significant to the most important, pursue desire, we fear lest – Holy Spirit forbid! – any of our successors be moved to recall the aforesaid persons because of the lure of wicked mammon. We wish and oblige ourselves and all our successors in those places not to recall any of the aforesaid persons and not to allow the dwelling or settling or advent of the aforesaid Jews, as has been stipulated above in regard to these Jews.

With the assent of our reverend fathers in Christ, Nicholas, bishop of Angers and Durrand, bishop of Nantes, of the chapters of Le Mans and Poitiers and Saint Martin of Tours, and of the abbots, Hospitaliers, Templars, barons, counts, knights, and others worthy of trust who live and dwell within the confines of those counties, it has been conceded to us freely and without duress that we ought to receive from each hearth three shillings once only and from each wage earner six pence once only, as some recompense for the profit which we lose through the aforesaid expulsions. This has been granted according to agreements made between them and our faithful Maurice, lord of Craon, our seneschal and vicar in the aforesaid counties. We note that they do this freely and without duress. We wish that, by this act, no prejudice be generated against them, even if they are commoners, and that no other right be acquired thereby by us or our successors of further seeking or levying hearth taxes beyond these taxes and dues which we have and should have according to the custom of the aforesaid counties.

We oblige ourselves, our heirs, and our successors to return to the
bishops, chapters, abbots, Hospitaliers, Templars, their subjects, and
our subjects, whoever they might be, all the money which we have
from the aforesaid hearth tax and wage earners tax, if it happen that –
110 God forbid! – we or our successors recall any Jew or Jewess to any of
the aforesaid places or consent to the recall, settling, or advent of any
of these, whether he engages in usury or not, or consent to the recall,
settling or advent of the Lombards, Cahorsins, or other foreigners,
when it is clear to us or our successors that they publicly engage in
usury . . . We wish that we and our successors be compelled to
observe all this by our superiors, even by financial loss. We agree
that, if it should happen that these stipulations be broken by our
successors, by instituting a recall of the aforesaid persons to any of the
aforesaid places, which are all part of our domain, when we or our
120 heirs or our successors or the other aforesaid persons had first
sufficiently warned and reproached, then – God forbid! – the prelates
of the area shall burden all our domain with an ecclesiastical interdict
and they shall continue with that interdict until proper satisfaction has
been made. We agree that none of our superiors shall hear us or our
successors or our officials as claimants, so long as the aforesaid persons
shall remain in the aforesaid places.

In testimony of this matter we have ordered the present letter to be
drawn up and to be strengthened by the appended seal of our
majesty.
130 Given at Angers, 1289 A.D., December 8, in the third indiction, in
the fifth year of our reign.

REFERENCES

MANUSCRIPT SOURCES

Canterbury Cathedral Library and City Record Office

Charta Antiqua manuscripts

A 68: an undated quitclaim in favour of monks of Christ Church.

A 90: an undated quitclaim in favour of monks of Christ Church concerning land at Hildinge.

A 93: an early thirteenth-century quitclaim in favour of the monks of Christ Church concerning land at Gore.

C 1211: letter patent 1291 granting former Jewish properties to Christ Church.

C 1213: letter patent 1291 granting former Jewish properties to Christ Church.

Eastry Correspondence no. IV, 13: advice from Hugh of Kendal to the prior of Christ Church concerning payment for former Jewish properties.

Letter Book II, no. 4: *starrum* including Hebrew version.

Devon Record Office

Crediton Tithe Map 1891.

Exeter Cathedral Muniments

Medieval Deeds nos. 3 and 4: land grant (early thirteenth century). John de Mouton grants land in Bilebirir to Bartholomew Boschet in return for quitting John of 40 marks owing to the Jews.

Medieval Deeds no. 52: land grant from John Quynel, rector of the church at Shobrooke, of land in the High Street, Exeter.

Hereford Cathedral Library and Muniment Room

Indexes of personal names and places in the above compiled by P. E. Morgan, 2 vols. (typescript).

MS 110: release by Emma widow of Hugh le Taillur to Isaac of Worcester of land in Hereford.

References

MS 334: grant from Hugh Freman of Shelwick to Thomas de Geyton of land in return for paying 40 shillings of a debt to Jews.

MS 335: grant from Hugh Freman of Shelwick to Thomas de Geyton of land in return for paying 5 marks of a debt to Jews.

MS 1635: lease for twenty years from Philip of Kynemaresbur to John abbot of St Peter's, Gloucester of the land called Yondercumb in consideration of 10 marks to acquit himself from Jewish debts in Gloucester.

Hereford County Record Office

MS AH81/34: a deed bought in 1981 from the collection of Thomas Phillipps of Middle Hill.

Bailiffs accounts 1272–91.

Lincoln Record Office

D II 80/3/25: land grant from William of Hepham *c.* 1250.

MCD 501 (a copy of PRO C/85/99): a letter from Bishop Richard of Gravesend stating his intention to excommunicate certain Christians for working (some as wet-nurses) for Lincoln Jews.

Foster Library Transcripts: Canon Foster's transcripts of Lincolnshire final concords.

Lincoln Public Library

The Banks Collection: the papers of Sir Joseph Banks (1743–1820).

The Ross Collection: handwritten unpublished Annales of John Ross (1801–70).

London, British Library

Additional MS 24,511: Hugh of Kendal's account.

Additional MS 32,085: copy of the Statute of 1275 and *Chapitles* purchased 1883.

Cotton MS Nero D II: fos. 80 and 183: the other folios are chronicles which refer to the Jews, particularly fos. 179, 183.

Harleian MS no. 957: legend or fable of a Jewish crucifixion of a Christian boy in Bristol.

Lansdowne MSS vol. 826, 4 part 5: papers originally belonging to William Cecil *et al.* Copies of grants of former Jewish property made in 1291 and 1292 to eighty-five recipients.

London, Public Record Office

Chancery

C/47   Miscellanea.

C/85   Significations of Excommunication.

C/146   Ancient Deeds.

C/241   Certificates of Statute Merchant.

C/255   Tower and Rolls Chapel Series Miscellanea.

References

Exchequer of Pleas
E/9   Plea Rolls of the Jews.

Exchequer
E/101   King's Remembrancer, Accounts Various.
E/352   Chancellor's Rolls

Exchequer of Receipt
E/401   Receipt Rolls.

Justices Itinerant
Just. Itin./1   Assize Rolls.

Special Collections
SC.1   Ancient Correspondence.
SC.8   Ancient Petitions.
SC.11   Rentals and Surveys.
SC.3.11 Special Collections Rolls Estate

Nottinghamshire County Record Office

MS M 24/182–8: the Lassman Papers collected by A. Lassman (1864–1944), former secretary of the Nottingham Hebrew Community.

Salisbury Cathedral Library and Muniments

MS 165 fos. 177 a/b: early twelfth-century manuscript written at Old Sarum, 'De puero judeo quem proprius pater pro susceptione corporis et sanguinis Christi in fornacem ardentem projecit'.

Westminster Abbey Muniments

Bonds in which Jew owes Jew: no. 6859
Material pertaining to Canterbury Jewry: nos. 6806, 6812.
Bonds owing to Canterbury Jews: nos. 9015, 9019, 9020, 9021, 9022, 9025, 9026, 9028, 9034, 9036, 9039, 9042, 9043, 9046, 9047, 9057, 9058, 9086, 9088, 9089, 9090, 9091, 9103, 9104, 9105, 9116, 9118, 9119, 9120, 9121, 9123, 9124, 9125, 9126, 9127, 9139, 9156, 9157, 9158, 9159, 9172, 9173, 9174, 9175, 9176.
Material pertaining to Colchester Jewry: nos. 6698, 9017, 9031, 9052, 9056, 9059, 9074, 9076.
Ketubboth: nos. 6797, 6847.
Bonds owing to Lincoln Jews: nos. 9014, 9027, 9032, 9054, 9087, 9092, 9093, 9094, 9095, 9097, 9098, 9100, 9117, 9130, 9131, 9132, 9135, 9137, 9140, 9142, 9143, 9144, 9145, 9146, 9147, 9148, 9150, 9160, 9161, 9162, 9163, 9164, 9165, 9167, 9168, 9169, 9170.
Material pertaining to the Norwich Jewry: nos. 9115, 6709, 6693, 6686, 6687, 9012.
Material pertaining to Nottingham Jewry: nos. 6783, 6784, 6799, 6800, 6831.

References

Wiltshire Record Office

Radnor Muniments 490/1491: appointment of Sarah de Hobotune as heir to two burgages (bought from William Luddok of Heytesbury) in Heytesbury by William de Heytesbury.

Radnor Muniments 490/1492: gift and quitclaim of a yearly rent issuing from properties formerly belonging to William Luddok of Heytesbury.

MS 132/1: grant of various lands in Heytesbury by William Luddok of Heytesbury.

PRINTED PRIMARY SOURCES

Abulafia, A. S. and Evans, G. R., *The Works of Gilbert Crispin, Abbot of Westminster*, London, 1986.

Annales Londinienses in *Chronicles of the Reign of Edward I and II*, ed. W. Stubbs, 2 vols, London, Rolls Series, 1882–3.

Annales Monastici, vols. I–IV, ed. H. R. Luard, Rolls Series, London, 1864–9.

Annales Theukesberia, in *Annales Monastici*, vol. I, ed. H. R. Luard, Rolls Series, London, 1864.

Bartholomew de Cotton, *Bartholomaei de Cotton Monachi Norwiciensis Historia Anglicana 449–1298 Rerum Eiusdem Liber de Archiepiscopis et Episcopis Angliae*, ed. H. R. Luard, London, Rolls Series, 1859.

Biblia sacra iuxtas vulgatam clementinam, Paris, 1938.

Calendar of Chancery Warrants, 1244–1326, Preserved in the Public Record Office, London, 1912.

Calendar of Charter Rolls, 1257–1300, Preserved in the Public Record Office, vol. II, London, 1906.

Calendar of Close Rolls of the Reign of Henry III, 1234–1272, Preserved in the Public Record Office, London, 1908–38.

Calendar of Close Rolls of the Reign of Edward I, 1234–1296, Preserved in the Public Record Office, London, 1900–4.

Calendar of Fine Rolls of the Reign of Edward I, 1272–1307, Preserved in the Public Record Office, vol. I, London, 1911.

Calendar of Fine Rolls of the Reign of Edward II, 1307–1319, Preserved in the Public Record Office, vol. II, London, 1912.

Calendar of Inquisitions Post Mortem and Other Analagous Documents Preserved in the Public Record Office, vols. I–III, *Edward I*, London, 1906–12.

Calendar of Inquisitions Miscellaneous (Chancery) Documents Preserved in the Public Record Office, vol. I, *Edward I, 1219–1307*, London, 1916.

Calendar of Patent Rolls of the Reign of Henry III Preserved in the Public Record Office, 1216–1272, London, 1901–13.

Calendar of Patent Rolls of the Reign of Edward I Preserved in the Public Record Office, 1272–1292, London, 1893–1901.

Calendar of the Plea Rolls of the Exchequer of the Jews Preserved in the Public Record Office, vol. I, *Henry III, 1218–1272*, ed. J. M. Rigg, Jewish Historical Society of England, London, 1905.

Calendar of the Plea Rolls of the Exchequer of the Jews Preserved in the Public Record Office, vol. II, *Edward I, 1273–1275*, ed. J. M. Rigg, Jewish Historical Society of England, London, 1910.

References

Calendar of the Plea Rolls of the Exchequer of the Jews Preserved in the Public Record Office, vol. III, *Edward I, 1275–1277,* ed. H. Jenkinson, Jewish Historical Society of England, London, 1929.

Calendar of the Plea Rolls of the Exchequer of the Jews Preserved in the Public Record Office and the British Museum, vol. IV, *Henry III, 1272 and Edward I, 1275–1277,* ed. H. G. Richardson, Jewish Historical Society of England, London, 1972.

Plea Roll of the Exchequer of the Jews, Michaelmas 1277–Hilary 1279, ed. S. Cohen (PhD thesis, University of London, 1951).

Plea Rolls of the Exchequer of the Jews, Preserved in the Public Record Office, vol. V, *Edward I, 1277–1279,* ed. S. Cohen, revised P. Brand, Jewish Historical Society of England, London, 1992.

Capgrave, John, *Johannis Capgrave Liber de Illustribus Henricis,* ed. F. C. Hungeston, London, Rolls Series, 1858.

Cartularium Rievallense, ed. J. C. Atkinson, Surtees Society 83, London, 1889.

Catalogue of Ancient Deeds Preserved in the Public Record Office, 6 vols., London, 1890–1915.

Catalogue of Anglo-Jewish Historical Exhibition, 1887, ed. J. Jacobs and L. Wolf, London, 1887.

Chronica Jocelini de Brakelonda, ed. J. G. Rokewode, Camden Society 13, 1840.

Chronica Johannis de Oxenedes, ed. H. Ellis, London, Rolls Series, 1859.

Chronicles of the Reigns of Edward I and Edward II, Commendatio Lamentabilis, vol. II, ed. W. Stubbs, London, Rolls Series, 1883.

Chronicles of St Augustine's Canterbury, ed. W. Thorne, in *Historiae Anglicanae Scriptores Antiqui,* ed. R. Twysden, London, 1652.

Cronica Maiorum, in *De Antiquis Legibus Liber. Cronica Maiorum et Vicecomitum Loniniarum,* ed. T. Stapleton, Camden Society 34, 1846.

Daniel, S., *The Collection of the Historie of England,* London, 1618.

Devizes, Richard of, in *Chronicles of the Reign of Stephen, Henry II and Richard I,* vol. III, ed. R. Howlett, London, Rolls Series, 1888.

Episcopal Registers of Richard de Swinfield Bishop of Hereford, ed. W. W. Capes, Canterbury and York Society 6, 1909.

Episcopal Registers of Worcester. Register of Godfrey Giffard 1268–1301, ed. J. Willis Bund, Worcestershire Historical Society 15, 1898–1902.

Eulogium (Historiarium Sine Temporis). Chronicon ab Orbe Condito usque ad Annum Domini 1366; a Monacho quodam Malmesburiensi Exoratum, vol. III, ed. F. S. Hayton, Rolls Series, 1863.

Gascon Register, A Series of 1318–19 edited from BM Cottonian Ms Julius E 1 ed. G. P. Cuttino, London, 1975.

Gervase of Canterbury, in *Historical Works of Gervase of Canterbury,* vols. I–II, ed. W. Stubbs, Rolls Series, 1879–80.

Gesta Regum Anglorum, in *Willelmi Monachi Malmesbiriensis de Regum Gestis Anglorum Libri V et Historiae Novellae Libri III,* vol. II, ed. W. Stubbs, Rolls Series, 1889.

Giraldus Cambrensis, *The Works of Giraldus Cambrensis,* vols. I–VIII, ed. J. S. Brewer, J. F. Dimmock and G. F. Warner, Rolls Series, 1861–91.

Grosseteste, Robert, *Epistolae,* in *Letters of Bishop Grosseteste,* ed. H. R. Lauard, Rolls Series, London, 1861.

Hemingburgh, *Chronicon Domini Walteri de Hemingburgh: De Gestis Regum Angliae ad Fidem Codicum Manuscriptorum Recensuit,* vols. I–II, ed. H. C. Hamilton, English Historical Society, 1848–9.

References

Hermes, E. (ed.), *The Disciplina Clericalis of Petrus Alphonsi*, Berkeley, 1977.

Historia Rerum Anglorum Willelmi Parvi Ordinis Sancti Augustini Canonici Regularis in Coenobio Beatiae Mariae de Newburgh in Agro Eboracensi ad Fidem Codicum Manuscriptorum, ed. H. C. Hamilton, English Historical Society, 1856.

Historia et Cartularium Monasterii S. Petri Gloucestriae, vols. I–III, ed. W. H. Hart, Rolls Series, London, 1863–7.

Howden, Roger, *Chronica magistri Rogeri de Howdene*, ed. W. Stubbs, Rolls Series, London, 1870.

H.W., *Anglo-Judaeus or the History of the Jews, whilst here in England, relating to Their Manners, Carriage, and Usage from their Admission by William the Conqueror, to Their Banishment*, London, 1656.

Israel, M. ben, *Spes Israelis*, London, 1650.

Leland, J., *Commentarii de Scriptoribus Britannicis*, Oxford, 1709.

Materials for the History of Thomas Becket, vols. I–VI, ed. J. Cragie Robertson, Rolls Series, London, 1875–85.

Matthew Paris, *Matthaei Parisiensis Historia Anglorum et sive ut Vulgo Dicitur Historia Minor (1067–1253)*, vols. I–III, ed. F. Madden, Rolls Series, London, 1866–9.

Matthew Paris, *Matthaei Parisiensis Monachi Sancti Albani Chronica Majora*, ed. H. R. Luard, 7 vols., Rolls Series, London, 1872–83.

Memorials of Fountains Abbey, vol. II, ed. J. R. Walbran, Selden Society 67, London, 1876.

Monumenta Franciscana, vol. II, ed. R. Howlett, Rolls Series, London, 1882.

Pecham, *Epistolae, Registrum Epistolarum Fratris Johannis Peckham Archiepiscopi Cantuariensis*, vols. I–III, ed. C. Trice-Martin, Rolls Series, London, 1882–6.

Peck, Francis, *Academia Tertia Anglicana; or the Antiquarian Annals of Stamford in Lincoln, Rutland and Northamptonshire*, London, 1727.

Pipe Roll 1191–1192, ed. D. M. Stenton, Pipe Roll Society, New Series 2, 1926.

Playford, H., *Rotulorum Originalium in Curia Scaccarii Abbreviatio Henry III – Edward III*, London, 1805–10.

Plea Rolls, see p. 307.

Political Songs of England, ed. T. Wright, Camden Society, 1839.

Prynne W., *A short demurrer to the Jews long discontinued barred remitter into England, comprising an exact and chronological relation of their first admission into their ill deportment, oppressions, and their final banishment out of England, collected out of the best historians and records. With reasons against their readmission into England*, 2nd edn, London, 1656.

Rapin de Thoryas, Paul, *Acta Regia being the account which Mr Rapin de Thoryas published of the History of England*, London, 1733.

Records of the Wardrobe and Household 1286–1289, ed. B. F. Byerly, London, 1986.

The Register of John le Romeyn 1286–1296, part I, Surtees Society 123, 1913.

Registrum Antiquissimum of the Cathedral Church of Lincoln, vols. I–X, ed. C. W. Foster and K. Major, Lincoln Record Society, 1931–68.

Registrum Hamonis Hethe, ed. C. Hohnson, Canterbury and York Society 48, 1937.

Roll of the Household Expenses of Richard de Swinfield Bishop of Hereford 1289–90, ed. J. Webb, Camden Society 59 and 62, 1853–5.

Rôles Gascons: Collections de documents inédits sur l'histoire de France: Rôles Gascons, ed. C. Bemont, Paris, 1900–6.

Rotuli Parliamentorum; ut et Petitiones, et Placita in Parliamento, 6 vols., London, 1783.

References

Ryan, W. G., *Jacobus de Voragine, The Golden Legend, Readings on the Saints*, vols. I–II, Princeton, 1993.

Select Cases in the Court of the King's Bench under Edward I, vols. I–III, ed. G. O. Sayles, Selden Society, 1936–9.

Seventh Report of the Deputy Keeper of the Public Records, London, 1846.

Speed, J., *The History of Great Britain*, London, 1611.

Srawley, J. R. (ed.), *The Book of John de Schalby Canon of Lincoln 1299–1303 Concerning the Bishops of Lincoln and Their Acts*, Lincoln, 1966.

Starrs and Jewish Charters in the British Museum, vols. I–III, ed. H. Loewe, H. P. Stokes and I. Abrahams, Cambridge, 1930.

Statutes of the Realm, Printed by Command of His Majesty King George the Third in Pursuance of an Address of the House of Commons of Great Britain from Original Records and Authoritative Manuscripts, vol. I, London, 1810.

Stow, J., *The Annales of England*, London, 1615.

Tout, T. F. T. and Johnstone, H., *State Trials of the Reign of Edward I 1289–1293*, London, Camden Society 9, 1906.

Triveti, Nicholas, *Annales sex Regum Angliae qui a Comitibus ad Egaversibus Orignem Traxerunt A.D. MCCXXXVI–MCCCVII ad Fidem Codicum Manuscriptorum Recensuit*, ed. T. Hog, London, 1845.

Walsingham, *Historia Anglicana*, in *Monasterii Sancti Albani I Walsingham Historia Anglicana*, ed. W. T. Riley, vol. I, 1372–81; vol. II, 1381–1422, London, Rolls Series, 1863–76.

Wilkins, David, *Concilia Magnae Britanniae et Hiberniae, a Synodo Verolamiensi, A.D. 446 ad Londiniensem A.D. 1717. Accedunt Constitutiones et alia ad Historiam Ecclesiae Anglicanae Spectantia*, London, 1737.

PRINTED SECONDARY WORKS

Abrahams, B. L., 1894a, 'The debts and houses of the Jews of Hereford in 1290', *TJHSE*, 1, pp. 136–59.

    1894b, 'The Expulsion of the Jews from England in 1290', *JQR*, 7, pp. 75–100, 236–58, 428–58. (Also published as an essay Oxford, 1895.)

    1895, *The Expulsion of the Jews from England in 1290*, Oxford.

    1896, 'Condition of the Jews of England at the time of their Expulsion in 1290', *TJHSE*, 2, pp. 76–105.

    1916, 'The economic and financial position of the Jews in medieval England', *TJHSE*, 8, pp. 171–89.

Abrahams, I., 1925, 'The Northampton Donum of 1194', *Misc JHSE*, 1, pp. lix–lxxiv.

Abulafia, A. S., 1981, 'An eleventh-century exchange of letters between a Christian and a Jew', *Journal of Medieval History*, 7, pp. 153–74.

    1984, 'An attempt by Gilbert Crispin, abbot of Westminster, at rational argument in the Jewish-Christian debate', *Studia Monastica*, 26, pp. 55–74.

    1989, 'Jewish-Christian disputations and the twelfth-century renaissance', *Journal of Medieval History*, 15, no. 2, pp. 105–25.

    1995, *Christians and Jews in the Twelfth-Century Renaissance*, London.

Addyman, P., 1984, 'Civilisation can now surely rest . . .', *Interim*, 9, no. 4, pp. 3–4.

Adler, M., 1903, 'History of the *Domus Conversorum* from 1290–1891', *TJHSE*, 4, pp. 16–75.

    1914, 'The Jews of Canterbury', *TJHSE*, 7, pp. 19–79.

References

1928, 'The Jews of Bristol in pre-Expulsion days', *TJHSE*, 12, pp. 117–87.

1931, 'The medieval Jews of Exeter', *Transactions of the Devonshire Association for the Advancement of Science Literature and Art*, 63, pp. 221–40.

1933, 'Aaron of York', *TJHSE*, 13, pp. 113–55.

1935a, 'Jewish tallies of the thirteenth century', *Misc JHSE*, 2, pp. 8–23.

1935b, 'Inventory of the property of the condemned Jews – 1285', *Misc JHSE*, 2, pp. 56–71.

1937, 'Medieval Jewish Mss. in the Library of St Paul's Cathedral, London', *Misc JHSE*, 3, pp. 15–33.

1939, *The Jews of Medieval England*, London.

1942, 'Benedict the Guildsman', *Misc JHSE*, 4, pp. 1–8.

Allin, P., 1972, 'Medieval Southampton and its Jews', *TJHSE*, 23, pp. 87–95.

1980, 'Richard of Devizes and the alleged martyrdom of a boy at Winchester', *TJHSE*, 27, pp. 32–9.

Almog, S., 1988, trans. N. H. Reishner, *Antisemitism through the Ages*, Oxford.

Arkin, M., 1955, 'When the Jewish goose stopped laying the golden eggs', *Jewish Affairs*, 10, part 3, pp. 16–20.

Aronsfeld, C. C., 1990, 'Exodus and return', *History Today*, March, pp. 7–9.

Atkinson, E. G., 1912, *The Jews in English History*, London.

Baldwin, J. W., 1970, *Masters, Princes and Merchants: The Social Views of Peter the Chanter and His Circle*, 2 vols., Princeton, New Jersey.

Barber, M., 1978, *The Trial of the Templars*, Cambridge.

Baring-Gould, S., 1872, *Curious Myths of the Middle Ages*, London.

Barrow, G. W. S., 1951, 'A twelfth century Newbattle document', *Scottish Historical Review*, 109, pp. 41–9.

Bartlett, R., 1993, *The Making of Europe: Conquest, Colonization and Cultural Change 950–1350*, London.

Barton, J. L., 1967, 'The Common Law Mortgage', *Law Quarterly Review*, 83, pp. 229–39.

Beardwood, A., 1955, 'Bishop Langton's use of statute merchant recognisances', *Medievalia et Humanistica*, 9, pp. 54–70.

Beit-Arie, M., 1985, *The Only Dated Medieval Hebrew Manuscript Written in England (1189 C.E.)*, London.

Belloc, H., 1928, *The Jews*, London.

Biles, M., 1983, 'The Indomitable Belle: Eleanor of Provence', in Bowers 1983b, pp. 113–31.

Bischoff, J. P., 1975, 'Economic change in thirteenth century Lincoln – the decline of a cloth industry', Yale University, PhD thesis.

Blumenthal, D. R. (ed.), 1984, *Approaches to Judaism in Medieval Times*, Brown Judaic Studies, 54, Chico, California.

Bowers, R. H., 1983a, 'From rolls to riches: king's clerks and moneylending in thirteenth-century England', *Speculum*, 58, pp. 60–71.

1983b, *Seven Studies in Medieval English History and Other Essays Presented to Harold S. Snellgrove*, Mississippi.

Brand, P., 1985, 'Edward I and the Judges: the "State Trials" of 1289–93', in Coss and Lloyd 1985, pp. 31–40.

forthcoming, 'Jews and the law in England, 1275–1290', unpublished paper given in Boston to the Medieval Academy of America.

References

Brewer, E. C., 1970, *Dictionary of Phrase and Fable*, London.

Britnell, R. H., 1981, 'The proliferation of markets in England, 1200–1349', *EcHR*, 34, pp. 209–21.

1993, *The Commercialisation of English Society 1000–1500*, Cambridge.

Britnell, R. H. and Bruce M. S. Campbell (eds.), 1995, *A Commercialising Economy: England 1086 to c. 1300*, Manchester.

Brown, C., 1904, *A History of Newark*, Newark.

Brown, E. R., 1991, 'Philip V, Charles IV and the Jews of France: the alleged expulsion of 1322', *Speculum*, 66, pp. 294–329.

Brunskill, E., 1964, 'The Jews in medieval York', *TJHSE*, 20, pp. 239–45.

Butcher, A., 1974, 'The origins of Romney Freemen 1433–1523', *EcHR*, 27, pp. 16–27.

Butler, L. H., 1952, 'Archbishop Melton, his neighbours and his kinsmen 1317–1340', *Journal of Ecclesiastical History*, 3, pp. 54–67.

Carpenter, D. A., 1992, 'King Henry III's "Statute" against aliens: July 1263', *English Historical Review*, 107, pp. 925–44.

Carpenter, D. E., 1986, *Alfonso X and the Jews: An Edition of and Commentary on 'Siete Partidas 7.24 De Los Judios'*, Berkeley.

Carus Wilson, E. M., 1965, 'The first half-century of Stratford upon Avon', *EcHR*, 8, pp. 46–63.

Chaucer, Geoffrey, *The Pardoner's Tale*, in *The Works of Geoffrey Chaucer*, ed. F. N. Robinson, London, 1976.

Chazan, R., 1969, 'Jewish settlement in Northern France 1096–1306', *Revue des études juives*, 128, pp. 41–65.

1973, *Medieval Jewry in Northern France: A Political and Social History*, Johns Hopkins University Press, Baltimore.

1977, 'The Barcelona "Disputation" of 1263: Christian missionizing and Jewish response', *Speculum*, 52, pp. 824–42.

1980, *Church, State and Jew in the Middle Ages*, New York.

1987, *European Jewry and the First Crusade*, Berkeley.

Chew, H. M., 1928, 'A Jewish aid to marry A.D. 1221', *TJHSE*, 11, pp. 92–111.

Childs, W. R., 1978, *Anglo-Castilian Trade in the Late Middle Ages*, Manchester.

Clanchy, M. T., 1979, *From Memory to Written Record: England 1066–1307*, London.

Clanchy, M. T. (ed.), 1971, *Civil Pleas of the Wiltshire Eyre, 1249*, Wiltshire Record Society 26, Devizes.

Clapham, J. H., 1933, 'A thirteenth-century market town: Linton, Cambridgeshire', *Cambridge Historical Journal*, 4, pp. 194–202.

Cluse, C., 1995a, '"Fabula ineptissima": die ritualmordlegende um Adam von Bristol nach der Handschrift London, British Library, Harley 957', *Aschkenas*, 5, pp. 293–330.

1995b, 'Stories of breaking and taking the cross: a possible context for the Oxford incident of 1268', *Revue d'histoire ecclésiastique*, 90, pp. 396–442.

Cohen, J., 1982, *The Friars and the Jews: The Evolution of Medieval Anti-Judaism*, Ithaca.

1983, 'The Jews as the killers of Christ in the Latin tradition, from Augustine to the Friars', *Traditio*, 39, pp. 1–27.

Cohen, S., 1932, 'The Oxford Jewry in the thirteenth century', *TJHSE*, 13, pp. 293–322.

Cohn, N., 1975, *Europe's Inner Demons*, London.

References

Cohn-Sherbok, D., 1979, 'Medieval Jewish persecution in England: the Canterbury pogroms in perspective', *Southern History*, 3, pp. 23–37.

Collins, A. J., 1946, 'The Northampton Jewry and its cemetery in the thirteenth century', *TJHSE*, 15, pp. 151–64.

Cooper, W. H., 1850, *History of Winchelsea*, Hastings.

Corcos, A., 1903, 'Extracts from the Close Roll 1279–1288', *TJHSE*, 4, pp. 202–19.

Coss, P. R., 1975, 'Sir Geoffrey de Langley and the crisis of the knightly class in thirteenth century England', *Past and Present*, 68, pp. 3–37.

Coss, P. R. and Lloyd, S. D. (ed.), 1985, *Thirteenth-Century England: Proceedings of the Newcastle upon Tyne Conference 1 1985*, Woodbridge.

   1987, *Thirteenth-Century England: Proceedings of the Newcastle upon Tyne Conference 2 1987*, Woodbridge.

Coulton, G. G., 1921, 'An episode in Canon Law', *History*, 6, pp. 67–76.

Cramer, A. C., 1940, 'The Jewish Exchequer: an inquiry into its fiscal functions', *American History Review*, 45, no. 2, pp. 327–37.

   1941, 'Origins and functions of the Jewish Exchequer', *Speculum*, 16, pp. 226–9.

Crook, D., 1980, 'The early remembrancers of the Exchequer', *BIHR*, 53, pp. 11–23.

Cutts, E. L., 1888, *Colchester*, London and New York.

Davies, R., 1875, 'The mediaeval Jews of York', *Yorkshire Archaeological and Topographical Journal*, 3, pp. 147–97.

Davis, M. D., 1881, 'The mediaeval Jews of Lincoln', *Archaeological Journal*, 38, pp. 178–200.

   1887, 'The Bodleian ewer', *The Jewish Chronicle*, 12 August, pp. 9–10; 19 August, p. 11; 26 August, p. 6.

   1888, *Hebrew Deeds of English Jews before 1290*, Publications of the Anglo-Jewish Historical Exhibition 2, London.

Denholm-Young, N., 1937, *Seignorial Administration in England*, Oxford.

   1944, 'Feudal society in the thirteenth century: the knights', *History*, 10, pp. 107–19.

   1947, *Richard of Cornwall*, Oxford.

Dickens, C., 1849–50, *David Copperfield*, 1983 edn, Oxford.

Dobson, R. B., 1974, *The Jews of York and the Massacre of March 1190*, Borthwick Papers 45, York.

   1979, 'The decline and expulsion of the medieval Jews of York', *TJHSE*, 26, pp. 34–52.

   1992, 'Booknotes', *JHS*, 32, pp. 373–6.

   1993, 'The Jews of Cambridge', *JHS*, 32, pp. 1–24.

du Boulay, F. R. H., 1966, *The Lordship of Canterbury*, London.

Edwards, L., 1958, 'Some English examples of the medieval representation of church and synagogue', *TJHSE*, 18, pp. 63–77.

Elman, P., 1936, 'Jewish finance in thirteenth century England with special reference to royal taxation', University of London MA thesis.

   1938a, 'The economic causes of the Expulsion of the Jews in 1290', *EcHR*, 7, pp. 145–54.

   1938b, 'Jewish finance in thirteenth century England with special reference to royal taxation', *BIHR*, 15, pp. 112–13.

   1939, 'Jewish trade in thirteenth century England', *Historia Judaica*, 1, pp. 91–104.

   1952, 'Jewish finance in thirteenth century England', *TJHSE*, 16, pp. 89–96.

References

Emery, R. W., 1959, *The Jews of Perpignan in the Thirteenth Century*, New York.

Essex, J., 1782, 'Observations on the origin and antiquity of round churches, and of the Round Church at Cambridge in particular', *Archaeologia*, 6, pp. 163–78.

Farmer, D. L., 1957, 'Some grain price movements in thirteenth-century England', *EcHR*, 10, pp. 207–20.

Farr, M. W. (ed.), 1959, *Accounts and Surveys of the Wiltshire Lands of Adam de Stratton*, Wiltshire Archaeological and Natural History Society 15, Devizes.

Finkelstein, L., 1924, *Jewish Self-Government in the Middle Ages*, New York.

Foster, C. W. (ed.), 1920, *Final Concords Suits in the King's Courts temp. Henry II – Henry III*, Lincoln Records Society 17.

Friedman, L. M., 1934, *Robert Grosseteste and the Jews*, Cambridge, Mass.

Fry, E. A. (ed.), 1908, *Wiltshire Inquisitions Post Mortem*, British Record Society 37, London.

Fuss, A. M., 1975, 'Inter-Jewish loans in pre-Expulsion England', *JQR*, 65, pp. 229–45.

Gerber, J. S., 1992, *The Jews of Spain: A History of the Sephardic Experience*, New York.

Gilbert, M., 1976, *Jewish History Atlas*, London.

Giuseppi, M. S., 1963, *Guide to the Contents of the Public Record Office*, vol. 1, London.

Golb, N., 1985, *Les Juives de Rouen au moyen âge: portrait d'une culture oubliée*, Rouen.

Grayzel, S., 1966, *The Church and the Jews in the XIIIth Century*, New York.

Greatrex, J., 1992, 'Monastic charity for Jewish converts: the requisition of corrodies by Henry III', in Wood 1992, pp. 133–43.

Gross, C., 1887, 'The Exchequer of the Jews in the Middle Ages', *Papers given at the Anglo-Jewish Historical Exhibition 1887*, pp. 170–230.

Gross, H., 1897, *Gallia Judaica: dictionnaire géographique de la France d'après les sources rabbinique . . .*, Paris.

Guttentag, G. D., 1977, 'The beginnings of the Newcastle Jewish community', *TJHSE*, 25, pp. 1–24.

Guy, J., 1992, *Tudor England*, Oxford.

Haberman, A. M., 1967, 'Hebrew poems of Meir of Norwich', in Lipman 1967, pp. 1–45.

Haes, F., 1899, 'Moyse Hall, Bury St Edmunds', *TJHSE*, 3, pp. 18–35.

1903, 'The Canterbury Synagogue', *TJHSE*, 4, pp. 230–2.

Hallam, H. E., 1981, *Rural England 1066–1348*, London.

Harding, A., 1993, *England in the Thirteenth Century*, Cambridge.

Hasted H., 1800, *History of Kent*, 12 vols., Canterbury.

Hatcher, J. and Miller, E. 1978, *Medieval England: Rural Society and Economic Change 1086–1348*, London.

1995, *Medieval England: Towns, Commerce and Crafts 1086–1348*, London.

Helmholz, R. H., 1986, 'Usury and the medieval English church courts', *Speculum*, 61, pp. 364–80.

Hill, J. W. F., 1965, *Medieval Lincoln*, Cambridge.

1979, *A Short History of Lincoln*, Lincoln.

Hillaby, J., 1984, 'Hereford gold: Irish, Welsh and English land – the Jewish community at Hereford and its clients 1179–1253, Part 1', *Transactions of the Woolhope Naturalists Field Club*, 44(3), pp. 358–419.

1985, 'Hereford gold: Irish, Welsh and English land – the Jewish community at Hereford and its clients 1179–1253: four case studies, Part 2', *Transactions of the Woolhope Naturalists Field Club*, 45(1), pp. 193–270.

References

1990a, 'The Worcester Jewry, 1158–1290: portrait of a lost community', *Worcestershire Archaeological Society Transactions*, 35(12), pp. 73–122.

1990b, 'A magnate among the marchers: Hamo of Hereford, his family and clients, 1218–1253', *JHS*, 31, pp. 23–82.

1990c, 'The Hereford Jewry 1179–1290 – Aaron le Blund and the last decades of Hereford Jewry 1253–1290', *Transactions of the Woolhope Naturalists Field Club*, 46(3), pp. 432–87.

1993a, 'London: the 13th-century Jewry revisited', *JHS*, 32, pp. 89–158.

1993b, 'Beth Miqdash Me'at: the synagogues of medieval England', *The Journal of Ecclesiastical History*, 44, pp. 182–98.

Hilton, C., 1989, 'St Bartholomew's Hospital, London, and its Jewish connections', *JHS*, 30, pp. 21–51.

Holderness, B. A., 1976, 'Credit in English rural society before the nineteenth century, with special reference to the period 1650–1720', *Agricultural History Review* 24, pp. 97–109.

Honeybourne, M. B., 1964, 'The pre-Expulsion cemetery of the Jews in London', *TJHSE*, 20, pp. 145–59.

Howell, M., 1987, 'The resources of Eleanor of Provence as Queen Consort', *English Historical Review*, 102, pp. 372–93.

Humphery-Smith, C. R., 1976, *Anglo-Norman Armory*, Canterbury.

Hunt, R. W., 1948, 'The Disputation of Peter of Cornwall against Symon the Jew' in Hunt, Pantin and Southern 1948, pp. 143–56.

Hunt, R. W., Pantin, W. A. and Southern R. W. (eds.), 1948, *Studies in Medieval History presented to Frederick Maurice Powicke*, Oxford.

Hunter, J., 1828, *History of South Yorkshire*, vol. 1, London.

Hyams, P. R., 1970, 'The origins of a peasant land market in England', *EcHR*, 23, pp. 18–31.

1974, 'The Jewish minority in medieval England 1066–1290', *JJS*, 26, pp. 270–93.

Jacobs, J., 1889, 'Une lettre française d'un juif anglais', *Revue des études juives*, 18, pp. 256–61.

1893a, *The Jews of Angevin England: Documents and records from Latin and Hebrew sources . . . for the First Time Collected and Translated*, London.

1893b, 'Little St Hugh of Lincoln, researches in history, archaeology and legend', *TJHSE*, 1, pp. 89–135.

1896, *Jewish Ideals and Other Essays*, London.

1899, 'Aaron of Lincoln', *TJHSE*, 3, pp. 157–79.

Jenkinson, H., 1913, 'William Cade a financier of the twelfth century', *English Historical Review*, 26, pp. 209–27.

1918, 'The records of the Exchequer receipts from the English Jewry', *TJHSE*, 8, pp. 19–54.

1922, 'Some medieval notes' and 'Tallies and Receipt Rolls', *TJHSE*, 9, pp. 185–92.

1955, 'Medieval sources for Anglo-Jewish history: the problem of publication', *TJHSE*, 18, pp. 285–93.

1968, *A Guide to Seals in the Public Record Office*, London.

Jenks, E., 1902, *Edward Plantagenet: The English Justinian or the Making of the Common Law*, London.

Johnson, C. P. C. 1978, 'A second Jewish *scola* in Lincoln', *Lincolnshire History and Archaeology*, 13, pp. 35–7.

References

Jolles, M., 1996, *A Short History of the Jews of Northampton 1159–1996*, London.

Jones, A., 1977, 'Harvest customs and labourers' perquisites in southern England 1150–1350 – the corn harvest', *Agricultural History Review*, 25, pp. 2–14, 98–107.

Jones, J. R. and Keller, J. E. (eds.), 1969, *The Scholar's Guide: A Translation of the Twelfth-Century Disciplina Clericalis of Pedro Alphonso*, Toronto.

Jones, N., 1989, *God and Moneylenders: Usury and Law in Early Modern England*, Oxford.

Jordan, W. C., 1978, 'Jews on top: women and the availability of consumption loans in northern France in the mid-thirteenth century', *JJS*, 29, pp. 39–56.

1989, *The French Monarchy and the Jews*, Philadelphia.

Kaeuper, R. W., 1973, *Bankers to the Crown: The Riccardi of Lucca and Edward I*, Princeton.

Katz, D. S., 1982, *Philo-Semitism and the Readmission of the Jews to England 1603–1655*, Oxford.

1992, 'The phenomenon of philo-Semitism', in Wood 1992, pp. 327–61.

Kaufman, D., 1893, 'The *Etz Chayim* of Jacob ben Jehudah of London and the history of the manuscript', *JQR*, 5, pp. 353–63.

Kedourie, E., (ed.), 1979, *The Jewish World: History and Culture of the Jewish People*, London.

Keith, K. E., 1959, *The Social life of a Jew in the Time of Christ*, London.

Kelly, J. N. D., 1986, *The Oxford Dictionary of Popes*, Oxford.

Kiewe, H. E., 1946, 'The earliest picture of an English Jew? A drawing of the Matthew Paris school', *The Jewish Chronicle*, 27 September 1946, p. 13.

King, E., 1970, 'Large and small landowners in thirteenth-century England: the case of Peterborough Abbey', *Past and Present*, 47, pp. 26–50.

1973, *Peterborough Abbey 1096–1310. A Study in the Land Market*, Cambridge.

Kingsford, H. S., 1920, *Seals*, London.

Kipling, R., 1906, *Puck of Pook's Hill*, 1951 edn, London.

Kirschenbaum, A., 1985, 'Jewish and Christian theories of usury in the middle ages', *JQR*, 75, pp. 270–89.

Kisch, G., 1957, 'The yellow badge in Jewish history', *Historia Judaica*, 19, pp. 91–101.

Kushner, T. (ed.), 1992, *The Jewish Heritage in British History: Englishness and Jewishness*, London.

Lacaita, P., 1887, *Comentum super Dantis Comoedium*, Florence.

Lamb, C., 1903, 'The two races of man', *The Works of Charles and Mary Lamb*, ed E. V. Lucas, vol. II, pp. 22–7.

Langland, W., 1974, *Piers the Ploughman*, trans. J. F. Goodridge, London.

Langmuir, G. I., 1963, 'The Jews and archives of Angevin England – reflections on medieval anti-semitism', *Traditio*, 19, pp. 183–244.

1971, 'Anti-Judaism as the necessary preparation for anti-semitism', *Viator*, 2, pp. 383–9.

1972, 'The Knight's Tale of Young Hugh of Lincoln', *Speculum*, 47, pp. 459–82.

1984a, 'Thomas of Monmouth: detector of ritual murder', *Speculum*, 59, pp. 820–46.

1984b, 'Historiographic crucifixion', in Blumenthal 1984, pp. 1–26.

1990a, *History, Religion and Antisemitism*, Berkeley.

1990b, *Toward a Definition of Antisemitism*, Berkeley.

Larking, L. B., 1886, 'On the alienation of the manors of Westwell and Little Chart by Peter de Bending and the tenure of the former manor', *Archaeologia Cantiana*, 6, pp. 305–21.

References

Leonard, G. H., 1891, 'The Expulsion of the Jews by Edward 1st – an essay in explanation of the Exodus A.D. 1290', *Transactions of the Royal Historical Society*, 5, pp. 103–46.

Lethieullier, S., 1700, 'A letter from Mr Smart Lethieullier to Mr Gale, relating to the shrine of St Hugh, the crucified child at Lincoln', *Archaeologia*, 1, pp. 26–9.

Levy, S., 1902a, 'Notes on Leicester Jewry', *TJHSE*, 5, pp. 34–42.

1902b, 'The Norwich Day-Book', *TJHSE*, 5, pp. 243–75.

Lewis, G. R., 1965, *The Stannaries: A Study of the Medieval Tin Miners of Cornwall and Devon*, Truro.

Lieberman, S. T., 1983, 'English royal policy towards the Jews' debtors, 1227–1290', University of London PhD thesis.

Liebeschutz, H., 1962, 'Judaism and Jewry in the social doctrine of Thomas Aquinas', *Journal of Jewish Studies*, 13, pp. 57–81.

Lilley, J. M. *et al.*, 1994, *The Jewish Burial Ground at Jewbury*, York.

Lipman, V. D., 1966, 'The Roth "Hake" Manuscript', in Shaftesley 1966, pp. 49–71.

1967, *The Jews of Medieval Norwich*, London.

1968, 'The anatomy of medieval Anglo-Jewry', *TJHSE*, 21, pp. 65–77.

1984, 'Jews and castles in medieval England', *TJHSE*, 28, pp. 1–19.

Lloyd, M., 1983, *Portrait of Lincolnshire*, London.

Lloyd, T. H., 1973, *The Movement of Wool Prices in Medieval England*, EcHR, supplement 6.

1977, *The English Wool Trade in the Middle Ages*, Cambridge.

Loewe, H., 1932, 'Two Hebrew charters at St John's College', *The Eagle*, 47, n. 209, pp. 73–82.

Loewe, R., 1953, 'The medieval Christian Hebraists of England – Herbert of Bosham and earlier scholars', *TJHSE*, 17, pp. 225–49.

Logan, F. D., 1972, 'Thirteen London Jews and conversion to Christianity: problems of apostasy in the 1280s', *BIHR*, 45, pp. 214–29.

McIntosh, M. K., 1988, 'Moneylending on the periphery of London 1300–1600', *Albion*, 20, pp. 557–71.

McLaughlin, T. P., 1939, 'The teaching of the Canonists on usury', *Medieval Studies*, 1, pp. 81–147.

1940, 'The teaching of the Canonists on usury', *Medieval Studies*, 2, pp. 1–22.

Maddicott, J. R., 1994, *Simon de Montfort*, Cambridge.

Maitland, F. W., 1912, 'The deacon and the Jewess: or apostasy at common law', *TJHSE*, 6, pp. 260–76.

Maitland, F. W. and Pollock, F., 1952, *History of English Law before the Time of Edward I*, 2 vols., Cambridge.

Marcus, J. R., 1965, *The Jew in the Medieval World*, New York.

Marmorstein, A., 1928, 'Some hitherto unknown Jewish scholars', *JQR*, 19, pp. 17–36.

1931, 'New material for the literary history of the English Jews before the Expulsion', *TJHSE*, 12, pp. 103–15.

Mate, M., 1973, 'The indebtedness of Canterbury Cathedral Priory 1215–1295', *EcHR*, 26, pp. 183–97.

1980, 'Profit and productivity on the estates of Isabella de Forz (1260–1290), *EcHR*, 33, pp. 326–34.

Meekings, C. A. F., 1955, 'Justices of the Jews 1218–1268: a provisional list', *BIHR*, 28, pp. 173–88.

References

1961, *Crown Pleas of the Wiltshire Eyre, 1249*, Devizes.

1981, *Studies in Thirteenth-Century Justice and Administration*, London.

Mellinkoff, R., 1973, 'The round shaped hats depicted on Jews in B.M. Cotton Claudius B iv', *Anglo-Saxon England*, 2, pp. 155–71.

Menache, S., 1985, 'Faith, myth and politics – the stereotype of the Jews and their Expulsion from England and France', *JQR*, 75, pp. 351–74.

1987, 'The king, the Church and the Jews: some considerations on the expulsions from England and France', *Journal of Medieval History*, 13, pp. 223–36.

1996, 'Tartars, Jews, saracens and the Jewish-Mongol "plot" of 1241', *History*, 81, pp. 319–42.

1997, 'Matthew Paris's attitude toward Anglo-Jewry', *Journal of Medieval History*, 23, pp. 139–62.

Mentgen, G., 1997, 'Die Vertreibungen der Juden aus England und Frankreich im Mittealter', *Aschkenas*, 7, pp. 11–53.

Metzger, T. and M., 1982, *Jewish Life in the Middle Ages*, Secaucus, NJ.

Miller, A. J., 1957, 'The Exchequer of the Jews', *Orthodox Jewish Life*, 25, part 1, pp. 63–5.

Miller, E., 1962, 'Review of H. G. Richardson's *English Jewry under the Angevin Kings*', *EcHR*, 14, pp. 342–3.

Milman, H. H., 1863, *The History of the Jews*, 3rd edn, London.

Moor, C. (ed.), 1929–32, *Knights of Edward I*, 5 vols., Harleian Society 80–4, London. Vol. I (1929), A–E; vol. II (1929), F–K; vol. III (1930), L–O; vol. IV (1931), P–S; vol. V (1932), T–Z.

Moore, R. I., 1987, *The Formation of a Persecuting Society: Power and Deviance in Western Europe 950–1250*, Oxford.

1992, 'Anti-Semitism and the birth of Europe', in Wood 1992, pp. 33–57.

Mundill, R. R., 1987, 'The Jews in England 1272–1290', University of St Andrews PhD thesis.

1990a, 'Anglo-Jewry under Edward I – credit agents and their clients, *JHS*, 31, pp. 1–21.

1990b, 'November 1, 1290: Expulsion of the Jews from England', *The Jewish Chronicle*, 26 October 1990, pp. 24–5.

1991a, 'English medieval Ashkenazim – literature and progress', *Aschkenas*, 1, pp. 203–10.

1991b, 'Lumbard and son: the businesses and debtors of two Jewish moneylenders in late thirteenth century England', *JQR*, 82, pp. 137–70.

1993, 'The Jewish entries from the Patent Rolls 1272–1292', *JHS*, 32, pp. 25–88.

1997, 'Rabbi Elias Menahem: a late thirteenth-century English entrepreneur', *JHS*, 34, pp. 161–87.

forthcoming, 'Medieval Anglo-Jewry: Expulsion and Exodus', *Judevertreibungen wahrend de Mittelalters Internationales Kolloquium an der Universitat Trier*.

Niewyk, D. L., 1980, *The Jews in Weimar Germany*, Manchester.

Nightingale, P., 1990, 'Monetary contraction and mercantile credit in later medieval England', *EcHR*, pp. 560–75.

Oliver, G., 1861, *The History of the City of Exeter*, Exeter.

Orange, J., 1840, *History of Nottingham*, Nottingham.

Ormrod, W. M., 1985, *England in the Thirteenth Century*, Harlaxton.

Ovrut, B. D., 1977, 'Edward I and the Expulsion of the Jews', *JQR*, 67, pp. 224–35.

References

Parker, R., 1979, *Men of Dunwich*, Newton Abbot.

Parkes, J., 1937, 'The Jewish money-lender and the charters of the English Jewry in their historical setting', *Misc JHSE*, 3, pp. 34–41.

    1938, *The Jew in the Medieval Community*, London.

    1962, *A History of the Jewish People*, London.

Parsons, J. C., 1995, *Eleanor of Castile: Queen and Society in Thirteenth Century England*, London.

Pearl, E. (ed.), 1990, *Anglia Judaica or a History of the Jews in England by D'Bloissiers Tovey*, London.

Pearson, N., 1983, 'Jewbury site news', *Interim*, 9, no. 3, pp. 3–5.

Picciotto, C. M., 1922, 'The legal position of the Jews in pre-Expulsion England as shown by the Plea Rolls of the Jewish Exchequer', *TJHSE*, 9, pp. 67–84.

Plucknett, T. F. T., 1949, *Legislation of Edward I*, Oxford.

Pollins, H., 1982, *Economic History of the Jews in England*, London.

Postan, M. M., 1928, 'Credit in medieval trade', *EcHR*, 1, pp. 234–61.

    1930, 'Private financial instruments in medieval England', *Vierteljahrschrift fur Sozial- und Wirtschaftsgeschichte*, 23, pp. 26–75.

    1966, *The Cambridge Economic History of Europe*, Cambridge.

    1972, *The Medieval Economy and Society*, London.

Potter-Briscoe, J., 1908, *Chapters of Nottinghamshire History*, Nottingham.

Power, E., 1941, *The Wool Trade in English Medieval History*, Oxford.

Powicke, F. M., 1947, *King Henry III and the Lord Edward: The Community of the Realm in the Thirteenth Century*, vols. I–II, Oxford.

    1962, *The Thirteenth Century*, Oxford.

Prestwich, M., 1972, *War, Politics and Finance under Edward I*, London.

    1980, *The Three Edwards: War and State in England 1272–1377*, London.

    1985, 'The piety of Edward I', in Ormrod 1985, pp. 120–8.

    1988, *Edward I*, London.

Pugh R. B., 1968, 'Some medieval moneylenders', *Speculum*, 43, pp. 274–89.

Pugh, R. B. (ed.), 1939, *Abstracts of Feet of Fines Relating to Wiltshire for the Reigns of Edward I and Edward II*, Devizes.

    1978, *Gaol Delivery and Trailbaston 1275–1306*, Wiltshire Record Society 33, Devizes.

Rabinowitz, J. J., 1956, *Jewish Law*, New York.

    trans., 1949, *Sepher Mispatim, The Code of Maimonides – the Book of Civil Laws*, Yale Judaica Series, Newhaven.

Rabinowitz, L., 1937, 'The origin of the Canterbury Treaty of 1266', *Misc JHSE*, 3, pp. 76–9.

    1938, 'The medieval Jewish counter-part to the guild merchant', *EcHR*, 8, pp. 180–5.

    1972, *The Social Life of the Jews of Northern France in the XIIth to XIVth centuries*, New York.

Reichel, O. J. (ed.), 1912, *Devonshire Feet of Fines 1196–1272*, Exeter.

Reynolds, S., 1977, *An Introduction to the History of English Medieval Towns*, Oxford.

Richardson, H. G., 1938, 'Glanville continued . . . ', *Law Quarterly Review*, 54, pp. 381–99.

    1960, *The English Jewry under Angevin Kings*, London.

Richmond, C., 1992, 'Englishness and medieval Anglo-Jewry' in Kushner 1992, pp. 42–59.

References

Rigg, J. M., 1903, 'Jews of England in the thirteenth century', *JQR*, 15, pp. 5–22.

Roberts, M., 1992, 'A Northampton Jewish tombstone, c. 1259 to 1290, recently rediscovered in Northampton Central Museum', *Medieval Archaeology*, 36, pp. 173–8.

Rokeah, Z. E., 1971, 'Shtar fragment in a sealing strip', *Tarbiz*, 40, pp. 513–17.

—— 1972, 'Drawings of Jewish interest in some thirteenth century English public records', *Scriptorium*, 26, pp. 55–62.

—— 1973, 'Some accounts of condemned Jews' property in the Pipe and Chancellor's Rolls, part 1', *Bulletin of the Institute of Jewish Studies*, 1, pp. 19–42.

—— 1974, 'Some accounts of condemned Jews' property in the Pipe and Chancellor's Rolls, part 2', *Bulletin of the Institute of Jewish Studies*, 2, pp. 59–82.

—— 1975, 'Some accounts of condemned Jews' property in the Pipe and Chancellor's Rolls, part 3', *Bulletin of the Institute of Jewish Studies*, 3, pp. 41–66.

—— 1982a, 'Crime and Jews in late thirteenth century England: some cases and comments', *Proceedings of the 8th World Congress of Jewish Studies*, pp. 13–18.

—— 1982b, 'The Jewish church-robbers and Host desecrators of Norwich (ca. 1285)', *Revue des études juives*, 141, pp. 331–62.

—— 1984, 'Crime and Jews in late thirteenth century England: some cases and comments', *Hebrew Union College Annual*, 55, pp. 95–157.

—— 1988, 'The state, the Church, and the Jews in medieval England', in Almog 1988, pp. 99–125.

—— 1990, 'Money and the hangman in late 13th-century England: Jews, Christians and coinage offences alleged and real (part I)', *JHS*, 31, pp. 83–109.

—— 1993, 'Money and the hangman in late 13th-century England: Jews, Christians and coinage offences alleged and real (part II)', *JHS*, 32, pp. 159–218.

—— 1997, 'A Hospitaller and the Jews: Brother Joseph de Chauncy and English Jewry in the 1270s', *JHS*, 34, pp. 189–207.

—— forthcoming, *The Memoranda Rolls 1266–1293*.

Roover, R. de, 1948, *Money, Banking and Credit in Medieval Bruges*, Cambridge, Mass.

Rosenau, H., 1936, 'The relationship of "Jews Court" and the Lincoln Synagogue', *Archaeological Journal*, 93, pp. 51–6.

Rosten, L., 1968, *The Joys of Yiddish*, New York.

Roth, C., 1934, *Medieval Lincoln and Its Jewry*, London.

—— 1946, 'Elijah of London', *TJHSE*, 15, pp. 29–62.

—— 1948, 'Rabbi Berechiah of Nicole', *JJS*, 1, pp. 67–81.

—— 1949, *England in Jewish History*, The Lucien Wolf Memorial Lecture, London.

—— 1950, 'Portraits and caricatures of medieval English Jews', *The Jewish Monthly*, 4, Supplement, pp. i–viii.

—— 1951, *The Jews of Medieval Oxford*, Oxford.

—— 1953, 'A medieval Anglo-Jewish seal?', *Misc JHSE*, 17, pp. 283–6.

—— 1957, 'Oxford Starrs', *Oxoniensia*, 22, pp. 63–77.

—— 1960, 'The middle period of Anglo-Jewish history 1290–1655 – reconsidered', *TJHSE*, 19, pp. 1–12.

—— 1962, 'The ordinary Jew in the Middle Ages: a contribution to his history', in *Studies and Essays in Honour of Abraham A. Neuman*, ed. M. ben Horim, B. D. Weinryb and S. Zeitlin, Philadelphia, pp. 21–33.

—— 1978, *History of the Jews in England*, 3rd edn, Oxford.

References

Roth, C. and Wigoder, G., 1975, *The New Standard Jewish Encyclopaedia*, Jerusalem.

Royal Commission on Historical Monuments, 1977, *Stamford*, London.

Ryder, M. L., 1981, 'British medieval sheep and their wool types', *Council for British Archaeology*, Research Report 40, pp. 16–29.

Saitz, R. L., 1960, 'Hugh of Lincoln and the Jews', *The Chicago Jewish Forum*, 18, pp. 308–11.

Salter, H. E. (ed.), 1930, *The Feet of Fines for Oxfordshire 1195–1291*, Oxford.

Salzman, L. F., 1931, *English Trade in the Middle Ages*, Oxford.

1968, *Edward I*, London.

Samuel, E. R., 1974, 'Was Moyses Hall, Bury St Edmunds a Jews' house?', *TJHSE*, 25, pp. 43–8.

Sayles, G. O. (ed.), 1936, *Select Cases in the Court of King's Bench under Edward I*, vol 1, Selden Society 55, London.

Scarfe, N., 1986, *Suffolk in the Middle Ages*, London.

Schechter, F. I., 1914, 'The rightlessness of medieval English Jewry', *JQR*, 4, pp. 121–51.

Scholem, G. C., 1969, *On the Kabbalah and Its Symbolism*, New York.

Schopp, J. W. and Easterling, R. C. (eds.), 1925, *An Anglo-Norman Custumal of Exeter*, London.

Schwarzfuchs, S. R., 1967, 'The Expulsion of the Jews from France (1306)', *JQR*, 75, pp. 482–9.

Scott, K., 1950, 'The Jewish arcae', *Cambridge Law Journal*, 10, part 3, pp. 446–55.

Scott, W., 1830, *Ivanhoe*, 1962 edn, New York.

Shaftesley, J. M. (ed.), 1966, *Remember the Days: Essays in Honour of Cecil Roth*, London.

Shatzmiller, J., 1990, *Shylock Reconsidered: Jews, Moneylending, and Medieval Society*, Berkeley.

Shimon, Z' Ev ben H., 1976, *The Way of the Kabbalah*, London.

Shohet, D. M., 1931, *The Jewish Court in the Middle Ages*, New York.

Simpson, A. W. B., 1966, 'The penal bond with conditional defeasance', *Law Quarterly Review*, 82, pp. 392–492.

Singer, S. A., 1965, 'The Expulsion of the Jews from England in 1290', *JQR*, 55, pp. 117–36.

Sombart, W., 1913, *The Jews and Modern Capitalism*, London.

Somner, W., 1640, *The Antiquities of Canterbury*, London.

Southern, R. W., 1958, 'The English origins of the "Miracle of the Virgin" ', *Medieval and Renaissance Studies*, 4, pp. 176–216.

1986, *Robert Grosseteste: The Growth of an English Mind in Medieval Europe*, Oxford.

Stacey, R. C., 1985, 'Royal taxation and the social structure of mediaeval Anglo-Jewry: the tallages of 1239–1242', *Hebrew Union College Annual*, 56, pp. 175–249.

1987a, *Politics, Policy and Finance under Henry III 1216–1245*, Oxford.

1987b, 'Recent work on medieval English Jewish history', *Jewish History*, 2, pp. 61–72.

1988, '1240–1260: a watershed in Anglo-Jewish relations?', *BIHR*, 61, pp. 135–50.

1990, 'The Expulsion of 1290: economics, sociology, politics', unpublished paper, Ithaca, New York.

1992a, 'The conversion of Jews to Christianity in thirteenth-century England', *Speculum*, 67, pp. 263–83.

1992b, 'Thirteenth-century Anglo-Jewry and the problem of Expulsion', in *Expulsion and Resettlement*, ed. Y. Kaplan and David Katz, Jerusalem.

References

1995, 'Jewish lending and the medieval English economy', in Britnell and Campbell 1995, pp. 78–101.

1997, 'Parliamentary negotiation and the Expulsion of the Jews from England', in *Thirteenth-Century England*, vol. vi, ed. R. H. Britnell, R. Frame and M. Prestwich, pp. 77–101.

Stenton, D. M., 1926, *Earliest Lincolnshire Assize Rolls*, Lincolnshire Record Society 22.

Stephenson, D., 1984, 'Colchester: a smaller medieval English Jewry', *Essex Archaeological and Historical Journal*, 16, pp. 48–52.

Stevenson, W. H., 1882, *Records of the Borough of Nottingham*, Nottingham.

Stokes, H. P., 1913, *Studies in Anglo-Jewish History*, Edinburgh.

1914, 'Records of manuscripts and documents possessed by the Jews in England before the Expulsion', *TJHSE*, 8, pp. 78–98.

1918, 'The relationship between the Jews and the royal family of England in the thirteenth century', *TJHSE*, 8, pp. 153–70.

1921, 'A Jewish family in Oxford in the thirteenth century', *TJHSE* 10, pp. 193–206.

1925, 'Extracts from the Close Rolls 1289–1368', *Misc JHSE*, 1, pp. 6–17.

Stone, E. H., 1920, *Devizes Castle*, Devizes.

Stow, K. R., 1981, 'Papal and royal attitudes toward Jewish lending in the thirteenth century', *Association for Jewish Studies Review*, 6, pp. 161–84.

1992a, *Alienated Minority: The Jews of Medieval Latin Europe*, London.

1992b, 'The good of the Church, the good of the state: popes and Jewish money', in Wood 1992, pp. 237–52.

Stow K. R. (ed.), 1989, *The Church and the Jews in the XIIIth Century (1254–1314)*, New York.

Strauss, R., 1942, 'The Jewish hat as an aspect of social history', *Jewish Social Studies*, 4, pp. 59–72.

Streit, K. T., 1993, 'The expansion of the English Jewish community in the reign of King Stephen', *Albion*, 25, pp. 177–92.

Stubbs, W., 1929, *Constitutional History of England*, 3 vols., Oxford.

Susser, B., 1977, 'The Jews of Devon and Cornwall from the Middle Ages until the twentieth century', University of Exeter, PhD thesis.

1993, *The Jews of Southwest England: The Rise and Fall of their Medieval and Modern Communities*, Exeter.

Synan, E. A., 1965, *The Popes and the Jews in the Middle Ages*, New York.

Tanner, L. E., 1936, 'The nature and use of the Westminster Abbey Muniments', *Transactions of the Royal Historical Society*, 19, pp. 43–78.

Tawney, R. H., 1937, *Religion and the Rise of Capitalism*, London.

Tawney, R. H. (ed.), 1925, *T. Wilson: A Discourse on Usury*, London.

Thrupp, S. and Johnson, H. B. (eds.), 1964, 'Earliest Canterbury Freeman's Rolls 1298–1363', in *Medieval Kentish Society*, Canterbury, Kent Record Society 18, pp. 173–213.

Tout, T. F., 1920, *Edward I*, London.

Tovey, de B., 1738, *Anglia Judaica*, Oxford.

Trabut-Cussac, J. P., 1972, *L'Administration anglaise en Gascogne, sous Henry III et Edouard I de 1254 à 1307*, Geneva.

Trachtenberg, J., 1943, *The Devil and the Jews*, New Haven.

Trice Martin, C., 1895, 'Gascon Rolls', *TJHSE*, 2, pp. 170–9.

Tuchman, B. W., 1982, *Bible and Sword*, London.

References

Tuck, G., 1934, Foreward and introduction in Roth 1934, pp. vii–14.

Turner, B. C., 1954, 'The Winchester Jewry', *Hampshire Review*, 21, pp. 17–21.

Usher, B., 1992, 'The Jew that Shakespeare drew', in Wood 1992, pp. 279–98.

Victoria County History, *Lincolnshire*, vol. II, Oxford.

Vincent, N. C., 1992, 'Jews, Poitevins and the Bishop of Winchester, 1231–34', in Wood 1992, pp. 119–32.

1996, *Peter des Roches: An Alien in English Politics, 1205–1238*, Cambridge.

Wade Labarge, M., 1980, *Gascony: England's First Colony 1204–1453*, London.

Walker, V. W., 1963, 'Medieval Nottingham: a topographical study', *Transactions of the Thoroton Society*, 67, pp. 28–45.

Watt, J. A., 1987, 'The English episcopate, the state and the Jews: the evidence of the thirteenth century conciliar decrees', in Coss and Lloyd 1987, pp. 137–47.

1991, 'The Jews, the law, and the Church: the concept of Jewish serfdom in thirteenth-century England', *Studies in Church History*, subsidia 9, pp. 153–72.

1992, 'Jews and Christians in the Gregorian Decretals', in Wood 1992, pp. 93–105.

Whitwell, R. J. 1903, 'Italian bankers and the English Crown', *Transactions of the Royal Historical Society*, 17, pp. 175–233.

Williams, A. L., 1935, *Adversus Iudaeos: A Bird's Eye View of Christian Apologiae until the Renaissance*, Cambridge.

Wolf, L., 1901, *Menasseh ben Israel's mission to Oliver Cromwell*, London.

1928, 'Jews in Elizabethan England', *TJHSE*, 11, pp. 1–91.

Wood, D., 1992, *Christianity and Judaism*, Studies in Church History 29, Oxford.

Wrightson, K., 1978, 'Medieval villagers in perspective', *Peasant Studies*, 7, pp. 203–17.

INDEX

Index

Cambridge Studies in Medieval Life and Thought
Fourth series

Titles in series

★ *Also published as a paperback*